Harvard Historical Studies, 107

Published under the auspices
of the Department of History
from the income of the
Paul Revere Frothingham Bequest
Robert Louis Stroock Fund
Henry Warren Torrey Fund

Episcopal Power and Florentine Society

1000–1320

George W. Dameron

Harvard University Press
Cambridge, Massachusetts
London, England
1991

Library of Congress Cataloging in Publication Data

Dameron, George W.
    Episcopal power and Florentine society, 1000–1320 / George
W. Dameron.
        p.   cm. — (Harvard historical studies; v. 107)
    Includes bibliographical references.
    ISBN 0-674-25891-6
    1. Catholic Church—Italy—Florence Region—Bishops—History.
    2. Patronage, Ecclesiastical—Italy—Florence Region—History.
    3. Church property—Italy—Florence Region—History.   4. Florence
Region (Italy)—Church history.   5. Florence Region (Italy)—Social
conditions.   6. Florence Region (Italy)—Economic conditions.
    I. Title.   II. Series.
BX1548.F55D33   1991   90-36715
945'.5103—dc20   CIP

To my wife and son, Deborah and Samuel

Contents

Preface

Much of the inspiration for the approaches taken in this book derives from two years of experience living in the West African countryside. As a Peace Corps volunteer in grain storage in the République populaire du Bénin between 1975 and 1977, I worked closely with Adja peasants in the Mono province in the southwestern part of the country. When I left in 1977—shortly after an attempted *coup d'état* by disgruntled Béninois exiles—I carried away with me certain salient observations, among which were the following: (1) the vast majority of the West African population faced an ever-present fear of famine; (2) the extended family was the primary point of reference for every type of social activity (marriages, funerals, land transactions, and religious ceremonies); (3) there existed a constant tension between the interests of the state for cash crops and the desires of the peasant farmer to be left alone to cultivate and market corn; and (4) the central government often manipulated traditional popular beliefs (especially the fear of witchcraft) to maintain or extend its power in the countryside during periods of political and economic crisis.

When I began my study of the Tuscan countryside in 1979, I brought to my analysis of the sources the first-hand experience of having lived in a world in which common western notions about politics and the economy were largely absent. I explored as much of the Tuscan countryside as I could by foot and Fiat, just as I had investigated the countryside in West Africa by foot and Motobécane. That experience in Africa equipped me with a set of questions rather than providing me with a set of answers. It goes without saying that West Africa in the twentieth century is very different from northern Tuscany in the thirteenth century. Nevertheless, the historian of medieval Tuscany can ask many of the same questions raised by the student of contemporary Africa. Indeed, issues such as the frequency and impact of famine, the relationship between traditional peasant culture and a central authority, the identity of the local elite, the nature of spirituality and its manipulation by that elite, the role of kinship—all are questions that analysts of both settings should be asking. The sources on medieval Tuscany cannot answer all those questions, but it is worth the effort to do the best we can with the resources available. It is my conviction that a narrative, interdisciplinary approach is the best method for describing and explaining the complex development of Florentine society before 1320.

There are many whose assistance and advice helped me prepare this manuscript, and I am very grateful to all of them. First, I would like to thank David Herlihy, who suggested this subject and offered me invaluable advice and inspiration over the years. James Given read an earlier version of this study and gave me helpful advice about how to improve it. Chris Wickham carefully read a draft of the text and offered me many constructive suggestions. William Bowsky has been a valued friend and adviser since I started working in the Florentine archives. To my Italian colleagues—Anna Benvenuti-Papi, Roberto Bizzocchi, Claudio and Metello Bonnano, Renzo Nelli, Paolo Pirillo, Emanuela Porta, Sergio Raveggi, and Giovanni Roncaglia—I owe a special debt of gratitude for their hospitality, guidance, and advice. Cinzio Violante was generous with his time when I visited him twice for consultations. Fellow American historians—Dan Bornstein, Richard Fraher, Patrick Geary, Carol Lansing, Duane Osheim, Paula Spilner, Richard Trexler, and Ron Weissman—have also offered assistance along the way. I am especially grateful to the staffs of the Archivio di Stato di Firenze (particularly Dr. Paola Peruzzi) and the Biblioteca Nazionale di Firenze. Without the cooperation and generosity of Dom Carlo Celso Calzolai (Archivio Arcivescovile di Firenze), Monsignor Ernesto Alba (Archivio del Capitolo Fiorentino), Dom Raspini (Archivio Arcivesvile di Fiesole), and the directors of the Vatican Library and Archive, this study would have been impossible. Saint Michael's College (and particularly its academic dean, Ronald Provost) graciously gave me financial and academic support to allow me to finish this and other projects, including several grants, a year of absence, and two course reductions. Kelly McDonald of Saint Michael's College provided an invaluable service preparing the final copy of the manuscript, and the inter-library loan service of the Durick Library was also very useful. Susan Kennedy of the University of Vermont Geography Department and her student, Kym Pappathanasi, generated the maps, based on my own drafts. Their help was invaluable. Finally, the Harvard

Center for Italian Renaissance Studies at the Villa I Tatti awarded me a fellowship in 1987–88 to finish the research and writing of the manuscript, and I especially want to thank the Leopold Schepp Foundation in New York and the Robert Lehman Fellowship for having supported that year in Italy.

Needless to say, all errors or mistakes are my own.

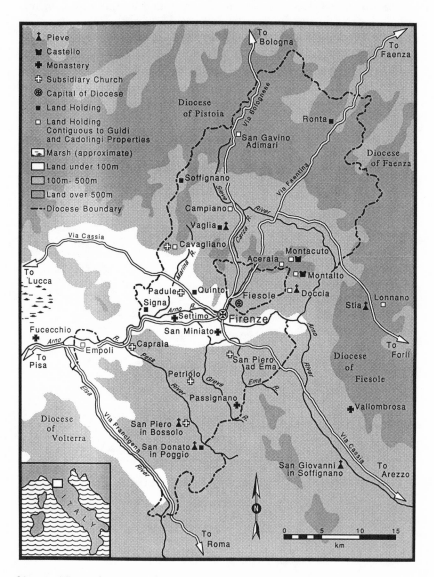

Map 1 The endowment of San Miniato al Monte, circa 1050.

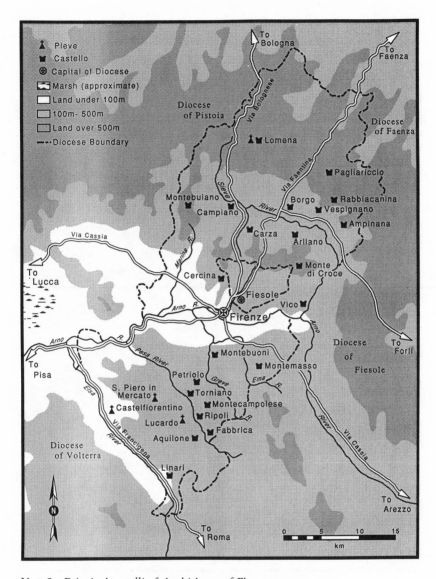

Map 2 Principal *castelli* of the bishops of Florence, 1000–1250.

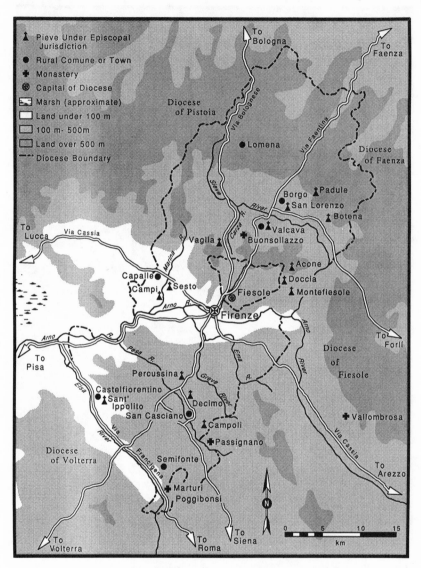

Map 3 The episcopal estate and the rural communes, 1200–1300.

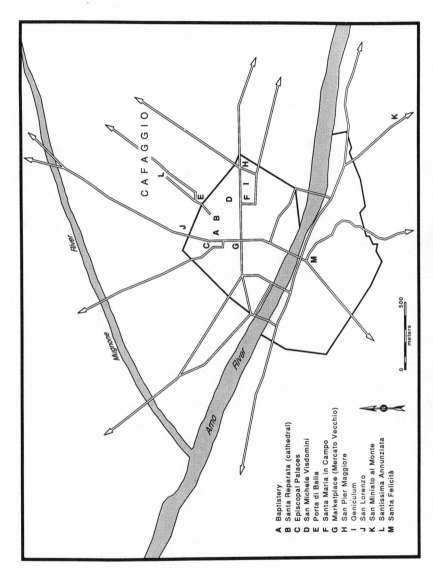

Map 4 Florence at the end of the thirteenth century (adapted from Spilner, 1987, plan 1).

A Baptistery
B Santa Reparata (cathedral)
C Episcopal Palaces
D San Michele Visdomini
E Porta di Balla
F Santa Maria in Campo
G Marketplace (Mercato Vecchio)
H San Pier Maggiore
I Geniculum
J San Lorenzo
K San Miniato al Monte
L Santissima Annunziata
M Santa Felicità

"I was going to ask you," I said, more to take his mind off the present painful proceedings than for any other good reason, "about your history of Lawnchester Cathedral."

"Oh, yes!" Cousin Timmy suddenly returned to life and his pale eyes sparkled with excitement. "I think I'm on the track of something interesting. . . . There seems to have been a gift of land to the Cathedral from the Crown in 1672."

"Sensational stuff! That ought to get you to the top of the best-seller list."

Cousin Timmy to Horace Rumpole—from
Rumpole and the Age of Miracles (1988),
by John Mortimer

Measurement, Money, and Dating

Land measurement. The principal unit of measurement was the *staio* or *starius*, equivalent to 525 square meters. There were 12 *pannora* in each *staio*. Other units included the following: the *braccio* (58.36 cm) and the *piede* (55 cm).

Dry and liquid measurements. The basic unit for dry measures (such as for grain) was the *moggio* (or *modius*), equal to 24 *staia*. Each *staio* or *starius* was 16.9–17.6 kilograms, equivalent to about 24.363 hectares of grain. The *cogno* was a unit of measurement for liquids, especially wine, and was composed of 10 *barils*. Each *cogno* was 407 liters. The *orcio*, the measurement for olive oil, was equivalent to about 28.86 kilograms.

Money. The basic money of account was the *lira* (or *libbra*), equal to 20 *soldi* or 240 *denari*. Its value was pegged to the gold florin after the middle of the thirteenth century. Between 1252 and 1321 the value of the *denaro* fell about 50 percent (Herlihy, 1968, p. 265). For more information, see Goldthwaite, 1980, pp. 301–303, 429–430.

Dates. The Florentines dated the beginning of the year on March 25 (the feast of the Annunciation). In the text, I have changed the dates to the common style, unless otherwise noted. In the notes, however, I have left the dates recorded on the documents in the Florentine style. The documents are classified in the archives according to the Florentine style of dating.

Introduction

On December 8, 1322, a specially appointed papal commission met in the Florentine church of Santa Maria in Campo to begin an extraordinary inquest about why the papal tenth collected in the diocese of Florence by the late Bishop Antonio degli Orsi—raised to finance military campaigns in the Holy Land—had curiously never made it to Rome. Though Bishop Antonio (1309–1321) had helped lead Florentine forces against the invading Holy Roman Emperor, Henry VII, and had attempted to reform the cathedral chapter in 1310, he also had kept two palaces and a household of servants. More than a year after Antonio's death, Pope John XXII sent two legates to Florence to track down the money and return it to Rome. In the course of the initial investigation—which lasted through March of the following year—the commission made a very careful survey of the former bishop's property, interviewing his family, his executors, and his administrative assistants. The testimony led them to focus their attention on the late prelate's father, Orso di Bartolo di Valentino da Firenze.[1]

Compared with the behavior of other Florentine bishops before him, the prelate's nepotism had not been unusual. In fact, throughout the three centuries which constitute the principal focus of this study, the channeling of ecclesiastical resources to enrich the kin groups associated with the episcopate had been a persistent pattern of behavior. From the early eleventh century to the arrival of Pope John XXII's commission, those in the Florentine community who opposed this type of favoritism often found themselves in a distinct minority. The careers of Andrea de' Mozzi in the thirteenth century and Ildebrando in the eleventh demonstrate an enduring symbiotic relationship between episcopal income and the economic and political well-being of kinship groups allied with the bishops.[2] In the *Paradiso* Dante directed his ire at a Florentine patrilineage associated with the episcopal power: the Visdomini, which from the early eleventh century administered the episcopal estate (*mensa*) during a vacancy. In Canto XVI of the *Paradiso* Dante wrote:

> Oh, how great have I seen those now undone by their pride! and the balls of gold adorned Florence in all her great doings. So did the fathers of those [the Visdomini] who, whenever your church is vacant, fatten themselves by staying in consistory.[3]

The Visdomini first appropriated the right to manage the vacant episcopate at the beginning of the eleventh century. Their use of the episcopal properties to benefit their family patrimony differed very little from the behavior of other kin groups linked to Florentine ecclesiastical resources.[4]

The traditional reliance on church offices, property, and honors to advance the interests of one's lineage consequently made the control of the episcopate a principal object of contention and struggle among the great families of Florence. The history of the estates of the bishops of Florence is therefore directly intertwined with the social history of the Florentine elite. The focus of conflicts within the elite was the patrimony of the See of St. Zanobi, consisting of landed properties and jurisdictional rights (*iura et bona*).[5] Access to that wealth gave to the bishops and their kin vast power—power both in the countryside and in the city. Indeed, episcopal lordship bound the city to the country.

The history of the patrimony (*mensa*) of the bishops of Florence between 1000 and 1320 is therefore a case study in the exercise of power in a very prosperous region of Europe. The key to unraveling the social, economic, and political history of any society is a close examination of those groups or institutions which control the economic resources of that community. Indeed, the historical record indicates that those who control the economic resources of a society also tend to dominate its political life. It follows that the dominant actors in the economic and political sphere are not institutions but the people who control the institutions and in whose hands most of the wealth is concentrated. A proper understanding of any advanced society therefore requires the historian to identify the groups who control the institutions.[6] However, those who exert economic and political hegemony in most societies are rarely united among themselves. In fact, ruling groups are often deeply divided, and they come together only when threatened by a common adversary (if even then). The acquisition and preservation of power by an elite are accomplished through several methods, among which are the following: the use of force, the role of law, the work of intellectuals to legitimize asymmetrical relations of power and privilege, and the possession and use by members of the ruling elite of a semi-mystical and influential quality known as *charisma*.[7] The economic power which the dominant families and organizations of any society possess—whether one is dealing with the bishops of thirteenth-century Tuscany, cloth-manufacturing capitalists in nineteenth-century Lancashire, or multi-national corporations operating in the developing world—allows them to exercise decisive influence over the development of the communities in which they exist. In the case of Florence, the dominant participants in political and economic life were the patrilineages of the ruling elite, many of whom depended on access to ecclesiastical offices and property for the maintenance of their privileged position. Consequently, the for-tunes of many members of that elite were inextricably linked to church property. The examination undertaken here of the patrimony of the bishops of Florence will therefore shed light on the distant past of the Arno city by focusing on one of its most important institutions.

Historians of Europe have long acknowledged that church property was closely linked to the history of European social and economic devel-opment. Emile Lesne's detailed survey of ecclesiastical property in France has not been equalled for any other country of Europe, although David Herlihy's 1961 article on church property had a continental scope, as it utilized the records of three hundred archives to describe the eco-nomic history of the church.[8] In the last half-century, historians have continued to examine ecclesiastical lordships as a way of commenting on general issues in economic and social history, including the nature of the seigneurial economy, socio-economic relationships on feudal estates, the impact of population movements on social structure, and the devel-opment of a feudal lordship.[9]

The study of ecclesiastical property in Italy has had a very unusual history. In Italian medieval studies in the two generations after the *Risor-gimento,* two of the most important concerns of historians have been the economic and juridical bases of the commune and the origin of the modern bourgeois state. For many nationalist Italian scholars, the church is seen as having exerted a negative influence on Italian history, contrib-uting to national disunity and later obstructing Italian unification. Conse-quently, many historians dealt with the church only in relation to the dominant issues of the day: the conflict of church and state, the origins of capitalism, or the emergence of the free commune. Few scholars wanted to study it on its own terms. Two of the first historians to exam-ine church history as an end in itself were G. Dinelli (1915) and Robert Endres (1916), both of whom exploited the rich archives of Lucca for information on the economic history of the Lucchese church. Although

Pietro Santini, Robert Davidsohn, Gioacchino Volpe, and A. S. Barbi examined episcopal power in Florence, Pisa, Luni, Massa Marittima, Volterra, and Pistoia, they were all interested primarily in the emergence of communal institutions, the clash between the country and the city, and the conflict of church and state.[10] The political legacy of the *Risorgimento* and the influence of Jacob Burckhardt on northern European and American historiography have also until recently tended to focus attention away from the study of the institutional and economic dimension of ecclesiastical life. Consequently, scholars have under-utilized the contributions that church history could make to an understanding of the social and economic history of medieval Italy.

Frustrated by the lack of interest in the economic history of the church among Italian historians, Carlo Cipolla published in 1947 a seminal article which made a convincing case that the study of ecclesiastical property should be a central concern for Italian economic historians.[11] Since the end of World War II several crucially important studies of church property in northern Italy have appeared. The works of Catharine Boyd on tithes (1952), Cinzio Violante on the bishop of Milan (1974a), Philip Jones on Tuscan monastic property (1954–1956), David Herlihy on continental church property (1961), Pierre Toubert on Latium (1973), Vito Fumagalli on ecclesiastical resources in the Po plain (1976), and Andrea Castagnetti on the parish (*pieve*) (1976) have all made notable contributions. Influenced by their peers north of the Alps (especially by the *Annales* "school" and their interest in local agrarian history), several Italian and French historians have published local histories of specific ecclesiastical lordships, using them to explore broader historical problems. The studies by Rosario Romeo on the lordship of Sant'Ambrogio at Origgio (1957; reprinted in 1971), by Giorgio Chittolini on the properties of the cathedral of Cremona (1965), by Elio Conti on the monastery of Passignano (1965), by Jean-Pierre Delumeau (1978) on the bishop of Arezzo, and by Gérard Rippe on the bishops of Padua (1979) are all local studies which addressed broad historical issues. For example, whereas Romeo was concerned with the relationship of the city to the countryside, Conti was fascinated by the origins of modern agrarian structures. Conti's magisterial analysis of Poggialvento near the abbey of Passignano has been a historiographical focal point for subsequent studies of specific regions, most recently Renzo Nelli's analyses of the Florentine episcopal lordship in the area around Monte di Croce (1985, 1988) and Christopher Wickham's study of the Garfagnana and Casentino (1988).[12] In the last two decades the literature on the economic history of the church has mushroomed. New contributions include Alberto Grohmann's work on Assisi (1981) and the Soviet historian L. A. Kotel'nikova's exploration of Tuscan agrarian history (1975).[13] Kotel'nikova (1975) studied the role of church property in her examination of the nature of a feudal economy and explored the transition from feudalism to capitalism. Regarding the study of Tuscan bishops and their estates in particular, the last quarter-century has been extremely important, as more historians have used the rich resources of the Tuscan archives to examine the histories of the episcopates of Volterra, Luni, Massa Marittima, Pistoia, Lucca, Arezzo, and Florence.[14]

Paradoxically, the church of the wealthiest and most powerful Tuscan city in the thirteenth and fourteenth centuries has received the least attention from historians, at least until recently. Whereas before the twentieth century, scholars such as F. Ughelli (1718), Giovanni Lami (1758), and Giusseppe Cappelletti (1861) published documents and collated specific information about specific churches and bishops, until recently historians since then have largely ignored the Florentine church.[15] To date the best surveys of the Florentine church are Robert Davidsohn's mammoth turn-of-the-century history of the city, Pietro Santini's analyses of the Florentine constitution, and the series of sketchy articles by Brunetto Quilici, published between 1938 and 1969.[16] In recent years, however, the landscape of Tuscan church historiography has been changing markedly. Johann Plesner, Philip Jones, Elio Conti, Richard Trexler, and Marvin Becker were among the first to turn their attention to the Florentine church. Whereas Jones focused on monastic property and Trexler on church law, Becker concentrated on heresy and the relation of the church to the commune. In the field of the history of spirituality, J. N. Stephens and Anna Benvenuti-Papi have made notable contributions to our knowledge about heresy, cults of the saints, and the mendicants.[17] The studies of the properties of the abbeys of Settimo, San Salvi, and Passignano by Philip Jones, Vanna Vannucci, and Elio Conti, respectively, were the earliest attempts to provide portraits of the estates of important ecclesiastical institutions. Recently, Renzo Nelli contributed to that series of local studies by publishing a study of episcopal lordship at Monte di Croce—a study which utilized the rich archival resources available for the late thirteenth and early fourteenth century to examine ownership of rural lands by city dwellers. William Bowsky's work on the chapter of San Lorenzo and Anna Benvenuti-Papi's on Bishop Ardingo (1205-1231) indicate a renewed interest in the church—unmatched since the eighteenth century. The recent book on the Florentine church in the fifteenth century published by Roberto Bizzocchi is a major contribution to our knowledge of the Renaissance church.[18] A thorough investigation of the history of the properties of the bishops of Florence is therefore both timely and crucial to this ongoing exploration of church history.

The purposes of this study are three. First, it will provide a portrait of episcopal power in Florence as it changed and developed over three centuries. It will explain those changes as well as describe them. Among the issues examined are the following: the acquisition of property and jurisdictional rights, the administration of the estate (including methods of accounting), the nature of the relationship of dependents to the bishop, and the interaction between the bishops and the commune of Florence. Implicit throughout this history of the episcopal estate is the assumption that episcopal lordship relied both on the bishop's jurisdictional and on his spiritual or sacramental power (*potestas jurisdictionis* and *potestas ordinis*). The concept of power used in this study, therefore, is a broad one, one that does not limit itself to material interests.

The second aim of this book is to use the study of the Florentine bishops to explore three of the most important issues in the historiography of Italy: the development of the elite patrilineages, the relation of the city to countryside (*contado*), and the nature of a northern Italian medieval lordship. The three centuries in primary focus in this study—1000 to 1300—framed a coherent phase in the history of elite patrilineages. Organized around ecclesiastical patrimonies at the beginning of the eleventh century, several patrilineages derived a great deal of their political and economic privileges from their access to ecclesiastical property. Among those were the Visdomini, whose name derived from their role as administrators of a vacant bishopric (*vicedomini*). Of central importance to the history of the Florentine elite, therefore, was the history of church property. With its estates in the countryside, the Florentine episcopate was also a link between the city and its surrounding region. The study of the Florentine bishopric (with its vast holdings in the major river valleys near Florence) can provide valuable insight into the nature of the interrelation between the city and its hinterland and allow us to test rival historiographical traditions regarding the nature of that relationship. (I define *contado* in a narrow sense as that part of the countryside around Florence subject directly or indirectly to the jurisdiction of the commune. The extent of the *contado,* therefore, will expand as Florence increasingly brings more and more of its hinterland under its control between the twelfth and thirteenth centuries. The territorial confines of the diocese is defined here as that part of the Florentine countryside subject to the spiritual and in some cases temporal authority of the bishop. At least from the twelfth century, it seems that Florentine

urban officials—and for that matter other northern Italian city leaders—assumed that the borders of the diocese defined the limits of expansion of the *contado*.)[19]

For the purpose of this study, we can distinguish two different approaches to this problem. An older generation of twentieth-century historians of Florence—Romolo Caggese, Robert Davidsohn, Gioacchino
Volpe, and Gaetano Salvemini—argued that the subjugation of the *contado* by the city marked the triumph of the urban "capitalist" bourgeoisie
over the rural "feudal" nobility. The oppression of the country by the
"feudal" elite was replaced by the exploitation of the countryside by the
commune. This approach viewed the commune of Florence essentially as
a center of mercantile interests—directly opposed to the landed "feudal"
elite.[20] Hence, the relationship between city and *contado* was antagonistic
and exploitive, pitting consumers (the city) against producers (the "feudal" nobility), with the final triumph of the city marked by the introduction of market controls, taxation of the *contado,* and usury.

A half-century ago, Nicola Ottokar, Johann Plesner, Enrico Fiumi, and
their students began to subject this interpretation to increased attack,
pointing out that there actually existed a continuity of interests between
rural and urban elites, that there was little class conflict between the
nobility and the urban elite, and that the relationship of the city with
the countryside was symbiotic rather than exploitive.[21] One of the most
articulate spokesmen of this view was Enrico Fiumi, who attempted to
demonstrate in a series of articles published in the *Archivio Storico Italiano* between 1957 and 1959 that the growth and prosperity of Florence
resulted not from the exploitation of its countryside but from the emi-
gration into the city of a vibrant rural bourgeoisie (*la gente nuova*) during
the period of demographic expansion. Consequently, when the demographic collapse occurred after 1348, Florence suffered an economic
decline. The growing consensus of opinion among historians today—most articulately and persuasively presented by Philip
Jones—stresses the interdependence of city and countryside, the absence of clearly drawn lines between feudal and mercantile interests,
and the importance of landed property to the communal elite (even to
the merchants).[22]

Italy is a country of contrasts and regional differentiation. As we shall
see in our discussion of feudalism, it is very difficult indeed to make
generalizations about the social or economic history of the peninsula
which are valid for most or all regions. This is certainly true for this
particular issue, and historians have to be very cautious when they gener-
alize about relations between the city and its hinterland. Two contrasting

examples from the historiographical literature serve to demonstrate this point quite well.

In his magisterial study of the territorial lordship of the Milanese monastery of Sant'Ambrogio at Origgio, Rosario Romeo (1971) argued that in the late thirteenth century there existed a separation between the city and certain areas of its *contado*. Following the breakdown of a social pact between the *popolo* and aristocracy in mid-century and the subsequent expulsion of some of the nobles into the countryside, there were few urban landlords in peripheral areas of the *contado*, such as Origgio (under the lordship of the abbots of Sant'Ambrogio). The commune exerted little influence, and the abbey had more in common with rural lords than with urban landowners.[23] The recent analysis of local societies in the Garfagnana and Casentino by Christopher Wickham (1988) during the four centuries between 800 and 1200 presents a different picture. In both valleys, the point of reference for the rural elite (both political and economic) was the city (Lucca and, to a lesser extent, Arezzo). In both areas, urban landholding was spread throughout the diocese, creating territorial cohesion and facilitating urban integration within relatively short periods of time.[24] Gérard Rippe's study of Padua indicated that no simple contrast existed between urban communes and rural communes.[25]

There are three major local studies of landholding patterns in specific zones of the Florentine *contado* that allow us to examine the extent of urban landholding in the contado before 1300: Plesner's analysis of Passignano and Giogole (1934), Conti's investigation of Poggialvento (1965), and Nelli's recent explorations of Monte di Croce (1985, 1988). Whereas Plesner makes the case that most immigrants from the two *castelli* he studied were rural landlords, the work of Conti and Nelli indicate that there were few urban landlords in the *contado* before 1250. If the conclusions of the latter historians regarding Poggialvento and Monte di Croce are true for the rest of the *contado*, then the urban ecclesiastical institutions (of which the bishopric was the richest) were among the few principal links of the city to the countryside before 1250.[26] At least by the early twelfth century, the Florentine elite viewed the borders of the diocese as the proper limits of its subject territory. Indeed, as we shall see, the jurisdictional claims of the Florentine bishops—temporal as well as spiritual—helped define the limits of communal expansion. A study of the episcopal estate may give us insight into the history of early communal development of Florence and the nature of the state.[27]

If an analysis of Florentine episcopal power can tell us something about the Florentine elite and the relation of city to countryside, it can also contribute to our understanding of the nature of social and economic developments in the Florentine *contado* before the Black Death. As a major property-holder in the *contado*, the Florentine episcopate was also a major participant in the integration of the *contado* into the urban-dominated regional economy between 1100 and 1300. For centuries the bishops of Florence presided over vast estates concentrated in the major river valleys of the diocese. Between 1000 and 1300 the rural economy underwent a slow but dramatic transformation—a process Philip Jones wrote took certain regions of Tuscany "from manor to *mezzadria*."[28] Since the jurisdictional and economic interests of the episcopate straddled both city and *contado*, an understanding of the nature of the evolution of the episcopal estate may illuminate the process of agrarian change in Tuscany between 1000 and 1300.

The study of lordship (the *signoria*) has been a central concern of Italian historians for generations.[29] For an earlier generation of scholars, the *signorie* evolved either from the judicial rights connected with private landowning or from public powers associated with the disintegration of the state. They were closely (but not necessarily) connected with the appearance of *castelli* (castles) and, later, with the emergence of rural communes. Until the mid–1950's, most Italian scholars believed that a "feudal system" composed of fief-holding and vassalage dominated all Italy after the break-up of the Carolingian state, but the publication of Cinzio Violante's *La società milanese nell'età precomunale* in 1953 helped shatter that consensus. Arguing that fiefs and vassalage emerged in Milan only in the tenth and eleventh centuries, Violante demonstrated that the formation of private local lordships after the collapse of the Carolingian state could depend on allodial holdings and not necessarily require membership in a hierarchy of fief-holding vassals. Greatly influenced by the work of Georges Duby (particularly his work on the Mâconnais in 1953), Violante and subsequent scholars have come to distinguish the existence of at least two models or "ideal types" of lordship in northern Italy during the three centuries covered by this book: landlordship (the *signoria fondiaria*) and the territorial lordship (the *signoria territoriale*).[30] Whereas the former implies the payment of rents in money or kind by tenants to a lord, the latter signifies the exercise by the lord of public or juridical rights over a subject population residing in a particular territory (the *dominatus loci*). Those subject to this latter type may include tenants as well as non-tenants. In a *signoria territoriale* the local population could owe, for example, any or all of the following: oaths of servile status (*fidelitas*), guard duty, taxes on immovable property, public (imperial) taxes (the *datium*), or court fines. The distinction between landlord-ship and a territorial lordship therefore is an important one, as a territorial lord could exercise lordship over a zone in which he did not own all the property. This study will explore the nature of a particular lordship in medieval Tuscany, examining the applicability of these two types of lordship to the power of the bishops of Florence.[31] An analysis of the presence or absence of feudo-vassalic relations will tell us about the role these social relations played in the episcopal lordship.

This book will define feudalism very broadly as a "mode of production": a way of producing at a particular historical stage of human development which was distinct from the mode of production which preceded it (the ancient economy) and from the mode of production which succeeded it (capitalism).[32] According to this conception, feudalism is the exploitive relationship between lords and a subject population by which the latter transfers to the former wealth beyond its needs of subsistence in the form of labor services, banal exactions, or rents in kind or money, often under the threat of coercion. Whereas the subjects want to retain as much of what they produce as possible, the lords want to maximize the amount of surplus product that they can extract. Consequently, there is implicit tension within this relationship, and this tension often erupts into open conflict. According to this conception of feudalism, the elite class of landholders is sometimes but not always organized hierarchically into vassalage relations, although these relations do not always involve fief-holding.[33] In other words, feudo-vassalic relations (what the Italians call *rapporti feudo-vassallici*) need not play a major role in the economy of a particular region, as the aforementioned work of Cinzio Violante first made clear in regard to Milan.

Defined in the narrow and strict juridical sense (and not as a mode of production), feudalism as a category of historical analysis is rapidly falling out of usage.[34] Defined as the establishment of reciprocal relations between two people in which one (the lord) grants property to another (his vassal) in exchange for certain services, feudalism cannot adequately describe the wide diversity of European social and economic relations between 1000 and 1300. Indeed, it appears that on a continental scale, the allod was actually more common than the fief.[35] A broader definition formulated by Marc Bloch and those influenced by him has linked the existence of fiefs and vassals with the economic exploitation of a subject peasantry, the *seigneurie*. Since the publication of Georges Duby's study of the Mâconnais in 1953, however, regional histories of France and Catalonia have called into question the relevance of vassalage and the fief as the formative component of European society.[36] The increasingly limited applicability of these definitions of *feudalism* has led more and more historians to reject the term feudalism altogether. Whether feudo-vassalic relations existed in particular regions still remains an important historical problem. Where Italian historians have looked for fiefs and vassalage in their own history, they have discovered incredible diversity and variation. Whereas in France there existed some dynastic continuity between the Carolingian period and the eleventh century, the lack of such in Italy led to a plurality of local situations. Italy lacked the large territorial lordships that existed in Anjou, the Mâconnais, and Normandy.[37] Whereas some communes used feudo-vassalic relationships a great deal in their political relations (such as at Arezzo and Piacenza), some communes used them sparingly (Florence), and some did not rely on them at all (Spoleto).[38] Rippe has argued that for Padua feudo-vassalic relations were constitutive elements in the formation of the commune.[39] Even within Tuscany itself, the situation was extremely diverse. Before 1050 there is little if any documentation for vassalage (only at Lucca and at Monte Amiata). After the eleventh century, it appears that the presence of feudo-vassalic relations in documents of some communes were frequent (Arezzo), minor (Florence), or somewhere in-between (Volterra, Pistoia, Pisa, and Lucca). For example, in his recent history of two mountain valleys in Tuscany, Wickham saw no evidence for feudo-vassalic relations in the Garfagnana and in the Casentino. They appear to have spread downwards to the peasantry in the twelfth century. Here, as elsewhere in Italy, the emergence of feudo-vassalic terminology did not correspond with a commensurate change in social relations. Rather, the emperors and regional lords used feudal terminology to define more precisely already existing social and economic relationships.[40] Exactly how important and prominent feudo-vassalic relations were to the exercise of a Florentine episcopal lordship will be one of the issues examined in this book.

The third aim of this book is to place the study of the bishops of Florence within a broader historiographical context. Indeed, the survey of the patrimony of the prelates of Florence affords the historian the opportunity to examine two problems of significance: the transition from feudalism to capitalism, and the origin and development of the European nobility. Capitalism, unlike feudalism, is a mode of production characterized by the exploitation of wage labor by an urbanized capital-owning elite for the production and international exchange of commodities. Crucial for the emergence of capitalism is the creation of a world market, dominated by Europe.[41] In the process of transition from one mode of production to another, Italy played a paradoxical but unique role. Indeed, in the thirteenth and fourteenth centuries, the economies of northern and central Italy were the most advanced and prosperous in Europe. The dramatic demographic increase and the urban expansion of the thirteenth century gave Italy a unique position in the later economic development of the West.[42] The transformation of the Italian economy from feudalism to capitalism, of course, lasted centuries. Nevertheless, the study of the estates of the bishops of Florence from the eleventh through the early fourteenth centuries allows the historian to chart the early stages of this process in the city and countryside of Florence on the local level.

In her examination of Tuscan agrarian history, *Mondo contadino e città in Italia dall'XI al XIV secolo* (1975), L. A. Kotel'nikova discerned two schools of thought on the nature of the late feudal economy in Italian historiography. On one hand, some historians (Chittolini, Jones, E. Cristiani, Violante, Romeo, and G. Luzzatto) have argued that agrarian change did not lead to a feudal crisis and decay and that the feudal economy continued to be vibrant. On the other hand, other scholars (most notably Cipolla, P. Vaccari, and L. Dal Pane) have argued that the rise of the communes and the agrarian crisis marked the decline of feudalism and the emergence of a new type of economy.[43] The study of the economic and jurisdictional powers of the bishops of Florence gives us a way of testing the validity of either of these two hypotheses—at least for the period before 1320.

The development of the feudal economy and the spread of feudo-vassalic relations after the eleventh century is directly linked in the minds of historians with the emergence of the nobility. What exactly was the nobility? What relationship did it have with knighthood? What was the chronology of its emergence? As was true for the historiographical debates regarding the nature of feudalism, the difficulty of resolving these issues derives from the incredible diversity of socio-economic relations in Europe after 1000. Scholars today tend to accept the following characteristics as central to a definition of noble status after 1200: aristocratic birth, the possession of jurisdictional powers (the authority to judge or the power of the ban, for example), freedom from outside exactions, knightly status (*via* dubbing), and public opinion. Most historians now accept that there was no break between the Carolingian nobility and the later elite of the twelfth and thirteenth centuries. Although the nobility and knights were separate before the thirteenth century, they began to fuse no earlier than the twelfth century, but not in the same manner everywhere in Europe. The emergence of an ideology of chivalry and the ritual of dubbing facilitated that union. Originally a moral term used by nobles to describe themselves, only around 1200 did *nobility* have any juridical validity, created partly to resist the challenges of the upwardly mobile mercantile elite.[44]

In Italy the situation was extremely complicated, making generalizations very difficult to make. Although the term *nobilis* had no precise meaning (it appears in documents interchangeably with the words *potentes* or *magnates*), it does seem to apply to that segment of the elite which represented the union of the great landowners (*proceres*) and the emerging knights (*milites*), united by a style of life, profession of arms, class consciousness, and the possession of privileged names (*dominus* or *Ser*). As such, the emergence of a hereditary nobility in Italy followed a pattern very similar to that of northern Europe. Unlike northern Europe, however, there were fewer social and economic distinctions between a landed and a mercantile elite, and the number of nobles among the aristocracy in Italy was very small indeed, relative to northern Europe. Consequently, there was a constant need for new blood. New members of the noble elite rapidly replaced those houses that either disappeared or fell to a lower level of the social scale. Also unlike their northern counterparts, Italian nobles sometimes made money from commerce and occassionally from money-lending. Whereas it was common for merchants to move into the nobility, it was uncommon for nobles to move into the mercantile elite. In some areas of northern Italy, many members of the nobility had been retainers of the margrave or powerful bishops after the disintegration of the Carolingian state. Similarly, in central Italy this group was present at the side of public officials during judicial proceedings, and many of them held episcopal and papal *castelli*.[45]

In Florence the nobility derived most of their wealth from the land, and they remained the richest group of the elite through the period covered by this study. Giovanni Tabacco has argued that in Bologna and Florence the nobility was closely connected with military service to the commune during the period of communal expansion into the countryside. It was there in the *contado* that the *militia* first emerged next to the rural population. Apart from marriage or dubbing, one was also able to enter the Florentine nobility by acquiring property with the juridical rights accompanying it. Knighthood and public opinion were the two crucial factors determining noble status in Florence.[46] Because the bishop was the lord of several *castelli*, the *dominus* of several regional lordships during the period of communal expansion, and a participant in Florentine military campaigns, a study of the lineages associated with him and his office allows us to explore from a different perspective the identity of a segment of the Florentine elite. The contribution that this study can make is not a general explanation for the origin, identity, or history of the aristocracy as a whole. Rather, the intent is to offer a new perspective on the proscriptive measures against that segment of the nobility juridically defined as *magnates* at the end of the thirteenth century. Not all the members of the Florentine nobility were classified as magnates. Scholarship has demonstrated in the last century that a clear definition and identification of the magnates is elusive, extremely problematic, and probably unnecessary. It seems to me, however, that we can use the study of Florentine episcopal power to offer new perspectives on the "magnate problem."

This survey of the episcopal estate begins with a brief discussion of the emergence, in the eleventh century, of the Tuscan patrilineage and the social and economic background for the foundation of the only monastery directly under episcopal jurisdiction (San Miniato al Monte). Chapter 2 will survey the twelfth century, particularly the origin of episcopal *castelli* and the conscious fostering of a network of episcopal clients in the countryside. The most crucial period for the future history of the episcopal *mensa*—the subject of Chapter 3—spanned the two generations between 1180 and 1250. This chapter will bring together several issues in agrarian and social history, including the origins of rural communes. The fourth chapter (1250–1320) will focus on the transformation of the bishops into urban and rural landlords at a time of dramatic political and social changes within Florence itself. Chapter 5—the conclusion—will weave together the many thematic threads into a coherent summary.

A history of the temporal lordship of the bishops of Florence must begin with five cautionary observations. First, the shortcomings of the sources themselves undoubtedly will condition the kind of conclusions reached in this survey. A fire in the sixteenth century in the Archivio Arcivescovile destroyed hundreds of parchments and left irreparable gaps in documentation. Consequently, there is precious very little information on the episcopal estate before 1000, relative to what is to be learned in the Luccan archive. The second cautionary observation is perhaps the most important, as well as the most easily forgotten by historians. Living in a society whose social relations and values differed so markedly from our own, the bishops of Florence and their households (*familia*) made economic decisions over the three hundred years surveyed by this book which do not correspond with the principles of neo-classical economics (supply and demand, maximization of resources, economizing, and cost/benefit analyses). As Karl Marx, Marcel Mauss, W. Kula, and Karl Polanyi have all warned (albeit coming from different directions), the historian must beware of applying capitalist categories (land, labor, capital) to the economies of pre-capitalist societies.[47] The imposition of contemporary ways of thinking distorts rather than illuminates one's understanding of non-capitalist economies. The economy of thirteenth-century Florence was embedded in the society of which it was a part. Cultural values and social relations were a major influence on the economic behavior of the Florentine bishops from the time of Ildebrando to Antonio degli Orsi. Similarly, cultural factors (such as belief among all classes that the bishops wielded sacramental power) greatly assisted the bishops to protect their interests. Though the bishops certainly modified over time the methods by which they attempted to exploit their patrimony (especially after 1175), they did not do so because they were necessarily becoming incipient capitalists.

Third, there are very few detailed monographs on other institutions of the Florentine church. Indeed, as we have seen, historians have largely ignored the history of the Florentine church. Though several scholars (like those mentioned earlier) are presently exploring this dimension of the history of the city, it will be several years before those studies are finished and a complete synthesis is possible. The history of the bishops, therefore, is only one piece of a large puzzle—a puzzle of which the other pieces are missing. As historians publish more studies of the Florentine church, they will fill in more of the pieces and provide answers for problems which this study must leave unresolved. Most important, we know very little about other church lords in the *contado* (other than those mentioned above)—especially the cathedral chapter and the bishopric of Fiesole. Where necessary in the narrative which follows, I will provide tentative and unsystematic overviews of the properties of those two lords.

The fourth observation is that we should not assume that the elite patrilineages or houses mentioned in this study acted as monolithic units. Indeed, as will become apparent, pressures within the patrilineage toward division were far stronger than the forces toward cohesion.[48] Finally, this is not a study which purports to provide a complete social and economic profile of the areas of the *contado* where the bishops had interests. We certainly need more local studies like those of Plesner (1934), Conti (1965), Nelli (1985, 1988), and Wickham (1988), but it will be a long time before we have an accurate picture of the entire *contado* for the period before 1300. Frankly, the type and nature of the sources largely dictated the scope and nature of this examination. What offers the historian an unprecedented opportunity to provide a general survey of Florentine episcopal lordship is the *Bullettone*, a summary of the episcopate's records. Though full of difficulties, it contains information on all aspects of episcopal lordship throughout the diocese from the ninth to early fourteenth centuries. The history of episcopal power is therefore primarily the analysis of this particular text.

The *Bullettone*

A fire in the archepiscopal palace in 1532 destroyed many of the most ancient documents and severely limited the written sources available to historians of the bishops of Florence.[49] The remaining principal source, however, is a rich one. It is the *Bullettone,* a register of all the documents related to the episcopal domain *(mensa episcopalis).*[50] Redacted in 1323, the *Bullettone* is a collection of abbreviated versions of documents collated and classified according to locality by notaries engaged after the death of Bishop Antonio degli Orsi in 1321 by the families which traditionally administered the bishopric during a vacancy. Among the types of records included in the *Bullettone* are lists of rents or obligations owed by tenants to the bishops, records of donations of properties and possessions to the bishopric, descriptions of episcopal rights and privileges on episcopal possessions, judgments by Florentine communal courts in cases involving the exercise of episcopal lordship, and records of disputes between the bishops and their tenants (and in some cases, rural communes). There are presently two fourteenth-century manuscript versions of the register: the original (1323) is in the Archivio Arcivescovile di Firenze and a later copy (1384) is in the Archivio di Stato di Firenze. This book is the first systematic attempt to use the entire *Bullettone* as a resource.[51]

In July 1321, Bishop Antonio degli Orsi died, and on August 3 the cathedral chapter came together to choose a successor.[52] Their deliberations led to a tense power struggle within the chapter, resulting from profound factional divisions existing within the hierarchy at the time. Eight canons supported five different candidates. Only after two months was the treasurer of the chapter, Guglielmo dei Frescobaldi, able to get a majority, but then Pope John XXII chose to overlook the chapter's choice and waited two years before naming someone to his liking. The pope's actions reflected the fact that the episcopal elections were no longer in the hands of the cathedral chapter; they were controlled directly by the papacy. As such, his decisions challenged the traditional rights of the Visdomini, Tosinghi, and Aliotti lineages to administer and manage the episcopal see during a vacancy.[53]

The growing strength of the papacy in Florentine ecclesiastical affairs was not the only threat to Visdomini interests. In 1276 the commune of Florence challenged the right of the Visdomini during the long vacancy of 1275–1286 to appoint administrators (*podestà*) in the rural communities under episcopal control. Legislation passed against magnates such as the Visdomini in 1281, 1286, 1293 (the Ordinances of Justice), and 1295 (a revision of the Ordinances) sharply circumscribed magnate power and placed the Visdomini under greater political pressure. Communal concern over the continued role of the Visdomini in episcopal affairs continued into the fourteenth century. Having served as administrators of a vacant seat for over three centuries and concerned that their rights were under attack, the three lineages engaged notaries to put together an abbreviated list of episcopal parchments to defend their traditional rights to administer the estate during a vacancy.

On the same day that Bishop Antonio degli Orsi died, the Visdomini met for the first time in the church of San Salvatore to choose four of their peers to serve as administrators for the first two months of the vacancy.[54] While the cathedral chapter was attempting to elect a successor, the Visdomini were hard at work, depositing in the care of the notary Ser Bindo da Calenzano an inventory of all the possessions of the deceased bishop.[55] On February 10, 1323, the *consorteria* deputized four of its members (Billiguardo della Tosa, Nepo della Tosa, Baddino dei Visdomini, and Ghino dei Visdomini) to collate material into a single register. Along with Lapo Aliotti, the four chose two notaries to do the job on March 30: Ser Giovanni Arrighetti da Pomino and Ser Giovanni Tieri da Castelfiorentino.[56]

By publishing an inventory of all charters, leases, privileges, and legal judgments affecting the episcopal estate from the ninth through early fourteenth centuries, the Visdomini wanted to create a written record of the traditional rights, possessions, and privileges the bishops and their administrators (themselves) held in the diocese at a time when they faced growing challenges to those rights. By doing so they also sought to prevent rural communities and tenants from challenging their jurisdiction during any interim vacancy period. As Trexler pointed out in a brief discussion of the *Bullettone* (1978), the *Bullettone* served the interests of the houses in at least three ways. First, records of annual episcopal gifts demonstrated that there existed a symbiotic relationship between the contributing lineage and the bishops. Second, lists of episcopal properties gave them an accurate picture of the extent and quality of episcopal wealth at their disposal during a vacancy. Finally, descriptions of past episcopal entries into the city before consecration—during which the three houses accompanied the newly chosen prelate—served to demonstrate to the entire Florentine community that their close ties to the Florentine bishopric were historically immutable. Indeed, the manuscript itself was proof of their special relationship with the episcopal office—an honor which they used to divert attention from their appropriation of ecclesiastical wealth.[57] We may add another reason for the redaction of the records: it served to protect the interests of those lineages associated with the bishopric from challenges issued by rival houses of the Florentine elite. The historical context for the redaction of the *Bullettone* was therefore rooted in the social, economic, and political history of Florence.

The *Bullettone* is a book of two hundred and eighty-six parchment folios and begins with a brief description of the material it contains as well as a list of those responsible for its creation. On the first folio Ser Giovanni Arrighetti wrote that the book is a register, repertory, and inventory of the properties and jurisdictional rights (*iura*) of the Florentine bishopric, written at the time that the Visdomini were custodians of the episcopal patrimony. In a passage dated February 10, 1323, Ser Arrighetti stated that the Visdomini wanted to compile the *Bullettone* for three reasons: to consolidate in one volume what existed in several, to conserve the many precious parchments from perishing, and to preserve the ancient rights of the Visdomini for future generations.[58]

The *Bullettone* has eight general sections. Following the introductory remarks, the notaries registered every type of document that related to the episcopal estate according to locality. A section that includes a list of all the annual payments (*affictus*) paid by episcopal tenants (*fideles*) precedes one of the most interesting documents: a description of the episcopal entry of 1286. A catalogue of community pledges of fidelity (*iuramenta*) made to the bishops is organized according to location and date. All of the documents included in the sixth section concern the interests of the Visdomini. After an inventory of episcopal property and the personal possessions of the bishop who died in 1321 (the seventh part), the notaries placed statements at the end to verify the accuracy of the register.[59]

The bulk of the register consists of abbreviated summaries of the charters, oaths of servile status or fidelity by episcopal dependents, lists of purchases, and papal privileges relating to the episcopal patrimony. Following the introductory folios,[60] the notaries classified each section of the *Bullettone* according to type (imperial privilege, papal bull, lists of rent payments) and according to locality. The notaries put all papal and imperial material in the same section. Though they chose to classify the summarized documents according to the parishes or rural communes to which they referred, they did not organize the material chronologically. Each entry is very concise and often does not include a date. Often it lists only the individual and the amount owed. This is apparent in the following example: "That the brothers Martinus and Corsus (sons of the deceased Lombardus) are required and ought to give and pay annually in perpetuity to the Florentine bishopric three *staia* grain for half of the *podere* of their grandfather, Bencivenni."[61] Only by locating the name of the tenant elsewhere in a datable entry in the register can we have any idea exactly when the episcopal notary made a record of the annual payment. Besides the two fourteenth-century manuscripts of the *Bullettone* (the 1323 original and the 1384 copy), there are three seventeenth-century copies in manuscript and one version published by Giovanni Lami in his *Sanctae Ecclesiae Florentinae Monumenta* (1758).[62]

In one of the notarial statements at the end of the *Bullettone*, Ser Giovanni Arrighetti da Pomino described the method by which he registered the original documents in the book. Following his own good judgment, he decided to collate and abbreviate the original parchments (*instrumenta*). Apparently, he followed the order and structure of the original collections as he found them.[63] The fact that Ser Arrighetti chose what to include and then summarized the original document underscores one of the most serious problems with the *Bullettone* as a source: one can never be sure that the entry of a document in the *Bullettone* is an accurate description of the original parchment.

We are fortunate that one of the collections of documents which served as a source for the register survived, for these documents allow us to check the degree of accuracy of Ser Arrighetti's summary. Around 1289 Bishop Andrea de' Mozzi (1287–1295) had his notaries record a series of sworn declarations (*recognitiones*) by episcopal tenants at Castelfiorentino acknowledging the annual payments they owed the bishop. Published in full by Michele Cioni, these *recognitiones* are examples of the documents the *Bullettone* notaries registered and abbreviated. One example will illustrate the differences between the *Bullettone* and Cioni's collection of *recognitiones*. The original document edited by Cioni not only names the individual involved (Gianni di Riccardino di Oddo di Palmiero) but also gives us a great deal of information on every aspect of the examination: the name of the church in which he was examined (San Blasio), the names of the witnesses, the name of the episcopal syndic to whom he made the statement, and the fact that the notary ordered the individual to make the annual payments which by the tenant's own admission his family had made in the past to the bishop. The entry in the *Bullettone*, on the other hand, provides us with only the sketchiest information: the name of the individual concerned and the fact that after confessing that his ancestors had paid three *staia* every August to the bishop he promised to resume payment every year in the future. The summary in the register gives us no indication that it was the episcopal syndic, a member of the Visdomini lineage, who questioned this recalcitrant tenant before several witnesses as part of a formal inquiry.[64]

The comparison of this one entry with its original is typical of all the entries in the *Bullettone*. They offer only a bare summary of the original document, including usually only the names of the individual involved and the notary. Sometimes there are no dates given at all. Often the abbreviation is so brief that one has only the vaguest idea of what the gist of the original parchment actually was. Often the *Bullettone* notaries chose to exclude the locations and the amount of land involved in the transactions involving the bishops or their tenants. In a recent publication, Conti observed that the *Bullettone* did not include descriptions of *datium* payments (originally an imperial tax), since the notaries assumed all episcopal tenants paid the levy in the thirteenth century.[65]

The lack of detail in the entries is only one of the several problems associated with the use of the *Bullettone* as a historical source. What compounds the difficulty in achieving a full picture of the episcopal estate is that documentation represented in the register is spotty for the centuries before 1300. I estimate the register contained roughly 3,347 entries, distributed in the following way: pre–twelfth century (103), twelfth century (196), thirteenth century (1,018), fourteenth century (809), and no date (1,221). I was careful to fix a date on an entry *only* if I was sure it was the correct date. That resulted in my count's having more entries in the "no date" category than were assigned by P. E. Palandri in a 1926 study. There are also serious problems with the dating of the entries: many have no dates, and if they do, the indiction often conflicts with the date given. Sometimes the discrepancies between the indictions and the dates given can be decades or even centuries. More seriously, the notaries did not choose to arrange the entries chronologically. Appendix D contains only these entries with known dates.

Aside from the problems of abbreviation and dating, there are at least two further difficulties. First of all, even if an entry states that an individual in a certain year acknowledged his obligation to pay a *census* annually for land he held, it is impossible to be certain that he or his family continued to pay the amount in subsequent years. Even if there are lists of people paying the *census* in 1299, we do not know if they were still making the payments in 1300. Furthermore, Conti suggested that the amount of the actual payments made to the bishops by their dependents were probably higher than those listed in the *Bullettone*.[66] Finally, the historian can never be sure that in the *Bullettone* we have a complete picture of the episcopal estate. The very fact that the Visdomini *consorteria* commissioned and oversaw its compilation presents the possibility that they excluded or added material to further their own interests rather than provide an accurate picture of the extent of the episcopal patrimony. They must have done a little of both. After all, it was in their interests to possess a full survey of properties and possessions to which custom allowed them access during a vacancy.

The shortcomings of the *Bullettone* as a historical source will strongly condition the kinds of conclusions reached in this study. Obviously, the abbreviated entries do not provide as complete a body of information as one would want. Indeed, *Bullettone* entries are not typical of those documents which do remain from the same period (1000–1300): they are much more abbreviated and incomplete. Furthermore, the abundance of documentation for the late thirteenth and early fourteenth centuries contrasts markedly with the lack of information we have for earlier periods. Only when more local studies of the *contado* before 1300 are completed (similar in scope to the work of Conti on Poggialvento, Nelli on Monte di Croce, and Wickham on the Casentino) will we be in a situation to place the information gleaned from the *Bullettone* within its full regional context. In the meantime, however, the historian can take a number of corrective measures.

To remedy the problems arising from the dating, I have rearranged the entries into chronological order within the proper geographical area, and I have corrected notarial mistakes in the dating by checking them with the indictions and the dates of the bishop mentioned in the entry. Furthermore, and perhaps more important, I have attempted to fill in the gaps of historical time not sufficiently covered by the *Bullettone* by drawing heavily upon other sources of primary material (published as well as unpublished).[67] Nevertheless, study of the *Bullettone* and documents in the public and private archives will tell us only part of the story of the economic history of the Florentine episcopate. Re-creating that history is therefore like piecing together a puzzle without having all the pieces.

The Emergence of the
Patrilineage and the Conflict
with Episcopal Interests

Geography, politics, and economic interests are principal actors in the
formation of the Florentine church. In his magisterial study of ecclesiastical life in England and Italy, Robert Brentano described the Italian
church as a church of cult centers and extended cities, with odd-shaped
diocesan borders. It stood in stark contrast to the English church, which
was territorial, tightly administered, and geographically well-defined. Be-
lieving that the two different church cultures evolved from two different
socio-economic environments, he observed that a dominant factor in-
fluencing the establishment of the form and outline of the Italian diocese
was geography.[1] As we shall see, the fortunes of the bishops of Florence
and their importance to the urban elite largely depended on access to
the road network in the diocese and on control of the economy of the
fertile valleys of the river basins.

The diocese of Florence is composed of river plain, mountains, and
hills (see Map 1).[2] Above all, it is dominated by the Arno River basin.
Originating on Monte Falterona in the Casentino, the Arno follows an
elliptical path through the Pratomagno until it reaches Pontassieve,
where it turns west to flow into the sea. Aside from the fertile river
valleys, the dominant geographical features are the mountains and hills
of the Florentine countryside. Florence is the geometrical center of the
arc formed by the Apennine range which stretches from the Mediterranean coast to the Adriatic. The region of the Florentine diocese, therefore, is part of a complex network of parallel mountain and hill chains
which extends from the southeast to the northwest and which are separated from one another by river valleys.[3]

Established no earlier than the fifth century B.C.E., Fiesole was a strategic point between the fertile valley of the Tiber and the Maremma region
in southern Tuscany. It was also a link between the settlements in southern Etruria and those in the Po Valley north of the Apennines.[4] Florence

probably was a Roman *colonia* founded in 59 B.C.E. Its chief importance lay in the fact that it was the site where the Via Cassia—the consular road connecting Rome, Arezzo, Bologna, and the Po plain—crossed the Arno River. Gradually Florence became one of the most important road intersections in central Italy. Joining the Via Cassia at Florence were the Via Pisana (which followed the course of the Arno to link Florence with Pisa), the Via Faentina (connecting the city with Faenza in the Po Valley), and the road to Lucca by way of Pistoia (see maps). The Via Cassia was not the only consular road passing through Tuscany in late antiquity: the Via Aurelia ran parallel to the western coast linking the ancient Etruscan cities of Roselle and Populonia with Pisa, and the Via Flaminia passed through a small section of eastern Tuscany.[5] After 800 the growing popularity of a new route between Rome and Piacenza—the Via Francigena—diminished the importance of the Via Aurelia and accelerated the decline of the Via Cassia.[6]

The Development of Ecclesiastical Organization

By the early seventh century, the basic ecclesiastical organization of the principal Italian bishoprics was in place. Following soon thereafter came the foundation of the rural parishes, most of which were equipped with baptismal founts. Although these rural churches might have emerged as early as the fifth century, the first documented reference to a baptismal church (*plebs*) comes from an eighth-century Luccan document.[7] Normally established by the bishops, baptismal churches (*plebes*) exercised spiritual and administrative jurisdiction over their surrounding territory.[8] By the eleventh century these churches had become the fundamental unit of ecclesiastical organization in the Tuscan countryside, exercising jurisdiction over the dependent satellite churches or oratories (*capellae*) in their immediate vicinity.[9] The oratories, like the baptismal parishes, were controlled by the bishops. Though a few references to the baptismal churches and oratories appear in documents as early as the eighth and ninth centuries, the majority of them date from a later period—probably from the twelfth century.[10] The city of Florence constituted one baptismal church district (*plebatus*), centered around the baptistery of San Giovanni and the cathedral of Santa Reparata (built at the end of the ninth century) (see Map 4).[11] At the close of the eleventh century, the diocese contained about sixty *plebes*. By the end of the thirteenth century, there were ninety-six.[12]

Having originally created many of the rural parishes to serve the needs of the local population, the bishops possessed by law and custom the right to choose or elect the priest or archpriest of the baptismal church (the *plebanus*). Normally the local congregations and lesser clergy were able to participate in the process of choosing an archpriest, as the bishop usually consulted them before making the final decision. Once elected, a senior priest of a baptismal church was in effect a "petty bishop" in his parish and exercised jurisdiction over the subject oratories.[13] The archpriests in turn had the right to appoint the rectors (*rectores*) of the subject oratories. Although the archpriests enjoyed a great deal of independence managing the parish patrimony, they were supposedly subordinate to the bishop in matters of discipline and policy.[14] A third and separate type of rural church emerged in the period of Lombard control: the proprietary church. Considered the possession of the owner of the land on which the church was situated, proprietary churches appeared throughout Tuscany in the eighth century. The proprietor of the church could be a layman, a monastery, a bishop, the royal family, or another church. Proprietors had the right to appoint the archpriest or rector of the churches under their control, effectively giving them direct access to church revenues. Most of the proprietors of this third group of churches were lay kinship groups.

The Restructuring of the Tuscan Elite and the Foundation of Proprietary Monasteries, 962–1020

When Otto I (936–973) and his Saxon Successors Otto II (973–983) and Otto III (983–1002) attempted to maintain a modicum of imperial control over Tuscany after the collapse of the Carolingian state in Italy, they necessarily had to cultivate political and economic ties with the three most powerful political players in the region: the margrave, the elite lineages, and the bishops.[15] From the reign of Otto I, the Saxon emperors engaged in a skillful game of playing off one member of the triad against the other two.[16] Theoretically, the margrave should always owe allegiance to the emperor, but in this period of political decentralization the lines of authority were not at all clear. The existence of a margrave in Tuscany prevented most of the Tuscan bishops (including the bishops of Florence) from acquiring the comital status achieved by their peers on the other side of the Apennines (with the exception of the bishop of Arezzo).[17] As a result, the margrave was a much more powerful and important ally for the Saxon emperors than was the bishop of Florence. Throughout the tenth century Saxon kings acted to consolidate and protect their bases of authority in Germany by placing their public lands into the endowments of newly founded monasteries. Forty-one years after Otto I had endowed a monastery at Magdeburg to protect many of his landed possessions,[18] the Tuscan margrave Hugh and his mother, Willa, began to follow a similar policy by establishing several monasteries throughout northern Tuscany and placing in their endowments the imperial fiefs. The first of those monasteries was the Badia in Florence, followed later by San Michele di Marturi in 997 (on the frontier of the Florentine and Sienese dioceses), San Michele sulla Rocca Verruca (near Pisa), and another monastery at Capolona (near Arezzo).[19] Hugh also founded the monastery of San Bartolomeo in Buonsollazzo in the Mugello.[20] Monasteries were founded for both political and religious reasons, but it was the former that was more important. They served as administrative centers for margraval possessions, and they also attracted donations.[21]

Out of the ranks of the late-Carolingian nobility there emerged to prominence in the tenth century four principal kinship groups in the diocese of Florence: the Aldobrandeschi, the Gherardeschi, the Guidi, and the Cadolingi. Of those four, the Cadolingi and the Guidi were the most important. In the early tenth century—at a time when the Carolingian administrative apparatus had largely collapsed—King Berengar I (888–924) of Italy attempted to counterbalance the growing power of the margrave by establishing the Cadolingi and Guidi as counts of Pistoia.[22] Originally Lombard, these two lineages had gradually become important allies of both the Italian kings and the margrave. Their political fortunes continued to rise in the early tenth century through the patronage of King Hugh of Provence (926–947). After 962 the Ottonian emperors simply built on the alliances already cultivated by their predecessors, the kings of Italy, and began to nurture extensive political ties with the powerful lineages as well as with the margrave.[23] In 964 the Cadolingi were close enough to Otto I to be able to sit in the imperial court of justice. By the end of the tenth century, the Cadolingi had become close allies and vassals of Otto III.[24] Whereas Guidi possessions were concentrated primarily around Pistoia and in the dioceses of Fiesole and Arezzo east of Florence, Cadolingi properties were located in the Valdarno Fiorentino west of Florence, the Lucchese, the Valdelsa, and in the dioceses of Pistoia and Volterra.[25]

Count Cadolo, who later gave his name to his descendants, first appeared in documents dated between 953 and 964. Having successfully built up a patrimony in the Arno plain west of the city, Cadolo founded the oratory of San Salvatore di Fucecchio before dying in 982.[26] The core of the Cadolingi possessions was concentrated in two areas: the region around Settimo (the *castelli* of Settimo and Montecascioli, the estate or *curtis* of Mantignano) and the zone around Fucecchio, where there were seven *castelli,* including one at Fucecchio itself.[27] The power exercised by the Cadolingi in these areas west of Florence was based on possession of the castles (*castelli*) and the dependent properties around them (the *curtes*). These possessions most likely derived from public (judicial) rights granted to them by the last kings of Italy, who appointed them counts in the early tenth century. In the early stages of Cadolingi expansion their economic base centered on the surrounding territory near the castle (the *circuitus castri*).[28] Indeed, following the dissolution of Carolingian power, lineages like the Cadolingi expanded their economic and political influence over the areas where first they had held public rights.[29] Suggesting that the Cadolingi were appropriating episcopal possessions at the end of the tenth century is the fact that they included Celiaula in the Val di Pesa—where the bishops had been leasing property—in the endowment made to one of their family monasteries, the Badia of Fucecchio.[30]

As this new elite coalesced around vast patrimonies after the final collapse of the Carolingian state, the structural organization of the families themselves underwent a transformation. The absence of any effective central authority in Tuscany in the tenth century created the conditions in which these changes took place. Tracing descent through the male line to a common male ancestor, the patrilineage or agnatic lineage emerged in order to preserve and protect the properties of its male members by limiting the number of possible heirs and by instilling in its members a strong sense of ancestral identity. The Tuscan families represented a particular type of patrilineage which appeared in Tuscan documents in the early eleventh century: the "consortial" lineage, or *consorteria.* A patrilineal descent group sharing a common patrimony, the emerging Tuscan *consorterie* of the late tenth and early eleventh centuries both benefitted from as well as hastened the demise of any remaining central power. As a reflection of the emergence of a patrilineal self-consciousness during this period, the kinship groups began to assume surnames. The Cadolingi genealogy began in the tenth century. The overriding goal of these patrilineages and *consorterie* was to preserve the unity of the patrimony from one generation to another.[31]

The territorial concentration of patrilineal patrimonies and the creation of proprietary monasteries as administrative centers to manage and protect those possessions hastened the localization of aristocratic power in certain areas of Tuscany. The success or failure of patrilineages in

Tuscany in the tenth and eleventh centuries depended on the balance of social forces present at the time in the region. At Populonia, Sovana, Massa Marittima, and Roselle the bishops were too weak to resist the pressure of the nobility (the Aldobrandeschi).[32] In the diocese of Lucca, episcopal land fell into the hands of the lay patrilineages between 850 and 1000. The bishops themselves came from those lineages.[33] In the diocese of Arezzo, however, the count-bishop effectively blocked the emergence of patrilineal power in the Casentino, making it easier for the commune of Arezzo later to expand its reach into the countryside with little noble resistance.[34]

The Cadolingi and Guidi fulfilled three of the requirements outlined by a recent historian for dynastic success: they possessed properties on the periphery of the diocese (composed of public lands and ecclesiastical property), they established proprietary monasteries in the heart of those holdings, and they received imperial protection of them.[35] The creation of those monasteries—although they were not proprietary establishments—provided a rational method of transmitting an undivided patrimony from generation to generation.[36] Like earlier proprietary monasteries established by the margrave and his wife, they served as administrative centers for possessions granted to them in usufruct from the imperial fisc. Furthermore, the monasteries functioned as adminstrative centers of the possessions of the patrilineage itself, administered as part of the monastic endowment.[37]

At the end of the tenth century—as the power of the margrave declined—both the Guidi and Cadolingi assumed greater importance to the emperor Otto III as political allies. Reflecting their growing wealth and self-confidence at the end of the tenth century, the Guidi founded abbeys at Sant'Ellero and at Strumi. Simultaneously, the two branches of the Cadolingi founded the two family monasteries in the Arno Valley west of Florence at Settimo (998) and Fucecchio (1001) (see Map 1).[38] Like the margrave and their peers, the Cadolingi and Guidi wanted their family monasteries to serve the spiritual as well as the material needs of the patrilineage.[39] Indeed, the two were so intertwined that they were indistinguishable. In each of the monasteries the founding lineage established a Benedictine community of monks led by an abbot. The primary purpose of the community was liturgical: to intercede daily through a life of prayer for the souls of the living and dead members of the founding patrilineage.[40] As Gerd Tellenbach has argued, the founders of these monasteries placed great confidence in the prayers of the monks. The more devout the monks were, and the more closely they followed their rule, the more they served the spiritual interests of the founder and his lineage. If the lord wanted to be buried in the monastery, he had even greater reason to want devout monks.[41] Furthermore, a monastic community with a reputation for holiness attracted donations from those members of the elite eager to commission prayers from the monks for the spiritual well-being of the donors. The success of monasteries therefore depended on the moral and spiritual integrity of the monks themselves. Because some churchmen believed that the buying and selling of ecclesiastical offices diminished the spiritual reputation of a community, several of the founders of the new monasteries wrote into the charters of foundation the right to remove an abbot guilty of the sin.[42]

In the Cadolingi abbey of San Salvatore di Settimo, Lotario di Cadolo (son of the patriarch of the lineage) appointed a certain Guarino as abbot.[43] Charged with safeguarding the spiritual life of the monastery for his patrons the Cadolingi, Guarino imposed a strict Benedictine discipline on his community in the early years of the eleventh century. Guarino, however, did not limit his concerns only to the community under his care. He came to see himself as a crusader against spiritual corruption, both inside as well as outside his monastery. In the early eleventh century he campaigned against sexual incontinence (nicolaism) among the clergy in the diocese of Florence. Among his targets was the bishop. The desire of the Cadolingi abbots to establish a spiritually "pure" environment at Settimo directly affected the fortunes of Bishop Ildebrando of Florence (1008–1024) and the material development of the episcopal estate.[44] Conflict between Abbot Guarino and Bishop Ildebrando in the early eleventh century set in motion events that challenged the spiritual primacy of the bishop and dramatically altered the way by which he organized and managed the episcopal *mensa*.

Bishop Ildebrando and the Struggle for Power in the Diocese of Florence, 1008–1024

The great lay kindreds were not the only lineages to treat church property as a principal political and economic resource.[45] For example, the Anselmi of Lucca are known to have transferred the episcopal title from uncle to nephew.[46] In Florence we have the case of a certain Giovanni, who founded the church of San Martino in Florence and appointed his brother and nephew as its rectors.[47] Of extreme importance for the story of the bishops of Florence is the behavior of one particular kinship group: the patrilineage of Davizo—later known as the Visdomini. They were to play an extremely important role in both the history of the bishopric and the commune. Appearing in the historical record in 1009, this Davizo was the first *lay* administrator (*vicedominus*) of the episcopal estate in the period between the death of a bishop and the election by the cathedral chapter of the successor. Before 1009 the administrator of the vacant bishopric had always been a cleric. But that changed in the early eleventh century, when Davizo managed to claim the office for himself and his descendants. Davizo's appropriation of the honor was a reflection on a lesser scale of the process of "lineage-building" associated with the social restructuring of the Tuscan elite at the beginning of the eleventh century. A similar development occurred at Luni, Lucca, Massa Marittima, and probably Siena, as several patrilineages enhanced their economic and political standing by appropriating this important office. Between 1009 and 1054, Davizo acted as the episcopal *vicedominus*. At his death in 1054, Davizo's patrimony (the office of *vicedominatus episcopi*) passed on to his three sons and a nephew. Guido, one of the sons of those four (Davizino), married a woman by the name of Tosa, daughter of a Meliorellus. Their son, Meliorellus della Tosa, became the ancestor of the della Tosa or Tosinghi family. These two lineages—the Visdomini and Tosinghi—shared with a third kinship group after 1200, the Aliotti, the traditional right to administer the episcopal estate during a vacancy.[48] Together, these three families formed an alliance (*consorteria*—united by blood and marriage) which transferred the *vicedominatus* as hereditary property to its descendants through the male line. They even took the office as their name. Even after the Second Lateran Council of 1179—in which the church hierarchy restricted the role of all but the cathedral canons in the election of bishops—the Visdomini continued to administer the episcopal patrimony during the vacancies.[49] By the early thirteenth century the vast *consorteria* therefore consisted of three branches (*casate*).

The use of ecclesiastical resources to serve personal interests was apparently also the practice of the first eleventh-century bishop of Florence, Ildebrando. Appearing first in the historical record in 1008 as prelate of Florence, Bishop Ildebrando apparently had obtained the See of Florence by tranferring funds to the emperor Henry II, subsequently becoming his loyal ally. Residing in the episcopal residence near the baptistery of San Giovanni, he shared his quarters with the mother of his four sons, Alberga. Abbot Guarino of Settimo, concerned primarily by the high public profile in the episcopal court assumed by Ildebrando's consort, launched a fervent campaign to force the removal of the prelate from office. Probably before the end of 1014, Abbot Guarino walked to the episcopal residence in Florence to demand an audience with the bishop,[50] perhaps to protest the presence of a woman and her children in the episcopal palace. According to the *Vita Johannis Gualberti* (composed long after the events described here), Guarino had a reputation before he met with Ildebrando and his court of speaking out freely against concubinage and the purchase of church offices.[51] Presenting his case before the bishop and his court, he awaited a response from the prelate. Instead, Ildebrando's consort, Alberga, responded to him: "My dear abbot, my husband has not yet discussed your concerns with his court. When he does, he will get back to you when it pleases him."[52] Enraged that Alberga had spoken to him and not the bishop in the episcopal court, Guarino gave the woman a verbal lashing: "You accursed and sinful Jezebel! How dare you speak (conscious of your sin) before the episcopal court! You ought to be consumed with fire for having presumed to slander a creature and a priest of God!"[53]

According to the sources, Abbot Guarino went forthwith to a sympathetic papal court and convinced Pope Benedict VIII (1012–1024) to withdraw Settimo from the jurisdiction of the bishop of Florence and put it directly under papal protection.[54] That act prevented the bishop thenceforth from having any power to confirm a new abbot and from receiving the customary tribute due him.[55] The Cadolingi had entrusted the abbot with the quality of spiritual life at their proprietary monastery. It was quite a responsibility, because the prayers of the resident monks for the living and dead members of the patrilineage were effective only when the community lived according to the highest standards of spiritual purity.[56] Guarino apparently took that responsibility seriously, even to the point of requiring the bishop to adhere to his spiritual standards.[57]

As we may well imagine, Guarino's work was beneficial to the Cadolingi on several fronts. First, his reputation for sanctity attracted new donations to the monastery, facilitating the creation or consolidation of networks of clients in the countryside.[58] Second, the Cadolingi realized that the spiritual environment their abbot fostered enhanced the reputation of the monks' prayers for their dead family members. And third—perhaps the most important of all—Abbot Guarino and his patrons shared a common desire to harass and even drive from office the presiding bishop of Florence. As we have seen, the Cadolingi achieved success partially at the expense of the economic well-being of the Florentine bishopric.[59] Both the bishops and the Cadolingi had possessions in the Valdarno Fiorentino, west of Florence.[60] By supporting Guarino's campaign against Ildebrando after 1011, the Cadolingi were able to apply greater political and economic pressure on the prelate to weaken his political position within the city and force him off disputed lands.

Who was the audience to whom Guarino directed his attacks on Alberga and her prelate-husband? To whom did he and his followers appeal? The sources do not allow us to offer definite answers to these questions, but we can suggest solutions. Guarino apparently was the leader of a community committed to a spiritual program embracing chastity, poverty, and asceticism. Although simony emerged later as the focus for the next generation of holy men, it did not apparently play a major role in Guarino's campaign against Ildebrando. Rather, the anti-episcopal faction was antagonistic to the bishop for at least two reasons. For Guarino and his followers, incontinence among the clergy elevated women to an unacceptable public position within the ecclesiastical establishment—a position which aroused in them serious fears of pollution and manipulation by females. At the heart of Guarino's spiritual ideal was patriarchy and hostility to women, a tradition within Christianity which became more prominent in the eleventh century throughout Europe.[61] At a time when communities were under severe economic and social strain as the economic expansion of the eleventh century was under way, disputes over land and marriage became very common. Desirous of a stable authority figure to arbitrate conflicts, many communities looked to their priests and bishops as leaders. Fearful of the influence of women on the guardians of the social order, Guarino and his followers perhaps perceived Alberga as a menace to stability and security. She represented the unwanted intrusion of female pressure in a world in which women were associated closely with pollution and sin.[62]

The second reason for hostility to the bishop possibly derived from the bishop's involvement in the development of a monetarized market economy within Florence. As we shall see, there is documented evidence that the bishop derived income from an urban market as early as 1024, and it is possible he was claiming market dues before then. Also, he began to require rent payments in grain instead of the customary money payments on at least one estate as early as 1013, implying that he was receiving more money from the sale of grain than he was from the money rents. For Guarino and his followers, the involvement of the bishop in a money economy conflicted with their embrace of poverty as the clerical ideal. After all, money was very closely associated with clerical avarice,which led directly to the impoverishment of local churches. Furthermore, the use of ecclesiastical resources by Ildebrando to benefit a concubine and her offspring disqualified him as an appropriate bishop in the eyes of the abbot of Settimo.[63]

The growing political pressure must have concerned the bishop very much, as he began to take steps to enhance his position within and without the city. In early 1014, Bishop Ildebrando approached his patron the emperor Henry II for financial assistance to rebuild the ancient and ruined oratory dedicated to St. Minias on the *Mons regis,* the first martyr of Florence.[64] The decline in the power of the Tuscan margrave after the death of Hugh (1001) upset the precarious balance of forces existing between the rural kin groups (especially the Guidi and Cadolingi), the bishops, and the margrave. Relying on all three as his allies in the diocese, Henry II saw Ildebrando's scheme to build a major basilica and monastery as a way of restoring a political equilibrium in the region. In the same year Heny II issued a charter of protection for the monastery at Settimo.[65]

Bishop Ildebrando's plan in 1014 to found a new basilica and monastery was actually part of a much larger scheme: to revive and develop the cult of the first martyr of the city, St. Minias. It is likely, although there is no evidence from the contemporary sources, that Minias had remained for centuries the object of a popular cult. The bishop's strategy therefore was to create a proprietary monastery to rival those created by the Cadolingi and Guidi. His program consisted of four components: the construction of a basilica and monastery, the endowment of said monastery with disputed episcopal properties located principally on the periphery of the diocese, the appointment of an abbot obedient to the bishop, and the composition by the abbot of a suitable *Passio Sancti Miniatis.*

Several concerns underlay Ildebrando's motives between 1013 and 1014. First, he wanted to establish and conceal a family patrimony which consisted largely of ecclesiastical property. Second, he wanted to create a basilica and monastery which would rival the nearby San Salvadore di Settimo in terms of its prestige and wealth, a monastery whose fame would attract donations from the Florentine elite and rival the reputations of the new monastic establishments founded by the major patrilineages. Because he wanted to place the monastery under the power of the bishop, he knew the growing wealth of the foundation would greatly enhance the episcopal *mensa.*

Third, Ildebrando believed that the successful "orchestration" of the cult of the first martyr of Florence would deflect attention away from the stinging accusations of malfeasance. If Guarino drew support from the Cadolingi and an anti-episcopal party, to whom did the bishop appeal? The revived cult of this model Christian soldier (*miles*) certainly must have appealed to the growing community of armed horsemen (*milites*) within and without Florence, many of whom might have been holding episcopal castles (*castelli*) in the countryside. Indeed, perhaps they (the *milites*) constituted the core of support for the bishop at this time.[66]

The *milites* first appeared in the sources in the Po Valley about the year 1000, and they were an elite and powerful group associated with the bishop and the king. Their power derived primarily from allodial holdings, estates, *castelli,* and banal rights. Out of this group around 1030 emerged an elite of vassals, whose social and political position was defined by feudal tenure.[67] Perhaps it was from this rural audience of *milites* that Ildebrando sought political support, protection, and donations.

Finally, and certainly not the least important, Ildebrando used the foundation of the new monastery either to reclaim or to protect properties disputed between the bishopric and the Cadolingi and Guidi, as well as to attract donations to the new establishment.[68] As we have seen, donations to a new monastery created or strengthened social and economic relationships between the monastery (or its patrons) and the donor. In other words, donations were one means of establishing networks of clients in the countryside. Since a fundamental source of conflict was over power in the countryside, Ildebrando's actions were crucial. His successors followed the same strategy.

The linchpin of his ingenious plan was promotion of the cult of St. Minias. The conscious reinterpretation and revival of the memory of the saintly first martyr of Florence afforded Bishop Ildebrando a method by which he could use his sacramental power (*ius potestatis*) to protect and enhance his material and political interests (*ius jurisdictionis*).[69] At a time when supernatural power translated easily into political power, the creators or "orchestrators" of saints' cults were able to tap that source of power to extend or protect their authority over the community.

One of the first steps he took was to send members of his entourage to the ridge overlooking the city to search for the bodily remains of the martyr, even though Bishop Deodericus of Metz sixty years before had supposedly already carted away the bones.[70] Probably associated with the *translatio* of 970, there existed a tenth-century *Passio* of the saint which mentioned that Minias had died alone.[71] Since the relics of the martyr were absolutely necessary to his plan, the bishop called on his first abbot, Drogo, to draft a new *Passio* to supercede the earlier one. The new *Passio* also served to embellish the memory of the saint, thereby enhancing Ildebrando's spiritual reputation as his orchestrator.[72] Furthermore, Drogo concluded that Minias suffered martyrdom not alone but with several associates.[73]

Having founded a basilica and established a monastic community at San Miniato al Monte, Bishop Ildebrando set about to endow it with properties from the episcopal *mensa* spread throughout the diocese. Among his aims were the following: to stakeout properties claimed by the Cadolingi and Guidi, to establish a central administrative apparatus for the management of episcopal holdings located on the periphery of the diocese, to attract donations to the new foundation, and to provide a convenient cover for the appropriation of ecclesiastical property for his sons. By placing these possessions under the protection of the saint, Ildebrando made it spiritually dangerous for anyone to tamper with them. In both 1018 and 1024 the bishop granted to San Miniato al Monte properties and jurisdictional rights in the diocese, some taken from the episcopal *mensa* in the previous century (see Map 1).[74] Several of the donated properties were located exactly where the Cadolingi and Guidi possessed interests, indicating that they might have been earlier objects of dispute. For instance, the bishop granted to the monastery in 1018 an estate (*curtis*) at Empoli, exactly where the Cadolingi also had a *curtis*.[75] The church of Santa Maria di Padule and the chapel of San Miniato at Capraia donated in 1024 were located in the middle of the territorial holdings of the Cadolingi in the Valdarno west of Florence. The fact that Ildebrando included a chapel at Capraia consecrated to St. Minias is very significant. Peppered throughout the diocese were several oratories consecrated to the saint (there may have been as many as forty in Tuscany at the time).[76] By reviving the cult of St. Minias Ildebrando reactivated the cult in those distant oratories, many of which were located in or near areas where the Guidi and Cadolingi had possessions.

The bishop was also motivated to protect or reclaim properties claimed by the Guidi. In 1024 Ildebrando transferred to the monastery a *curtis* and oratory at Lonnano in the Casentino and the oratory of San Pietro di Cavagliano in the Bisenzio Valley with its possessions. The Guidi had properties both at Lonnano and Cavagliano.[77] As we shall see, Ildebrando's successors continued to include in their donations to the monastery properties located in areas of Cadolingi and Guidi strength. Unfortunately, the sources do not allow us to speculate further about the nature or history of these possessions, but it seems reasonable to assume that the properties at Empoli, Lonnano, and Cavagliano (and perhaps those at Capraia) were originally episcopal possessions lost and appropriated by the two patrilineages in the tenth century (Lonnano was in the diocese of Arezzo). According to a recent study of the Casentino, Lonnano was among the gifts of Guido II to the Guidi proprietary monastery of Strumi in 1029. Ildebrando tried to confirm the inclusion of Lonnano in the endowment of San Miniato al Monte in 1024. Apparently, his attempt was unsuccessful, and the estate fell out of episcopal hands forever.[78]

A glance at Map 1 indicates that the bulk of the endowments of 1018 and 1024 were located on the edges of the diocese, areas of greatest pressure by the rural lords. In the Mugello the bishop put one-half of the castle (*castellum*) of Montacuto (*plebatus* of San Martino di Viminiccio) and property in the *plebatus* of Vaglia into the monastic endowment in 1018 and 1024, respectively.[79] The bishop also might have intended the inclusion of possessions in the Bisenzio Valley near San Giovanni Soffignano to protect episcopal interests from Cadolingi encroachment on the western frontier of the diocese. Episcopal interests in the Val di Sieve extended back at least to the early tenth century. In that region of the diocese—a stronghold of the Guidi—Ildebrando placed under the protection of the saint a landed holding (*sortis*) at Aceraia, and the castle (*castrum* or *castello*) and manor (*curtis*) at Montalto, *plebatus* of Sant'Andrea di Doccia.[80] This is the first episcopal *castello* to appear in the historical record. In the *contado* of Florence, the bishop might have had a low profile, but—if Conti's study of Poggialvento is indicative of the *contado* as a whole—he might have been one of the only urban lords in the countryside until the thirteenth century. Clearly, the prelate designed the endowment to attract new donations to the monastery in areas of Cadolingi and Guidi strength, thereby enhancing his clientelar networks and economic power.

Many of the donations listed in the 1018 and 1024 documents were urban possessions, and the prelate included them in the grants for reasons different from those which motivated his donations of rural properties. The bishop intended the urban component of the endowment to benefit his immediate family. Sometime before 1024 Ildebrando established an urban market, the proceeds of which he gave in 1024 to San Miniato al Monte. As we shall see, the bishops in the early eleventh century had direct interests in at least one other market, located in the Valdelsa at San Piero in Mercato. Ildebrando wanted the new Florentine market to serve two purposes. First, he wanted the proceeds to be divided equally among his sons. Second, like his contemporary the bishop of Pistoia, he might have wanted to put economic pressure on the Cadolingi, who would have to market the produce of their lands in the episcopal market.[81]

The bishop also included in the two documented grants the two urban churches of Sant'Andrea sul Mercato and Santa Felicità. Originally donated by Bishop Podo (989–1002) to the cathedral chapter, Sant'Andrea and its attendant possessions were included by Ildebrando in the 1018 donation. The bishop apparently entrusted the church to his four sons (Gerardo, Pietro, Sichelmo—a priest, and Ildebrando) and to a member of the cathedral chapter for two *soldi* per year. He included the canon only to deflect attention away from his real intent. By the end of his tenure (1024) his sons exercised full control over the income of the church.[82] Santa Felicità was part of the original 1018 endowment, and it also ended up under the control of Ildebrando's family, as did the proceeds from the market created by the bishop.[83] By the time of his death in 1024, Ildebrando perhaps felt satisfied that he had successfully set apart enough income deriving from selected ecclesiastical properties under his control to provide for his family.

Most historians of eleventh-century Florence in the last century have been very critical of Bishop Ildebrando.[84] Until recently, scholars have seen him through the eyes of later reform propaganda. We must resist evaluating the early eleventh century in terms of the Gregorian program of the last quarter of that century. Indeed, we cannot talk of the emergence of a Gregorian program *per se* until decades later. If we evaluate his contribution to the history of the Florentine bishopric on its own terms, we see that he made some positive contributions to the later development of the episcopal estate. In terms of his own goals, to protect and enhance the patrimony entrusted to him and to provide for his family, Ildebrando was successful. A proper perspective on Bishop Ildebrando—the one developed in this chapter—sees him as an innovator who set in motion the process of reclamation, reconstitution, and creation of the episcopal *mensa*. He recognized the inextricable connection between religious interests (represented by the cults of local saints) and material interests, and later bishops attempted to follow his example. Although he enjoyed only mixed success realizing his goals, as we shall see, he greatly influenced the policies of his successors. By founding San Miniato al Monte and reviving the cult of the saint, Ildebrando initiated a campaign against the rural lords of the diocese and their allies, like Guarino, because he viewed them as the principal threats to the health and stability of the properties under his control. He recognized that the establishment of Cadolingi and Guidi proprietary monasteries had seriously threatened the future of episcopal holdings in the diocese. By placing episcopal properties under the protection of San Miniato, he hoped to prevent the loss of those properties to the rural counts and to shore up the declining profile of the bishop in the countryside. Later bishops—even Bishop Gerardo (Pope Nicholas II)—carried on this struggle for the next century and a half. Florentine bishops added to the endowment of San Miniato al Monte lands and jurisdictional rights which they sought to reclaim or protect from the the rural patrilineal elite.

The first appearance of a grain rent on episcopal land, the existence of interests in the market at San Pietro in Mercato, and the creation of an urban market during the tenure of Ildebrando mark him as the first bishop to see that involvement in the emerging commercial economy offered distinct advantages. In his evaluation of the state of episcopal wealth in the diocese of Lucca around the year 1000, Duane Osheim wrote, "The episcopal administration was passive, reacting to the changes and conditions created by others."[85] The Florentine bishopric might not have been as wealthy as its Luccan counterpart, but evaluations of the career of Ildebrando do not allow the historian a similar perspective on the state of Florentine episcopal administration around the turn of the millennium. If we distinguish two aspects of the later eleventh-century program of ecclesiastical activists—the abolition of clerical marriage and of the purchase of church offices on one hand, the reconstitution of church property on the other—Ildebrando played a major role in contributing to the latter.

Episcopal Expansion and Consolidation in the Diocese, 1024–1113

There is evidence that at the end of the first quarter of the eleventh century the Florentine bishopric possessed limited interests in six areas of the diocese: the Mugello, the Val di Pesa, the Val di Sieve, the Valdarno, in or near Florence itself, and in the Valdigreve. However, the vast majority of agrarian contracts (*libelli, feuda,* and perpetual leases) was concentrated in the Valdarno Fiorentino and on the outskirts of Florence (see Appendix D). Bishops Lamberto (1025–1032), Attone (1032–1046), and Gerardo (1046–1061) attempted to extend their previously limited presence in the countryside into some of the most important areas of the *contado.* Between 1026 and 1050 documented donations to the bishopric increased 60 percent (from five to eight), with almost half the donations involving property in the Mugello (see Appendix D). Previous to that date episcopal presence in the Mugello had been negligible. Donations of property in the Mugello to the bishops continued for the remainder of the eleventh, twelfth, and thirteenth centuries. Although the bishops continued to accumulate property in Florence itself, they also began receiving grants of land and jurisdictional rights in the Val di Pesa from the middle of the eleventh century. The increase in the economic power of the bishops in the countryside between 1024 and 1113 resulted primarily from donations rather than purchases. Several factors might account for this accumulation of property. First, it is possible that some members of the rural aristocracy donated property to the bishopric purely for religious reasons. Perhaps some of the donors were armed horsemen (*milites*), for whom St. Minias became a patron saint. In exchange for gifts, they expected protection and intercession from him. Second, some members of the minor landed elite came under increased and sustained demographic pressures in the eleventh century and were forced to break up their properties as they slipped into impoverishment. Some of those properties undoubtedly were donated to the bishopric. This process benefitted other ecclesiastical lords in the diocese in the early twelfth century, such as the monastery of Passignano (see Map 1). Originally one of three lords in the area around the present-day Poggialvento, the monastery became the major landholder in the twelfth century as the two minor noble families in the region fell into financial debt and poverty.[86] Both religious and economic factors seem to have played a role in the growing number of donations of property to the monastery, especially after 1040. After 1126, when the bishops of Florence acquired property primarily by way of purchase, they began to rely on their own monetary reserves and treasure to finance their purchases—a practice followed by most bishops in this period.[87]

In a recent study of the Garfagnana and Casentino before 1200, donations appeared to be "the religious element in a clientelar chain."[88] Perhaps beginning with a single donation made for religious reasons (prayers for the dead, for example), the process of gift-giving spread throughout the network of friends of the original donor and continued until the donors believed it was no longer in their interest to continue making the gifts. The recipient of those donations, either a church or proprietary monastery, was willing to trade its patronage and protection of specific individuals in a certain community for an increase in its local power and influence. To maximize its attractiveness as a recipient, ecclesiastical institutions tended to cultivate the attentions and interest of particular factions within the communities over which they sought influence.[89] Although we can reach no firm conclusions about why the bishopric began receiving donations in this period until historians have completed more local studies, we can venture some hypotheses.

In the diocese of Florence, it appears that after the first quarter of the eleventh century the bishops took an active role in encouraging donations of property and jurisdictional rights in areas where they already had possessions. They attempted to entice the minor aristocracy as well as small to medium landowners away from the patronage network of the Guidi, Cadolingi, and Aldobrandeschi. What the bishop had to offer was important to these landholders: defense of their interests with the margrave and with public officials in Florence. In effect, the bishops wanted to substitute their patronage for that of the rural lineages. As we shall see below, the bishops counted among their clients in the twelfth century several of the most important lineages in the *contado*, the Ubaldini and the Aldobrandeschi. The primary concerns of the bishops in the period between 1025 and 1113 appear to have been twofold: to continue the policy begun by Ildebrando to reclaim and protect episcopal properties claimed by the rural lords, and to expand and consolidate episcopal power in the countryside by creating a network of centers of power based on the possession of *castelli, curtes,* and patronage rights in local parish churches. This century therefore marks a watershed in the history of the episcopal *mensa*. The basis of power in the countryside in the eleventh century was possession of *curtes,* residences of the lord with all its associated buildings and properties. In the twelfth and thirteenth centuries these *curtes* were often surrounded by a wall and boasted at least one tower. Contemporary documents referred to these complexes as *curtes et castella*.[90] Following the lead of Bishop Ildebrando before them (who had before followed the lead of the rural lords and margrave), Bishops Lamberto and Attone continued to make donations of disputed *curtes et castella* to San Miniato al Monte to shelter them from outside interference. The Florentine bishops used their full moral and spiritual *charisma* to entice the minor rural lords to cede or to restore to them important properties in the major river valleys of the diocese. Particularly successful were Bishops Gerardo and Ranieri (1073–1113). Those donations for the most part took the form of the twelve *castelli* in areas where the bishops had previously enjoyed a low profile. Three of those *castelli* carried with them the acquisition of patronage rights to the oratories associated with them. These rights to appoint the local parish clergy played a prominent role in the establishment and extension of clientelar relationships in the countryside. Those relationships, as we shall see, had very real advantages for the prelates, as they often facilitated the purchase of property. In the Valdelsa Bishop Attone actually created a new *plebs* (Sant'Ippolito di Castelfiorentino in 1036), which gave later bishops the right to appoint the arch-priest. By 1113—a pivotal date both for the death of Bishop Ranieri and the death of the last Cadolingi—episcopal power in the diocese had grown markedly in the Mugello and in the Val di Pesa. Those two areas remained for several centuries to come the principal sources of income for the Florentine bishops. The growing presence of the bishops in the region of the Valdelsa around Castelfiorentino also dates from this period.

Bishops Lamberto, Attone, and Gerardo were all political *protégés* of the German emperor. Lamberto, a former prior of Sant'Apollinare in

Classe, was appointed by Conrad II (1024–1039). A follower of Romu-ald, Lamberto left the responsibilities of being bishop after seven years to return to monastic life.[91] Conrad II also was responsible for the elec-tion of Bishop Attone. Like Lamberto, Gerardo was an outsider (he was a Burgundian), and he was elevated to the See of St. Zanobi during the reign of the reform-minded Henry III (1039–1056).[92] They opposed clerical marriage, limited and eventually ended the claims of the sons of Bishop Ildebrando to the income of the church of Sant'Andrea, at-tempted to reorganize the affairs of the cathedral chapter, and extended the economic and jurisdictional reach of the bishops far into the coun-tryside.

Agreeing with the major tenets of the program initiated by Abbot Guarino and his circle, these bishops attempted to sever the access of ecclesiastical families to church property. All three were uncomfortable with the provisions made by their predecessor for his four sons. Sensitive to the demands to end clerical marriage in the diocese, they acted to circumscribe the access of the sons to ecclesiastical property. Although Lamberto confirmed the transfer of the Florentine church of Sant' An-drea to the sons of Ildebrando in 1025, he did so on the condition that they pay 24 *denari* annually to San Miniato al Monte, reconstruct the church, and assure that the church offer the divine services.[93] Lamberto's overall concern—although he did not attempt to disinherit the sons—was to assure the physical and spiritual well-being of the church. He attempted to make the requirements for the fulfillment of the *libellus* concerning Sant'Andrea so difficult to fulfill that private control of the church would effectively end. Only one son, Sichelmo, managed to fulfill Lamberto's stipulation. The *primicerius* Pietro either outlived the sons or bought them out, as the four sons no longer appeared in the docu-ments. When Bishop Attone restored possessions to the cathedral chap-ter in 1036 as part of his attempt to restore that body to economic health, he referred to this same Pietro as a "usurper."[94] Santa Felicità also seems to have fallen out of the hands of the family of the former bishop by the middle of the century. Under the efforts of Bishop Gerardo the church was refurbished and rebuilt as a convent by 1056.[95] Bishop Ge-rardo, like Lamberto, was hostile to the provisions made by Bishop Ildebrando for his sons.

By the middle of the eleventh century the successors of Bishop Ilde-brando had successfully ended the control of ecclesiastical assets by the descendants of the prelate. After 1026 there is no further documentary evidence that the market established by the prelate continued to exist. Hence, one may infer that family control of that operation also ended.

The reasons for its disappearance from the historical record are mysterious. One theory proposes that hostility to the new market by Florentine merchants led to its eclipse. We can only speculate that there had been intense local opposition to the involvement of the bishop in a mercantile economy, accounting for some of the popular support for the religious program associated with Abbot Guarino, Romuald, and later even Giovanni Gualberto.[96]

Although Bishops Lamberto, Attone, and Gerardo were hostile to the attempts of their predecessor to provide for his family at the expense of the Florentine church, they certainly embraced his practice of using donations to the new episcopal monastery of San Miniato al Monte to protect and reclaim episcopal properties and to create administrative centers for episcopal holdings. Many donations were situated in localities where the Cadolingi and Guidi also had possessions. In 1028 Bishop Lamberto donated to the monastery a *mansus* (a holding large enough usually to support a household) at Cellole near the site of a Cadolingi castle (Colle Muscioli), probably a holding absorbed by the Cadolingi into the orbit of their *castello*.[97] In 1037, Bishop Attone placed under the care of St. Minias a *castello* at Colleramole (Collis Romuli) in the *plebatus* of Sant'Alessandro di Giogole, the site of a Cadolingi landed holding perhaps usurped from episcopal possession in a prior time. Bishop Attone also reclaimed property at Quinto in the *plebatus* of Sesto, located in the midst of concentrated Cadolingi power.[98] Donations of property located in areas of Cadolingi strength were not the only grants given to the monastery. In the 1037 donation, Attone included Sant'Andrea di Doccia and half the *plebs* of San Giovanni di Remolo in the Val di Sieve—located in the heart of Guidi possessions.[99] The 1028 documents also ceded to San Miniato al Monte several Sienese churches which probably were claimed by both the Florentine and Sienese bishops.[100]

The emperors realized that a recharged and strengthened bishopric suited their interests appropriately, especially as a check on the increasingly independent margrave. Consequently, Conrad II and Henry III assisted San Miniato al Monte to settle property disputes in its favor. At a time when anti-imperial revolts broke out in Parma and Milan in 1038, the imperial chancellor confirmed for the monastery the possession of the church of San Gavino Adimari in the Mugello. In that same year the margrave Boniface—representing the emperor—confirmed the possession of San Piero ad Ema. That decision was later reconfirmed by an imperial court.[101] Finally, when Henry III attempted to end Boniface's attempts to create an independent principality, he cemented a political alliance with the bishop of Florence in 1043 by taking the possessions of the monastery under imperial protection.[102]

San Miniato al Monte consequently played a principal role in the promotion of episcopal interests, contributing to the reconstitution and protection of episcopal properties. Furthermore, its wealth and prestige attracted donations from all over the diocese, including the church of San Pietro ad Ema.[103] Consequently, it is not surprising that the eleventh-century bishops wanted to keep a close rein on the management of its endowment. Their proprietary right to elect the abbot allowed them to make sure that the monastery was managed according to the interests of the bishopric. When Abbot Leo (who had followed Drogo in the post) died in the middle of the 1030's, Bishop Attone therefore appointed Uberto abbot after apparently receiving a sum of money from the candidate. While the transfer of such funds was a normal occurrence in most proprietary monasteries, it shocked and appalled one of the monks, Giovanni Gualberto.[104]

The continued practice by Florentine prelates of granting "gifts" to their patrons in exchange for the episcopal see infuriated the young Giovanni Gualberto. A native of the Pesa valley, he had been influenced by the spiritual zeal of men such as Abbot Guarino of Settimo and Romuald. Some of Abbot Guarino's associates had retreated to the remote Aquabella in the diocese of Fiesole during a period of political tension, and over twenty years later, Giovanni Gualberto returned to the same place after his own public challenge to Abbot Uberto of San Miniato al Monte. It was at Aquabella that he founded the monastery of Vallombrosa sometime before 1037.[105] Within a very short period of time, Vallombrosa and other monasteries under its jurisdiction began perhaps to receive the lion's share of new donations by laymen. His opposition to simony made him famous throughout Tuscany. For the first time in the history of Florence, simony—the buying and selling of church offices—was elevated to a priority position in the religious and spiritual discourse in the diocese.

True to the ascetic ideal and the vow of poverty, Giovanni Gualberto believed simony had a morally corrosive effect in ecclesiastical life, a practice which aroused the sins of avarice and pride. Associated with the growing importance of cash in Florentine society, simony identified the priesthood with an increasingly monetarized economy. Perhaps it is no accident that this crusader against simony came from an area of the *contado* that shows some of the earliest traces of the development of a market network: the Pesa valley. Giovanni Gualberto found many allies in his campaign, including many on the upper and lower ends of the social scale who feared its practice because it facilitated rapid social mobility.[106] Those on the upper level showed their enthusiasm for his program by donating property to the monasteries associated with him. Building on the political base first established by Abbot Guarino, Giovanni Gualberto became so powerful that he later was able to expel a bishop from the city of Florence.

The Projection of the Episcopal Presence into the Countryside: The Castelli

Many of the castles which came into the possession of the bishops in the eleventh century were donations; only two were constructed by the bishops themselves. Episcopal castle-building (*incastellamento*—a process which played a major role in the economic and social changes of central and southern Italy) seems to have been virtually non-existent in the diocese of Florence. The first documented record of episcopal *castelli* in the diocese of Florence comes from the first and third set of episcopal donations to San Miniato al Monte in 1024 and 1037 (Lancisa and Collis Romuli).[107] The first documented instance of a contract for an *incastellamento* dates from 1104 (Pagliariccio in the Mugello). For example, the bishop of Lucca leased part of a castle in return for the completion of its construction in 1005 at Anchiano.[108] Documented Florentine episcopal possession of *castelli* post-dated documented instances of the same in Lucca by at least a century. In the diocese of Florence the acquisition of rural *castelli* by bishops was partially a reaction to lay possession of *castelli* (particularly by the Guidi and Cadolingi)[109] and to the growing economic strength of the monasteries in the diocese associated with Vallombrosa. These *castelli* and their surrounding properties (the *curtes*) became the centers of economic and jurisdictional power in the countryside in the tenth century (a period particularly marked by political instability and decentralization). Indeed, the *castello* and the administrative district around it (the *curia*) became the fundamental economic and political unit in the countryside.[110]

Concerned by the territorial power wielded by the rural lay elite, the bishops were also disturbed by the rise to local power of the monasteries under the jurisdiction of Vallombrosa. The new community had rapidly attracted vast donations of property and churches. In 1039 the abbess of Sant'Illari in the Mugello granted extensive properties to the monks, perhaps to avoid episcopal interference in the affairs of the abbey. Giovanni Gualberto also received the following monasteries under his direction: San Piero in Moschetta, San Paolo in Razzuolo, and San Cassiano di Monte Scalari. In 1048 a Florentine by the name of Rolando donated to Vallombrosa a small church which became the convent of San Salvi and quickly spread the economic and jurisdictional reach of the monastery into the Valdigreve, the Mugello, the Val di Pesa (Lucardo), and the area immediately south of Florence (Antella and Arcetri).[111] Finally, and perhaps most important for the bishops, the Cadolingi appropriately placed the San Salvatore di Settimo of the late Guarino under the direction of Giovanni Gualberto sometime between 1040 and 1046.[112]

In the fifth decade of the eleventh century, therefore, Bishops Attone and Gerardo faced formidable rivals for economic and jurisdictional power in the diocese: the monasteries under the protection of Vallombrosa, the Guidi, and the Cadolingi. The bishops found themselves squeezed by two Vallombrosan monasteries on the west and the east of Florence itself and in the Mugello. Furthermore, these establishments were receiving the bulk of new donations. Cadolingi, Guidi, and Ubaldini power kept the bishops out of the southwestern part of the diocese (Cadolingi), the Valdarno around Settimo and Empoli (Cadolingi), the Val di Sieve near Monte di Croce (Guidi), the western Mugello (Ubaldini), and other areas throughout the diocese (possessions of the Vallombrosan monasteries).[113]

Given these circumstances, it is not surprising that Bishops Attone and Gerardo proceeded to acquire *castelli* and to develop a following in certain areas of the diocese on the periphery of the estates of these powerful lords: the eastern Mugello and the Val di Pesa. Concentrating on those areas allowed the bishops to create concentrations of territorial power to preserve, protect, and extend episcopal interests in the diocese. The majority of castles which appear in the sources therefore were located for the most part in the eastern Mugello. In both areas the bishops could appeal to the minor aristocracy or to the small to medium landowner as their protectors against the pressures of the more powerful lords, the Guidi and Cadolingi. One way that we can see this process work concerns a minor lineage in the eleventh century, the Ubaldini. First mentioned in the sources at the end of the eleventh century, they show up as episcopal "vassals," implying perhaps that the bishops enfiefed them with land or *castelli* in return for military and administrative services. They also were vassals of the margrave and the Guidi. The absence of a local history of the Mugello prevents us from drawing conclusions, but we can speculate that the Ubaldini were an up-and-coming lineage which initially joined the ranks of episcopal clients in this period of rapid episcopal penetration of the eastern Mugello. Episcopal protection possibly served as a buffer against the Guidi, effectively preventing the Guidi from swallowing the Ubaldini estates.[114]

We see a similar process at work in the Pesa valley (see Map 2). The acquisition of Ripoli in 1054 was the first of many acquisitions of *castelli* in the Val di Pesa. And in 1098 a branch of the Aldobrandeschi transferred lands, possessions, and *castelli* (*terras, possessiones, et castra*) to the bishop. A valley with no significant Cadolingi, Guidi, or Vallombrosan interests, the Val di Pesa became a fertile area for episcopal penetration in the eleventh and twelfth centuries.[115] Although the sources are silent on this point, we can speculate that the rural lineages which donated their *castelli* to the bishops and received them back in fief were chiefly responsible for managing the *castelli* and rendering military services to the bishop when called upon to do so (see Chapter 2). If so, these are among the few examples of military service in exchange for grants of land.

The fact that the bishops of Florence between 1024 and 1061 acquired all or portions of several rural *castelli* indicates that they were aware that the territorial units organized around them were the keys to their economic prosperity. The *castelli* of Lancisa and Collis Romuli were probably constructed by the bishops themselves (although we have no corroborative proof of that). Before the death of Bishop Gerardo in 1061, the bishops managed to acquire interests in five *castelli*. In the Mugello, they received all of portions of the *castelli* of Ampinana (1041), Vespignano (1050), and Cerliano (1059).[116] Vespignano was close to the *curia* of Borgo San Lorenzo, where the bishops had been leasing land at least as early as the episcopacy of Rambaldo (929–964).[117] They also received rights in the castles of Ripoli in the Val di Pesa (1054) and Cercina in the Valdarno (1047, 1072, 1074).[118] The bishops designated these castles and their *curiae* as organizing centers for the episcopal estates in the Valdarno Fiorentino, the Val di Pesa, and the Mugello. As we shall see, they most likely were centers for the collection of rent (especially Vespignano).

Episcopal power in those areas increased by way of donations of property as well. Donations of property situated in the Mugello increased slightly between 1026 and 1076 (and they were to continue to increase on into the twelfth century) (see Appendix D). In the Mugello, Bishop Gerardo received two donations of property in the *curia* of Borgo San Lorenzo.[119] The acquisition of the *castelli* and their dependent properties enhanced a significant episcopal presence in local parish affairs in the Valdarno Fiorentino, Val di Pesa, and Mugello. In the Valdarno the rector of the church at Padule was paying 24 *denari* for lands and tithes leased by the bishops at the end of the tenth century, and the arch-priests of San Martino di Brozzi and of San Martino di Sesto were also leasing episcopal land. In the Val di Pesa, near the recently acquired *castello* of Ripoli, the arch-priest of Santa Cecilia di Decimo had been paying eight *soldi* for episcopal property at the end of the tenth century. We also know that the arch-priest of Santa Agata in the Mugello north-west of Borgo San Lorenzo was paying rent to the bishop at the end of the tenth century.[120] All in all, the economic and jurisdictional connec-tions between the bishops and local churchmen in areas where the bish-ops were acquiring *castelli* and clients were another level of episcopal power in those zones. During the tenure of Pietro Mezzabarba (1062–1068) acquisition of *castelli* and jurisdictional rights in the diocese ended, but they resumed under the bishopric of Ranieri.

Bishop Attone extended the reach of episcopal jurisdictional power into the Valdelsa by actually *creating* a *plebs,* Sant'Ippolito di Castelfio-rentino.[121] This is the only instance of the creation of a *plebs* by a bishop in the sources, and it was one of the first steps toward the creation of an episcopal lordship. Located on the right bank of the Elsa northwest of Marturi (the site of the margraval abbey of San Michele), the new *plebs* of Sant'Ippolito di Castelfiorentino was on or near the Via Fran-cigena. North of there, on the hilly spine which separated the Valdelsa from the Val di Pesa, was the episcopally controlled *plebs* of San Pietro in Bossolo, which also was located on a major road artery: the secondary road linking it with San Pancrazio in Lucardo and San Pietro in Mercato (see Map 1). The new church was situated twenty kilometers north of present-day Poggibonsi, and we know that the bishops had been leasing property there since the tenth century (see Appendix D).[122] Shortly after the middle of the tenth century, Bishop Sichelmo granted to Rodolfo di Ildibrando the former demesne (*donicatum*) at Pisano for 24 *denari*.[123] Earlier in the century, the arch-priest of San Pietro in Mercato (1008) had also been leasing land and probably tithes from the bishop. The creation of the *plebs* of Castelfiorentino therefore marked an attempt to enhance a growing episcopal presence in the region, no doubt linked to a desire on the part of Bishop Attone to profit from access to the markets on the Via Francigena located at or near the new *plebs*.

The bishops also hoped to weaken Cadolingi power in the region or to reclaim lost properties from them. The formation of the *plebs* served to create a network of clients rivaling that of the Cadolingi accross the river. The Cadolingi possessed vast properties on the left bank of the Elsa: six *castelli* (Catignano, Pulicciano, Casaglia, Germagnano, Ridarotta, and Colle Muscioli) and a *curtis* (Mucchio). They also exerted some control over three *plebes* (Chianni, Cellole, and San Gimignano). We have already seen how Bishop Lamberto placed a *mansus* at Cellole under the control of San Miniato al Monte. The creation of the episcopal *plebs* of Sant'Ippolito di Castelfiorentino was therefore part of the process of resisting or competing with Cadolingi regional power in that commercially important part of the Valdelsa. To guarantee its financial security and independence, in 1059 Pope Nicholas II confirmed to the arch-priest the possession of its tithes and half the testaments, exempting the *plebs* from all jurisdiction except that of the bishop.[124] The arch-priest was an important member of the episcopal clientelar network, but the *plebs* was not always in episcopal possession after 1036. In 1050 Bishop Gerardo donated it to the cathedral chapter as part of his plan to reform and reconstitute the economic interests of the chapter. Shortly thereafter, however, given its significance, the *plebs* returned to episcopal control.

It is possible that the bishops constructed the seven *castelli* we know initially were in their possession: Montalto, Montacuto, Ancisa (in the endowment to San Miniato al Monte), Collis Romuli, Campiano, Cavagliano, and Bossolo. Two *castelli*—Campiano and Cavagliano, which Bishop Attone donated to the cathedral chapter in 1036—also show up on the list of Guidi *castelli,* indicating that the Guidi might have absorbed them later into their possession. The remainder of the *castelli* in which the bishops held interests before 1115 came into their possession by donations (except for Pagliariccio), usually from local lay lineages. Even then, episcopal possession was not total; the bishops usually received only fractional parts of the *castelli.* Two *castelli,* Montebuoni and Fabbrica, were originally in the possession of a minor branch of the Aldobrandeschi. Of the 130 known *castelli* in the diocese before 1100, the bishops therefore held documented interests in only twenty (15 percent), and they initiated the construction of no more than eight (6 percent) (see Appendix C).

This was quite a different situation from what occurred in the dioceses of Lucca and Arezzo, where castle-building was started by powerful institutions (the bishops, the churches, or public powers) before being taken up by lay families.[125] As Duane Osheim has demonstrated for the diocese of Lucca, tenth- and eleventh-century bishops occasionally leased portions of *castelli* to local individuals in exchange for a money payment and on the condition that the leasee complete the castle.[126] In a recent study, Wickham argues that *castelli* in the Garfagnana (near Lucca) emerged out of the *curtes* and were rent-collection centers, not centers of socio-economic control. In the Casentino (diocese of Arezzo), they had slight economic but a great deal of political importance. Indeed, the local aristocracy crystallized around them.[127] In the diocese of Florence during the episcopacy of Ranieri there is only one recorded *libellus* (a documented lease) in which the leasees agreed to help construct the castle (at Pagliariccio in the Mugello) for an annual payment of *denari*.[128] How do we account for this rather limited role played by the bishops, relative to the greater role played by their counterparts in other Tuscan dioceses?

The appearance of *castelli* throughout the Italian countryside after 850 is a major issue in contemporary Italian historiography.[129] The publication of Toubert's analysis of *incastellamento* in Lazio (1973) has drawn maximum attention to the importance of this process in Italian medieval history. Toubert made the case that *incastellamento* marked a decisive social and economic "rupture" in the history of tenth- and eleventh-century Lazio: lords consciously reorganized previously dispersed settlements into concentrated centers (*castelli*) to maximize the amount of surplus they could extract from a subject peasantry.[130] Since 1973 historians have acknowledged the crucial importance of *incastellamento* in the social and economic development of Italy, but they have questioned whether a single theory (Toubert's) can account for the process throughout the peninsula. Recent scholarship has demonstrated great variation and complexity in each region of Italy. It appears that *incastellamento* appeared first in the north (ninth century in the Val Padana) and then spread south (Lazio after 920, Campania after 950). In Tuscany demographic movements were both the cause and consequence of castle-building, which was primarily initiated (at least at Lucca) by the bishops and local inhabitants. In the diocese of Florence, many *castelli* became walled *curtes*.

Although our conclusions must remain provisionary until we have completed more local studies, it appears that the acquisition of *castelli* by the bishops was linked primarily to the desire on the part of the bishops to dominate particular zones of the countryside.[131] Specifically, since landholding was the source of power, the bishops sought possession of *castelli* for two reasons: to create alliances and clientelar relationships with the local elite to augment their political and economic presence (and facilitate donations of property), and to use them as administrative centers for the management of their estates. Examples of the latter probably included Borgo (1080) and Pagliariccio (1103) in the Mugello, and Decimo (1105) and Fabbrica (1098) in the Val di Pesa.

They were especially useful for controlling previously dispersed properties, which were in the process of being consolidated by the bishops to
prevent their alienation by episcopal tenants.[132] Many if not most of the
episcopal *castelli* were originally *curtes*. Since all but one already existed
before the bishops acquired them, it appears that the desire to clear land
or concentrate the population played a minor role in their thinking.
These processes had probably already occurred. Many *castelli* were also
defensive in nature and controlled access to very important roads in the
diocese (Ampinana, Borgo, Carza, Cercina, Montebuoni, Decimo, and
Fabbrica). For that reason they must have had received tacit support (if
not explicit promotion) from the public authorities, the margraves and
their allies in Florence. It is hard to believe that the acquisition of the
castelli of Montebuoni (by way of enfiefment of the original owners) in
1092 and of Fabbrica in 1098 occurred without outright support and
encouragement from the Countess Matilda, who dominated Tuscan political life until 1115. After all, both bishop and city had a common
interest in weakening the localized power of the rural elite in the countryside and bringing them into the sway of the Arno city. Although the
bishop was one of the only urban lords with possessions in the countryside, he did not control as much territory as his Lucchese counterpart
possessed. Hence, he was not in a position to create *castelli;* he had
to acquire already existing ones. By bringing the local aristocracy (the
Ubaldini, the Buondelmonti) into his clientelar network, the bishop acquired their *castelli,* enfiefed the *castelli* back to the lineages, and relied
on them to administer and defend the *castelli.*

Capitular Property in the Eleventh Century

Opposed to clerical marriage and the "misuse" of church property, Bishops Attone and Gerardo brought the same energy to the reorganization
of the cathedral chapter as they had to their reorganization of episcopal
properties. As they ended the access to church income enjoyed by the
descendants of Bishop Ildebrando, they attempted to terminate the same
diversion of episcopal property in the chapter. They relied greatly on
what the they had learned from similar attempts to reform the chapters
in the dioceses of Fiesole and Pistoia. Bishop Gerardo later used this
knowledge gained as a bishop to push for continental reform as Pope
Nicholas II.

    In the diocese of Florence, Bishop Attone attempted in 1036 to imitate
the example of Bishop Jacopo of Fiesole by imposing a strict form of

common life on the canons and designating a provost to oversee capitular income. He also gave the canons the right to appeal any episcopal violation of capitular economic sovereignty to the papal court.[133] In that same document he restored to the chapter the church of Sant'Andrea sul Mercato (formerly controlled by the sons of Ildebrando). Desirous of putting the financial affairs of the chapter on a sound footing, Bishop Attone donated to the chapter in 1038 the castle, estate, and baptismal church of San Pietro in Bossolo (*castellum, curtis,* and *plebs*) with all its dependencies in the Val di Pesa. Important as it was, it returned to episcopal control a century later.[134]

In July of 1050 Bishop Gerardo confirmed all the possessions of the chapter, and required the canons to use the possessions of the chapter as a community. This document required that they had to eat and live together in a shared dormitory. As part of the confirmation he ceded to the canons full possession of the *plebs* of Sant'Ippolito di Castelfiorentino. Desirous of placing ecclesiastical establishments throughout the diocese on a sounder economic footing, he made donations to the patrimonies of the following churches: San Pietro in Quarto, Sant'Andrea di Empoli, Sant'Andrea a Mosciano, and Sant'Ippolito di Castelfiorentino.[135] Sant'Ippolito di Castelfiorentino returned to the episcopal *mensa* less than a century later. These donations not only strengthened the economic base of the chapter, but they also solidified the political alliance between the chapter and the bishop. This alliance was especially important to the bishop in areas where both bishop and chapter had interests: the eastern Mugello and the Valdarno Fiorentino.[136] In the Mugello the chapter had possessions at Ronta, houses and landed holdings at Borgo San Lorenzo, and a *curtis* at Susinana. It leased the tithes and properties of the *plebs* of Signa from the bishop, and it received the Badia of Sant'Andrea in Florence from the bishop as well. Among other holdings leased from the bishop were some land at Piscinale and Quinto in the Valdarno Fiorentino and the *plebs* of San Pietro in Bossolo. A papal confirmation in 1076 of chapter property included the following: possessions in Florence and vicinity (*Prato Regis, Campo Regis,* the *curtis* of Sant'Andrea, Sant'Ambrogio, Santa Maria Novella, the Campo Orto near Santa Reparata, *curtes* at Cintoia); in the Valdarno Fiorentino (Quinto, Signa—including tithes, and a *mansus* at Lanciano); in the Mugello (*curtes,* churches, and *castelli* in the *plebatus* of San Giovanni Maggiore, San Lorenzo, San Pietro di Vaglia, and San Cassiano); in the Valdelsa (the *plebs* of Sant'Ippolito); the church of San Martino in the *plebatus* of Santa Maria Impruneta; and miscellaneous possessions elsewhere (including in the diocese of Fiesole).

The Episcopacy of Pietro Mezzabarba and the
Foundation of San Pier Maggiore, 1062–1068

After the deaths of Pope Nicholas II and Humbert of Silva Candida, conservative voices again were heard in Rome. Lombard bishops demanded at the imperial diet at Basle that one of their own succeed Nicholas II as pope, and it is possible that they also nominated at that same meeting Pietro Mezzabarba as the next bishop of Florence. His father had once bragged that he had purchased the office for his son at the imperial court. A member of a noble family from Pavia, Pietro Mezzabarba became a major ally of the margrave Godfrey, who used the prelate as his political agent in the city. Politically allied with the margrave, Pope Alexander II was willing to turn a blind eye to the role simony played in the professional life of the new prelate.

Giovanni Gualberto, however, was unwilling to ignore that fact. Simony, tainted as it was with the stain of greed, worldly pride, and the contemporary demands of lordship, disqualified the new bishop as a worthy occupant of the See of St. Zanobi in the eyes of Gualberto. To him, even the sacraments administered by the simoniac bishop were invalid. This position clearly worried even the reformers within the papal court,[137] as they believed that the sacraments were valid regardless of the character or personal history of the priest administering them. If this were not so the entire ecclesiastical hierarchy would collapse. It was therefore in the interests of the papacy to keep the independent-minded founder of Vallombrosa in check.

The anti-episcopal party in Florence, however, was not willing to ignore the bishop's reputation as a simoniac. Led by Giovanni Gualberto, they lobbied vigorously against the prelate at the papal court and in the court of public opinion. The crowd or *populus* in the documents which supported Giovanni Gualberto, according to a recent study, was non-knightly in character and held no independent role in public affairs. For the monk and his supporters, perhaps, simony was associated with episcopal involvement in the land market and the cash economy.[138] In other words, the crusade against Pietro Mezzabarba was at least in part a reaction to the economic and social demands of episcopal lordship, made more acute by the aggressive acquisition and consolidation of property initiated by Pietro's predecessors. Giovanni Gualberto recognized the close link between material power and religious authority, and he wanted nothing less than the prelate's expulsion.

The bishop seems to have followed a three-track policy to resist the challenges of the Vallombrosan party, a policy which gradually evolved

over the course of the eight years of his episcopacy. Unlike Bishops
Attone and Gerardo (and Ranieri after him), Pietro Mezzabarba attempted to develop a network of clients primarily in the city, not in the
countryside. Perhaps this strategy resulted from his recognition that the
aggressive economic strategies of his predecessors in the countryside
had elicited a strong negative reaction from the *populus*. While pursuing
his own and his father's ambition by becoming a bishop, he faithfully
represented throughout his tenure the interests of his patron, the margrave. There is no record of any acquisition of property, *castelli*, or
jurisdictional rights during his episcopacy. Apparently, he sought to
undercut the work of Bishops Attone and Gerardo regarding the cathedral chapter by removing any administrative autonomy that the chapter
enjoyed over its own *mensa* and by renting freely possessions of the
chapter to his clients and political allies. The prelate took the offensive
by trying to capture his enemy Giovanni Gualberto in the Vallombrosan
monastery of San Salvi sometime in 1065 or 1066.[139] The attempt failed
and only made the followers of Giovanni Gualberto (many of whom
were wounded) even more popular.[140] Many historians (such as Milo or
Davidsohn) have dismissed this action as foolhardy and unprovoked. No
doubt that it was. We must not forget, however, that the bishop felt that
the Vallombrosan party in the diocese threatened the economic life-
blood of the bishopric. By attracting donations to its monastic establishments (San Salvatore di Settimo, San Salvi, San Pietro in Moscheto in
the Mugello, San Cassiano di Monte Scalari south of Florence in the
diocese of Fiesole), the Vallombrosan monasteries might have denied
the Florentine bishops donations of property and exerted tremendous
economic pressure on episcopal lordship in vulnerable areas (the Valdarno Fiorentino and the Mugello). Pietro Mezzabarba's action was violent, but it was also comprehensible. By January 1066, perhaps even
before the attack at San Salvi, the prelate had forbidden the provost of
the cathedral chapter the right to manage its own possessions. The result
of this decision was predictable: he alienated a significant group of cathedral canons, who then decided to join the Vallombrosan party.[141] Furthermore, the bishop leased eight separate sets of episcopal property to
individuals in the Valdarno Fiorentino at Carraria Marittima (two in
1065), Careggi (1067 and 1068), and Sesto (four between 1065 and
1067).[142] No doubt he hoped to win support from important lay figures
in the city as well.

Facing continued opposition, Bishop Pietro took a most dramatic step
a year later (March 1067). He collaborated with a female member of the

Firidolfi family to establish a new monastery, San Pier Maggiore.[143] We cannot understand the foundation of this monastery unless we see it as a dramatic and conscious re-enactment of the creation of another monastery, San Miniato al Monte. Like Bishop Ildebrando, Bishop Pietro felt besieged by enemies. He felt a special kinship with his distant predecessor, as they both were locked in combat for their survival with a faction of the Florentine clergy associated with the monastery of San Salvatore di Settimo—supported by the Cadolingi patrilineage. The creation of San Miniato al Monte had successfully shored up the political fortunes of Bishop Ildebrando. The basilica to the first martyr of Florence was still—fifty years later—an extremely popular center of worship for the Florentine masses. Pietro intended the foundation of San Pier Maggiore to have the same effect.[144] We may also speculate about another motive behind this collaboration as well. By identifying himself with a prominent Florentine female and taking an active role in the creation of a new monastery for Florentine women, the bishop was perhaps trying to appeal to women, who must have seen the misogynistic attitudes of Giovanni Gualberto (like those of Abbot Guarino) as a threat to their own status and spiritual welfare. Within the city, Bishop Pietro perhaps attempted to forge a political alliance with the female religious community.

In March of 1067 the prelate presided over the elaborate ceremony of consecration of the new convent (see Map 4). He chose the site for at least two reasons: the church (San Pier) was associated with St. Peter (the symbol of orthodoxy) and the neighborhood in which it was located was connected with St. Zanobi (the fifth-century bishop-saint).[145] Located near the eastern gate of Florence, the convent was built with funds provided by the elite families of the city. The margrave Godfrey and his wife, political allies of the bishop, were present at the ceremony. Like Ildebrando, Bishop Pietro probably endowed the new establishment with some episcopal properties, but the bulk of the endowment came from the patrimony of a certain Ghisla dei Firidolfi, who became the first abbess of the convent. Her four daughters became the first nuns.[146]

The foundation of San Pier Maggiore bears an uncanny resemblance to the foundation of San Miniato al Monte fifty years earlier. Like Ildebrando—assuming the endowment did include some of the episcopal properties—Pietro intended the monastery to protect episcopal interests from his enemies, the Vallombrosan party and the Cadolingi. Also like his predecessor, he used the document of foundation to underscore his own qualities, affirming his adherence to orthodoxy and beseeching the

Florentine community to live in harmony. The political overtones of that document—which Davidsohn believed resembled the speech he gave at the actual ceremony—were not lost on his enemies.

The bishop's actions differed from those of Ildebrando in one major way, however. The prelate probably initiated at the ceremony of foundation a symbolic marriage between himself and the abbess, which took place during the ritual entry into the city of the bishop.[147] It symbolized a union of this particular bishop with the Firidolfi, and it symbolized the joining together of the bishop with his diocese. Henceforth, perhaps for several centuries, successive bishops repeated that ceremony of entry at the beginning of their tenure.[148] One can approach the ritual marriage on two levels. First, it symbolized an alliance of the bishop with the Firidolfi family. Second, it affirmed publicly the liturgical and ceremonial *charisma* of the bishop. This was not the only instance of an episcopal entry involving the ceremonial "marriage" of a bishop and a local abbess. The ceremony surrounding the entry of the bishop of Troyes into the city—including the night he spent at the convent of Nôtre-Dame-aux-Nonnains—was very similar to the Florentine episcopal procession.[149]

The outcome of the bishop's actions, however, was not successful. The political atmosphere within the city continued to get more tense as the two sides became more polarized. Pope Alexander II reacted by dispatching Peter Damian to Florence to calm the stormy seas in the spring of 1067. Concerned by Giovanni Gualberto's insistence that the sacraments administered by a simoniac bishop were invalid, Peter Damian stressed that only the forthcoming Roman synod was the proper place for the resolution of the conflict.[150]

The followers of the Vallombrosan party proceeded to press hard to expel the bishop from the city. Given full jurisdiction over San Salvatore di Settimo granted by Guglielmo di Bulgaro di Cadolo sometime between 1040 and 1046, Giovanni Gualberto thought of himself as the latter-day Guarino. Both of them stood for the same principles; both were abbots at Settimo; both were supported and sponsored by the Cadolingi; both saw the bishop of Florence as their enemy. The significance of the drama acted out by the bishop and his allies was therefore not lost on Giovanni Gualberto and his followers. They recognized correctly that the outcome of the struggle between themselves and the bishop depended primarily on whether they or the prelate won the hearts and minds of the Florentine "crowd" (*populus*). Drawing on the popular memory of Guarino's attack on Ildebrando, Giovanni Gualberto chose to continue to press his attack on Bishop Pietro. Holding fast to his spiritual ideal, he sought to expel the prelate by undercutting his *charisma.*

Significantly, Giovanni Gualberto chose as the site for the final act of the "drama" the symbolic heart of the reform tradition in Florence: the abbey of Settimo. A trial by fire undergone by the young Vallombrosan monk, Pietro Igneo, was an attempt to demonstrate that the party of Giovanni Gualberto could marshall more supernatural and spiritual power than the partisans of the bishop. The successful resolution of that ordeal in favor of the Vallombrosans apparently won the support of the Florentine community (probably the Florentine elite, minus the allies of the margrave, including the Firidolfi). Mindful of the bishop's precipitous loss of political support within Florence and of its betrayal by a former ally the margrave, the papal synod in the spring of 1068 merely confirmed the deposition of the bishop. Practical politics—not the merits of the case—led to that decision by the papal court.[151]

Renewed Expansion in the Countryside:
The Episcopacy of Ranieri, 1071–1113

Following the departure of Pietro Mezzabarba, the See of St. Zanobi was vacant for three years.[152] In 1071, however, Ranieri became bishop of the Arno city. His origins are obscure, although he was probably not a Florentine. Aside from being very close to the margrave, he also was a favorite bishop of Gregory VII (indicating that he was sympathetic to the papal side in its conflict with the empire).[153] Like his predecessor, Ranieri was closely allied with the Countess Matilda, but his politics were quite different. Like Matilda he found common cause in the struggle against the emperor. Both countess and bishop agreed on the need to limit or weaken the power of the principal imperial allies, the rural patrilineages. The significant number of donations in the eleventh century was transforming the episcopate into a major presence in the countryside, and Matilda saw in Ranieri a dependable representative of Florentine interests.

The tenure of Ranieri is important for several reasons. He continued the policies of strengthening the economic base of the cathedral chapter, initiated by his predecessors. He resumed the process of acquiring *castelli* and their adjacent properties in the diocese, particularly in the Mugello and Val di Pesa. His interest in those two regions made them the most important zones of episcopal economic and jurisdictional power for centuries to come. He recognized after the expulsion of his predecessor that the maintenance of episcopal power depended on a strong presence in the countryside. When he died in 1113, the episcopal estate was more extensive and stronger than it had been in 1071.

One of the most important acts of Bishop Ranieri's administration was to convene a diocesan synod at Santa Reparata to reconsecrate the convent of San Pier Maggiore, perhaps because the previous ceremony had been associated with a discredited prelate.[154] On November 27, 1073, he confirmed the donation by Ghisla to the convent and added some possessions of his own to the establishment (Santa Maria Ferlaupe, San Pietro in Scheraggio, San Remigio, San Felice prope Fiumine, San Benigne, and all the properties and *curtes* pertaining to them).[155] Besides attempting to solidify political connections between the bishopric and the Firidolfi and their new convent, the bishop also apparently wanted to use the monastery as a way of shielding certain episcopal possessions from outside threats (as Ildebrando had done). Whether he controlled any of those properties placed in the endowment of the monastery is impossible to know. Many of the properties included in the endowment were located in the Mugello (Vaglia and Carza), in the Valdema (San Felice ad Ema), in the Valdigreve, and in Florence itself (or just west of the city walls).[156] The episcopate had its own interests (*iura*) in San Piero ad Ema, Carza (a *castello* in episcopal possession at least since 1080), and Vaglia, indicating that Ranieri believed as did his predecessors that donating property to the convent was a convenient shelter for safeguarding certain episcopal properties.[157]

Ranieri recognized that the close political, spiritual, and economic ties between the bishopric and the convent added weight to the episcopal presence—both economic and moral—in the diocese at a time when the Vallombrosan monasteries were attracting donations. In 1085 Vallombrosa itself became directly dependent on the papacy, effectively making Settimo entirely free of any tie to the bishop of Florence.[158] Ranieri's consecration of the church of Santa Maria Novella in the fall of 1096 underscored the role of the bishop as the spiritual leader of the diocese.[159] The moral and spiritual image of the bishop was extremely important to insure that laymen continued to transfer property into its *iura*. The new Vallombrosan establishments continued to grow and expand throughout the end of the eleventh century, putting pressure on the bishop's financial resources and making it more difficult for the bishop to use monastic resources for his own ends. For example, in 1102 Pope Paschal II issued a bull of protection to the abbot of San Salvi, specifying that he wanted to prevent episcopal meddling in the monastery's affairs.[160]

Bishop Ranieri worked to repair the damage done to episcopal-capitular relations by making several donations of episcopal property to the cathedral chapter, thereby solidifying his alliance with it. He learned a valuable lesson from the experience of his predecessor that a bishop could not afford to alienate the cathedral chapter or a significant faction within it for short-term gains. In 1077 he refereed a dispute between the monks of San Miniato al Monte and the chapter over the division of offerings obtained during the public processions of churches within the diocese.[161] Within the next few years the prelate made significant grants of property to the chapter, hoping thereby to enhance his political position within the city. In 1084 he gave them wooded land at Capiteto, and five years later he donated some land at Quarto to the hospital of the chapter. Finally, in 1113, just prior to his death, he transferred to the cathedral clergy episcopal possessions in the *curtis* of Cintoia near Florence.[162] That last grant did not in any way diminish episcopal economic interests in the diocese, because the bishopric had very few possessions to begin with in that region (see Map 2). By 1113, those interests were heavily concentrated in the eastern Mugello, the Val di Pesa, and the Valdarno Fiorentino.

The major contribution Bishop Ranieri made to the formation of the episcopal *iura* was the acquisition of several *castelli,* adjacent lands, and patronage rights to local churches concentrated in the Mugello and the Val di Pesa (see Map 2). As one can see in Appendix D, during the tenure of Ranieri, donations of property continued precisely in the areas where Bishops Attone and Gerardo had first increased the episcopal presence: the Val di Pesa and Mugello. Ranieri received some property by way of donation at Montughi, in the northwest suburbs of the city.[163] He recommenced the penetration of the Val di Pesa and the Mugello and acquired important rights in the Valdigreve just south of the city.

Located seven kilometers from Florence on the right bank of the Greve, the *castello* of Montebuoni was the possession of the Buondelmonti, perhaps a branch of the Aldobrandeschi. Possibly as a result of the economic and political troubles besetting them, the family yielded the entire *castellum* to the bishop on August 23, 1092. Perhaps desiring episcopal protection and patronage in Florence, they made themselves vassals of the prelate. Receiving back their property in fief, they were required to render military service when necessary, as they did in the twelfth century.[164] The location of the castle on the Via Senese was of extreme strategic importance to the city of Florence. Prior to the donation the Buondelmonti were collecting tolls on the road, implying that they were able to obstruct commercial traffic on that artery and to exert

military and economic pressure on nearby Florence. The Florentines—with the support and acquiescence of the Countess Matilda—preferred Bishop Ranieri to control the road rather than the Aldobrandeschi. After all, the Florentines, Countess Matilda, and the bishop were
close allies.[165] Six years later the same parties constrained the Buondelmonti to relinquish Fabbrica in the Val di Pesa. As we shall see, the
Florentines had their own reasons for applying political pressure on the
Buondelmonti: submission to the bishop carried with it submission to
the city of Florence.[166]

Expansion into the Val di Pesa added to the properties and rights the
episcopate possessed in the area since the tenth century. In the eleventh
century the bishops shared control of the valley with the margrave,
the emperor, the Cadolingi, the Guidi, and the Aldobrandeschi. The
margrave regularly stayed at the *plebs* of Santo Stefano di Campoli while
traveling in the valley, and the bishop eventually used it as a residence
as well.[167]

In the Val di Pesa Bishop Ranieri began accumulating rights in the
following *castelli:* Petriolo (1076), Fabbrica (1098), and Decimo (1105).[168]
Located in the parish of Santo Stefano di Petriolo in the *plebatus* of
Decimo on the road between Siena and Florence, the castle of Petriolo
had been in the possession of one Tedaldo di Ranerio. In 1076 the
widow of Tedaldo ceded it to the bishop (perhaps for religious reasons,
but also perhaps she did not want her property to fall into the hands of
more powerful local lineages like the Cadolingi).[169] Located further
south on the same route, Fabbrica and its parish church came into episcopal possession in 1098. Just one kilometer from the Pesa, Fabbrica was
originally a possession of the Aldobrandeschi and later passed into the
dominium of one of their minor branches, the Buondelmonti.[170] In 1098
Uguccione di Aldobrandino degli Scolai-Buondelmonti donated all his
properties and jurisdictional power there to Bishop Ranieri. Growing
indebtedness, increased pressure from church reformers to restore ecclesiastical property, and coercion from the Florentines (who preferred
the bishop to the Buondelmonti) might have constrained the family to
grant the *castello* to the bishop.

The acquisition of the *castello* at Decimo (1105)—which followed the
acquisition between 1054 and 1098 of major *castelli* or portions of major
castelli in the Val di Pesa, namely Ripoli, Petriolo, and Fabbrica (see Map
2)—was especially important. Located on a hill two-and-a-half kilometers
from the Pesa, the *plebs* (Santa Cecilia) and *castello* of Decimo was on
the old road to Siena on the site of the tenth Roman milestone (see Map

3). At the end of the tenth century the *plebs* of Decimo was paying rent for episcopal land, as we have seen.

The acquisition of these *castelli* was not haphazard nor fortuitious. Perhaps originally an idea of Bishop Gerardo, the intent behind their acquisition was clear: to acquire important *castelli* which controlled the road from Siena to Florence on the right bank of the Val di Pesa. Coupled with dominion over the other former Buondelmonti *castello* at Montebuoni (located also at an important strategic point near the city), the possession of these castles made the bishops strategic players in the southern part of the diocese.

In acquiring at least three of those cases *castelli*—Petriolo, Fabbrica, and Montebuoni—the bishop also acquired patronage rights to the local parish churches. The possession of these properties and jurisdictional interests strengthened the episcopal presence in the two river valleys. Especially important to the bishop was the fact that these castles and their dependencies were located on or near the major arteries linking the city to its hinterland (see Maps). Although the sources do not suggest it, it is possible that the bishop was also attempting to assert his power over the local markets emerging on these roads.

The episcopate extended its reach primarily in the Val di Pesa during the tenure of Ranieri, but the bishop was also very interested in the central and eastern Mugello.[171] Certain individuals donated shares in the castles of Casole (1079), Carza (1080), Borgo (1080), and Pagliariccio (1103, 1104).[172] At Pagliariccio he contracted with the local population to build part of the castle (see below).[173] Adding to previous possessions (the *castelli* of Ampinana and Vespignano), these castles allowed the episcopate to control the road system in that part of the Sieve Valley. Borgo, located at the crossroads of two major arteries (see Map 1), effectively allowed the bishops to control the road over the Apennines to Faenza and Imola. Again, it appears that the acquisition of these particular castles was not fortuitous. Their possession rendered the bishops the effective lords of the road system in the eastern Mugello. It was certainly in the interests of both the countess (whose political base was on the other side of the mountains) and the city of Florence to see that their ally the Florentine episcopate, and not members of the rural nobility, controlled those castles. Linked closely to the bishop, the chapter also possessed property at Borgo San Lorenzo and in the northeast Mugello, and the Ubaldini were solidifying their control of many passes at this time as well.[174]

The possession of patronage rights, control of several castles, leasing of property to local arch-priests, and the rental of lands to local peasants effectively made the bishop of Florence at the beginning of the twelfth century the regional lord of the east bank of the Pesa and of the left bank of the Sieve from Borgo San Lorenzo to Ampinana. The possession of several *curiae* in those valleys made the bishop the primary power-broker—politically and economically. The bishop was prosperous enough apparently to construct for himself a larger episcopal residence in Florence by 1105.[175]

The Estate of the Bishops of Fiesole in the Eleventh Century

As we have already discussed the connection between Florentine episco-pal property and the possessions of the Cadolingi, Guidi, and the monas-teries under the jurisdiction of Vallombrosa, it remains for us now to discuss the patrimony of another ecclesiastical lord, the bishop of Fie-sole. Indeed, the location of many of his properties directly north of the city and along the Sieve Valley made it difficult for the bishops of Flor-ence to penetrate those regions in the eleventh century (see Map 1),[176] even if they had wanted to do so. Before 1000 we can document that there were episcopal holdings in the island of Fiesole at Montereggi, Trespiano, and Montefanna, as well as along the Mugnone (Campo-longo). At Larciano (Mugello) and Lonnano (diocese of Arezzo) the episcopàte also had at least two landed holdings (*sortes*).[177] In 1018 Bishop Regembaldo donated and confirmed properties in his diocese to his chapter, perhaps for the same reason that Ildebrando donated much of his property to San Miniato: to organize the patrimony in such a way as to administer it more efficiently and to protect those properties from being appropriated by the Guidi. Among those properties were Tizzano (the valley of the Godenzo) and Tatti (below Monte Careggi northeast of Florence).[178]

A year later the bishop transferred his cathedral from outside the city to inside, renaming it San Bartolomeo Apostoli and endowing it with substantial properties (one-third of the episcopal estate). Among those lands donated were properties at Careggi and holdings adjacent to that monastery. Again, we can see similarities between this case and that of San Miniato. That same year the prelate established an administrative center for his properties in the Godenzo Valley by founding the monas-tery of San Gaudenzio in Alpe.[179] The concentration of landed holdings of the bishop of Fiesole in or immediately near Fiesole itself, along the Mugnone north of Florence, and in the Godenzo Valley effectively prevented Florentine episcopal penetration of this part of the Florentine *contado*.

Sources of Income and Administration, 1008–1113

Episcopal income in the eleventh century included tithes, urban rents, market dues, fees from religious activities (of which there are no records), rents from agrarian leases, and payments for the leasing of tithes. Unfortunately, unlike the sources for the history of Lucca, the Florentine archives offer us very little information about tithes or fees resulting from religious activities in the diocese. There were very few if any labor services still required of episcopal dependents at this time, and most of the income the bishops enjoyed came from the annual fixed dues (mostly in money) coming from the *libelli* and customary contracts. Unlike their counterparts at Lucca—who began commuting fixed, perpetual dues to grain rents in the eleventh century—the bishops of Florence did not begin commutations until the late twelfth century. There was only one documented rent rendered in grain in the eleventh century, perhaps reflecting the fact that the Florentine urban economy was a good century behind that of Lucca.

Many arch-priests and the chapter leased property from the bishop (presumably including tithes). Among the properties were the following: Sant'Alessandro di Giogole (12 *denari* documented in 1005),[180] San Pietro in Mercato (20 *soldi* in 1008), San Sepolcro near Florence (one pound of oil in 1020), San Pancrazio di Lucardo in the Val di Pesa (10 *denari* in 1025), and San Lorenzo (30 *soldi* for certain lands in 1045).[181] Leases of property in the city and in the Valdarno Fiorentino also played an important role, especially (as we have seen) during the tenure of Pietro Mezzabarba. These leases created and solidified political and clientelar alliances between the bishop and the most important arch-priests in the region. Leases of tithes and property by the bishops to the chapter also consolidated close ties between the two. Among the property leased to the chapter included urban possessions (the Badia of Sant'Andrea) and property in the Mugello (houses and *sortes* at Borgo San Lorenzo and the tithes of the *plebs*). In the Val di Pesa the chapter leased the tithes and *curtis* at Bossolo and property adjacent to the city (as at Cintoia and Quinto) and in the Valdarno Fiorentino (tithes of the *plebs* of Signa).[182] All of these leases underscore how important the Mugello, the Valdarno Fiorentino, the Val di Pesa, and increasingly the Valdelsa were to the interests of the bishops.

The location of the properties being leased was not fortuitous: the bishops let out those tithes or lands in areas where they were actively attempting to build up the bases of their local power, which relied on the possession of *castelli,* land, and of a network of clients (the arch-priest being the most important). Ildebrando or his managers leased property in at least four areas of the diocese: the Val di Pesa (1015), the Valdelsa (two in 1008), the Valdarno (three contracts), and in Florence itself (at least five contracts). At least two of the lessees were churchmen: the rector of the Florentine church of San Sepolcro and the arch-priest of the *plebs* of San Pietro in Mercato in the Valdelsa.[183] On the north-south artery linking Florence with Siena are two important *plebes:* San Pancrazio in Lucardo and San Pietro in Mercato. The bishops apparently had interests in both. As for San Pietro in Mercato—one mile from modern Montespertoli and located on a hill between two branches of the Pesciola—it was paying the episcopate 20 *soldi* in 1008. The location of a regional market there might explain the high *census* paid to the bishop. Either the bishop was charging a high rent to skim off some of the wealth acquired by the arch-priest from the proceeds of the market, or it was leasing the market itself to the arch-priest. In any case, San Pietro in Mercato—along with Borgo in the Mugello and *Curtis Elsae* (Castelfiorentino)—is the first evidence that a bishop had interests in a rural market.[184] According to the work of Charles de la Roncière, San Pietro in Mercato is the *first* market in the diocese to appear in Florentine historical sources.[185] Similarly, the bishop might have leased to the arch-priest of Borgo San Lorenzo in the Mugello the market dues from that important market. If that is true (and our sources are silent—we can only speculate), then a prosperous group of middlemen (the arch-priests and minor aristocracy) effectively had direct control over episcopal resources. The bishops managed those sources of income indirectly, receiving a fixed rent (usually in money) in return.

Drawing on his spiritual authority, the bishop required his tenants and dependents to pay their rents on the eighth day (*ottava*) after the feast-day of St. John, the patron saint of the bishopric, since the middle of the tenth century. From at least 1127 his tenants came to the city to present wax offerings to him on the feast-day itself as a symbol of their submission. Throughout the tenth, eleventh, and twelfth centuries, the day of St. John (June 24) developed into an elaborate ceremony during which episcopal dependents came to the city to submit themselves to their patron saint and bishop. The authority of the bishop was indistinguishable from that of the saint; it required obedience and assent. Eventually, as we shall see, the ceremony became the occasion for the submission of dependent communities to the commune.[186]

The bishop's expectations of his tenants or those living within his *curiae* were not onerous. From the Ubaldini or Buondelmonti, he probably expected military services when called. But from his tenants, he expected only fixed and unchangeable levies for the property they held from him. In return, they received protection from hostile rural lords and representation of their interests in Florence. Significantly, it was during Ildebrando's tenure that a *census* payment in grain appears in the historical record (1013), indicating he was interested in selling it himself. Not surprisingly, the property leased for the grain payment was located in the the city, indicating that the episcopate was leasing land for grain payments in that area as early as the beginning of the eleventh century.[187] It is apparent that the bishop was beginning to take advantage of the urban grain market about the same time he began thinking about founding San Miniato al Monte. The establishment of a new market by the bishop in 1024 reveals a keen interest in involving the episcopate in the developing market for grain in the city.[188] By the time that Ranieri was bishop, the manorial system (*sistema curtense*) in northern Tuscany had virtually disappeared. Rents in kind had been commuted to rents in money. Labor services disappeared, and managers were paid by salary or leased commercial properties on easy terms.[189]

Several factors contributed to that transformation: subdivision of the *mansus* as the result of population pressure, the need of lords like the bishop for cash, and changing forms of political organization (among others).[190] By the end of the tenure of Bishop Ranieri in 1113, there were few if any labor obligations on the episcopal estates.[191] Like the other rural lords in the diocese—lay and ecclesiastical—Bishop Ranieri and his managers were content to use their jurisdictional power to derive income from the collection of tithes (usually one-fourth went to the bishop) and of rents in money from the tenants on their properties. Annual dues (*census*) in the leases and *libelli* were money payments. As we shall see in the next section, the bishops came to rely more and more in the eleventh century on hereditary, long-term leases for money rents as their preferred source of income. As several of the most recent studies of church property have indicated, this was true elsewhere as well.[192] Despite the build-up of episcopal interests in the Mugello and Val di Pesa between 1024 and 1113, the majority of the leases of episcopal property still involved land located in the Valdarno Fiorentino. Between 1051 and 1075, eleven of seventeen leases were in that region west of the city. The bulk of the property leased by the bishops, however, was located within the city walls or just outside, especially along the Mugnone (see Map 4). For instance, in 1044 there is a record of the leasing of episcopal property by San Lorenzo for 30 *soldi*.[193] All in all, 90 percent of all leased property was in or near the city. It is likely that the economic position of the bishop of Florence was not unlike that of his counterpart at Lucca at the end of the eleventh century. The prelate of Lucca was not in a strong position. His rents were fixed and modest, and a significant amount of his property was still in the hands of the rural elite.[194]

We know very little indeed about the administration of the episcopal holdings before 1113. Like his peer at Lucca, the bishop probably handled most of his affairs himself, relying occasionally on the cathedral chapter and his *vicedominus* and *avvocatus* (legal representative). We know very little indeed about accounting methods. Presumably, the bishops kept what charters existed in the episcopal palace. Most of the entries in the *Bullettone* for the period before 1100 concerned property near Florence, *castelli,* or leases of pievan tithes in the countryside. There were at least two important offices in this period. The first one, the Avvocati, represented the bishop and chapter in legal proceedings, since priests could not take oaths. The second office, that of the steward or *vicedominus,* is better documented but still appears rarely in the sources before 1113.[195] Stewards were common throughout Tuscany, at least for Lucca, Massa Marittima, and Siena. In Lucca a cleric originally administered during a vacancy, but by the late tenth century laymen—the Avvocati patrilineage—took over the office and made it hereditary.[196] At Massa Marittima the Vicedomini were the Aldobrandeschi, whose territorial power extended throughout that part of southern Tuscany. They shared responsibilities with other patrilineages, and by 1200 a *consorteria* of fifteen families served as episcopal *vicedomini.* Visdomini at Siena left few traces of themselves, but they seem to have been linked closely to the Aldobrandeschi and church of Massa Marittima. A certain Rolando Vicedomino appeared in the eleventh century, second son of Guido *vicecomes et saligo.*[197] The Florentine *vicedomini* (known later as Visdomini) were therefore not exceptional. Their history is indeed the history of the Florentine bishopric, and their fortunes tied directly to the development of the city.

This is precisely the kind of situation which led the First Lateran Council in 1123 to forbid stewards to be anyone other than a cleric. Needless to say, in Florence the canon was disregarded; the political and economic ties of the bishops with the Visdomini *consorteria* were just too strong.[198] The Visdomini first appeared as administrators of the temporal possessions of the bishops in the eleventh century, but references to them are rare. Among the few references is an entry in the *Bullettone* which mentions that a Pietro Visdomini received the donation of *iura* at Noce and Sant'Antonio in 1112.[199] The Visdomini became especially important as administrators during episcopal vacancies, and their uncanonical control of the office often led to friction with the cathedral chapter, which was supposed to be consulted and to assist the bishop to manage his properties.[200] Unfortunately, we know very little about how the bishops managed their *castelli,* but those rural lineages such as the Ubaldini in the Mugello or the Buondelmonti in the Val di Pesa who commended themselves to the bishop do seem to have played major roles overseeing those *castelli* for their *dominus* the bishop. Later in the twelfth century, however, the office of *castaldus* emerged as the chief administrator of the episcopal *curiae,* those territorial complexes of *castelli* and their dependent properties.

The Bishop and the Emerging Commune, 1008–1113

At the beginning of the eleventh century the four major power brokers had reached a precarious balance in the diocese: the emperor, the margrave, the principal rural lords, and the bishop. By the beginning of the twelfth century a new authority had begun to eclipse those four: the commune of Florence. The emergence of jurisdictional autonomy of the commune of Florence at the end of the eleventh century is one of the major themes in Florentine history, and it is linked very closely with another major historical development. The political importance of Florence to the Countess Matilda (1076–1115, who succeeded her father, the margrave Boniface, after the deaths of her siblings) in her struggle with the emperor Henry IV (1056–1106) motivated her to transfer directly to the city major jurisdictional powers, which helped transform Florence by the time of her death in 1115 into an autonomous commune. Unlike the prelate of Arezzo, the bishop of Florence had never possessed comital powers. Therefore Florence, unlike other Tuscan communes, did not go through a period of episcopal dominance before attaining communal autonomy.

When local Tuscan and Roman interests coincided in the 1070's as the great clash between the papacy and empire erupted, the party of Giovanni Gualberto unambiguously sided with the papacy. It counted among its allies both the Cadolingi and the Guidi, and when Matilda became countess in 1076, they clearly supported her in the pursuit of a pro-papal and anti-imperial policy.[201] In fact, Florence became the only city in Tuscany which remained faithful to Matilda throughout the later investiture controversy.[202] There were several reasons for its fidelity. First, as we have seen, the parties of Guarino and later Giovanni Gualberto—opposed to incontinence and later simony within the church—had always been strong in the Arno city. Second, the elevation of Florence to capital of the Tuscan march in 1057 by the margrave Godfrey tied the city closely to the fortunes of that office. At a time when the Florentine elite was feeling acutely the growing commercial and economic pressures coming from nearby Lucca and Pisa, it saw that affiliation with the pro-papal cause of the countess was the best guarantee for its future prosperity. When the emperor Henry IV issued charters of privilege in 1081 to the commercial cities of Lucca and Pisa, Matilda realized that the protection of her own interests required her to strengthen her own political base in Florence.[203] The favor of the emperor toward other Tuscan cities brought the countess and the Florentines together.

Another reason the alliance between the Florentine elite and Matilda endured was their common desire to check the power of the rural patrilineages. According to a recent study, Lucca and Arezzo dominated their hinterlands. Apparently, in the Garfagnana and the Casentino the rural aristocracy was directly involved in the political and economic life of the city; indeed, the rural elite had both rural and urban interests, rendering the territories cohesive and receptive to urban penetration. In the diocese of Arezzo, the decline of episcopal power in the countryside coincided with the entry of the rural aristocracy into the urban sphere of influence.[204] The contrast with nearby Volterra is also instructive. The bishop—unlike his counterpart in Florence—was effectively the count of the countryside. Furthermore, he was consistently a member of the Pannocchieschi patrilineage (which had its own interests to protect). When the commune (composed of traditional residents of the city and newer inhabitants who moved into Volterra from the countryside) expanded its influence into its *contado,* it had to overcome the power of its bishops. The same thing occurred at Pistoia, where the relations between commune and bishop had been conflictual.[205]

The situation in the diocese of Florence was different. There were few urban property-owners in the eleventh century, but the episcopate and the chapter were among those few. Because Matilda had to worry about the challenges posed by the rural patrilineages who were imperial clients, she found a natural ally in the bishop of Florence. Both wanted to encourage a weakening of the power of the rural lords. Furthermore, the importance of the episcopate to Matilda and later to the commune was underscored by the fact that the bishops and the Visdomini *consor-*

teria were few of the only urban dwellers who held land in the *contado*. Defending the episcopate meant defending the Florentine presence in the countryside. Such close relations were evident in the relationship between Matilda and Bishop Ranieri and between Matilda and his successor, Goffredo (1113–1136).

Matilda began to transfer to the civil authorities jurisdictional power formerly reserved for officers of the margravial administration. By 1079 the city probably possessed its own system of measures and weights, a privilege formerly reserved for officials of the margrave. More important for subsequent history (especially for the history of the episcopal estate), by the last decade of the eleventh century (between 1090 and 1093) the Florentines were able to collect the public (imperial) taxes in their *contado*. Only the emperor and the margrave had formerly reserved the right to collect these dues.[206] The concession of these privileges, probably by the countess, at the end of the eleventh century set Florence on the path of communal autonomy. The popularity of the papal party within Florence itself weakened imperial power, as it loosened and eventually severed the economic and political connection between the bishops and the emperor.[207] The bishop and the secular power in Florence both saw that a pro-papal and anti-imperial alliance best served both their interests. By the time of Matilda's death in 1115, the Florentine communal authorities enjoyed unparalleled independence. The unique political history of the city—its deep-seated loyalty to the movements of Guarino and Giovanni Gualberto and to the Countess Matilda—allowed it to exercise full sovereignty by 1115 without having to experience an intermediate stage of episcopal rule (as occurred in nearby Pistoia, Massa Marittima, Arezzo, and Volterra).[208] After Matilda's passing, the commune and the episcopate continued to find common ground: they both wanted—for different reasons—to expand their influence into the countryside and to weaken the power of the independent rural aristocracy. Like Ildebrando, Guarino, Pietro Mezzabarba, and Giovanni Gualberto, the nascent commune recognized that the acquisition and preservation of economic and political power depended on religious and sacramental authority as well as material interests. The commune had to acquire more than jurisdictional influence. It needed its own *charisma;* it needed to be "at the center of things," and that meant a close association with the cults of the most important saints in the diocese. Therefore, the commune began consciously to promote the cult of St. John and supplant the bishops in the role of the saint's champions. In 1084 the first submissions of rural communities and lineages to the commune were made in his name.[209]

The Bishop, the City, and the *Contado* in the Twelfth Century

When Volterra and Pistoia challenged and successfully tamed their bishops, they inherited jurisdictional rights and a functioning communications system (roads) which extended throughout their hinterlands. The commune of Arezzo was rapidly able to fill the political void in the countryside left after the disintegration of its bishop's comital powers.[1] In the diocese of Florence, however, the situation was different. At the beginning of the twelfth century the Florentine elite possessed very little control over the hinterland of the city. As Elio Conti observed, the majority of landlords in the *contado* in the eleventh century were rural, not Florentine. This lack of urban orientation among the rural elite is one reason why Florentine subjugation of its hinterland took such a long time and why it relied so heavily on military conquest, relative to the history of other Tuscan cities.[2] The bishops played a very significant role in this process.

Also to be considered is the great increase in population between the eleventh and thirteenth centuries.[3] The population pressures within the city were a cause of great concern to the ruling elite, as the inability to feed or employ the masses could lead to political instability. To obtain military security as well as access to the resources necessary to feed an expanding population, the Florentine elite realized it needed to expand its influence into the countryside and weaken that of the rural patrilineages. The city leaders inherited from the Countess Matilda a close collaborative relationship with the episcopate, which—by 1100—had acquired a notable presence in the major river valleys of the diocese. That relationship continued throughout the twelfth century. The extension of the bishops' influence in the *contado* by way of purchase and donation in the twelfth century complemented the military campaigns of the young commune to strengthen the bonds of city and country. Another reason for the collaborative rapport between the episcopate and the commune was the simple fact that the Visdomini and Tosinghi—the episcopal administrators during a vacancy—were also members of the Florentine consulate (urban officials): members of these patrilineages served in the consulate in 1190, 1194, 1198, 1200, 1201, and 1203.[4] Furthermore, the Visdomini were active participants in events of central importance to communal security and interests. For instance, in 1173 Davizio di Meliorello della Tosa was witness to the donation of a *castello* and possessions of a certain Guiscardo di Bernardino to the consuls, and Catalano della Tosa played a principal role receiving the submission and fidelity of the Alberti counts to the commune of Florence in 1184.[5]

The Development of Florentine Regional Hegemony: An Overview, 1113–1197

The strategy developed by the Florentine elite toward the city's country-side stemmed from the desire for grain, security, troops, and revenue.[6] In the early eleventh century the Florentines sought to control the major highways in the diocese, gain access to the major regional markets, and prevent independent challenges to its hegemony by the rural aristocracy. The need for economic and military security was paramount, as the urban and rural economies were becoming more and more interdepen-dent.[7] In many ways, the policies of the Florentines mirrored those of Pistoia and other cities, which also attempted to control the major high-ways and mountain passes.[8] The achievement of territorial sovereignty by the Florentine ruling elite does not imply that there existed a "plan" for the subjugation of the *contado*. Indeed, the attainment of its goals did not require direct rule, nor did it entail a policy of "subjugation." Rather, the Florentines pursued first and foremost their immediate inter-ests on a case-by-case basis. The episcopal presence in the Mugello, Val di Pesa, and Val di Sieve assisted the consulate to achieve its goals: the bishops apparently provided troops, perhaps brought grain to the city, secured strategic portions of several regional highways, and even col-lected taxes for the commune.

The primary challenges to Florentine goals in the countryside came from neighboring Fiesole, Siena, and the powerful territorial lords: the Cadolingi, Guidi, and later the Alberti and Ubaldini. Indeed, the com-mune and the rural aristocracy were rival systems of power, vying for hegemony along the strategic river valleys and roadways of the diocese. It took Lucca only three years (1170–1173) to take the Garfagnana, a region where the economic and political power of the local lineages were not exclusively rural-based (as in the Florentine countryside) and where the rural elite remained oriented towards the city. In some areas of the diocese of Milan, however, the commune had to rely on military conquest after the middle of the thirteenth century to subjugate outlying areas of the *contado,* where some members of the urban nobility had fled and ensconced themselves after their expulsion from Milan.[9] As in the Milanese countryside, the Florentine rural nobility maintained a degree of autonomy from the city, requiring the commune to rely heavily on force to achieve its goals. One of the first territorial goals of the Florentines, therefore, was to control the road system in the *contado* (see Map 2), which basically followed the major river valleys.[10] For example, conflict over the control of the river and the highway from Florence to Lucca (the old Via Cassia) led to Florentine military campaigns against the Alberti at Prato in 1107 and the Adimari at Monte Gualandi in 1114.[11] Apparently, the primary goal of the commune was to control the highways and assure themselves access to the emerging market centers.[12]

In 1113 the last of the male members of the Cadolingi lineage died, leaving his widow Cecilia to probate the will. Count Ugo stipulated that all the Cadolingi allods were to go to the Alberti (including Mangona and Vernio) and that the ecclesiastical properties taken from the churches of northern Tuscany be restored to the bishops. The imperial fiefs went to the emperor. In 1113 the bishops of Florence, Volterra, Pistoia, Pisa, and Lucca divided the ecclesiastical possessions, and conflict immediately erupted among them. First, the Florentines contested the acquisition of the Cadolingi allods by the Alberti. Second, the Alberti wanted to prevent the bishop of Florence from receiving Montecascioli, located in the Arno Valley west of the city and included in the list of ecclesiastical properties Ugo meant to be returned to the churches. To keep the peace, Matilda appointed an Alberti family member as bishop, a certain Goffredo dei Conti Alberti. With little influence in the countryside, Countess Matilda and the commune needed to seek an alliance with one of the major rural lineages (the Alberti) and attempt to exploit the rivalry between the two lineages, the Alberti and the Guidi. The election of Goffredo meant that the Florentines had taken sides with the Alberti over the disputed Cadolingi estate. Elected without canonical approval and accused of simony, Goffredo was opposed by the lineages associated with the bishopric (the Ughi and Visdomini), who feared the Alberti would seek to take over their access to episcopal resources. Nevertheless, his election was a logical part of the countess's policy: it exerted pressure on the Guidi holdings in the Val di Sieve (where the bishops already had possessions at Galiga), and it was a way of extending urban control into the countryside.[13]

Bishop Goffredo was unpopular. The clergy and people (*populus*) of Florence argued that sacraments administered by Goffredo were invalid, marshalling many of the same arguments used earlier by Guarino, Romuald, and Giovanni Gualberto. Furthermore, Goffredo apparently attempted to extort huge sums from the clergy of the diocese and impose taxes. Reminiscent of the events half a century before, the warring factions went before a papal court in Rome, where the pope reaffirmed the authority of the bishop. Why was the bishop able to remain in office, given the strong tradition against simony in the city? Perhaps the Vallombrosans did not oppose the bishop because they were too closely tied to the Alberti. Also, the papal/imperial conflict over the Cadolingi patrimony seemed to take precedence. For the Florentines, political exigencies made the alliance with the bishop imperative. The Florentine-Alberti alliance lasted until 1136, when the city forced the bishop into exile.[14]

To limit the influence of the Alberti, Countess Matilda adopted a member of the Guidi lineage as her son (Guido Guerra). The Guidi in turn gave some of their rights in the Val di Sieve at Galiga, Monte di Croce, and Fornello to the bishop of Florence. There was peace among the various parties as long as the countess lived.[15] In 1115, however, Matilda passed away. Her allods went to the papacy and her imperial fiefs reverted to Emperor Henry V. During Matilda's reign the Guidi had maintained peaceful relations with Florence. After her death, however, they immediately refused to accept any Florentine jurisdiction and found common cause with the emperor. In 1122 the Guidi forged an alliance with nearby Fiesole at the same time that the margrave was also currying favor with the ancient city. War between Fiesole and Florence began in 1123, ostensibly over the alleged seizure by Fiesole of Florentine property. Fearing an alliance between Fiesole and the Guidi, the Florentines attacked Fiesole in 1125.[16] War against the Guidi by Florentines continued off and on between 1120 and 1157.

By the mid–1130's the Alberti realized that the alliance with Florence no longer served their interests. In fact, they feared domination by the city and were eager to assert their autonomy. Consequently, the bishop and several of his kinsmen sought imperial help to remove the possessions of the family from urban jurisdiction. The prelate and his family were emboldened by the support they received from the emperor himself. In 1133 the emperor Lothar II (1125–1137), a close associate of the Alberti, confirmed for the bishop the possession of four castles in the *contado:* Monte Giovi, Monte Buiano, Montacuto, and Montazzi.[17] These are the only documented *castelli* given to a bishop by a public authority.

Fearing Florentine encroachment, the Alberti cultivated a close relationship with Rabodo, the margrave after the death of Matilda. Concerned with the growing antagonism of the Alberti, in 1135 the Florentines moved against the castle of Montegufoni near modern
Montespertoli, which was controlled by vassals of the Alberti, the Or-
manni. Located in the Val di Pesa on the road to Castelfiorentino, Montegufoni was strategically important. After thoroughly destroying Montegufoni, the Florentines next turned their attention to Montebuoni in
the Valdigreve. Although officially vassals of the bishops of Florence,
the Buondelmonti of Montebuoni refused to fight with the Florentines
in the battle for Montegufoni. The Florentines therefore decided to raze
the strategic castle of Montebuoni in 1135 to punish the Buondelmonti
for their treachery and to send a signal to other episcopal vassals that
the commune did not tolerate such behavior.[18]

The conflicts between the Alberti and Florence intensified in 1136,
culminating in the expulsion of Bishop Goffredo from the city. With
support from Lothar II and the margrave, the bishop had tried to eliminate urban influence over the properties of his patrilineage. At stake
was episcopal jurisdiction over the *castelli* granted the bishop by the
emperor in 1133. At this point the commune decided to expel him,
using as justification his reputation as a simoniac and extortioner.[19] Dis-
trustful of Alberti motives and aware that the lineage no longer served
communal interests as they had done before, the commune used and
perhaps even orchestrated a campaign against the bishop. The combination of the margrave, the Alberti, and the bishop was just too threatening
to the consulate, so the Florentines expelled the bishop from the city.
The bishop went into exile, although he was able to return shortly thereafter.[20]

Although he did not spend much time in Tuscany, the emperor Conrad III (1137–1152) posed a continual threat to Florentine independence
by allying himself with the Alberti. He sided with the rural houses and
strengthened the power of the margrave, bishop, and counts to enhance
imperial influence in the region. In 1138 the bishop and the Alberti
allied with the margrave Henry of Bavaria to limit urban jurisdiction in
the *contado*. Also in August of 1138—angered that the commune was
violating ecclesiastical rights in the newly conquered *castelli*—Goffredo
placed the city under an interdict. Again, the major point of contention
was the episcopal (formerly imperial) *castelli*. Recognizing the importance of rural *castelli* to Florentine interests, the commune feared losing
them to Alberti control. Furthermore, the clergy of the city continued
to be outraged by the bishop's onerous taxes and fees. At a synod in

June of 1139 the city and the bishop came to an agreement. Adhering to the judgment of a commission composed of the *vicedomini*, the archdeacon of the cathedral chapter, and eight parishioners, the bishop agreed not to impose any more taxes on the clergy other than those imposed by his predecessor. To strengthen the episcopal hold on the *castelli* in question, the new margrave Ulrico confirmed for the bishop in August of 1139 the lodging rights (*albergaria*) and public powers granted the prelate by the emperor several years earlier.[21]

Conflict between the Guidi and the Alberti over the patrimony of Count Arduino Guidi again elicited Florentine intervention, offering the commune another justification to weaken Guidi power in the Val di Sieve near Monte di Croce and in the Valdelsa near Marturi.[22] The bishop himself activated his vassals to protect the interests of his family. Aligning themselves with the Alberti and the bishop, the Florentines moved against the Guido Guerra and his family at Monte di Croce and at Marturi. The bishop was eager to contribute to the military campaign, as nearby Doccia had been refusing to pay its rent to San Miniato al Monte. The Val di Sieve had been the center of Guidi holdings in the diocese since the tenth century. In the Val di Sieve the war focused on the struggle for control of Monte di Croce. It was a conflict which lasted from 1143 to 1147. In 1143 episcopal vassals attempted to take the stronghold by force. In spite of the Florentine support they received, they failed to dislodge the Guidi and suffered a serious setback. Later that same year the Florentines—backed by the Alberti and the Pisans—attacked the citadel and finally took it. According to the 1147 compromise, the Guidi agreed to pay an annual tribute to Florence and to the bishop as an acknowledgment of urban jurisdiction. In exchange, the Guidi were able to keep a viscount at Monte di Croce. Because the city had attacked the family of a crusader (Guido Guerra), Pope Eugenius III placed an interdict on the city which lasted from 1148 to 1153.[23]

Because Frederick I (1152–1190) was so preoccupied with Lombardy, he seldom intervened in Tuscany, but he carefully developed close relations with both the Guidi and the Alberti. In 1155 and 1164 he issued charters protecting the possessions of the Alberti, and in 1164 he did the same for the Guidi. He also re-issued a decree of his predecessor Lothar, removing from urban jurisdiction all lands won by war or treaty.[24] The first documented appearance of imperial taxes levied in the diocese (the *foderum*) dates from this time (between 1156 and 1158).[25]

In an area of still undefined jurisdiction, Poggibonsi became a major test of political will on the part of the Florentines. Situated between the Staggia and Elsa rivers on the Via Francigena, Poggibonsi was of strategic importance to the Florentines.[26] At the end of the eleventh or the beginning of the twelfth century, Countess Matilda granted to the family of Guido Guerra (her eventual heir) properties near the ancient *castellum* of Marturi. Alarmed by the erection of a well-fortified castle on the Via Francigena near the Sienese frontier, the Florentines attacked and destroyed the castle in 1115. Guido Guerra forthwith established an alliance with the Sienese and began to rebuild the fortress, naming it Podio Bonitii. He donated the castle to Pope Adrian IV in 1155, who took the *plebs* under his protection, excluded the bishop of Florence from exercising any rights there, and gave full jurisdiction to the Sienese bishop.[27] Apparently, the bishop of Florence was requiring the *plebs* of Santa Maria di Marturi to make certain undefined payments.[28] On July 21, 1155, the pope granted Bishop Ranieri of Siena permission to build the church of Sant'Agnese in return for the payment of one bizant a year. Seriously concerned by both the strategic threat posed by the castle on its southern frontier and by the loss of episcopal jurisdiction, the Florentine consulate (with Alberti support) again sent a military expedition against the fortress.[29]

On December 3, 1156, the conflict took a decisive turn. Adrian IV suddenly switched sides in the dispute, revoking the privileges awarded the bishop of Siena and awarding the *plebs* of Marturi to the bishop of Florence. The summarization of the papal act recorded in the *Bullettone* reads as follows: "Pope Adrian IV revoked the concession which he had made to the Sienese bishop at Monte Bonizi which had been prejudicial to the rights of the Florentine bishop."[30] The reason for the reversal lay not with the intrinsic merits of the Florentine case *per se*. Rather, the key to this "about-face" was the fact that Florence was a far more effective ally against the emperor Frederick I than was Siena.

Pressured by a combination of Florentine and papal interests, the commune of Siena granted to the commune of Florence in 1176 half of all the houses, the square, and properties that it possessed in Poggibonsi (with the exception of the church of Sant'Agnese).[31] Pope Alexander III (1159–1181)—himself the member of a prominent Sienese family—agreed with the exemption and restored all *iura spiritualia* in that church to the bishop of Siena.[32] Apparently, the controversy over the parish continued, necessitating the intervention of Clement III, who reasserted in 1188 the decision of his predecessor.[33] Not until the beginning of the thirteenth century did the Florentines and Sienese actually reach an accommodation over property at Poggibonsi and its surrounding territory.

After neutralization of Milan in 1162, Frederick created a system of imperial control in Tuscany inspired by the advice of his counselor, Rainald. His policy found ready support from both the Alberti and the Guidi. Frederick established a network of imperial agents (*potestates*) throughout the province who were responsible for maintaining stability and collecting imperial income. They were responsible only to the imperial governor residing at San Miniato al Tedesco in the Arno Valley between Florence and Pisa. After 1167, when Frederick was again so preoccupied with Lombardy, the *potestates* lost much of their power. Florence exploited that vacuum of power to subjugate Figline and Empoli in the Valdarno in 1168 and 1182, respectively. After the Peace of Constance settled the conflicts between the Lombard communes and the emperor in 1183, Frederick turned his attention to Tuscany. In the early 1180's, Florence had managed to subjugate the Alberti fortresses of Empoli (1182), Pogna (1182), and Mangona (1184), successfully securing the roads to Pisa, Siena, and the Romagna.[34] As a symbol of Florentine sovereignty, Empoli and Mangona had to pay an annual tribute, and at Pogna the Alberti had to make other fiscal concessions. The Florentines imposed the same arrangement on Certaldo (Valdelsa) in 1198 as they had at Empoli and Mangona: as tribute the Alberti paid to the commune the former imperial tax (*foderum*). For the lands between the Arno and the Elsa, the Florentines and the counts divided the tribute. By 1184 half of all Alberti revenue went to the city.[35]

Perturbed that the Florentines enjoyed a *de facto* independence without a charter, the emperor re-imposed the system of *potestates* throughout the province (headquartered at San Miniato al Tedesco) and confirmed the possessions of the rural lineages. The reign of Henry VI, Frederick's son, lasted only seven years (1190–1197). At his death the communes immediately pressed for full independence from imperial control.[36] The formation of the Guelf League after the death of Henry VI (an alliance of bishops, communes, and counts) is the first evidence that there existed a juridical relationship between the city and its *contado*. This pact—signed by the consuls of Florence, most counts (Guidi and Alberti included), and the bishops of Arezzo, Volterra, and Florence—included a clause which recognized the theoretical domination of each commune over its *contado*. The death of Henry VI severely weakened the imperial cause, and the rural lineages had little choice but to reach an accommodation. By 1200 the Alberti ended their resistance and agreed to live one month a year in Florence.[37]

As the Florentines extended their influence into the countryside, they developed a system of direct taxation to pay for the increased military and administrative costs. Already by 1093 Florence was levying a tax (*audiutorium*) in its *contado* alongside public taxes raised on behalf of the margrave.[38] In the years between 1156 and 1183 there co-existed the imperial direct tax (*foderum* or *datium*) and a communal direct tax (*foderum* or *datium*). In some cases the bishops and other rural lords collected the imperial levy for the emperor, even as late as 1195. In the twelfth century the name of the communal tax was the *audiutorium*, known also as the *foderum*. Whereas Arezzo abolished the imperial tax in 1197 and doubled the urban *foderum* from 12 *denari* to 24, the Florentines by 1198 apparently had abandoned the original urban tax (probably also 12 *denari* per hearth) and assumed the full imperial tax of 26 *denari* as their own. As he had done for the emperor, the bishop collected the urban *foderum* or *datium* in some areas of the *contado* for the commune. After 1198 it appears that a *datium* was levied on all episcopal lands. The bishop was effectively responsible for paying the tax to the commune for those under his jurisdiction, at least in certain places such as Monte di Croce. As we shall see, the bishops had their own *datium* (or *accattum*) to collect, derived from former public taxes as well.[39]

As urban influence in the *contado* increased, the bishops became more useful to the Florentines. First, they continued to represent a Florentine presence in hostile areas on the edges of the diocese (the Val di Sieve and the Val di Pesa). Second, the bishops occasionally provided troops to the Florentines. For example, the Florentines used episcopal vassals in the sieges at Montegufoni and at Monte di Croce. Third, the bishops possibly contributed to the provisioning of the city. The *Bullettone* documents that grain was cultivated at Vaglia (1142), Montecampolese (1142), Valcava in the Mugello (1144, 1172, and 1178), and at the Ospedale del Calzaiuolo (1149). Much of that grain possibly made its way to the Florentine markets. Fourth, by the end of the twelfth century and certainly by the beginning of the thirteenth, the commune was using the bishops to collect the imperial (now urban) *foderum* or *datium* of 26 *denari* per hearth (*foculare*) at Monte di Croce. Fifth, and perhaps most important, the growth of episcopal power in the Val di Pesa and the Mugello enhanced Florentine control of the major highways in its *contado*. By 1168 the roads along the Pesa were considered a public highway (*via pubblica*).[40] The string of episcopal castles and the extensive landed holdings in that valley made that route more secure for the consuls in Florence. However useful the bishops were, they were not simply tools of Florentine policy. Indeed, they always retained some autonomy.

The behavior of Bishop Goffredo and his family the Alberti frightened the consulate. The circumstances surrounding the expulsion of Bishop Goffredo had made it clear to the Florentines that never again could they tolerate the formation of an alliance between the bishop and the rural aristocracy. Therefore, the consulate attempted to insert itself more directly into the internal affairs of its bishops.

The Development of the Episcopal Mensa, 1113–1190

From the middle of the eleventh century the bishops had acquired property in the Mugello, the Val di Pesa, and in Florence itself. As Appendix D shows, the twelfth-century bishops continued to receive substantial donations of property in those two valleys (especially in the Val di Pesa). Although there were few if any purchases of property by the episcopate in the Mugello, there were very many purchases in the Val di Pesa between 1126 and 1225. After 1126 (and at an increasing rate) the bishops began supplementing their donated properties with purchases. Possession of patronage rights in the *plebes* of Castelfiorentino, Borgo San Lorenzo, Sesto, Campoli, and Decimo facilitated the buying up of land in those areas. As we have seen, concentration of property helped prevent local residents from selling or giving it away to kinsmen. Perhaps the inheritance of properties bequeathed to the episcopate by the last of the Cadolingi in 1113 made some of these purchases possible. Income from those possessions might have facilitated the consolidation of episcopal lands. The extension of episcopal landed holdings in those areas, the expansion of an episcopal network of clients in the countryside (specifically achieved by way of the careful appointments of arch-priests and rectors), and the acquisition of property formerly controlled by members of the rural nobility—all complemented communal military actions. We must not assume, however, that the bishops were loyal dependent servants of the Countess and commune; often (especially during the tenure of Goffredo dei Conti Alberti) the alliance lasted as long as both bishop and commune shared a common set of interests.

The Mugello

In the twelfth century the episcopate acquired part or all of the following castles in the Mugello: Monte Giovi (1133), Monte Buiano (1133), Montazzi (1133), Lomena (1159), and Buonsollazzo (1176). The first three were donations to the Alberti bishop from Lothar II (1125–1137). The transfer of public power was an attempt on the part of the emperor to detach the bishop from the city. Aside from interests in those *castelli*, the bishops were also leasing property located within their shadow and developing clientelar relationships with local inhabitants. Some of those lands were leased to local arch-priests.

In the *plebs* of San Piero di Vaglia, the bishopric, the cathedral chapter, the monastery of Buonsolazzo, and several lineages exercised *dominium* over vast properties.[41] Located on the Via Bolognese north of the city, Vaglia was an important strategic point in the Sieve Valley. Episcopal holdings in the area extended back at least to 1080, when Bishop Ranieri granted to a client the castle of Carza and the *curia* of Bivigliano. In 1103, 1123, and 1158 the episcopate received more possessions at Bivigliano, Carza, and Fortuna, respectively.[42] Though most local families were making the bulk of their donations to the local monasteries, the episcopate was also benefitting from the networks of clients it had developed in the eleventh century who continued to donate property.[43] In fact, donations increased markedly in mid-century. It is likely that the close relationship between the arch-priest and the bishop made the acquisition of property easier for the prelate. Specifically, the arch-priest leased the tithes of the *plebs* from the bishop, paying him four *moggi* of grain.[44] The task of the arch-priest was to act on behalf of his patron and facilitate the acquisition of property, either by purchase or donation.

Northwest of the *plebs* of Vaglia in the *plebs* of Pimonte was the *castello* of Monte Buiano. The *plebs* of Pimonte itself enjoyed a very close relationship with the episcopate. During the tenure of Bishop Ambrogio (1155–1158) it leased the tithes and income in the area for an annual payment (*census*).[45] After 1145 the episcopate began acquiring property (houses, *fideles,* and land) at Molezzano from several lay families, the *plebs* of San Giovanni Maggiore (1161), and the monastery of Crespino (1197).[46] The *castello* of Montegiove, located within the *plebs* of Valcava, also became very important for episcopal interests. Located on the mountainous spine dividing the Mugello from the Arno basin, it complemented episcopal possessions in the area, including the *castello* of Carza. As in the *plebatus* of Vaglia and Pimonte, the local arch-priest leased tithes and property from the bishop, paying him a rent in grain (1144). These grain rents are among the first we have encountered on the episcopal estates. The Valcava lease was the first documented *locatio in perpetuo* made in the *plebs* of Valcava, and the arch-priest paid the bishop in grain and money.[47] All in all, episcopal possession of several *castelli* and the close relationships with local arch-priests gave the episcopate a great deal of military and economic influence in a strategic part of the diocese: the major north-south road into the city. The imperial donation of the *castello* included the right to collect the imperial *datium,* which appear in the sources in 1195.

The episcopal possessions at Monte di Croce served as a bridgehead of Florentine influence in the lower Val di Sieve. As we have seen, some of the estates of the bishop of Fiesole were located on both banks of the Sieve. The strengthening of the Florentine episcopal presence in this part of the *contado* weakened the economic power of a lord who had declared himself willing to cooperate with an enemy. Montalto (a *castello*) and Aceraia were part of the original endowments of San Miniato al Monte (mentioned first in 1013 and 1024, respectively). It might have fallen out of episcopal hands, however, for in 1133 Lothar II conceded it to Bishop Goffredo. Its acquisition carried with it the right to collect imperial *datia* in the area, which turn up in sources at Monte di Croce in the thirteenth century. In 1113 Galiga became part of that endowment as well.

Two decades before the major Florentine assault on the fortress in 1147, two local families offered their lands and jurisdictional rights in the *curia* and *castello* of Vico, perhaps restoring to the church possessions taken by their ancestors generations before. Among the donors were the Guineldi, who originally exercised *dominium* in the area with the Guidi. This was the first documented episcopal *castello* acquired in that area of the Val di Sieve. Although their holdings were minor compared to what they possessed in the Mugello and Val di Pesa, they began leasing property in the region for money rents (*a livellario*) in 1140 at Montefiesole. At Montefiesole south of Monte di Croce the episcopate received its first documented donation in 1160. There is the record of at least two other leases in the twelfth century (1156 and 1179).[48] Acquired during the period of cooperation between the Alberti bishop and the commune (1113–1136), the castle of Vico served as the episcopal foothold in the stronghold of Guidi strength. Indeed, Vico was not far from the daunting Monte di Croce. Again, episcopal penetration of the area by Bishop Goffredo coincided with Florentine policy. In fact, as we have seen, episcopal vassals besieged the Guidi fortress. At the time that the Florentines reached an accord with the Guidi over Monte di Croce in 1147, the bishop of Florence was creating a small pocket of power centered at Vico.

The Val di Pesa

No area of the *contado* received more attention from the bishops than the Val di Pesa. Although donations continued (especially between 1126 and 1150), the bishops acquired most of their new possessions in the valley by way of purchase. Between 1126 and 1225 the bulk of episcopal purchases concentrated on the Val di Pesa (see Appendix D). Many of those donations and purchases involved members of the minor landed elite who perhaps wanted to free themselves from the power of the

Alberti counts.[49] On the whole, these acquisitions were attempts to round out and consolidate formerly disparate properties acquired through donations. Between 1113 and 1190, the episcopate acquired interests in the castles of Aquilone (1127), Montacuto (1156), and Petroio (1165).[50] Located near the castle of Fabbrica, these castles allowed Bishops Goffredo, Attone, and Giulio to expand episcopal power on the right bank of the Pesa River in the southern part of the diocese. Their acquisition was intentional. Twelfth-century bishops enhanced their economic and political power in the valley by acquiring castles and surrounding satellite properties. Near the castle of Ripoli Bishop Ambrogio decided to build a *castello* in order to take advantage of the commercial opportunities there, and it served most likely as a rent-collection and administrative center. Although there is mention of a *libellus* in the area from 1130, the *Bullettone* indicates that there was only a minor episcopal presence at Montecampolese before 1156. Yet, cognizant of the commercial possibilities in this rich grain-growing area, Bishop Ambrogio received land via four donations in the vicinity from several individuals for the purpose of constructing an episcopal *castello*.[51] The concentration of episcopal interests in this region of the Val di Pesa was linked to the desire by the bishops (especially Bishop Ambrogio) to take advantage of the increasingly lucrative market in grain in that area of the valley. As such, the *castello* might have served as an administrative center for the collection of rent, but it probably had a military purpose as well in that part of the *contado*. It served as an defensive outpost near Alberti and Guidi possessions, close to the Sienese frontier. The bishop had the *castello* built at the height of tension between the Florentines and Sienese over the *castello* of Poggibonsi, and between the bishops of Florence and Siena over the *plebs* of Marturi.

Adding to the number of castles possessed by the prelates since the eleventh century, these castles greatly increased the economic and jurisdictional presence of the bishops in the area. A glance at Maps 2 and 3 indicates their strategic significance: most of them were located on the Via Senese on the right bank of the Pesa. The bishop also acquired lodging rights (*albergaria*) from the margrave Conrad in 1127 in the *plebatus* of Campoli, Decimo, and Bossolo. The margrave wanted to cultivate an alliance with the Florentines at a time when he was supporting Genoa in its war with Pisa (at that time an ally of Florence).[52] As the commune of Florence began to move militarily against the minor nobility in the Pesa Valley after 1110, growing episcopal power in the region served as another instrument of communal interests (especially during the alliance of Bishop Goffredo and the commune between 1113 and 1136). As the commune moved against Vignale (1129) and Montes-pertoli (1135), Bishop Goffredo acquired the castle of Aquilone and lodging rights at Decimo, Bossolo, and Campoli in 1139.[53]

Most of the new acquisitions were located in the two *plebatus* of Campoli and Decimo on the right bank of the Pesa. Typically, the episcopate built up its holdings adjacent to or near the *castelli* it had acquired or was acquiring. For instance, in the *plebatus* of Bossolo, the bishops acquired the *castello* of Petriolo in 1076. By donation and purchase they expanded the amount of their possessions around that castle between 1076 and 1222, effectively creating an episcopal *curia*.[54] Having already possessed patronage rights to the local parish (which it received in the original 1076 donation), the twelfth-century bishops were in a good position to purchase local properties and monopolize the economic resources of the region. Similary, at Fabbrica (acquired in 1098), Bishops Goffredo and Pietro purchased property in 1116 and 1195 to consolidate their properties.[55]

The bishops developed a presence in the entire *plebatus* of San Pietro in Bossolo. Located high on the Elsa plain near a small stream called the Virginio, Bossolo was situated on the road leading north from Poggibonsi and Sant'Appiano to Florence (see Map 1).[56] Episcopal holdings there date at least from the tenth century, when the daughter of Rolandino di Paladino granted the bishops unspecified possessions (*iura*) in the *plebatus* of Sant'Appiano and San Pietro in Bossolo. As we have seen, Bishop Attone relinquished the episcopal portion of the castle of Bossolo in 1038 to the cathedral chapter. A century later, however, it was back in episcopal possession. The 1127 grant of lodging rights by Conrad III added to episcopal possessions there. The donation to the bishop in 1165 by a certain Minigarda (the widow of a certain Gattolino di Gentile) of landed properties (*feuda et terras*) in the *castello* of Petroio as well as patronage rights to the local parish added to episcopal possessions. The tie between the bishop and the arch-priest was doubly strong. The *plebs* leased property and tithes from the bishop for a monetary payment (documented in 1121).[57]

As important as the zones around Decimo, Campoli, and Bossolo were to the bishops, most of the twelfth-century acquisitions were related to a hospital on the Via Senese. Located on the west bank of the Pesa slightly west of Bibbione, the hospital came into episcopal possession on April 15, 1146. It is of special interest to the historian, because the acquisition of this hospital indicates for the first time that the episcopate was deriving income from mills. On that day, Giovanni di Pietro (a shoemaker or *calzaiuolo*) and his daughter donated it with all its possessions to Bishop Attone for the sake of their souls.[58] Although the hospital passed into the hands of the episcopate in 1146, records of purchases and grants to the institution go back to 1139, when Giovanni di Pietro either bought or received as donations nine separate pieces of property from different local families. Four were purchases by Giovanni himself, and five were outright donations. All acquisitions were of lands, mills, and aqueducts near the hospital. From 1139 to 1146, there were twenty-four separate acquisitions, of which ten were purchases.[59]

The acquisition of the hospital is evidence that the bishops were interested in diversifying their income. The mills associated with the hospital undoubtedly served the local community, already a grain-growing region by 1150. The bishops probably used these mills to grind their own marketable grain. There is no evidence at this time that there was any imposition of banal rights requiring the local population to use the episcopal mills at this time. The bishops did contribute greatly toward the development of the local economy of this part of the valley by building the *castello* of Montecampolese—a *castello* which probably served principally as a market site. During the tenure of Bishops Attone, Ambrogio, and Giulio, the patrimony of the hospital continued to grow. In 1151 Rolandino di Ubaldino da Figline and his wife sold land to the hospital on which a mill was to be constructed.[60] Spinello di Alberico and his brother sold to Giovanni di Pietro the shoemaker part of an aqueduct for the construction of a mill below Pergoleto. The evidence of the existence of at least two mills on this land (1151 and 1159) indicates that the hospital was grinding its own grain. The ongoing importance of mills at the site is evident from the fact that of the thirteen donations and purchases of property associated with the hospital from 1163 to the end of the twelfth century, five concerned mills.[61]

Aside from the possession of land, the acquisition of patronage rights to local parishes in the two *plebatus* of Decimo and Campoli increased episcopal jurisdictional power in the region. The earliest acquisition of property in the parish of Sant'Andrea in Percussina (*plebatus* of Decimo) was a donation made by Pesigolo di Rodolfo and others to Bishop Giulio in 1159. In 1165 the prelate received patronage rights to the parish.[62] In the same year he received patronage rights (*ius patronatus*) to the parish of Petroio. The possession of *castelli*, landed properties, and patronage rights in the *plebatus* of Decimo and Campoli effectively made the bishop of Florence the dominant lord in the middle Pesa Valley.

Leasing of property in the valley became much more frequent in the twelfth century, as Appendix D demonstrates. As the bishops were acquiring property, they were also leasing it out on *libellus* contracts. For instance, the first recorded leases in the region around San Casciano di Decimo were in 1123 (a *libellus* at San Casciano), in 1140 (another *libellus*, near the castle of Decimo), and in 1150 (an "enfiefment" at Bagniuolo). This last lease, an enfiefment, indicates the extent to which feudal terminology had creeped into the language of agrarian leases, perhaps as a result of the resurgence of imperial power throughout northern Italy and the revival of Roman law. This "fief" was not a fief in the strict legal sense of the term. It probably had nothing to do with military or administrative service. All three leases involved payments in currency.[63] The first lease (*libellus*) at Montecampolese dated from 1130.[64]

In the Valdigreve the episcopate acquired some new holdings in the course of the twelfth century. In 1131 Brunetto di Gherardo sold to the prelate all his houses, possessions, and lands in the *plebatus* of Giogole. Twenty-seven years later, the "patron" of San Zenobio di Casignano donated the patronage rights of the church to Bishop Giulio.[65]

The Valdelsa

Compared with the amount of purchases made by the bishops in the Val di Pesa, the acquisitions in the Valdelsa were negligible. During the period of conflict between Florence (with its ally the bishop) and the Guidi, the episcopate acquired valuable properties in the vicinity of modern Poggibonsi. Donating the *castelli* of Catignano, Linari, and Pogna, a noblewoman named Zabollina also gave to Bishop Goffredo the two estates (*curtes*) of Cinciano and Linari in 1126. Zabollina was the widow of Ridolfino di Catignano da Pogna, an associate of the Cadolingi. Located between two branches of the Drove in the *plebatus* of Sant'Appiano, Cinciano had originally been part of the Cadolingi patrimony. The acquisition of these properties from the last surviving member of a local noble family indicates just how important the demise of the Cadolingi was to the fortunes of the Florentine bishops.[66] Donations of those castles were equivalent to donations to the city of Florence. Having been made in 1126 (thirteen years after the death of the last Cadolingi), they are evidence that Zabollina wanted to keep the property from falling into the hands of the Alberti, at that time rapidly consolidating their regional power. Perhaps she also had no children, and the primary intent was spiritual. In any case, the bishop proved himself to be a more effective patron to Zabollina than the Alberti. By enticing the minor nobility away from the Alberti, the bishop made them more sensitive to urban interests.[67]

In the early twelfth century Bishop Goffredo used his control of that *plebs* to increase his possessions in the Castelfiorentino area. A major boost to episcopal penetration of the region was the donation in 1126 by Zabollina of her share in the *castello* of Timignano.[68] In an area of concentrated Alberti power, episcopal control of a *plebs* and part ownership of a *castello* posed a threat to continued Alberti hegemony.

As in the *plebatus* of Decimo and Campoli in the Val di Pesa, the bishops set about in the twelfth century to accumulate properties in the region around the castle. In 1143 Ugolino di Vulpello sold the procurator of Bishop Attone all houses, lands, and mills that he held in the *curtis* and *castello* of Timignano. Shortly thereafter, the *vicedominus* of Bishop Giulio bought all jurisdictional rights in 1181 in the parishes of San Michele di Valecchio and San Quirico a Monteravoli from Guido, Enrico, and Alamanno di Ildebrandinello da Sambuco.[69] The earliest *libellus* in this region dates from 1128.[70]

As the population increased in the area around Timignano and the *curtis Elsae,* the name Castelfiorentino began to appear in the documents—probably because of its position on the border of the *contado* and because of its association with episcopal jurisdiction.[71] The extension of episcopal jurisdiction in the zone was of great interest to the Florentines, as the Alberti held the bulk of the lands there as an imperial fief.[72] San Miniato al Monte, the bishop of Lucca, the bishop of Volterra, and the Badia of Florence all had landed interests and jurisdictional rights there.[73] Indeed, Castelfiorentino was a jumble of competing jurisdictions. Situated at the narrowest point on the river aside the Via Francigena, Castelfiorentino became a flash point between Florence (with its bishop) and the traditional lords. In the second half of the twelfth century—when the Florentine consulate was worried about Guidi intentions at Marturi (Poggibonsi) and Alberti aims in the Valdelsa—a strong episcopal presence at Castelfiorentino gave the Florentine rulers extra political and jurisdictional leverage on that portion of the Via Francigena and complemented Florentine attempts to control Colle Valdelsa (1138) and Poggibonsi.

Florence and the Valdarno

A glance at Appendix D indicates that the bishops in the twelfth century received a steady stream of donations of property located in or near Florence. There were very few if any actual purchases of new property, as the episcopal administrators—with full support of the Florentine consulate—concentrated primarily on accumulating property in the Val di Pesa. Nevertheless, in 1124 Bishop Goffredo acquired more property at Montughi, and in 1121 Santa Maria Maggiore was paying the bishop 18 *denari* for three plots of land located inside or just outside the city walls.[74] All in all, the bulk of episcopal property leased to churches and individuals was located along the Mugnone or just west of the city walls, a situation which had prevailed since the tenth century (see Map 4).

In the Valdarno Fiorentino west of the city, Bishops Goffredo, Attone, Ambrogio, Giulio, and Bernardo leased (*a livellario*) at Sesto and in the immediate vicinity for payments in money. In 1125, 1132, and 1139, Bishop Goffredo made three contracts (*libelli*) at Trevalle, Sesto, and Truncholi—all for Luccan *denari*. By far the heaviest concentration of *libelli* and perpetual leases accrued during the tenure of Bishop Ambrogio, especially in 1155 and 1156. Most of the leases were at Sesto and involved annual payments in Luccan currency. For Sesto we have the most complete information for the twelfth century—information which reveals that the bishops were leasing a lot of property for money throughout the last three quarters of the twelfth century.[75] For example, the bishops leased tithes (and perhaps landed properties as well) to the arch-priest of San Donato di Calenzano for eight *denari*.[76]

The Business and Administration of the Episcopal Estate, 1113–1200

Expenses

The expenses of the twelfth-century bishopric were very varied, but unfortunately we know very little about them because the sources tell us so little. Needless to say, the episcopal *castelli* had to be maintained, as did the household in Florence. The *castaldus* (a local episcopal official) probably received his payment from the local community, which was required to shoulder the bill. A special kind of episcopal tenant (the *masnaderius*) often had to serve in the *castelli* as guards or assistants to the bishop. Although purchases of new properties must have been among the most expensive expenses, the bishops also had to bear the military costs of several sieges. We know that episcopal vassals were present at two sieges, Montegufoni and Monte di Croce. Furthermore, some of the expenses incurred during the tenure of Bishop Goffredo might have concerned disbursements to his lineage or its allies.

As far as we know, the payment of taxes by the bishops to the commune of Florence or to the papacy—perhaps the heaviest financial burdens for the thirteenth-century bishops—did not exist in the twelfth century. There is no evidence that the city taxed monasteries in the twelfth century or the bishop and chapter before 1240, but perhaps the bishop had to contribute some funds toward the construction of local walls and fortifications, just as the Florentine monasteries were required to do.[77] It is also possible that the bishop had to provide grain to the commune when it was deemed necessary by communal authorities. This was true at Lucca, where in 1180 Bishop Guglielmo I had to pawn some of his treasure to assist the city in time of need. The first evidence in the sources for the sale of grain by a church or monastery to a commune also comes from the Luccan documents: in 1139 the Badia sold 24 *moggi* of grain to the consuls for 24 Luccan *lire*. Although the Luccan prelate might have had more responsibility for provisioning the city than his counterpart from Florence, it is not unlikely that the bishop of Florence had to sell or give away grain to the city when the consuls requested it. After all, before 1150 he was already receiving grain rents from tenants in the Mugello (Valcava, Monte Buiano) and in the Val di Pesa (Monte-campolese).[78]

Income: The Bishops as Landlords

To make the extensive purchases in the Val di Pesa between 1126 and 1225 (see Appendix D), the bishops relied both on traditional sources of wealth as well as on newer resources. Although there is no documentation of it, it is also possible that they dipped into church treasure as well. We can start with the more traditional (and the primary) sources of income: perpetual leases (both *libelli* and *concessiones ad fictum perpetuum*), or perpetual contracts with fixed payments. As Appendix D indicates, the bulk of those leases were situated in the city Florence, its immediate environs, the Valdarno Fiorentino, the Mugello, and the Val di Pesa. Of the thirty-four twelfth-century *libelli* documented in the *Bullettone*, about a third of them involved property in or around Florence, and another third concerned property leased in the Valdarno Fiorentino. Primarily requiring money payments, these leases provided a steady but not dependable source of income for the bishops. They also leased tithes to several arch-priests (at Calenzano, Pimonte, and Valcava), and two of those leases were the first examples of grain rents paid to the bishopric in the countryside (in 1142 and 1144). The major conflict over the *plebs* of Marturi with the bishop of Siena undoubtedly concerned the desire to control the tithes of that *plebatus*.

In the twelfth century there was still some difference between the perpetual contracts (*concessiones ad fictum perpetuum*) and the *libelli*, but by the thirteenth they were virtually indistinguishable.[79] The payments required by these contracts had become nothing more than symbols of the bishop's lordship. If the tenant refused to pay, according to canon law, he had two or three years to comply. Even then, if he refused to pay, he often did not have to relinquish his holdings.[80] By 1150, therefore, episcopal property in many areas of the diocese had effectively fallen out of the hands of the bishops and into the control of the tenants.[81] Episcopal demands on tenants were comparatively very light. Presumably, the bishop had the obligation to protect his tenants militarily—something that must have been very important in this period of constant warfare in the *contado*.

Although the tenants on his estates had to provide fixed payments every year (predominately in money), tenants enjoyed a great deal of independence from their landlord. For those who were sensitive to the commercial possibilities of growing grain and marketing it, the situation facing episcopal tenants had specific advantages. They received increased income as the price of grain rose (stimulated by increased demand resulting from demographic pressures), while they paid a fixed money payment to their landlord. Labor services, the bane of their Carolingian ancestors, were virtually non-existent. Lease-holders were cultivating grain on episcopal lands by the middle of the century in the Val di Pesa (Ospedale del Calzaiuolo in 1149, Campoli in 1142) and in the Mugello (Vaglia and Valcava by 1142, Monte Buiano by 1172).[82] Perhaps local peasants were themselves marketing the grain in the nearby markets at Montecampolese and Vaglia. By the next century virtually all rents were paid in grain. This practice had already begun on the estates of the bishop of Lucca (where the first instances date from the eleventh century) and was nearly universal by the end of the twelfth century.[83] In 1142 Bishop Goffredo leased landed property at Campoli on a perpetual basis for one *moggio* grain and one *orcio* of oil.[84] Apparently, this region of the Val di Pesa—the *plebatus* of Decimo and Campoli—was very advanced economically and becoming increasingly integrated into the burgeoning regional market economy. The bishop had recognized by 1150 that it was in his interests to acquire access to some of the new wealth created by this urban-dominated market economy.

The two centuries between 1000 and 1200 saw the virtual emancipation of the Tuscan peasantry from the vestiges of any remaining manorial obligations. Personal servitude declined as labor services became more scarce. Free settlers on colonized land and free lease-holders replaced the servile laborers of the Carolingian estates. In some cases, the bishop leased former demesnes (the *pars dominicatum* or *donicatum*) for perpetual dues, usually in money, but—as we have seen—sometimes in grain.

Again we should return to the example of the lease at Campoli. In 1142 Bishop Goffredo leased a former demesne at Campoli (*fictus nomine*) to Melliorello di Guido di Tottoli for the above-mentioned grain and oil rents.[85] Even if the tenants were paying predominately in grain instead of money rents, they benefitted from the fact that the dues were fixed and perpetual. In an increasingly prosperous economy in areas of the *contado* like the middle Val di Pesa and the west-central Mugello, peasants and medium to small landholders saw the amount of surplus product available to them continue to increase.

In the twelfth and early thirteenth centuries, material conditions favored the peasantry and rural merchants as a network of markets developed in the countryside. The price of land perhaps increased, allowing some to buy their freedom. Land transactions between kinsmen and neighbors enhanced local social networks, often to the exclusion of outsiders (including the bishop). Prosperous peasants were able to accumulate more land and eventually enjoy a modicum of self-government during this period.[86] Therefore, the peasant tenants of the bishop were relatively autonomous of the bishop, enjoying the distinct advantage of paying fixed dues as a growing economy benefitted them tremendously. However, increased urban taxation, the political pressures emanating from Florence, and inflationary pressures by the end of the century rendered much of this independence precarious.

Other Sources of Income

The expenses outlined above perhaps explains why Bishop Goffredo dei Conti Alberti attempted to diversify and tax the clergy of the city. It is likely also that he was channeling those resources to the members of his lineage, as had so many of his predecessors. Political pressure made it impossible for him to continue to extort the clergy, so in 1139 he agreed to the recommendations of the commission appointed in 1139 and promised to require only the taxes exacted by his predecessor.

Although rents constituted the bulk of episcopal income in the twelfth century, the bishops possibly also drew income from regional markets such as Castelfiorentino, Borgo San Lorenzo, Sesto, and Montecampolese (now Mercatale). Although the records do not indicate it, it is likely that Bishop Ambrogio actually had the market near Montecampolese (Mercatale) created, and we must presume that he then drew some income from the customary taxes levied on the proceeds. The *castello* near Montecampolese which Bishop Ambrogio had constructed probably served as an administrative center as well as a rent and tax collection center. Although these revenues were not uncommon for other episcopal estates, such as that of Lucca, they probably constituted a minor source of income.[87] Aside from market dues, payments resulting from the grinding of grain in episcopal mills might also have provided some income. As we have seen, the rapid economic development of the Val di Pesa attracted the bishops also to the ownership of mills as a means of diversifying and enhancing income. In the twelfth century, the only episcopal mills which appear in the sources were located in the Val di Pesa near Bibbione and in the Valdelsa at the *curia* of Tignano.

After the middle of the century, the bishops began to collect a former imperial or public tax, the *datium*. Most lords in the *contado* had managed after 1150 to appropriate this tax as their own, and it probably did not exceed ten *soldi* on episcopal lands, but it could also vary from time to time, depending on the needs of the lord. By 1200 it appears that the bishop was levying the tax on all his lands. When the commune directly integrated zones such as Monte di Croce into its sphere of influence, it relied on the bishop to collect its own public tax (the *foderum* and also called the *datium*) as a symbol of the dependence of the community on the city.[88] Apparently, the bishops simply transferred the taxes to the proper authorities.[89]

Administration

By the end of the twelfth century, the episcopal patrimomy was organized into *curiae*, and the historical record documents the existence of at least four in the Mugello and Val di Pesa: Borgo, Petriolo, Decimo, and Tignano (near Castelfiorentino). An episcopal *castaldionus* managed the properties to make sure that the tenants made their annual payments promptly, and he also received donations or bought property on behalf of his patron. The power wielded by the bishops at the end of the twelfth century was the result of 150 years of careful consolidation of previously dispersed properties grouped around *castelli*. Accomplished at first by donations and later by money purchases, this process of creating great properties began in the early eleventh century as a response to the emergence of the rural patrilineages and accelerated during the eleventh and twelfth centuries.

During the twelfth century a more sophisticated administrative network emerged to manage the increasingly complex episcopal *mensa*. These officials could be local (*castaldi* or *ad hoc* representatives) or come from the Visdomini or Tosinghi clans. The bishops still appeared to be doing many of the day-to-day transactions, however. They kept records of donations, leases, and conflicts and stored them in the episcopal palace. Presumably communal officials had copies of some of those documents (at least the ones which were relevant to pending legal disputes). In 1175 a certain Ingemmato di Ugo bought property at Petriolo on behalf of the bishop.[90] The primary episcopal representatives on the local level in the diocese, however, were the focal points of the episcopal clientelar networks: the arch-priests and rectors of the local churches. The abbot of San Miniato al Monte never appears as an administrator, but it is certain that his role as administrator of the *mensa* of the episcopal proprietary monastery was extremely important to episcopal interests. As we have seen, properties of that monastery in the lower Val di Sieve around Monte di Croce served as a bridgehead for further episcopal penetration of the region in the twelfth century.

Occasionally syndics and procurators appeared in the sources, but they were not as important nor as visible until after 1200. Sometimes the documents simply indicate that a certain individual transacted business for the bishop (*vice et nomine dicti Iohannis Episcopi Florentini et Episcopatus*). For example, a certain Galiasso bought property at San Martino Episcopi (Val di Pesa) from Giovanni Angiolelli, other unmentioned men, and their wives.[91]

We hear nothing of an *advocatus episcopi* (staffed by members of the Ughi lineage), but the Visdomini and Tosinghi appear often in the sources doing episcopal business, especially during vacancies. Unlike the other officials mentioned, the Visdomini were not local residents; they were working diocese-wide. We see a member of the Visdomini acting for the episcopate in 1180, receiving the pledge from a certain Angiolerio di Periugoli from Petriolo (Val di Pesa) that he would not sell or exchange lands there without permission from the bishop. And a year later Visdomini were both buying properties and jurisdictional rights at Vallecchio and San Quirico near Castelfiorentino for the bishop and receiving donated possessions at Noce and Sant'Antonio.[92] These transactions occurred in 1181, indicating how important the Visdomini were to the affairs of the episcopate during the twelfth century. They became even more prominent in the thirteenth century.

Unrest in the Countryside, 1113–1119

Because the bishop was responsible in some areas for the collection of urban taxes (*datia*), he became associated in the local community with urban intrusion. Furthermore, the pressures of the development of a sophisticated urban fiscal bureaucracy encouraged many episcopal tenants to attempt to avoid paying the customary annual rents (*afficti*) to their landlord the bishop. The successful consolidation of previously dispersed properties by the prelates made it more difficult for the local population to alienate plots of land to benefit themselves and their kinsmen. Perhaps these are the reasons we begin finding after 1150 documented evidence of local opposition to the episcopal presence in the countryside. All of the earliest cases were isolated and usually did not involve more than a few people. There is documentation in the *Bullettone* for resistance to episcopal authority at the following sites: Monte Buiano (1130), Cafaggio (1147), Vico (1151), and Sesto (1158).[93] At Monte Buiano, Vico, and Sesto, as we have seen, the bishops were actively attempting to acquire more property.

Theoretically, *libellarii* could not alienate the plots without receiving permission from the bishop first. Those assuming perpetual leases sold to them had to shoulder the same responsibilities and requirements.[94] The documents indicate that these tenants were exchanging parcels of land with kinsmen and neighbors, hoping to enhance their status and power within the community. This sort of activity led to social differentiation within the community and also diminished the status and power of the bishop as chief dispenser of favors and land. Inflationary pressures also could have encouraged the local tenants to resist pressures from the bishops (see Chapter 3). Perhaps fears about the threats to the episcopate's local base of power posed by these transactions led to the actual prohibition of any transfer of land without the expressed opinion of the bishop. Pronouncements requiring the bishop's approval of transfer were made in the Val di Pesa (Decimo and Petriolo in 1180 and 1188), Montebuoni (1183), and the Mugello in 1188 (Borgo).

Unrest on episcopal lands made it imperative for urban authorities to keep a check on episcopal rural interests. It is probable that it was during the early decades after the death of Matilda that the ruling elite (the *boni homines*) first required the bishops to handle their affairs by clearing them first with the civil authorities.[95] Indeed, church law required the bishop to submit disputes with delinquent lessees to regional courts.[96] During this same period, when the Alberti bishop and the *boni homines* were working together, bishops and the commune found common interest in forcing the bishop of Fiesole to make massive territorial and jurisdictional concessions in the Mugello to the bishop of Florence. The transfer of the holdings of the bishop of Fiesole in the lower Val di Sieve to the bishop of Florence must have occurred at this time.[97] The occupation of episcopal property at Sesto was the most egregious and the most threatening to both the episcopate and the commune. The sons of Morentano di Campi and others occupied ecclesiastical lands. Unable to handle it himself, Bishop Giulio came before the communal courts.[98] To the episcopate, unrest on its lands interfered with the orderly collection of needed income. To the Florentines, it threatened the stability and peace of the *contado* at a time of continued tension with the rural houses, the margrave, the emperor, and Siena. Also, the city was increasingly relying on the bishops to collect the urban *datia*, at least at Monte di Croce.

Whereas the commune of Arezzo gradually and successfully brought its rural lineages into its orbit after the decline of its bishop's comital powers, the commune of Florence faced a much more independent and defiant hinterland, autonomous of the authority of the city precisely because its bishops had possessed no public authority and because they had been too weak to hold the *contado* under their sway. In 1159 the city officials decided to act. In that year the consulate passed an ordinance which effectively gave the bishop free rein to repress opposition on its lands. No one could alienate church land, and no communal official could override episcopal measures designed to stop it. The consulate pledged itself to protect church property.[99] In matters involving episcopal tenants, however, the bishop apparently had to bring the cases to a communal court.[100] Further measures apparently limited the right of the bishops to dispose of property.[101] Actually, the bishops were in danger of losing control of their their own lands and possessions to increasingly independent peasants, who were chafing under increased demographic and inflationary pressures. That the situation was desperate is evident from the fact that Bishop Giulio appeared in the communal court at Or San Michele to defend his claims in 1159.[102]

3 Rural Communes and the Challenge to Episcopal Hegemony in the Countryside, 1180–1250

At the end of the twelfth century, the bishop of Florence was the largest urban landowner in the diocese.[1] With his properties organized into *curiae*—districts formed from landed estates (*curtes*) grouped around *castelli*—he exercised power in the central Mugello, the lower Val di Sieve, the upper Val di Pesa, the Valdarno Fiorentino in the *plebatus* of Campi, and in the Valdelsa in the *plebatus* of Sant'Ippolito di Castelfiorentino. Of course, there were other major ecclesiastical lords in the dioceses of Florence and Fiesole as well: the cathedral chapter of Florence and the bishops of Fiesole. Whereas the former had most of its holdings between 1180 and 1250 in the Valdarno Fiorentino (Signa, Quinto, Solicciano, Campi, Colonata, Sesto, and Quarto) and the Mugello (Pulicciano and Molezzano), the latter had most of its holdings in the island of Fiesole, at Monte Ceceri, Ontignano, Trespiano, Montereggi, Montefanna, and Montebonello.[2]

The late twelfth century, however, found many ecclesiastical lords chafing under fiscal pressures. The sources indicate that many Florentine church lords were falling into debt in the last decades of the century,[3] and two of the principal reasons were taxation and inflation (resulting partly from increased demographic pressures in the countryside and city). As we have seen, monasteries and convents occasionally had to pay levies for the erection of walls and military defenses. It is also likely that the consolidation of formerly dispersed properties in the diocese required the taking out of loans to finance purchases. Bishop Pietro in 1193 was under pressure to pay his creditors, so he sold the *castello* of Montemasso in the Valdigreve to the monastery of Montescalari to pay his debt to the Tornaquinci. It is apparent from a glance at Map 2 that Montemasso was located far from a region of concentrated episcopal power. Indeed, the bishop could have afforded to let that *castello* go much easier than *castelli* in the Mugello or Val di Pesa.[4] The last one hundred years of consolidation might have overextended the financial capacities of the bishops.[5] Since most of the rents on episcopal lands represented fixed money payments, episcopal income in the last quarter of the twelfth century might actually have gone down as market prices increased (surviving documents at Lucca indicate that prices increased fourfold).[6] Buying and selling of episcopal property during the vacancies of 1182, 1187, 1190, and 1205 by the Visdomini and Tosinghi also could have harmed the financial health of the *mensa*.

The historian must be very careful not to assume that the Florentine bishop was seriously in debt. The documents indicate that the bishops were accumulating and consolidating property in the first quarter of the thirteenth century, especially in the Mugello, Val di Pesa, Valdarno Florentino, and Florence (see Appendix D). Episcopal penetration of these areas stimulated some local resistance. Appendix D reveals that documented cases of opposition to episcopal power increased in the last half of the twelfth century. On the episcopal estate, documented references to opposition to episcopal rights in the *Bullettone* increased from nine for the period 1176–1200 to fifty-seven for the period 1201–1225. Most of those instances occurred in the Mugello (40 percent for 1201–1225) and in the Val di Pesa (25 percent), the central *foci* of episcopal interests. The increase in the population of Tuscany pressured many peasants to open up previously uncultivated tracts of land. Growing prosperity in the countryside, coupled with the fact that episcopal leases required fixed money rents as their primary form of payment, allowed the holder of an episcopal lease to retain a margin of independence from his lord which would have been unthinkable a century before. Exchanges of land among these tenants created a great deal of concern among the bishops and abbots of the twelfth and early thirteenth century—concern arising from the realization that ecclesiastical property was again falling out of the control of ecclestical landlords and into the hands of laymen (specifically, prosperous peasants and Florentine creditors).

In the entire region of northeast Tuscany ecclesiastical institutions were encountering outright resistance on the part of their tenants to make the customary payments. In some cases peasants refused to accept the lordship of a church or monastery; in other cases, local peasants simply sold ecclesiastical property. Between 1172 and 1225 there are twelve documented instances in which Tuscan churchmen approached the court of the Florentine *podestà* for assistance in reclaiming their land or enforcing the payment of annual dues. These cases testify to the climate of disorder which seems to have spread throughout the diocese on ecclesiastical estates and to the importance of communal jurisdiction in those cases.[7] To the present, few scholars have recognized the degree to which ecclesiastical lords in the diocese were in trouble.[8] Typical of this situation is the example of the monastery of Settimo, once the proud and powerful family monastery of the Cadolingi. In 1211 it had to pawn all of its possessions at San Martino alla Palma to contract a six-year loan for 300 *lire* in order to pay its debts.[9] In one of the most celebrated cases, discussed below, the bishop of Fiesole was unable to pay his debts to Florentine citizens in the second decade of the thirteenth century.

To resolve the difficulties facing them, the bishops of Florence initiated major innovations in the administration and nature of their lordship at the end of the twelfth and beginning of the thirteenth centuries. As we shall see, those changes included the requirement that episcopal dependents swear servile oaths (*iuramenta fidelitatis*), commutations, and the assertion of seigneurial rights by the bishop. In this chapter, we will examine how this transformation and the reactions it caused actually worked out on the local level in the Mugello, the Valdelsa, the Val di Pesa, and in Florence itself.[10]

The Valdarno Fiorentino

The Valdarno west ofhe city was the first area of episcopal holdings where there is documented evidence of opposition to episcopal power (see Chapter 2), and it was one of the earliest regions where collective opposition emerged in the form of a rural commune to challenge episcopal interests. Perhaps the reason was that it was the area of the *contado* where the economy was most advanced and the location of a major source of grain for the city. At the end of the twelfth century and the beginning of the thirteenth episcopal economic interests were concentrated primarily in two *plebatus:* Santo Stefano di Campi and San Martino di Sesto. In addition, the bishops possessed scattered properties (but exercised no rights in any *castelli*) in several other of the ten *plebatus* in the Arno plain. The bishops were not the only lords in the plain. Between 1180 and 1250 the cathedral chapter had property at Signa, Quinto, Quarto, Mantignano, Campi, Colonata, Sesto, and Lonciano (*plebatus* of Settimo). Before the middle of the tenth century, the *plebs* of San Giovanni di Signa was part of the episcopal estate, but Bishop Rambaldo granted Signa to the cathedral chapter in 964. In 1235 Bishop Giovanni da Velletri reconfirmed that grant.[11] The Badia of Settimo, endowed as it was with Cadolingi property from the end of the tenth century, also dominated the economic life of the plain west of the city.

At the end of the twelfth century the Alberti still possessed much property there. In 1183 the populations of Ugnano and Settimo swore obedience to the commune of Florence, but in 1187—as the city was fixing its boundaries—it left out of its purview the possessions of the Alberti near those two parishes.[12]

In the *plebatus* of Sesto the bishops followed a concerted strategy to diversify and increase their income. They required oaths from their dependents (*iuramenta fidelitatis*), increased the pace of consolidating their holdings, purchased mills in the area in order to lease them, and commenced requiring grain rents instead of money or mixed rents. This strategy did not win friends among the local population. The first evidence of resistance in the thirteenth century to the episcopal presence at Sesto dates to 1208 and 1209. Sometime in those two years, the episcopal syndic appeared before the Florentine consuls to complain about some men at Querceto who claimed they were not episcopal *fideles*.[13] In 1209 the episcopal notary first referred to the rebellious *fideles* as a "commune." By that date individual instances of resistance coalesced into collective challenges to episcopal power, with the commune of Sesto as the *locus* of that resistance. Although the sources are vague, it appears that the men of Sesto (*omnes homines de Sesto et ipsius plebatus*) sought to remove themselves from episcopal jurisdiction and declare independence from any obligation. They apparently resorted to violence to protest their displeasure; an entry in the *Bullettone* indicates that they "injured and molested the bishop and the episcopal office by damaging his properties and rights."[14]

Local opposition to the massive amount of purchasing by the episcopate and the Visdomini *consorteria* in the area perhaps led to the conflicts between bishop and tenant. The rebellion led to an episcopal excommunication, but the excommunication did not in itself end the controversies. In 1220 witnesses appeared before a Florentine court to argue that the *castellare* (former castle) and men of Sesto were subject to the bishop. Florentine intervention ended the conflict in 1220, as the entire episcopacy of Ardingo Foraboschi (1231–1247) was free of any challenges (except for one case in 1234 involving land).[15] The twelve-year conflict at Sesto, however, was extremely important for the fate of episcopal properties throughout the *contado*. It marked the first documented moment when the consuls of Florence intervened in a conflict involving the bishop and a *commune*. It was certainly not the last, and the lessons learned by the Florentine elite in this case affected the resolution of the controversies involving the three most important rural communes: Castelfiorentino, San Casciano Val di Pesa, and Borgo San Lorenzo.

The attempt of the bishops to consolidate their properties, diversify their income, collect the *datia,* and purchase mills in the *plebatus* of Campi met with concerted resistance from the local inhabitants. Perhaps inspired by the example of the Sestesi who opposed episcopal presence in the *plebatus* of San Martino in 1158 and 1209, the population of Capalle began to act on its own behalf against the bishop as early as 1230. In that year they appointed a syndic to argue their case in the Florentine courts.[16] Apparently, the conflict involved the refusal on the part of the inhabitants to pay a sum of money to the bishop, perhaps representing the *datia* or payments stemming from the use of the local mills. In 1232 the commune of Florence intervened to order that episcopal mandates be prepared for the governance of the community.[17] Having learned that the redaction of such mandates worked well to end the unrest in both Borgo San Lorenzo (1227) and Castelfiorentino (1231), the Florentine consuls followed the same pattern at Capalle. However, the conflict continued into the 1240's. In April of 1240, Bishop Ardingo commanded certain men of Capalle to pay 30 *lire.* This sum represented payment for loss of seigneurial rights in the community, and might have included the value of annual rents (*pensiones*) as well. In an undated entry (but most likely from the same period), the bishop excommunicated the citizens of Capalle for having been "perjurors." That is to say, they swore an oath to uphold episcopal rights, only to violate it later.[18]

The Mugello

At the end of the twelfth century there were four principal regional lords in the Mugello: the Ubaldini in the west, the bishops in the center, and the Guidi and the cathedral chapter in the east.[19] In the eleventh and twelfth centuries the Ubaldini were *fideles* of the Tuscan margrave, the bishop, and the Guidi. Especially close were the relations between that lineage and the bishops, as the Ubaldini held many lands in fief from the bishops from the eleventh through the thirteenth centuries.[20] Whereas the properties of the Guidi and the Ubaldini go back at least to the tenth and eleventh centuries, the *castelli et curiae* controlled by the bishops were largely the creation of the eleventh and early twelfth centuries. Besides the episcopate and the two rural patrilineages, there were five major monasteries with interests in the valley in the thirteenth century: Santa Maria di Vigesimo, Santa Maria e Bartolomeo in Buonsollazzo, San Piero di Luco, San Piero in Moscheto, and the Servite establishment at Montesenario. The bishops of Fiesole, as we have seen, possessed properties directly north and northeast of the city.

As the bishop was battling the commune of Sesto in the Florentine courts in 1220 and worrying about imperial support for the Ubaldini, he had to contend with one of the first expressions of collective opposition in the Mugello.[21] In 1159 the episcopate had acquired the *castello* of Lomena, which controlled a strategic route through the Mugello and was located near Ubaldini properties in the *plebatus* of Sant'Agata. In 1220 Lomena refused any longer to make required unspecified payments to the bishop (*debita usitata, servitia annuatim*). The episcopal syndic then brought the case before the courts of the Florentine *podestà*, which ruled in favor of the bishop (just as it did in the controversy at Sesto).[22] This refusal could have been linked to the imperial confirmation of 1220, which local residents might have taken as an opportunity to shirk off episcopal authority in a part of the Mugello close to or in the Ubaldini territory.

The example of Lomena probably set an example for the citizens of Borgo San Lorenzo and Valcava when they attempted to declare independence of episcopal control in 1226 and 1232, respectively. When rural communes throughout the *contado* actively resisted the episcopal presence in their communities in the 1220's, the collective movement at Lomena resurfaced at least one more time in 1224 (when the Florentines were summoning men from Lomena to testify).[23] The experiences of the bishop dealing with Sesto and Lomena, however, did not prepare him for what was to come from the inhabitants of the *castrum et curia* of Borgo.

The Plebatus of San Lorenzo di Borgo

In the early part of the thirteenth century the *Bullettone* gives us very little evidence of actual leasing, but it is clear from the source that the bishops and their administrators began tightening up the jurisdictional bonds that tied them to their tenants and dependents at the end of the twelfth century.[24] Indeed, it was at this time that the bishop claimed seigneurial power over the entire area, above and beyond his powers as a landowner. In 1188 the bishop forbade his tenants there to sell or alienate episcopal land, perhaps indicating the presence at the end of the twelfth century of a land market in the region in which episcopal tenants freely exchanged properties nominally leased from the bishop.[25] This was not the first such prohibition to be made in the entire valley; Bishop Gerardo had imposed a similar prohibition against the inhabitants of the episcopal *castello* of Vespignano in 1050. Bishop Giovanni da Velletri attempted to maintain episcopal control there by requiring a large number of oaths of *fidelitas*. Typical of these acknowledgments was the one made by a resident of Borgo, Ugolino di Bellamoglia, who in 1219 swore his *fidelitas* to the bishop and promised to pay annually one pair of capons and unspecified *servitia* every year.[26] In 1205 appears in the sources the first documented rent in grain: Agimmato di Geso leased perpetually land at Novelleto for one *moggio* of wheat and one of spelt.[27] By the end of the thirteenth century tenants paid virtually all their dues in grain. The year 1240, as we shall see, was a crucial year for commutations of *affictus* in the region. It is the first documented commutation for Borgo.

In the early thirteenth century arises the first evidence of unrest in this area of episcopal control. Initially, disgruntled individuals challenged episcopal interests, automatically bringing in Florentine intervention. In 1206 the imperial vicar for Florence ruled against one Siminetto di Siminetto in a case which the notary of the *Bullettone* leaves undefined. By 1207, two years after the first documented grain rent in the area, the Bishop Giovanni da Velletri resorted to excommunication to deal with the notaries of the syndic of Borgo. This case constitutes the first evidence that the political leaders of Borgo were acting collectively. Relying on his spiritual power of excommunication, the bishop hoped to end opposition to his authority. He supplemented that measure by requiring further *iuramenta* at Borgo in 1219.

By 1222 the nature of that opposition had definitely shifted from expressions of individual complaints to collective resistance. The origins of the clash between the commune and the bishop which was to last seventeen years are not difficult to isolate: the collection of the *datium*, which dates from the second half of the twelfth century, the appointment of a *podestà* for Borgo, and the levy of grain rents. The first documented evidence that the bishop was collecting the *datium* is from 1213, when the magistrates of Borgo swore to collect the *datium* and pay it to the bishop.[28] To enforce the collection of this traditional public tax, Bishop Giovanni da Velletri first appointed a *podestà* for Borgo in 1223, modeled after the *podestà* sent to San Miniato al Tedesco by Frederick I.

In 1222 Bishop Giovanni ordered the men of Borgo to accept Ghezzio and Restuccio as *rectores* or *consules* of Borgo. Instead, at the end of the year, the commune elected its own rectors. Apparently, the men of Borgo took the case themselves to the Florentine courts. Two years after the outbreak of hostilities, witnesses were still appearing before the court. Among those appearing was Ughetto di Pietro di Gherardo da Borgo, a notary, who testified that Bishop Giulio and his successors possessed, dominated, and held Borgo and its entire district (the *burgum*, *castrum,* and *curiam*).[29] In the face of an order by the Florentine *nuptius* in 1226 to obey Marsoppo, the people of Borgo—called by the episcopal notary a *commune*—rejected the legitimacy of the episcopal appointee and elected their own syndic. In 1227 the bishop was forced by the circumstances of this challenge to his authority to compromise on the issue of *podestà* appointments: at the end of the year the two parties agreed on a formula (*pactum*) whereby the bishop agreed to appoint his own *podestà* every fourth year (giving the commune the right to appoint the official the other years). The agreement worked out at Borgo San Lorenzo was the first compromise engineered between a comme and the bishop. It set the precedent and model for later agreements between the bishop and other communes: Castelfiorentino (1231) and San Casciano Val di Pesa (1241).

The nature of the *pacta* created an extremely unstable environment at Borgo San Lorenzo. Effectively, the commune lost its right to self-government for one out of every four years. Recognizing that fact, it attempted to block the appointment of the episcopal official in 1232 (perhaps—according to the provisions of the compromise—the first time the bishop was allowed to appoint his own man). To force compliance, the bishop resorted to excommunication. The measure apparently worked. In 1232 Bishop Ardingo therefore directed his *podestà* to order Borgo to swear allegiance to the new *pacta,* which they did on February 14.[30] Also on that day the *podestà* pledged to collect the *datia,* perhaps the original reason for the outbreak of hostilities.

Four years later in 1236—exactly when the bishop again was guaranteed the right to appoint the *podestà*—the commune refused to pay him the taxes and rents he claimed were his. The pro-Ghibelline *podestà* in Florence (who served for the first half of the year), Guglielmo Venti, refused to protect episcopal authority in the area because of the bishop's allegiances to the Guelfs.[31] The election of a Guelf *podestà* in May of 1236 was good news for the bishop, for he immediately came to the aid of the embattled prelate.[32] In August of that year the Florentine magistrates intervened to order Borgo to pay the taxes and rents (*datia et affictus*) which it was withholding. The Guelf *podestà* stepped in to maintain order in that strategically important part of the *contado* and to support the interests of its ally the bishop.

On the eve of another episcopal appointment to the *podesteria* in 1239, the commune of Borgo swore to observe the statutes of the bishop and to pay him due reverence. Bishop Ardingo appointed a member of the Ubaldini family, Ubaldino da Pila, as rector or *podestà* in 1239. Appointment to the office cemented the political alliance between the bishop and his potential rivals the Ubaldini. Unabashedly anti-Florentine in their sympathies, the Ubaldini were Ghibelline when Florence was Guelf (as in the second half of 1236) and Guelf when the city was Ghibelline.[33] The appointment of a member of that family as *podestà* (a post which normally went to the Visdomini) made peace between the prelate and its major political rival in the area. The *podestà* then proceeded to forbid the enclosure of land without episcopal license and the construction of buildings above the height of 15 *braccia*.

Protected by the agreement of 1227 and its affirmation in 1239, Bishop Ardingo set out in 1240 to commute the traditional *servitia* to grain rents. Commutations, therefore, did not lead to the clashes between 1226 and 1239. The principal causes were the collection of annual rents and the levy of the former public taxes (*datia*). Only after the situation was stabilized was the bishopric able to attempt to enhance its income by commuting traditional rents and services. After 1239 the evidence of conflict is insignificant. In 1252, shortly after the entry of Bishop Giovanni de' Mangiadori, the men of Borgo, Culcelli, Carza, Monte Giovi, and Grezzano swore to obey the episcopal mandates. By 1240, therefore, the bishops had managed to beat back the challenges of collective opposition. It was able to collect the *datia* and commute several rent payments into grain payments. However, its ability to act as absolute lord of the region had ended with the compromise of 1227.

Pagliariccio, Molezzano, Rabbiacanina

From the middle of the eleventh century to the early thirteenth, the Florentine episcopate actively acquired jurisdictional rights in the lower slopes of the Apennines northeast of the *plebatus* of San Lorenzo di Borgo. In the *plebatus* of San Casciano di Padule and Santo Stefano di Botena the bishops possessed several *castelli* and their districts (*curiae*): Rabbiacanina, Casole, Molezzano, Pagliariccio, Ampinana, Loncastro, and Vespignano (see Map 2).[34] The possessions in this area do not seem to be as ancient as those in the *plebatus* of Vaglia or Borgo. Throughout the twelfth and early thirteenth centuries, the bishops accumulated properties through donation and purchase (see Appendix D) to round out their possessions and strengthen their regional power. Pagliariccio was one of two *castelli episcopi* (the other being Montecampolese) actually constructed by the bishop, indicating a clear attempt to establish a regional lordship in the area. As we have seen previously, several noble families and the bishop of Fiesole had interests in the area around Molezzano.[35] The bishops acquired property there (houses, land, *fideles*) in

1156, 1203, and 1218. Also, a canon in the *plebs* of San Giovanni Maggiore donated possessions to the bishop at Molezzano, Pagliariccio, San Casciano di Padule, and Valcava in 1161. In the early thirteenth century Bishop Giovanni da Velletri attempted to round off his properties in the area by accumulating more possessions at Padule, Monte Acutolo, and Loncastro.[36]

At the end of the twelfth and the beginning of the thirteenth centuries, the bishops and their syndics were consolidating and concentrating their holdings in northeastern Mugello. A reasonable explanation is that families preferred to hand over their properties to the bishop than remain under the jurisdictional pressure of the Guidi, whose stronghold was contiguous to episcopal lands (the castle of Ampinana). Also, it is possible that they were seeking relief from the growing burden of debt and preferred to sell their lands or cede them to the bishop. Perhaps they believed the bishop (and by extension the Florentine elite) to be a more reliable and effective patron for the protection of their interests than the Guidi.

The bishop's position as lord in the contado was expressed on several levels. Aside from the many *castelli* they possessed, the bishops also had the patronage rights in the parishes of Molezzano and Pagliariccio at least from 1197. Local churches routinely rented or donated property to the episcopate (Padule, 1218; Loncastro, 1244; Vitigliano, 1254). Also, the bishops were appointing canons to the churches of Padule and Botena.[37] Before 1207 all episcopal *fideles*—like Drudolo and Gianni del Pesce di Orlandino and the men of Loncastro—held land of the bishop and paid dues on a perpetual basis in grain, meat, chickens, and money. The first appearance of a rent paid in grain dates from 1204. The year 1207 was a pivotal year in the history of the episcopal lordships at Molezzano and Pagliariccio, as Bishop Giovanni da Velletri made several commutations of traditional "services" (*servitia*)—which included labor services—into payments in grain.[38] Though the bishops continued to lease on a perpetual basis, they had to require their *fideles* to swear oaths of fidelity (*fidelitas*) to assure that the tenants continued to make the necessary payments. The first such oath in the area dates from 1211, and it was repeated in 1219. The oaths might have been directly related to the commutations. Most of the oaths, however, date from the beginning of the terms of new bishops. In 1231 and 1252–53—immediately after the accession to the bishopric of Bishop Ardingo and Giovanni de' Mangiadori, respectively—episcopal administrators required oaths at Rabbiacanina in and throughout the *plebatus*.[39] To prevent local tenants from escaping their obligations, Bishop Giovanni da Velletri issued an order in 1222 forbidding the alienation or selling of episcopal property. These measures indicate that the bishop was encountering resistance to his interests in the area shortly after the initial commutations in 1207. Opposition to the payment of dues apparently peaked in the first year or two of a bishop's term. The *fideles* took that opportunity to challenge episcopal jurisdictional rights, requiring the bishops to act through their representatives to force their *fideles* to acknowledge *in writing* that they were dependents of the bishop. Hence, most of the *iuramenta* date from the early years of a new bishop's term: at Loncastro (1230, 1232, 1254); Pagliariccio (1251–1253, 1273); and Molezzano (1231, 1253).

One may wonder why there did not emerge in this area of northeastern Mugello a rural commune to challenge episcopal lordship. Perhaps the answer lay in the fact that this small valley in which we find the *castelli* of Casole, Vitigliano, Pagliariccio, Molezzano, and Rabbiacanina was less commercialized a region (less integrated into the market network of the Mugello) than the area around Borgo. The control of numerous castles, the ability to appoint clergy to churches, patronage rights, and the successful consolidation of local properties made the bishop a very powerful lord indeed. This concentration of power perhaps prevented the tenants from organizing collectively as their counterparts at Borgo and Valcava had been able to do.[40]

The Plebatus of San Cresci in Valcava and the Commune of Valcava

Located directly south of the two *plebes* of Padule and Botena across the Sieve, the baptismal church of San Cresci is one of the oldest in the diocese. Only in the early thirteenth century does a record of donations begin, including (for example) one by a certain Barone di Gherardino di Perdipasso in 1208.[41] Episcopal ties to the arch-priest of Valcava were very close and extend back into the last quarter of the twelfth century. As was true in the *plebatus* of Padule and Botena and Borgo, the episcopate was rapidly accumulating property and consolidating dispersed holdings at the end of the twelfth and beginning of the thirteenth centuries. For example, in 1209 the arch-priest sold Bishop Giovanni da Velletri unspecified payments (*servitia*), and in 1218 he sold several men (*fideles*) and the rights to collect their rents (*affictus*).[42] These sales continued in 1220, when the arch-priest sold all the possessions in his control in the district around the *castello* of Oliveta.[43]

The first grain rent appears in 1144, and the bishops were collecting the *datium* as early as 1195 (though perhaps for the emperor).[44] Although only one *castello* shows up in the episcopal *mensa* (Arliano), the bishops exercised a great deal of power in the local affairs of the area. That power derived primarily from their relationship with the arch-priest, some of whom held the land in fief (*nomine feudi*), as did the sons of Martinizzo da Cerverde (who perhaps rendered military service for the bishop at the castle). Like other *fideles* in the nearby *plebatus,* the arch-priests pledged fidelity to the bishop and paid a yearly perpetual rent. In the first decades of the thirteenth century, the bishops began requiring their tenants to pay exclusively in grain instead of in payments of grain and money. The last perpetual payment in money that we see in the *Bullettone* dates from 1224, when Bernardo di Rustico and Gerardo di Angioello acknowledged that they owed one-and-one-half *denari* and three *denari,* respectively.[45]

The extensive influence of the bishop in the local affairs of the community elicited local resistance, which followed the pattern of opposition found in other areas. Opposition began first as acts of defiance by individuals. In 1218—the year of the oath of obedience to the commune of Florence—a certain Venuto di Gianno di Gregorio refused to acknowledge that he was a dependent of the bishop. Although the sources do not allow us to be certain, it might not have been a coincidence that Venuto's resistance occurred the same year as the sale of property by the arch-priest to the bishop. If so, it would indicate that the close relationship between the bishop and the arch-priest was at the heart of the troubles at Valcava, and local tenants of the arch-priest resisted their transformation into dependents of the bishop. The dispute was settled by a Florentine judge a year later in a decision which favored the bishop. Concurrently, the bishop began requiring specific tenants to acknowledge in writing that they indeed were dependents in order to end such disputes.

By 1227, the men of Valcava were refusing to swear fidelity to the bishop and obey his mandates. As a consequence, the bishop fined them one hundred *soldi.* There is no further evidence of conflict. In 1229 the episcopal *podestà* appeared for the first time.[46] Another *podestà* compelled the men of Valcava to swear loyalty in 1231—the year after Bishop Giovanni da Velletri's death. In the next year the new bishop tried to collect the *datium* of one hundred *lire* from the community, which certain representatives of Valcava accepted to pay. It was at this time—1232—that the word *commune* was used for the first time in the episcopal documents to refer to Valcava. Probably inspired by the example of nearby Lomena and Borgo San Lorenzo, the episcopal tenants residing in the *plebatus* of Valcava organized themselves into a commune to resist having to pay the customary *datium* after the death of Bishop Giovanni.[47]

By 1243 the *podestà* of Valcava proposed that the rural commune of Valcava make a set of statutes that it could submit for episcopal approval.[48] It is likely that the bishop was following the precedents set by the resolution of other conflicts involving rural communes, specifically the drawing up of statutes for Borgo San Lorenzo (1227), Castelfiorentino (1231), Capalle (1232), and San Casciano Val di Pesa (1241). By 1250 the bishop had approved a set of statutes to govern the community, seven years after the commune had sworn to obey the episcopal *podestà* and his mandates. The commune was given some autonomy within the umbrella of episcopal sovereignty.

The Plebatus of Acone, Doccia, and Montefiesole

Corresponding roughly to the southern slopes of Monte Giovi, this entire area had previously constituted a Guidi lordship.[49] Although the bishops enjoyed some properties in the region, it was not until 1227 that they took possession of Monte Giovi, Monte di Croce, Monterotondo, and Galiga.[50] With the financial backing of the commune of Florence, Bishop Giovanni da Velletri was able to make himself lord of Monte di Croce and edge out the Guidi from that fertile and strategically located region of the *contado*.[51] To understand the reasons for that purchase and the reasons for Florentine involvement, we must remember that from the death of the last Cadolingi the Florentines had attempted to neutralize Guidi power in the lower Val di Sieve. The formation of the Guelf League in 1197 regulated the relationship between Florence, the Guidi and Alberti counts, and the bishops of Volterra, Arezzo, and Florence. Each of the rural families and the bishops agreed to recognize the overall *dominium* of the city over the *contado*.[52] Regarding Monte di Croce, the act of submission by the Guidi to Florence did not completely dissolve the bonds between the traditional lords of the area and their local dependents (*fideles*). Although the commune required each *borghata* to pay the *datium,* in 1226 the Guidi were still collecting it for themselves, a fact which forced the inhabitants to elect representatives to seek a loan to enable them to pay it.[53]

Under pressure from the Florentines, the Guidi sold all their possessions at Monte di Croce to intermediaries—the Adimari—who in turn sold them to the bishop. Aside from the strategically located *castello,* the purchase included Galiga and Monterotondo. By late October, the commune of Florence had extended financial assistance for the purchase, and on December 1, all inhabitants of Monte di Croce swore to obey the mandates of the newly appointed *podestà,* Marsoppino di Rusti-chello.[54] With a century of conflict behind them, the Florentine consulate saw the acquisition of Monte di Croce as a means of further weakening the power of the Guidi at an extremely vulnerable point in the *contado.* Seventy years after the razing of the Guidi *castello* in 1154, the Florentines replaced one lord whom they could not control with another whom they could. As we shall see, one principal reason for this action was to be able to rely on a dependable surrogate for the collection of the *datium.*

The last major *plebatus* in which the bishop exercised a large degree of economic and jurisdictional power was San Giovanni di Montefiesole. The *Bullettone* reveals that the bishops had properties concentrated at Pievevecchia, Vico, and Montefiesole. The first documented grain rent in the lower Val di Sieve turns up in a 1197 lease at Pievevecchia. By 1210 Bishop Giovanni da Velletri was continuing to lease property there for grain, as in that year he rented (*locavit in perpetuo*) several plots for four *staia* of grain.[55] Bishop Giovanni increased his interests in local lands and mills by making purchases in 1193, 1203, 1208, 1209, 1212, and 1213. The first mill appears in the sources in 1207.[56]

Episcopal interests in the parish of San Niccolò di Vico extended back to the early twelfth century, when two families offered their lands and jurisdictional rights in the area around the *castrum* (*curia et castrum*) of Vico. In the first quarter of the thirteenth century, Bishop Giovanni eagerly purchased more land and men (*fideles*) from the local nobility.[57] The local elite might have been desirous of escaping the pressures of the Guidi, or Florence could simply have pressured them to sell to the bishop. In any case, Bishop Giovanni actively sought to create a lordship there, centered around the castle of Vico and its district. Most men held land perpetually as *fideles* and paid a yearly rent.[58]

At Monte di Croce, resistance by the local inhabitants emerged immediately after the purchase of 1226. At the heart of the controversy was the payment of the *datium* and annual *servitia* (probably rent payments and court fines). Apparently, from 1226, the commune of Florence was using the bishop to collect the *datium* at Monte di Croce, just as it had occasionally collected for the emperor.[59] Refusal to pay the tax increased significantly at the death of Bishop Giovanni da Velletri. Therefore, the new bishop went to the Florentine courts for relief. In 1231 the Florentine *podestà* fined certain men for not paying the episcopally imposed *datium,* a right which the Guidi previously possessed but which the

Florentines—through the bishop—had usurped. In 1232 there is the record of a collective oath (*iuramentum*) at Monte di Croce taken by a hundred men. Nevertheless, two years later at least fifty-six residents refused to pay certain unspecified *servitia*, requiring intervention by the *podestà* again in 1233.[60]

The community of Monte di Croce had refused to accept the legitimacy of an episcopal lordship and welcome the episcopal deputy, the *podestà*. They rejected his authority to raise the *datium* and to collect the former *servitia* of the Guidi. The timing of this conflict is significant: 1231 and 1233—years which coincided with the beginning of the episcopacy of the new bishop, Ardingo Foraboschi. The interventions by the Florentine courts and the fines which they imposed allowed the new bishop to introduce a further "novelty" in the nature of his lordship. In 1235, Bishop Ardingo made four separate commutations of former dues (*servitia antiqua*) into grain payments.[61] As we shall see in the example of the Val di Pesa discussed below, commutations like these could create opposition as well.

In the *plebatus* of Montefiesole, the first set of clashes occurred in the 1230's, simultaneous with the conflicts elsewhere on episcopal lands. Here the point of contention was the episcopal appointment of a *podestà*, in 1229 for the parishes of Vico, Pievevecchia, Monte Rinaldi, Valcava, Pagliariccio, Monte Acutolo, and Botena.[62] The initial cause of the disturbances probably centered on the collection of the *datium* by the bishop. In 1236 the communities refused to swear obedience to the bishop and accept his representative; perhaps the refusal was related to the series of commutations made in the area in 1235. Consequently, the bishop requested the *podestà* to require the men at Montefiesole, Vico, Monte di Croce, and San Cresci in Valcava to proffer the necessary oaths.[63] They did so, and in 1251 (at the beginning of the term of office of Bishop Giovanni de' Mangiadori) Montefiesole swore to another set of oaths of obedience. The situation then stabilized—at least until a new cycle of conflict arose in the early 1290's.

The Valdelsa

The upper Valdelsa was dominated by several diverse powers competing for hegemony: the Alberti, the communes of Siena and Florence, and the bishops of Florence. In comparison with the Val di Pesa and the Mugello, episcopal interests in the Valdelsa were not as extensive. The upper Valdelsa was a stronghold of the Alberti, who inherited much of the Cadolingi property on the left bank of the river in 1113. Because they were lords of Certaldo and exercised some power in Castelfiorentino, they were able to control traffic on the Via Francigena.[64] Encouraged by Frederick I, the Alberti began the construction of Semifonte in 1181 both to take advantage of the growing commercial potential of the area and to create an imperial foothold in the diocese of Florence. Indeed, Semifonte was one link in a series of *castelli* which formed a ring to separate Florence from Siena. Along with Montegrossoli, San Miniato al Tedesco, and Fucecchio, Semifonte served to protect and enlarge the presence of the Alberti in that area and their ally the emperor. Eventually attaining a population of ten to fifteen thousand, Semifonte was located strategically near the Via Volterrana and the Via Francigena (see Map 3). After the death of Henry VI, Count Alberto sold the *castello* to the Florentines in 1200. Nevertheless, the Florentines continued to fear its strategic and commercial power. In 1202, therefore, allied with the bishop of Volterra, the Florentines laid siege to Semifonte and completely obliterated any trace of the community from the face of the earth.[65] The destruction was a signal to all rural lords that the consulate would not tolerate a pro-imperial, commercially powerful outpost in its *contado*. Using a phrase taken from contemporary political language, the destruction of Semifonte by the Florentines was an act of "state-sponsored terrorism."

The Plebatus of Sant'Ippolito di Castelfiorentino

In the early thirteenth century the bishop acquired rights in mills and began taxing property in the prosperous community of Castelfiorentino. Patronage rights in the *plebs* of Sant'Ippolito gave him enormous power to consolidate and acquire property. However, there is no evidence that Bishop Giovanni da Velletri was trying to collect the *datium* at Castelfiorentino. The first recorded conflicts between the bishop and his tenants occurred in the first quarter of the thirteenth century (see Appendix D). Specifically, the first clash between the local inhabitants and the bishop occurred when Bishop Giovanni and one Errigo di Sirimanno agreed that indeed the bishop had *dominium* over one-fourth of a mill at Timignano. Apparently, this was not an isolated incident. Other local residents were also challenging episcopal jurisdiction and evidently went to the Florentine *podestà* for justice. In support of episcopal interests, the *podestà* ruled in 1217 that he would accept no more complaints (*querimoniae*) against the bishop.[66] The first use of the word *commune* to refer to Castelfiorentino by episcopal notaries appears in a 1218 document, but the first use to refer to the community dates from 1195.[67] In 1218 the community as a whole refused to accept the legitimacy of the appointment of an episcopally elected *podestà*. The election of that official, therefore, seems to have been a principal reason for collective opposition to episcopal rule.

On April 18, 1218, Bishop Giovanni excommunicated the commune of Castelfiorentino for its contumacy.[68] Five months later the representative (*iudex*) of the *podestà* of Florence, Alberigo, ruled that the bishop could indeed send a rector to Castelfiorentino—a decision which the commune itself accepted a few months later.[69] The several oaths (*iuramenta*) taken by local residents in 1220, 1223, and 1224 reveal that the episcopal *podestà* was determined to avoid any withholding of annual payments in the future. In 1221 and 1224 the Florentine courts continued to support episcopal interests in the region, ruling in favor of the episcopal side in two cases involving the refusal of two locals to make the necessary rent payments in grain for property held from the bishop.

Perhaps emboldened by the determination of San Gimignano to seize castles of the bishop of Volterra in January of 1230, Castelfiorentino escalated its own conflict with the bishop of Florence.[70] Shortly thereafter, Bishop Giovanni da Velletri of Florence died. As we have seen, episcopal dependents often took the opportunity of the death of a bishop to assert their independence. The death of the bishop gave the commune of Castelfiorentino the breathing space it needed to challenge episcopal rights in the area. Specifically, the issue of the day concerned the right of the bishop to tax the inheritance and transfer of private property within the commune.[71] The commune continued to oppose the appointment of an episcopal *podestà*, whose duty no doubt was to collect the taxes. As in San Gimignano, the consuls of the commune called into question the right of the bishop to tax the community. Located at a major commercial crossroad in the *contado,* the mercantile community of Castelfiorentino had good reason to oppose the attempt of the bishop to dip into the growing wealth of the commune.

In November of 1231 the two parties reached a compromise. There is preserved in the Archivio di Stato di Firenze a copy of the agreement in the *Diplomatico fondo.*[72] First, two pro-episcopal arbitrators—the *capellanus* of the bishop and a canon from the *plebs* of Sant'Ippolito—set the terms of assessment for each house bought and sold in the commune (so many *denari* for each *lire* of the price paid by the buyer).[73] The second issue settled was also decided in favor of the bishop: the property of those who died intestate went to the bishop. Third, the bishop could collect a third of all income from court fines and legal cases.[74] Lastly, the agreement allowed the commune to elect its own *podestà,* but the candidates had to be referred to the bishop for approval. Individuals with complaints could appeal to the *podestà* and consuls of the commune, or directly to the bishop.[75] The agreement of 1231 clearly favored the episcopate. It guaranteed to the successors of Bishop Giovanni da Velletri access to a profitable source of income generated in a commune situated at the crossroads of the Via Volterrana and the Via Francigena. Castelfiorentino constituted a bridgehead of Florentine communal power and influence at the portals of the diocese of Volterra. The loss of episcopal power in the community would have been a blow to Florentine influence in the southwestern part of its *contado* and to control of the Via Francigena.

Following the agreement of 1231, there was much less conflict between the commune of Castelfiorentino and the bishop of Florence. During the tenure of Ardingo (1231–1247), the nature of the payments changed. After his tenure most were made in grain. In the two decades of his power, there were seven leases of property in and around Castelfiorentino: three *emfiteosim* (1242), three *locationes in perpetuum* (1236 and 1242), and one *affictus* (1242). What is striking about these references in the *Bullettone* is that the rents were all in grain and that most of them were done around the year 1242. During the tenure of Ardingo, there were several such admissions, and in 1241 over two hundred people from Castelfiorentino swore fidelity (*fidelitas*) to the bishop.[76] The register also records thirteen acknowledgments by local residents that they owed the bishop annual payments—all clustered as well between the years 1240 and 1242.

The Val di Pesa

Whereas the creation of an episcopal seigneury (specifically involving the imposition of taxes and the election of the regional *podestà*) led to the establishment of the communes of Borgo San Lorenzo and Castelfiorentino, the extensive commutation of cash rents or mixed rents into rents in grain at Montecampolese in 1236 appears to have played a major role in formation of the commune of San Casciano sometime before 1241.[77] Along with the Mugello, the Val di Pesa was the area of the *contado* where the bishop enjoyed the greatest amount of jurisdictional and economic power. As Map 2 demonstrates, by 1181 the bishop had control of a vast array of *castelli* on both sides of the valley. It also had the patronage rights in the two *plebes* of Santa Cecilia di Decimo and Santo Stefano di Campoli, allowing it to appoint the local arch-priest.[78] To strengthen his connections with the *plebanus* of Campoli, Bishop

Giovanni da Velletri donated to him the lucrative hospital of Calzaiuolo (which was acquired in 1146). By 1230—after following a conscious policy of consolidation and acquisition of new properties—the bishop wielded enormous strength over a regional lordship which extended over most of the middle Pesa Valley.[79] The number of documented purchases increased from twelve for the period between 1176 and 1200 to eighteen for the quarter-century between 1201 and 1225 (see Appendix D).

Documented oaths of *fidelitas* go back to 1217. In order to maintain order on episcopal estates after the death of Bishop Giovanni and at the beginning of his tenure, Bishop Ardingo required seventeen men from Fabbrica to swear *fidelitas* in April 1232. Another set of oaths date from the beginning of the term of office of Giovanni de' Mangiadori (1252). These *iuramenta* were done to assure that episcopal tenants continued to fulfill their commitments to the bishop. The 1232 oaths, however, were especially important, as they occurred as Castelfiorentino and San Casciano were resisting episcopal power and Florence continued its war against Siena.[80] Of four purchases of property made by Bishop Ardingo at Fabbrica in 1234, 1235, 1237, and 1245, at least two and possibly three were made from men who had taken oaths. Episcopal jurisdiction in the region extended to the patronage rights in the parish. In fact, the bishops in the first half of the thirteenth century relied a great deal on the rector of Sant'Andrea di Fabbrica to facilitate the episcopate's penetration of the area. From at least 1225 Fabbrica was a major market in the region,[81] the creation of episcopal policies of acquisition and consolidation. Between Bibbione and Fabbrica on the right bank of the Pesa was the *castello* of Torniano.[82] On October 12, 1217, Bishop Giovanni acquired the castle. Two sets of brothers sold all their property and rights (including their dependents) to the prelate.[83] On the same day the bishop "enfiefed" the property back to the brothers, just as he had done at Fabbrica in 1098.[84] Bishop Pietro was especially interested in accumulating more property in the region of Montecampolese. Located on the hill of Mercatale (formerly Monte Falco) was a community to which the *Bullettone* notaries referred as Montecampolese.[85] In 1191 an episcopal procurator purchased vineyards, fields, and unspecified immobile property in 1191. In 1200 and 1203 the bishop acquired several dependents (*fideles*) of a local lord. Bishop Pietro's successor continued the policy of purchasing property in the area, for he acquired property (including *personae*) at Rignolla (1209) and at Montecampolese (1211, 1213, and 1214).[86] Both bishops rented property at Montecampolese. For example, in the last two decades of the twelfth century, there were four leases (*locationes in perpetuo*), and we know in the early thirteenth century Iunta di Guerneri and Fasciano da Nuovole promised to remain episcopal *fideles* and make the necessary payments (*servitia consueta*).[87]

Bishops Pietro and Giovanni da Velletri were pursuing the same policy of acquisition and consolidation in the *plebatus* of Decimo as they were in that of Campoli. Reference to Map 2 indicates that by 1181 the bishop had jurisdiction over a large number of *castelli* in the area: Petriolo, Decimo, Ripoli, and Montecampolese. A donation in 1183 and purchases of property in 1194 and 1195 in the parish of the *plebs* rounded off episcopal holdings there.[88] Between 1076 and 1222 the episcopate was particularly concentrating on the acquisition of property in the area around the castle of Petriolo, which they had originally assumed in 1076,[89] and in the parish of San Martino del Vescovo (Argiano) (1194, 1201, and 1204). In fact, Bishop Giovanni acquired some interest in the *castello* of Argiano in 1202 and 1248.[90] There is evidence as well in this period of some leasing and donations of land acquired in the *plebatus* of San Piero in Bossolo.

In the area around San Pietro in Bossolo, direct conflict between the bishop and his tenants is evident in the first two decades of the thirteenth century. In 1210, 1214, and 1219 there were clashes between Bishop Giovanni (or his representative) and local residents. Except for one, all the people concerned came from the *plebatus* of Bossolo. The individuals involved in these cases apparently claimed that the bishop did not have authority (*dominium*) over them or the land they were cultivating.

In 1219 the Florentines sent an army to the *castello* of Bossolo to destroy it. The sparse documentation, unfortunately, allow us only to speculate as to the reason. A reasonable hypothesis is that the consulate and *podestà* decided to raze the castle to prevent or destroy the emergence of a community (rural commune?) at Bossolo, which wanted independence from the bishop and hence from Florence. Bossolo was small enough that it did not pose a serious threat. With the experience of Semifonte in 1202 fresh in their minds, the Florentines refused to allow the emergence in the *contado* of communities that they could not control. Bossolo was small and could be destroyed. Other communes, like San Casciano, could not be repressed so easily.[91] By the end of the thirteenth and beginning of the fourteenth centuries, the Florentines had found more effective ways to limit the independence of local communities.

The bishops attempted to end or at least to cripple the land market among the episcopal tenants to prevent properties from falling out of their control. In 1180, therefore, in the district of the castle of Petriolo, we have one example of a pledge by a local tenant—Angiolerio di Peringello—not to sell or alienate properties of the bishop. Apparently, such independent behavior continued there; in 1218 the episcopal syndic seized the lands of several *fideles* (located at Petriolo, Giogoli, and Cigliano) for not making their yearly payments (*debita servitia et fidelitates*).[92] Three years later Bishop Giovanni thought it important enough to make an accurate record of the *servitia* owed him each year. Individual opposition at Petriolo, however, soon led to collective resistance. As in the Mugello and at Castelfiorentino, the bishop sent a *podestà* to Petriolo to enforce the episcopal will. The community refused to accept his legitimacy. Consequently, Florence intervened to condemn the men of Petriolo for their disobedience in 1244.[93]

Resistance and opposition continued to increase elsewhere in the *plebatus* of Decimo. In 1207 two tenants of the bishop—Bencivenni and Aldobrandino—denied they were *fideles*, and episcopal representatives called in witnesses to prove that they were.[94] Evidence of conflict still appears in the sources after 1207. Whereas the *Bullettone* says very little about leasing of property in the parish of the *plebs* of Decimo, it does include at least twenty-eight entries describing four decades of conflict between the inhabitants of the area around the parish and the bishop. Before 1230 the conflicts were exclusively between the bishop and individuals. The causes of the clashes varied. They involved land (1212), grain payments (1221), gate duty (*scaraguates*) at Decimo, and the customary payment of a shoulder of pork. In the last two conflicts, the *podestà* of Florence intervened and settled in favor of the bishop.[95] In 1230 the nature of the clashes changed dramatically from conflicts involving individuals acting singly to conflicts motivated by an expression of collective resistance by the men of San Casciano. In that year the *podestà* of Florence ruled against the men of San Casciano (*homines Sancti Cassiani*). The *Bullettone* notary does not explain the reason for this decision, but it might have concerned the refusal of the local residents to accept the authority of the episcopal *podestà*, who exercised authority there as early as 1223.[96] Challenges to episcopal power continued to increase, especially after Bishop Giovanni da Velletri began to commute his rents in the region around Argiano (1218) and Fabbrica (1209).[97]

The first recorded commutation of perpetual traditional payments (*servitia consueta*) to grain payments appears at Montecampolese in 1211.[98] Perhaps in a related development, by 1212 Bishop Giovanni had sent Lotterio dei Visdomini to serve as the episcopal *podestà* for the communities of Argiano—and perhaps also Montaguto, Montecampolese, Luciano, Ripoli, and Fabbrica.[99] Ostensibly, his responsibility was to assure the continued payment of episcopal *servitia* in the face of opposition by requiring periodic *iuramenta.*That task became especially important because the bishop was beginning to commute traditional payments from the mixed variety to grain dues. For San Martino Argiano he received those oaths in 1212.[100] *Iuramenta* are also recorded for Fabbrica in 1217, eight years after the appearance of the first grain rent. Significantly, a year after the *podestà* shows up in the documents for San Martino Argiano, Bishop Giovanni commuted a traditional *servitium* at Argiano to grain. There is no evidence of commutations at Petriolo, but the growth of episcopal power in the region met with some degree of resentment. Certain tenants lost their lands in 1218 in Petriolo for not having paid their required dues (*debita servitia et fidelitates*), indicating that local tenants were refusing to pay their yearly rents as well as were selling property claimed by the bishop.[101] To enforce discipline among the tenants (*fideles*) Bishop Giovanni sent *podestà* to other areas of the region. They appear at Decimo and Montecampolese in 1223. There is no evidence that Bishop Giovanni was collecting the *datium* there.

The story of resistance to episcopal lordship in the *plebatus* of Campoli is no different from the story regarding the *plebatus* of Decimo. Especially galling to the residents of the castle of Fabbrica and its district (*curia*) was the tremendous amount of land purchased by the bishop between 1195 and 1245. It is possible but not certain that the arch-priest of Campoli, Bene, either shared the concerns of his parishoners or was not as zealous a representative of episcopal interests as Bishop Ardingo had wanted. After the death of Bishop Giovanni in 1230, discontent with the role of the bishop in the area increased. In 1232, therefore, Bishop Ardingo removed the arch-priest Bene and replaced him with someone who would more suitably protect his interests (buy and sell property, end challenges to episcopal lordship, and work closely with the *podestà*).[102] Bene's replacement was a certain Bernardo, arch-priest of Panzano.

Four years later, Bishop Ardingo embarked on a bold and dangerous policy to commute the traditional payments in money or mixed dues into grain rents. Understandably, it created a furor. In 1236 (fourteen years after the first episcopal *podestà* came to the Val di Pesa), Bishop Ardingo da Pavia orchestrated a "massive" series of commutations in June and July of that year. The *Bullettone* records fifty-three, occurring over several days (June 22, June 30, July 1, and August 23).[103] The commuted payments ranged from one to twenty-eight *staia* with the average payment being about three *staia* per year. At San Martino del Vescovo Bishop Ardingo began to lease property for grain payments also at the same time, 1236. To Caroccio di Pancetto the bishop leased (*locavit et concessit ad affictum perpetuum*) two pieces of property (one in the *curia* of San Martino and another on the Pesa) for twelve *staia* of grain and six of spelt due every year in August.[104] These commutations at Campoli and the introduction of grain rents at Argiano in 1236 did not represent reductions in the annual dues required of episcopal tenants. They were increases which deprived many families of much of their marketable grain.[105]

Three very interesting observations can make about these changes. Most important, the commutations came after the appointment of the pro-episcopal *podestà* in Florence, Rubaconte Rossi, in May of 1236. The previous *podestà,* the pro-Ghibelline Guglielmo Venti, had refused to intervene to support the bishop in his disputes with his tenants. Bishop Ardingo took advantage of the protective umbrella offered by the *podestà* to jack up the rent on his properties near Montecampolese. Second, the increases occurred at the end of the harvest of the grain planted in the fall of the previous year. That sent a signal to the tenant that next year some of his grain would go to the episcopal representatives sent to collect it. Third, the bishop began the commutations two days before the feast of the patron saint of Florence, St. John. Because he was responsible for the promotion of the cult in the diocese, the bishop benefitted from the timing of the commutations, as the feast day greatly accentuated his spiritual power and prestige (*ius ordinis*). Bishop Giovanni's use of his sacramental role to protect his material interests, however, did not succeed. In a *contado* where heterodoxy flourished, episcopal excommunications in the Val di Pesa and elsewhere fell on deaf ears. Loyalty to the episcopal will did not come.

On October 15, 1236, Rolando, the Guelf *podestà* of Florence, sent his judge, Jacopaccio, to San Casciano to investigate the cause of the dispute between the bishop and the residents of San Casciano.[106] Specifically, the disagreement stemmed from the refusal of the residents to accept the episcopal *podestà.* On that score, the men of San Casciano found support in the cathedral chapter, which was opposed to the appointment of a *podestà* to the community without its permission and approval. But there also might have been another reason for the rebellion: the commutations at Montecampolese—formalized four months before. There was a link between the two issues. The *podestà*'s job was to collect the commuted payments and assure fidelity and obedience. On November 3, 1236, Iacopaccio ruled that indeed the episcopal *podestà* was legitimate and deserved the loyalty of the community.[107] A month later Iacopaccio ordered San Casciano to submit to the authority of the bishop, and the Florentine *podestà* confirmed it.[108] San Casciano remained opposed.

Meanwhile, the cathedral chapter decided to sue the bishop before the papal court for issuing excommunications and absolutions without its consent and for having refused to confirm the grant of property made by a predecessor of Ardingo. Meeting outside the gate of San Frediano, the chapter made the decision to denounce the bishop to the pope in order to recover its rights.[109] Those disputes—the question of property and the excommunications—appear to be associated with the Val di Pesa. In early 1237 Bishop Ardingo excommunicated the men (*homines*) of San Casciano, just as he had done before in similar cases. When excommunication failed to weaken local opposition, a papal representative arrived to warn San Casciano that it had to pay its withheld dues to the bishop.[110] In May and December of 1237 the Florentine courts continued to rule against San Casciano and for the bishop. In that last judgment, the *podestà* (still the Guelf Rolando Rosso) ordered the men to obey the *podestà* of the bishop and swear fealty. The next day he condemned San Casciano.

The decisive intervention of Florence broke the back of the resistance to episcopal authority . . . temporarily. In 1238 local residents, angry over the commutations and opposed to the *podestà* of the bishop, finally gave in. The episcopal *podestà* for Montecampolese and Ripoli convened a meeting to require all tenants to swear oaths of *fidelitas* to the bishop.[111] These oaths, however, did not guarantee obedience after 1238. In the parish of Percussina (*plebatus* of Decimo), residents who were inspired by the tradition of resistance to episcopal rule challenged the right of the prelate to appoint the parish priest. On August 13, 1239, procurators of Sant'Andrea conferred the right to name the priest to the bishop. This was simply a formal recognition of what always occurred. That same day, Bishop Ardingo appointed as the rector a canon of San Jacobo di Mosciano (*plebatus* of Decimo), a man who was also the episcopal *capellanus*. An anti-episcopal party formed to resist the election of Berto. Consequently, the bishop quickly excommunicated the anti-episcopal faction, just as he had done two years previously at San Casciano. Warning the parish against naming its own priest, he threatened the arch-priest of Decimo with excommunication if he confirmed a new rector. By February 7, 1240 (or 1241), the *podestà* of Florence intervened, just as he had done at San Martino Argiano and San Casciano. His representative personally confirmed the episcopal rector in his new post.[112]

The opposition to episcopal rights of patronage in the parish of Percussina underscores how deeply opposed and despised was the continuation of episcopal lordship in the region. It also explains why resistance to episcopal rule continued in the two *plebatus*, even after the oaths of

1238. The establishment of an episcopal *podesteria,* the commutations, and the continued manipulation of local parish appointments continued to trouble local residents. It is therefore not surprising at all that in 1241 a new stage of resistance began—one organized around the commune of San Casciano.

There is no documented characterization of San Casciano as a commune in the *Bullettone* before 1241. The community continued to refuse to pay the bishop his rent payments and to recognize the legitimacy of his representative, the *podestà.* Consequently, the Florentine courts took action. In the entry which uses for the first time the word commune to refer to San Casciano, there is recorded the fact that Rolando dei Rubei fined the commune (*universitas et communis*) three hundred *lire.* By the middle of the year the commune had apparently given up. On May 12 the bishop appointed a *podestà* for the community, and on June 1 the residents formally agreed to obey his mandates. A week later the *podestà* of Florence ruled that no one could enter into any agreement which could do harm to episcopal interests. The ban might have been designed to prevent an alliance between San Casciano and the cathedral chapter or between the commune and the Ghibelline faction.[113]

Three days later the bishop issued statutes for San Casciano, which Florentine officials had of course previously approved.[114] This did not mean the end of the disputes, however. Two years later the commune took advantage of the election of a new episcopal *podestà* to contest his legitimacy again. On August 26, 1243, the *podestà* of Florence reconfirmed the right of the bishop to send a *podestà* to the community. Two months later the syndic of Decimo and San Casciano dropped the suit, and there is no further evidence of conflict for several years.[115]

For Florence the stakes in this twenty-year-long conflict were very high. But Florentines did not speak with a united voice. For the Guelfs, support of episcopal rights was indispensable. The Florentine Guelf elite realized early that it could not afford to lose its influence in that region of the Val di Pesa. Since the eleventh century the episcopate had been a dependable instrument of Florentine power, and it assumed an extremely important role in the 1220's and 1230's. At that time the city was involved in a war with Siena, and the Val di Pesa and the Valdelsa were major theaters of that war. The city's Guelf sympathies required that it play a principal role in the affairs of that part of its *contado.* Also, the city was attempting to enhance its influence in the diocese of Volterra by strengthening San Gimignano against its powerful neighbor Volterra. Florence, therefore, could not afford to lose control of the Val di Pesa. Its access to grain, taxes, and troops and the maintenance of its

military security at a time of war depended on its control of San Casciano. The bishops of Florence were its surrogates—the guardians at the
gate. Furthermore, several urban lineages (like the Visdomini, Tosinghi,
and Aliotti) depended on its connections to the episcopacy.

The Ghibelline elite, however, saw the situation differently. It did not
want to see the territorial power of a papal ally (the bishop) strengthened
in the diocese at the expense of imperial protégés (the Alberti, the
Guidi, the Ubaldini). The Ghibellines wanted to see a diocese controlled
by their allies, not those of the Guelfs. Consequently, whenever a Ghibelline *podestà* was in power (as in January to April, 1236; 1237 and the
first half of 1238; and 1244), he resisted episcopal pressure to repress
local opposition to his power. Local communities were aware of the
internal conflicts, and often rebelled, knowing the Ghibelline leadership
in Florence was sympathetic.

Between 1209 and 1243 isolated cases of individual resistance to the
exercise of episcopal power in its territorial lordships developed into
collective, organized challenges to that rule. At least since the middle
of the twelfth century, the struggle over local control and influence
between the bishops and their dependents was constant. The formation
of new coalitions in the first decades of the thirteenth century was therefore rooted in several generations of conflict. The social forces which
led to the emergence of the rural communes were but one part of a
broad historical process which involved the local farmers, the bishops,
the cathedral chapter, "heretics," and, especially, the Florentine consulate. The clash of interests in the Florentine *contado* was of tremendous
concern to the divided Florentine elite. The history of episcopal property in the city and of the role of the bishop in the political history of
the commune is therefore an important and necessary part of Florentine
history.

Political and Institutional Constraints on
Episcopal Power within Florence

Between 1180 and 1250 a new and prosperous association of non-nobles
(the *popolo*) was challenging the power of the consular elite.[116] In the
late twelfth century the membership of the consulate was aristocratic
and included very few merchants.[117] Between 1150 and 1180 the merchant guilds formed as Florence thrived as a manufacturing and banking
center. Accompanied by the emergence of armed neighborhood military
companies, the guilds gradually challenged the power wielded by the
aristocracy. As the *popolo* demanded a greater share in political power,

it exacerbated tensions within the aristocracy until it broke into several factions in the 1170's and 1180's (later leading to the Guelf/Ghibelline fracture).[118] As tensions between the Guelfs and Ghibellines increased in the city, the bishop found himself more and more limited politically, jurisdictionally, and sacramentally by five institutions or groups: the guilds, the papacy, the mendicant orders, the commune of Florence, and the Cathar heretics. The growing power of the guilds was especially damaging. Since long before the foundation of San Miniato al Monte in 1018, the bishops of Florence had exercised influence in the city through their jurisdictional and their sacramental powers. Of great importance was their maintenance and promotion of the urban cults, especially those of St. John, St. Zanobi, and St. Minias.[119] Their orchestration of the cult of St. John was crucial, as they traditionally required their tenants to make the annual rent payments on his feast day (June 24). When the guilds and the consulate began to demand a greater role in the political life of the city, they gradually inserted themselves into the sacramental life of the city as well. They understood that sacramental and jurisdictional power worked hand in hand. Submission to the bishop meant submission to the city.

At the end of the twelfth century, therefore, the principal craft guilds began to take over the responsibilities of protecting and managing the principal churches in the city. By 1157 the Calimala (the cloth finishers' guild) had charge of the Baptistery, the center of the urban cult of St. John.[120] In 1192 the major guilds had charge of the leprosarium of Sant'Eusebio. The increased economic clout of the major guilds facilitated their ascent to power, at the expense of the episcopate, as managers of the major churches. The success of their attempts to participate in the ritual life of the city limited the power of the bishop to manage funds which previously were his alone to disburse.

This takeover, however, did not occur without opposition and resistance from the bishops. In the second decade of the thirteenth century Bishop Giovanni da Velletri resisted the diversion of the tithes from Settimo, Calenzano, Remolo, Pane, Empoli, and Ripoli to the Opera Sancti Johannis, the civic organization controlled by the Calimala guild responsible for the cathedral. The settlement of that dispute by the papacy in 1217 was a serious blow to the bishop. It removed a source of income (the tithes), and it enhanced the power of the Calimala at the expense of the bishop.[121] A second blow to the sacramental and spiritual power of the bishops came shortly thereafter, when the Calimala took charge of the Opera Sancti Miniatis. Again, Bishop Giovanni resisted the Calimala; he attempted to use the funds available to the Opera for his own use without conferring with the Calimala. In 1228 the arch-priest of the chapter (the representative of the abbot of the monastery) and the consuls of the Calimala came to an agreement which forbade the abbot in the future from diverting funds from the Opera and circum-venting the Calimala.[122] Since the abbot was appointed and controlled by the bishop, the decision placed limits on the freedom of the bishop to use the resources of the Opera of San Miniato al Monte for his own interests. Like the case involving San Giovanni in 1216 and 1217, the defeat of the bishop over the Opera Sanctis Miniatis in 1228 marked the end of an era—an era when the bishop was the supreme religious figure in the city. By that date the Calimala controlled the financial resources of the Opera, not the bishop.

The rise of a "papal monarchy" in the twelfth and thirteenth centuries also limited the ability of the Florentine bishops to act independently. From the middle of the twelfth century the papacy increasingly con-trolled the appointments of the bishops of Florence and used them as instruments of papal policy. Bishop Giulio (1158–1182) was a close ally of Pope Alexander. When he refused to support the imperial pretender to the See of St. Peter, the imperial party attempted to overthrow him, forcing him to seek refuge in his *castello* at Pagliariccio.[123] Bishop Gio-vanni da Velletri (1205–1230) was also a papal appointee. A native of Velletri (near the home of Pope Innocent III), he was a very close associate of the pope, who executed a program of reform of the local monasteries. He was also very close to the emperor. As a papal legate, Bishop Giovanni re-established in May of 1220 a semblance of peace between the bishop of Volterra (and his ally San Gimignano) and the commune of Volterra. He enjoyed the favor of three popes.[124] Finally, Bishop Ardingo da Pavia (1231–1247), another papal appointee, also received the support of Frederick II.[125]

The control of the elections of the bishops of Florence gave the papacy added leverage in Florence in the first generation of the Guelf and Ghi-belline clashes. Indeed, in the Guelf commune, the bishop was a prime representative of the papacy—at least until the arrival of the mendicants. Papal political interests in the diocese, however, created problems for the bishops and indirectly weakened their financial condition. Preferen-tial treatment for the mendicants by the papacy most clearly exemplifies this situation. The papacy promoted the mendicants for several reasons. For one, their loyalty made them effective instruments of papal policies. That in and of itself would not have been important if it was not also accompanied by the growth of their financial and economic resources. Politically, the bishops were not as dependable as the mendicants; they

were sensitive to local political interests at a time of growing Guelf/
Ghibelline rivalry.[126] Finally, the Dominicans were effective crusaders
against heterodoxy at a time when episcopal sacramental power was
weakened by unrest on its lands and by the growing power of the guilds.
The spiritual power of the mendicants and the weakness of the bishop
were exemplified most clearly in the emergence in the early thirteenth
century of the popular cult of Umiliana dei Cerchi, a young widow
profoundly influenced by the friars. Appealing to a female audience, the
cult provided Florentine women with a role model embodying the vir-
tues of simplicity, orthodoxy, and charity.[127] The arrival of the mendicant orders, therefore, was facilitated by the economic and spiritual crisis
of the bishopric, but it also exacerbated that crisis by placing greater
economic and jurisdictional strains on the prelate.

With full papal backing, the Dominicans and the Franciscans insinu-
ated themselves into the religious and economic life of the city, and
their involvement created conflict between the regular clergy and the
mendicants. Florence had been one of the first places the Franciscans
visited (1209), and St. Dominic had come to the city at least once before
1219. In 1218 a certain Forese Bilicuzzi Mergulliesi donated land at
Monticelli for a Clarist convent. Ten years later (in 1228) Gregory IX
gave the Franciscans special protection at Santa Croce.[128] In the region
immediately east of the city and just outside the walls, Bishop Giovanni
received the church of San Jacopo di Ripoli from a certain Diomitici
in 1214. Under a papal directive, the prelate conferred the church to
Dominican nuns for the establishment of a convent. In 1229 the bishop
absolved the new convent of any and all episcopal exactions.[129] The
major grant to the Dominicans, however, occurred in 1221, when the
cardinal legate gave the Dominicans Santa Maria Novella, which had
been originally consecrated in 1096. Shortly thereafter the cardinal legate gave Giovanni da Salerno instructions on how and when to move
against the heretics.[130]

By the end of the twelfth century, the commune had intervened extensively in ecclesiastical affairs it believed were central to its own interests.
In 1197 the commune elected its own rector of Santa Maria Novella to
end the alleged corrupt mismanagement of the church. The canons of
the cathedral chapter and the bishop joined forces to oppose that intervention, but they failed to convince the consulate to respect ecclesiastical
immunity.[131] The commune did not hesitate to settle disputes between
the chapter and the bishop. In 1210 the bishop and the chapter were in
conflict, leading the *podestà* to intervene in 1214. As mentioned above,
the power of the guilds in the political and economic affairs of the city

led the *podestà* in 1216 and 1217 to force the bishop to concede to the Calimala the tithes he was refusing to give to the Opera San Giovanni.[132]

As the commune usurped more and more of the institutional responsibilities of the bishops, it slowly appropriated for itself the cult of St. John. Indeed, overshadowing the episcopal patron saint, St. Zanobi (whose cult became more important in the late eleventh century than that of St. Minias had been earlier in that century), St. John came to symbolize and embody the *charisma* of communal authority. Communal offerings to St. John began in the twelfth century, and by the thirteenth city officials were formally making ritual submissions to the patron saint. On his feast day the rural communes and lords of the *contado* submitted themselves to the saint just as episcopal tenants had done to the prelates as early as the tenth century. The slow evolution of the communal cult of St. John symbolized the growing strength of public authority and the economic and political marginalization of the bishop.[133] The commune's achievement replicated the experience of other Italian cities. At Bologna the commune consciously orchestrated the cult of St. Petronio in the twelfth and thirteenth century to replace the former episcopal saint; at Pistoia the authorities encouraged the cult of St. Jacobo, just as at Perugia the city developed the official cult of St. Ercolano.[134]

Circumscription of episcopal authority also occurred on the economic and administrative level. The commune placed limits on the use of ecclesiastical property in 1225, when it passed a statute refusing to allow anyone to touch Florentine church property without communal permission, even if they had papal letters which allowed them to do so. The statute was the result of communal protection of the creditors of the bishopric of Fiesole. After 1220 the bishop of Fiesole was unable to repay loans, and the pope—concerned about the jurisdictional issue—attempted to prevent the Florentine creditors from keeping possession of church property that had fallen into their hands as security for the loans. At this point the commune intervened, resisting the papal attempts to take church property out of the hands of the creditors. Eventually, the bishop settled with the commune. He paid back 3,000 *lire* of the 10,000 *lire* loaned and agreed to live in Florence permanently in the church of Santa Maria in Campo. The bishop lost all direct jurisdiction over his *mensa,* except for Turicchi.[135] His forced residence in the city began a process meant to force the bishop and his allies to favor the city's interests over those of the countryside.

During the first half of the thirteenth century the commune of Florence sought to push back the power of the neighboring communes of

Volterra and Siena. For many of those years Florence was at war. Between 1200 and 1210 the commune enjoyed a period of peace, but in 1220 it attacked Montenanno, and in 1222 Pisa. In 1225 it went to war against Figline and Incisa, and in 1228 again against Pisa. But the most important conflict—certainly for the story of episcopal lordship in the *contado*—was the war against Siena. Between 1228 and 1235 the two communes fought in the Valdelsa and the Val di Pesa.[136]

In 1197 the Guelf communes, the bishops of Arezzo, Volterra, and Florence, and the Guidi and Alberti concluded a pact which regulated relations among the communes, the bishops, and the rural elites in their respective dioceses. In 1218 all men of the *contado* had to swear allegiance to the commune of Florence, and the census defined the fiscal condition of all. Following the first commission on revenue in 1224, the Florentines sought to find newer ways of collecting the revenue needed to pay for its widening military and domestic endeavors. In the midst of the war with Siena, the city decided to hold a census between 1230 and 1233 in order to tax every household.[137] The new taxes which resulted from the survey directly affected the ability of Bishop Ardingo to collect his rents every August. There can be no doubt that the growing tax burden on the *contadini* (rural population) intensified their already strong tradition of opposition to episcopal lordship, associated directly with the urban penetration of the countryside.[138] A recent historian has written that the 1233 census and tax actually *caused* the episcopal tenants (*coloni*) to resist episcopal collection of the *datium* and led the bishop to intensify his efforts to commute his traditional rents. The communal tax (26 *denari*) was far less than the episcopal *datium* of 10–12 *soldi*. Resistance to the episcopal presence might have been only one part of a much larger tradition of opposition to the growing power of Florence and urban lords in the *contado*.

For the history of episcopal power in the city, the decade of the 1230's was crucial. The triumph of the Ghibellines in 1244–45 had disastrous results for the political and economic position of the bishop in the city. The 1230's, however, did not begin so inauspiciously for the bishop. When Bishop Giovanni da Velletri died in 1230, relations between the emperor and the commune were amiable. The new bishop, Ardingo da Pavia, was favored by both.[139] As tension between pope and emperor increased in the middle of the decade, so did the conflicts within the city of Florence. For example, Ardingo issued in 1231 a new constitution to govern the affairs of the cathedral chapter—measures which cracked down on the misuse of church property by members of the chapter (such as Pagano, the arch-priest of Figline). Understandably, its issuance exacerbated tensions between the bishop and the chapter.[140] During the *podesteria* of Guglielmo Venti (1236), the Guelfs were placed on the defensive. This Ghibelline *podestà* found support from the rural allies of the emperor: the Alberti, the Ubaldini, the Guidi, and the rural communes opposed to Florence.

At this point the exercise of episcopal lordship in the countryside and the demands of Florentine urban politics intersected at a crucial conjuncture. Increasingly, from 1217 to 1243, Bishops Giovanni da Velletri and Ardingo turned to the commune of Florence for support as new forms of social organization (the rural communes) called into question episcopal regional control. The more they turned to the commune, the more dependent politically they became. At the same time, it was in the interest of the Ghibelline faction within the city of Florence to weaken or prevent the ability of the commune to exert its power over the *contado* at the expense of the Ghibellines and allies. The pro-imperial party wanted to prevent the emergence of a centralized territorial state under Guelf leadership. Consequently, when San Casciano resisted the pro-Guelf bishop, Guglielmo Venti refused to assist the bishop to repress the rebellion and sided with San Casciano. Apparently the cathedral chapter—still angry at Ardingo's initiatives—intensified its pressure on the bishop by appealing to the papacy to protest what it perceived was the violation of its rights.[141]

Within the communal elite, a power struggle between Guelf and Ghibelline factions resulted in the ouster of Guglielmo Venti and the installation of a Guelf *podestà* in May of 1236: Rolando Rossi.[142] The Guelfs believed fervently that they had to come to the aid of their bishop for two reasons. First, he was a Guelf and a valuable ally. Second, and most important, the power he wielded in the outlying areas of the *contado* counteracted the rural power of the Ghibelline rural elite.

In May of 1236 the new *podestà* immediately confirmed ecclesiastical rights and came to the aid of the besieged bishop. Indeed, the prelate also promised the *podestà* his support and loyalty.[143] However, Bishop Ardingo's hope that the commune would continue to protect episcopal power suffered a setback with the election of the pro-Ghibelline *podestà*, Rubaconte di Mandello. Apparently, the Guelf victory of May 1236 was followed by a Ghibelline reaction. Rubaconte, like Guglielmo Venti, refused to come to the aid of the bishop in defending his rights at San Casciano. Bishop Ardingo thereupon cited him for heresy.[144] The connection between heresy, Ghibelline policy, and the failure to support episcopal interests in the diocese was not fortuitious.

Heresy and Episcopal Power in the Diocese of Florence

The weakening of episcopal influence created a vacuum in the country-side. Certainly one of the most important developments in Italian eccle-siastical history in the twelfth and thirteenth centuries was the popularity of Catharism in the cities and countryside.[145] Catharism appeared first in Lombardy sometime before 1167, probably brought by missionaries coming from northern France, and it reached Florence by 1173.[146] Along with the Cathars, the Waldensians were also present in Florence (they first appear in 1206).[147] Catharism apparently was most popular among merchants and residents of suburbs between the new and old walls of northern Italian cities. One scholar has found close links between the heresy and pursemakers in Bologna at the end of the thirteenth century. Although artisans seem to have been the major transmitters, the aristoc-racy became important patrons of the Cathars (as the Uberti did in Florence). First interdicted in 1173 in the diocese of Florence, the heresy was popular in the countryside before spreading to the city itself. At that point the city became a principal point of diffusion, especially after the Cathars found shelter among many Ghibelline residents.[148] In the thirteenth century Florence was the seat of a Cathar bishopric, the juris-diction of which embraced all of Tuscany.[149] Unlike the situation in Languedoc, in Tuscany peasants were apparently not attracted to the heresy.[150] In 1250 the documents recorded only one hundred professed adherents.[151]

The sources allow us to draw only indirect connections between her-esy, episcopal lordship, and political developments within Florence.[152] We know that Cathars were numerous in the diocese of Volterra, in the Valdelsa, at San Gimignano, and at Poggibonsi, where there was a school. There is no evidence from the documents that Cathars were present in any of the rural communes challenging episcopal lordship in the first half of the thirteenth century. Nevertheless, Catharism did influence the political fate of the bishop in the city and *contado*. The tenure of Bishop Giovanni da Velletri began and ended with two signifi-cant acts designed at least in part to support the forces of orthodoxy in the diocese. In 1204—around the time Giovanni became bishop—he arranged for the arm of the apostle Philip to be transferred from the east to Florence, and in 1230—at the end of his tenure—there occurred in the city the miracle of the eucharist. In 1206 the city integrated into its statutes certain anti-heresy statutes promoted by the pope.[153] In 1227 Gregory IX asked Giovanni da Salerno to initiate proceedings against Florentine Cathars. Although in 1233 Bishop Ardingo failed to convince the urban authorities to pass new anti-heresy statutes, by 1235 the Domenicans had taken over the responsibility of the inquisition. The chief inquisitor, Ruggero Calcagni, was responsible for sentencing ten people to the stake.[154]

The extremely sensitive balance of political forces (pope and emperor) unravelled in 1242 and 1243. Bishop Ardingo, favored by both parties, had attempted to retain a position of cautious neutrality as the tensions mounted. In Florence itself, the bishop confronted the two Ghibelline *podestà* for failing to uphold his jurisdictional rights and for being associated with heresy. Ardingo did what he could to prevent the outbreak of civil war, but in 1242 that war began. The Guelf lineage, the Adimari, attacked the towers of the Ghibelline Bonfanti clan. Ardingo maintained a very tentative peace. Nevertheless, after the election of Innocent IV in 1243 the bishop could no longer maintain his neutrality and he split with the emperor definitively.[155]

As the Ghibellines increased their power in the city, the bishop, the Dominicans, and the Guelfs went on the offensive. Although Florence was dominated by the Guelfs, there were many Ghibellines in the city sheltering Cathars. The emperor Frederick II, wanting to weaken the Guelf commune of Florence and its ally the bishop, lent his support to the Ghibelline *podestà* in 1244. Meanwhile the pope named as inquisitor for Tuscany Ruggero Calcagni of Santa Maria Novella. Bishop Ardingo named him his vicar in matters of faith. In 1244 the two accused a prominent Ghibelline, Barone di Barone, of sheltering and giving aid to Cathars in the city. The *podestà*, Pace Pesanuola, refused to arrest Barone, and a dramatic confrontation ensued.

The Guelfs, allied with the bishop and the Dominicans, attempted to pressure the *podestà* to resign. In 1245 the emperor intervened to support his allies, and the pope immediately excommunicated him. The heresy tribunal thereupon condemned the *podestà*. The bitter controversy ended finally when Pace and Barone broke into the cathedral with the support of a mob and forced the episcopal forces to back down. The final triumph of Pace and Barone left Florence more Ghibelline than it was before. Thenceforth, the Cathars were left alone. Eventually, imperial troops under Pandolfo entered and subjugated the city. Frederick of Antioch was named *podestà*, and responsibility for the *contado* was removed from the city administration. The *contado* was divided into three parts and managed by an imperial functionary.[156]

On one hand, the pro-papal party wanted a city governed by the orthodox Guelfs and a countryside administered by a Guelf administration and its ally, the bishop. On the other hand, the pro-imperial party desired a city managed by allies of the emperor who encouraged and supported heterodoxy as a way of weakening Guelf influence in the city and countryside. The imperial party probably supported the efforts of the rural communes in the episcopally dominated areas to attain more autonomy. The oscillation between Guelf and Ghibelline forces in the mid–1230's also explains why disputes with the bishop re-surfaced at Borgo San Lorenzo and Valcava after the 1227 settlement, and why the conflict with San Casciano intensified after 1236 and was not settled until 1241.

The example of San Casciano Val di Pesa is especially instructive. During Guglielmo Venti's tenure as *podestà*, from January to May of 1236, the residents of San Casciano refused to accept the legitimacy of episcopal lordship. Guglielmo Venti, who refused to support the bishop, encouraged by his inaction the rebellion of the community. San Casciano watched political developments in Florence closely, perhaps knowing it would get the support of the Ghibelline *podestà*. When the Guelfs and the bishop expelled Guglielmo Venti in May of 1236, the new *podestà* (Rolando Rossi da Parma) immediately pledged to support episcopal rights. Bishop Ardingo da Pavia, relying on this pledge, then began in June of 1236 the series of commutations which led to more resistance in the community. The successor of Rolando, the pro-Ghibelline Rubaconte di Mandello (*podestà* for all of 1237 and half of 1238),[157] returned to a policy of inaction, wanting as he did to weaken the Guelfs and their ally the bishop. The bishop then accused the *podestà* of heresy to exile him from office. Once he left office, his Guelf successors oversaw the resolution of the conflicts on episcopal lands at San Casciano (1241), Valcava (1243), and Borgo San Lorenzo (1272).[158] The connection between jurisdictional power (*ius iurisdictionis*) and spiritual power or *charisma* (*ius ordinis*) was inextricable: the exercise of one depended on the exercise of the other. The heritage of resistance to episcopal lordship—a heritage which extended back at least to the middle of the twelfth century—provided an environment in which Catharism could flourish. The two merged in the mid–1230's, encouraged and supported by the Ghibelline faction in the city and Ghibelline allies in the countryside. The triumph of the Ghibelline commune in 1244 and the momentary victory of the urban Cathars contributed to a further weakening of the political and liturgical power of the bishops.

The Ghibelline Commune, 1244–1250

In 1248 the Guelfs left the city to Frederick of Antioch. Although some went to Lucca, others fled to *castelli* in the countryside. In Florence itself the Ghibellines went on a rampage of revenge, destroying the towers of prominent Guelf families (the Cerchi and Tosinghi, for example).[159] To generate revenue, the Ghibelline elite began to tax ecclesiastical institutions. The first evidence of prior taxation of the church was in 1203, when the commune had taxed the abbey of Passignano. In 1242 the Guelf leadership imposed a tax on the urban church. But in 1246 and 1247 the new leaders of the commune initiated very heavy taxes on the Florentine church, their enemies in the heresy trials of the 1230's and 1240's.[160]

The impact of the Ghibelline triumph on the bishop was severe. Having abandoned the emperor in 1243, he was open to the full brunt of Ghibelline vindictiveness. To punish him and to cripple his political base within the city, the Ghibelline elite stripped him of most of his income. In 1247 he found refuge in the monastery of San Miniato al Monte, where he died a broken man. The picture of Ardingo at the end of his life is a sad one. Sick and poor, he was constrained to sell episcopal property at San Martino alla Palma to the monastery of Settimo to provide for his medical needs in his dying days.[161] Even his holdings in the city were under increased pressure and scrutiny from the urban elite. The prelate died on May 3, 1247.[162]

Episcopal Property in Florence, 1180–1250

Most urban episcopal possessions were located in the Cafaggio (the zone north of the second circle of walls), at Montughi (a hill northwest of the city), and along the Mugnone west of Florence (see Map 4). Our sources are silent on the Cafaggio for most of the twelfth century. However, both Bishops Pietro and Giovanni da Velletri were actively acquiring properties by purchase in the Cafaggio between 1201 and 1216, including a piece of land near the Mugnone in 1219.[163] A *finitio et refutatio* of a piece of land in 1214 by Davizio della Tosa indicates that the bishop was leasing property in the thirteenth century, but unfortunately there is no further information on leasing in the Cafaggio for the remainder of the thirteenth century.[164] Apparently, some of these acquisitions did not sit well with the local residents. Opposition to episcopal lordship in the Cafaggio is evident from the end of the twelfth century. Between 1192 and 1197 Bishop Pietro went before the courts of the commune to recover lands seized by certain unnamed men.[165] These suits resulted from the opposition by local residents to the extensive amount of purchasing of property by the bishop in the area (see Appendix D). The bishop wanted to organize and consolidate into single pieces of property the lands that a predecessor had originally received in 898. Aside from the Cafaggio, the bishops after 1205 acquired more property at Montughi, primarily by donation. The episcopate does not seem to have controlled any property *within* the city at all (within the second communal wall, that is). Only at the end of the thirteenth century do we find evidence of episcopal leasing inside the city walls around the Baptistery.

The Bishop and the Urban Churches and Monasteries

Of no small importance was the bishop's authority over and the urban churches and monasteries. Unfortunately, the sources tell us little about the urban churches before 1251. All Florentine churches were obliged to swear obedience to the bishop, and the symbol of that relationship was the payment of a pound of wax every year to the bishop on the feast day of St. John. A few churches actually leased from the bishop. Under papal pressure, Bishop Giovanni da Velletri had to make important concessions of Santa Maria Novella and Santa Croce to the mendicants (against the will of his clergy). San Miniato al Monte continued to be the only monastery under his control, but he lost some of that control over San Miniato and the cathedral to the Calimala at the beginning of the thirteenth century.[166]

It appears that papal and episcopal concern with the debt of churches and monasteries in the diocese played a major role in the series of changes initiated by the bishop in the first half of the thirteenth century. Under papal directive, the bishop oversaw the installation of the Cistercians at Settimo in 1236. Located just west of the city was the convent of Monticelli, and the monastery of San Donato a Torri was northeast of the city in the *plebatus* of Remole. Just outside the San Frediano gate, Monticelli became the convent of the Poor Clares in 1218. On the other side of the city was the church of San Donato a Torri, to which the bishop moved the Umiliati in 1239. Concerned with the disintegration of the church, the bishop granted the church to the Umiliati for its improvement and restoration. Known for their economic vitality, the Umiliati were originally an eremetical sect close to the ideals of the Poor Men of Lyons and had developed into an acceptable orthodox order. After taking San Donato, they acknowledged episcopal jurisdiction and agreed to pay 30 Pisan *soldi* every November.[167] Twelve years later, in 1251, the bishop transferred the Umiliati from San Donato to the church of Sant'Eusebio in the city itself, agreeing with the order that they needed more space and a better environment for their activity as wool finishers.[168] The Umiliati concluded a formal contract with the Tornaquinci, who possessed land there, and they began to enlarge the church that was later to be known as the Ognissanti.[169] As for the abandoned San Donato (also called San Donato Polverosa), the bishop gave it to the Augustinian nuns from San Casciano a Decimo, since their convent had become decidedly unsuitable for their needs.[170] The changes made by the bishop between 1236 and 1251 underscore the fact that the ecclesiastical establishment found itself in an economically weak position just as new social forces benefitting from commercial prosperity were demanding a greater role in the political life of the city.

Conclusion: The Transformation of Episcopal Lordship, 1180–1250

Expenses

In the two generations after 1180 there was a dramatic increase in the expenses required of the Florentine bishops. Rising prices most likely acounted for most of that increase. Furthermore, constant withholding of rent payments by episcopal tenants created an unstable financial situation, in which the bishops were unable to be certain how much money or grain would come into their possession in any one year. They still had to pay to manage their *castelli* and to operate their Florentine palace in the Piazza del Duomo. In the case of Pagliariccio in the Mugello and Montecampolese in the Val di Pesa, the prelate had to spend some of his own money to build *castelli*. Presumably, grain payments by tenants had to be marketed, another cost for the bishops. Although they paid no papal taxes (not until the second half of the thirteenth century), in 1244 and 1245 they were required to pay some taxes to the commune. By the middle of the thirteenth century the bishops also had to share some of the costs of the inquisition. Finally, although documentation is incomplete, the episcopate must have been shouldering at the end of the twelfth and beginning of the thirteenth century the burden of paying the debt contracted in the previous decades.

All in all, it became increasingly difficult for the bishops to rely on traditional sources of income to meet their growing expenses. Indeed, it was a difficult situation, for virtually every aspect of episcopal lordship depended on a vast network of local agents. Consequently, the prelates tried in the thirteenth century to create innovative techniques for paying their local officials. For example, once they had established a *podestà* on episcopal lands, they apparently had him paid with grain (one *staio* per household) from the local inhabitants so as to avoid any direct expense for themselves.[171] The arch-priest of Campoli received the hospital of Calzaiuolo as part of his payment.

Income

As this chapter has demonstrated, after 1180 Bishops Pietro, Giovanni da Velletri, and Ardingo followed a systematic strategy to consolidate, engross, increase, and diversify their scattered possessions. The prelates did not embark on this strategy to acquire and consolidate in areas where they did not already possess holdings. Rather, they consolidated and increased their possessions in areas of strength—the *curiae*. New purchases declined after 1225, as by that date the bishops and their representatives had largely fulfilled their goal. Resistance to their accumulation of land and rights by local communities also helped to slow down the acquisitions. The principal means of acquiring new land were purchase and permutation (exhange of land with other landholders). The Val di Pesa (Fabbrica, Petriolo, Montecampolese), the Valdarno (Padule and Sesto), the lower Sieve Valley, and the Mugello were the principal areas of concentration and purchase.[172]

Some of the income of the bishops undoubtedly came from tithes and fees from religious duties (such as the ordination of priests). The bishopric seems to have leased many of its tithes to arch-priests and rectors of churches of which the bishop was the patron (such as Santa Cecilia di Decimo, San Lorenzo di Borgo, or Santo Stefano di Campoli), and in at least one case the commune seized the tithes from the *plebes* of Settimo and Calenzano and gave them to the Opera San Giovanni. Therefore, tithes might have been important primarily for solidifying political relationships rather than for providing a direct source of income. Rents in the rural communes must also have provided some disposable cash. By far, however, most of the income came from rural rents, at the end of the twelfth century paid in fixed payments in money or kind.

Rising expenses coupled with an undependable source of income (rents from agrarian leases) convinced the bishops at the end of the twelfth century to integrate their *mensa* more fully into the growing wealth in the countryside and the city, produced by an increasingly urban-dominated regional economy. They did so by diversifying the sources of their income at the same time that they asserted seigneurial rights in areas of the *contado* under their traditional jurisdiction. To bring the management of their estates into line with the urban economy, the bishops asserted their personal powers as lords of a territory (banal rights) to increase sharply the demands on those living within their domain. In effect, after 1150, the power of the bishops increasingly relied on their territorial seigneurial rights (*signoria territoriale*) and less on private landholding (*signoria fondiaria*). The sources tell us little about when this process began. Perhaps it began in the late eleventh century, as it had in the Casentino. As we have seen, the bishop received many juridical rights from the emperors in the early twelfth century (*castelli* and *albegaria*). The collapse of imperial authority allowed the bishop to appropriate the imperial public tax in certain areas at the end of the century.

What seems clear, however, is that the scope of episcopal power had by 1200 become more territorially oriented and less focused on scattered plots of land. In the documents, *castelli* and their *curiae* began to appear with the word *districtus,* the judicial territory over which the bishop extended his seigneurial control.[173] When this actually began is impossible to say. The revival of Roman law in northern Italy fostered by the imperial policies of Frederick I offered a legal mechanism by which the bishops could loosen their hold on land but tighten their hold over men. It was at this time that the bishops introduced feudo-vassalic terms (*fidelitas*) and oaths of servile status or fidelity (*iuramenta*) into their relations with those living within the region subject to their control. The bishops intended these oaths to insure local obedience to their demands to pay the rents and dues, obey episcopal officials, and avoid the alienation of episcopal property.[174] On one level, this was an *ideological* innovation designed to define and clarify already existing relations. In terms of the quantitative nature of the relationship between bishop and dependent, however, effectively these oaths placed far heavier burdens on the people than earlier bishops had required of their ancestors. The introduction of vassalic terminology allowed the bishops to seek redress more effectively in the urban courts from reluctant dependents, as we have seen. If and when local residents resisted and appealed to the Florentine courts, they found the Florentine elite was usually unsympathetic to their complaints. After all, Florence wanted, for its own reasons, to strengthen the episcopal presence in the countryside, not weaken it. Qualitatively, therefore, these policies marked a decisive change in the nature of the relationship between the bishop and those living in his territories. They were the means by which the bishops sought to enhance their access to the wealth created by the peasant and merchant populations on their lands. Ironically, the bishops relied on vassalic terminology to integrate their estate into a market economy.[175]

Increasingly from the end of the twelfth century, the bishops required those living within their territories (now defined in writing in the *iuramenta* as *fideles*) to pay the *datium,* market dues (Borgo San Lorenzo, Montecampolese, Castelfiorentino, and Fabbrica after 1225), rents (which only tenants paid), and a portion of the fees of justice (Castelfi-

orentino and Borgo San Lorenzo). At Monte di Croce, Borgo San Lorenzo, San Cresci in Valcava, and Campi—they collected the *datium,* a
descendant of a public tax first levied by Frederick I in the mid-twelfth
century and appropriated by many rural lords at the end of the twelfth
century. It is possible that all episcopal *fideles* paid that tax.[176] At Castelfiorentino, Bishops Giovanni and Ardingo claimed the right to tax property transfers, wills, and the property of those who died intestate. In the
Valdarno and the Val di Sieve the bishops purchased grain mills, which
provided a dependable income from fees for the grinding of grain des-
tined for the Florentine market. A flourishing land market among the
tenants of the bishop existed, and episcopal dependents did not hesitate
to deny their dependent status after the death of a bishop (as in 1181,
1205, and 1230). The bishops at the end of the century therefore tried
to bring the situation back into their control by defining their tenants as
fideles, requiring them to agree in documents never to sell or alienate
episcopal property at Decimo (1180), Petriolo (1180), the hospital Calzaiuolo (1214), Borgo (1188), Molezzano (1222), and San Giovanni Maggiore (1206). Such documents were valid in urban courts largely sympathetic to the bishop. As Christopher Wickham found in the Casentino,
feudo-vassalic terms entered the language of social relationships from
the top down[177] and were designed to make legal prosecution of recalcitrant *fideles* more effective and easier. Nevertheless, these changes
marked a decisive *qualitative* change in the nature of the relationship
between the bishop and the local communities within his jurisdiction.

By far most of the bishops' income came from agrarian rents. As they
tightened their juridical hold over men and loosened their hold over
land *per se,*the prelates in the opening decades of the thirteenth century
began a process of commuting fixed rents in money and/or kind into
grain rents to take full advantage of the burgeoning market in grain.
Florentine public authorities encouraged or supported the move to enhance its own access to the grain in the *contado:* they forbid the exportation of grain out of the *contado* in 1219–20, 1223–25, and 1239. The
Sienese did the same in 1227 and 1230 (during its war with Florence).[178]
Effectively, the commutations at Montecampolese (1211, 1236), San
Martino del Vescovo (1213), Monte di Croce (1235), Borgo San Lorenzo
(1240), Molezzano (1207, 1236), and Monte Buiano (1231) forced episcopal tenants to set aside for the bishops some of the grain that otherwise
they would have marketed.[179]

Scholars have carefully charted this process of commutation from traditional dues in money and kind into grain payments throughout northern Italy. At Lucca, a much more advanced and urbanized economy than

that of Florence before 1200, these commutations began in the eleventh century and were virtually complete by the end of the twelfth. Siena, Arezzo, Pisa, Volterra, and Pistoia followed that pattern shortly thereafter. Some ecclesiastical lords made the transition later: the bishop of Luni commuted between 1230 and 1250, the Milanese abbey of Sant'Ambrogio commuted dues on its estates at Origgio between 1250 and 1260, and the chapter of Cremona did not commute extensively until the end of the thirteenth century. In the Sienese *contado* grain rents were also common from the early thirteenth century, but in the Casentino they were not customary until the second half of that century.[180]

At the end of the twelfth century several of the major ecclesiastical institutions in the *contado* responded to the growing crisis and the needs of the urban market for grain by beginning to require rents in grain rather than in currency or mixed payments. Then, beginning in the first decade of the thirteenth century, several of the larger monasteries began actually to commute their rents into grain. On the estates of the monastery of Settimo, the first rent exclusively in grain dates from 1200. San Miniato al Monte began to transform its rents as early as 1195. Passignano commenced in 1188, and in 1204 Buonsollazzo made several commutations of rents from money to grain. One of the most dramatic sets of commutations—besides those made by the bishop of Florence—occurred on the estates of the monastery of Luco in 1235. Fifteen leases were commuted to grain.[181] Initially, the attempt to switch exclusively to grain rents at the end of the twelfth century elicited some resistance on the part of the tenants, as had occurred in 1195 between tenants and the abbot of San Miniato al Monte.

Administration

The emergence of territorial lordships on certain episcopal lands, the assertion of seigneurial rights, and the commutation of agrarian rents required a sophisticated and complex bureaucracy. Episcopal *castaldi, vicarii,* and *nuptii* continued to do important business on a diocese-wide basis. Specifically, the last two officers bought and sold land, as well as acted as episcopal representatives in courts of law. The arch-priests and rectors of episcopal *plebes* (such as Campoli, Decimo, or Castelfiorentino) were also extremely important episcopal players in local strategies. By far, however, the most important official to appear at this time was the episcopal *podestà,* whose very reason for being derived from the bold assertion of territorial rights by the prelates at the end of the twelfth century.

After succeeding in bringing together dispersed holdings and consolidating property in areas of jurisdictional and economic strength, the bishops needed an official representative to manage that territory in their interests.[182] The *podesteria* (modeled after that of the German emperor and the commune of Florence), therefore, was an office charged with overseeing the territorial lordships of the bishops in the Val di Pesa, the Mugello, the Valdarno, and the Valdelsa. Whereas it was very difficult to eliminate the threat of individual resistance to episcopal power on scattered and dispersed holdings, it was much easier to force tenants to pay their required dues when the leased properties and taxable property were located within one jurisdictional and territorial unit, a unit presided over by an official acting on the bishop's behalf.[183] These officials, therefore, had among their tasks the responsibility of assuring that the *fideles* fulfilled their yearly obligations. Consequently, at the beginning of the thirteenth century the bishops and later the *podestà* began to require formal, written oaths from the *fideles*. The first oath dates from 1200 (Decimo) and the second from 1211 (Molezzano). Oaths were especially important after the death of a bishop and at the beginning of another prelacy—a time when many *fideles* took the opportunity to deny the bishop the obligation of *fidelitas*. The *podestà* also ultimately were responsible for overseeing and managing the episopal *castelli*. No longer did the bishop entrust local lineages (such as the Buondelmonti or Ubaldini) or local residents with the management of their *castelli* and properties. Instead, they appointed representatives directly loyal to the bishopric—individuals who came from the city and were not as sensitive to local political pressures. Of great importance—indeed of crucial importance—to the later social and ecclesiastical history of Florence was the identity of these *podestà:* for the most part, they were all members of the Visdomini, Tosinghi, and Aliotti houses (after about 1203). Their access to episcopal resources (property and offices) helped make the Visdomini one of the most important in the city.

There are at least two reasons why the bishops of Florence appointed *podestà* in the early thirteenth century.[184] First, it was a natural outgrowth of the attempt by the bishops to tighten up their hold on their dependents. Because of the heritage of resistance to episcopal power, the appointment of a *podestà* was especially important. Second, the growing need of the Florentine commune to determine the legal status of those living in its *contado* for administrative and financial reasons made it imperative for the bishops to find ways to enforce the jurisdictional dependence of their tenants or risk losing them. In the 1220's and 1230's, when Bishops Giovanni da Velletri and Ardingo were faced with opposition, the *podestà* acted as liaisons with the Florentine communal authorities.

Indeed, they were the spokes of authority emanating from the city into the far reaches of the *contado*.The emergence of this bureaucracy led to more efficient accounting techniques (including the *iuramenta*—lists of dependents paying annual rents), intended to preserve an accurate record of episcopal rights and to press claims in communal courts against obstreperous tenants. It was obviously in the interests of the city between 1230 and 1233 to have an accurate record of all the episcopal *fideles* for purposes of taxation.[185]

Conflict with Episcopal Fideles and Rural Communes

The social and economic changes initiated by the bishops on their estates had a tremendous impact on their relations with their tenants. Initially for the bishops, that impact was positive: it increased and diversified their income. But for the peasant tenant and local merchant (of whatever social position) who lived where the bishop claimed *dominium,* the result was negative. The strategy begun at the end of the twelfth century tended to increase the episcopal income at the expense of the local peasantry and merchant community. The new measures led to the imposition and enforcement of new exactions in the form of the *datium,* milling rights, judicial fines, and property transfer taxes. The episcopal *podestà* attempted to limit the freedom and independence of the local community to buy and sell property as it chose or market its surplus free of episcopal constraints. Above all, the commutation of traditional rents into grain payments (the earliest in 1207 at Molezzano and the most extensive in 1236 at Montecampolese) sharply increased the amount of surplus transferred to the bishop and decreased the amount of grain a peasant tenant could market for himself. If the episcopal *datium* was ten *soldi,* it was equivalent roughly to the value of forty days of work by the peasant. Furthermore, for every *staio* of grain the peasant had to relinquish, he lost at least two *soldi,* as the value of a *staio* on the market in the early thirteenth century was about 2.222 *soldi;* the *datium* would therefore be the equivalent of 4 to 5 *staia* of grain.[186] Consequently, the introduction of the *datium* and the commutation of traditional rents into grain payments must have irritated all *fideles,* especially the poorer peasant.

Instead of enhancing episcopal power, however, these steps exacerbated tension on the episcopal estates. Furthermore, after the death of Henry VI in 1197, the Florentines extended to each *borghata* the communal *datium* of 26 *denari* per household.[187] In areas of the *contado* where the bishop had estates, he was probably responsible for the collection of this tax (*foderum* or *datium*) for the Florentines—an activity which made him even more unpopular among his dependents. After 1200 conflict and struggle increasingly characterized the relations between the episcopate and its tenants. Before that date resistance took the form of individual challenges, marked by a refusal to pay rents and to accept the lordship of the bishop. After 1200, however, those challenges assumed a collective aspect. At Sesto, Capalle, Borgo San Lorenzo, San Casciano Val di Pesa, Castelfiorentino, and Valcava entire communities sought to shirk off the jurisdictional and economic might of the Florentine bishop. The reasons for those rebellions and the emergence of rural communes on those lands were complex and diverse in every case. Nevertheless, there were several common denominators in each situation. Each community was a market center. The underlying reason for the collective resistance was opposition to the ongoing episcopal strategy to increase its income at the expense of the local residents through the consolidation and concentration of older properties, the purchase of new possessions (especially mills), the appointment of regional *podestà,* taxation, and commutation of traditional rents. Determined to retain control over the fruits of their own labor, the communities refused to pay the rents or the taxes, precipitating the clashes. From the perspective of the local population, it was the bishop who was breaking tradition and precedent—not themselves. Besides reducing the amount of disposable grain available to the tenant, the commutations broke with revered tradition. Many of the communities in which these pressures existed transformed themselves into rural communes: Castelfiorentino (1195), Sesto (1209), Lomena (1220), Borgo San Lorenzo (1226), Capalle (1231), Valcava (1232), and San Casciano (1241).

In the last century historians have explained the origin of rural communes by citing several different factors: the link to older public rights (Schneider), the desire for freedom (Volpe), the drive for economic and juridical independence (Caggese), the influence of population growth (Herlihy), social and economic forces (Fiumi), the role of the bishops in creating the *curiae,* the alliance of *rustici* and *milites* (Jones), and the need for defense from seigneurial pressures. It is clear, obviously, that no single factor accounts for their emergence. For example, a recent study of the Casentino and the Garfagnana found that rural communes emerged as a response to the example of the city (Florence and Arezzo), the importance of territorial identity after the disappearance of the state, the integration of a silvo-pastoral economy into an urban market network, and the sharpening of seigneurial rights.[188]

The diocese of Florence shares several characteristics in common with the rural communes that appear in this study. It is evident that regional lordships of the bishop of Florence in the Val di Pesa, the Mugello, and the Valdelsa provoked the formation of the rural communes. However, the bishops played both a positive and a negative role in their formation. On the negative side, the drive for more income on the part of the bishops created the conflict which led eventually to the formation of the communes. Each commune which emerged on episcopal territory was the site of a prosperous market on a major road in the diocese. Demographic expansion by that date had expanded greatly the market for grain, of which the residents of those communities sought to take advantage. It was this sense of communal solidarity and shared interests that clashed directly with the policy of the bishops to rationalize its estate and increase its income. This survey has demonstrated, however, that the conflict was not a clash between a reactionary power (the bishop) and a progressive capitalist rural commune. Rather, it was a conflict over access to the wealth created by the commercialized, urban-dominated economy, a conflict that pitted the interests of the bishops against those of the local communities. The bishops introduced feudo-vassalic terms and oaths of fidelity to define their juridical status and the status of those living within their territorial lordships (*signoria territoriale*). What the prelates wanted was what the local communities desired as well: grain, taxes, rents, court fines, and milling fees. The bishops, therefore, were not reactionary representatives of a by-gone era. The economic strategies they followed from the end of the twelfth century were rational and creative responses to the demands of a regional, market-oriented economy. The struggle over which party had the right to tax (the bishop or the rural commune) and the conflict over rent (recently commuted to grain) led to the collective rebellions. Also significant in some areas was the bishops' collection of the communal *datium*. Episcopal economic strategies may explain why conflict arose, but it does not fully explain why communes emerged as a response to conflict.

The history of these particular rural communes in the diocese of Florence also indicates that the bishops paradoxically exerted a positive influence on the formation of communes. Some communities (Bossolo and Pagliariccio, for example) actually developed from *castelli* constructed by the bishops. Fabbrica and Campoli (location of a *mercatale*)—communities which did not become communes but most likely played a role in the birth of San Casciano—began as episcopal *castelli* and became two of the most important markets in the Val di Pesa.[189] The location of episcopal *castelli* there certainly concentrated the social and economic forces which created the market, but it is also possible that the bishops originally *created* the markets there. Furthermore, the maintenance and management of episcopal *castelli* and the establishment of the *podesteria* functioned also as a training ground in administration and eventually in self-government for the officials of the future commune. By 1225 the peasants, merchants, and knights (*milites*) in rural communities already had in their midst a functioning model for communal government: the episcopal *podesteria*. The appointments of episcopal *podestà* conferred a political and administrative structure where none had ever existed before. The example of the episcopal *podestà* seems to be a much more decisive influence on the development of the rural commune than the ideology of communal government emanating from Florence. The history of the communes was therefore inextricably linked to the history of episcopal *castelli* and to episcopal lordship. The political, social, and economic conditions for the emergence of a commune were present, but episcopal lordship transformed those communities into rural communes. It is for these reasons that we must conclude that it was no accident that the principal rural communes in the diocese of Florence—Borgo San Lorenzo, San Casciano Val di Pesa, Castelfiorentino—emerged where there had once been an episcopal *signoria territoriale*. The most important factors, however, must lie within the communes themselves: the desire for independence and autonomy from outside powers.

The communes first emerged after the coming of the *podestà*, but the conflicts that gave rise to them sharpened during three periods: the death of Bishop Giovanni da Velletri (1230), the war between Florence and Siena (1227–1235), and the appointment of Ghibelline *podestà* in the 1230's. Documents give us little information, but famine also might have exacerbated tension between the bishop and his *fideles*. There apparently had been a serious famine in 1227.[190] The decision on the part of the commune to conduct a census of the personal status of all male residents of the territory between 1230 and 1233 might have resulted from the concern shared by all members of the Florentine elite stemming from the unrest in the countryside.[191] Related to the political struggles with the bishop in a very complex and still not understood way, the popularity of the Cathars eroded episcopal power just as it must have benefitted from the weakening jurisdictional position of the bishop. The frequent use of excommunication in the disputes at Castelfiorentino (1218), Borgo San Lorenzo (1232), San Martino del Vescovo (1236), San Casciano (1237), and Percussina (1239) appear largely to have fallen on deaf ears (or souls, as it were). The economic and political decline of episcopal power in the countryside created a vacuum in which heterodoxy could flourish, but the presence of the Cathars in Florence certainly contributed to the weakening of episcopal lordship by undercutting the credibility of episcopal excommunications.

The commune of Florence did not support the rural communes against the bishop "in the spirit of liberty."[192] Underlying Florentine policy was the desire to maintain order in the countryside. Essential to Florentine interests—especially during its war with Siena—was access to grain, revenue, a pool of draftable young men, and the guarantee of military security. Warfare gave rural communities an opportunity to assert their independence and challenge traditional authorities. Determined to maintain its hegemony in parts of an unruly *contado* where it had neither the will nor the means to govern directly, the Guelf elite in Florence supervised and oversaw a set of power-sharing agreements which maintained the lordship of its Florentine surrogate the bishop but kept the exercise of that power circumscribed within a framework which also granted some autonomy to the communes.[193] The resolution of the conflicts between the bishops and the rural communes required the redaction of statutes which defined the balances of political forces in the life of the community. The first documented pact was achieved at Borgo San Lorenzo in 1227, which must have served as the precedent and model for the others. Often with Florentine assistance, the bishops and local leaders worked out agreements for Castelfiorentino (1231), Capalle (1232), San Casciano Val di Pesa (1241), and Valcava (1243). The Guelfs were determined to prevent the emergence of pro-Ghibelline rural communes located at strategic points in the contado. The Ghibellines, however, were willing to tolerate independence of the communes from the bishop because it weakened episcopal (and hence Guelf) power in the countryside. But the Ghibellines did not want totally independent communes either. They wanted the rural communes to exist within a *pax ghibellina*—controlled ultimately by the Ghibelline forces in the *contado:* the Guidi, Alberti, and the Ubaldini. These families and the Ghibelline *podestà* in the 1230's and 1240's nurtured the Cathar tradition to cripple the ability of the forces of orthodoxy to use their spiritual and sacramental power to defend their material and political interests. Behind the resistance to episcopal lordship in the diocese, therefore, was another protagonist: the rural *patrilineage*.[194]

4   Episcopal Property and the Transformation of Florentine Society, 1250–1320

Fiscal Pressures on Church Property

There is some indication that by 1256 the commune of Florence was taxing the following ecclesiastical institutions: the bishopric, the chapter, and the monasteries of Mantignano, Luco, Passignano, and Coltibuono.[1] This violation of ecclesiastical liberty concerned the papacy very much, and in 1257 the papal representative in Florence received word from the communal syndic that the city had confirmed the ecclesiastical liberty of the Florentine church.[2] The papacy needed to maintain the exemption of church property from urban taxation to be able to use it as a lucrative taxable resource itself. Military expenses in southern Italy and plans for a crusade led to growing papal demands on the Florentine church from the middle of the thirteenth century.[3] As a result of these burdens, the bishopric faced a 5,600 *lire* debt by 1255.[4] As we will see, the bishop attempted to pay off the debts by selling property in the Cafaggio. Perhaps the best known of the papal exactions were those collected in the closing years of the thirteenth century, detailed information of which appears in the *Rationes Decimarum*.[5] In the early years of the *trecento*, the conflicting needs of the papacy and the commune exacerbated the tension and disrupted severely the financial management of the Florentine church. In 1306 the papacy imposed a tax on the entire diocese. By 1307 the commune attempted to tax the churches very heavily to support its bureaucratic and military needs, an attempt which led to an extensive controversy.[6]

Another very important source of pressure on the churches and monasteries of the diocese was their responsibility for the cost of the ceremonial entry of the bishop into the city of Florence. The first account of an entry (that of Jacopo da Perugia in 1286) reveals how sumptuous and impressive the event must have seemed to observers and participants alike.[7] Faced with challenges to the power of his spiritual, charismatic, and sacramental power (*ius ordinis*), the bishops and the families associated with them attempted to embellish and elaborate upon the ceremony of the first entry of the bishop into the city to impress and inspire the faithful of the diocese. In the previous two generations the rural communes, Florence, the Cathars, and the mendicants had diminished and circumscribed the jurisdictional, economic, and charismatic authority of the episcopate. The prelates attempted to compensate for that loss of power by embellishing and expanding their roles in formalistic public ritual. As we learn from the historical record, in the late thirteenth century the bishops required the clergy of the city of Florence to shoulder the cost of the ritual entry, but their demands led to severe conflict.[8] In 1304 Bishop Lottieri della Tosa (1302–1309) decided to take a step toward resolving the dispute. On January 8 of that year he acceded to the demands of his clergy and ruled henceforth that they would not be responsible for more than 2,000 florins of the costs of the bishop in Rome and of the entry into Florence.[9] Further evidence of the sensitivity of the clergy to episcopal expenses is the declaration by Bishop Andrea de' Mozzi (1286–1295) that the funds for the palace he built for himself next to San Miniato al Monte came from family money and not from the resources of the monastery.[10]

For several reasons, then, many of the Florentine churches were seriously in debt.[11] Often the bishop had to grant permission to a church or monastery before it could sell land to repay a loan or simply to take out a loan. In some cases the bishop annexed one ecclesiastical entity to another to strengthen the economic base of the former, as he did when he gave the church of San Cresci near Fagna in the Mugello to the monastery of San Pietro di Moscheto in 1255.[12] Most of the indebted churches were rural, although the bishops did act on several occassions to provide for an urban indigent convent, like San Donato a Torri in 1256, or to allow an urban institution to sell property to pay a debt, as Santa Maria Nuova did in 1296.[13] The widening fiscal burden forced many religious establishments to squeeze their sources of revenue as much as possible. In some cases, that attempt led to conflict over property and jurisdiction between churches themselves—conflicts involving control of tithes, taxation, clerical appointments, and rents. For example, in 1261 the requirement to pay taxes to the commune of Florence brought the *plebs* of Signa and the chapter of San Martino di Gangalandi into conflict over whether four local churches should pay their share with the *plebs* or with the chapter of Gangalandi. Many ecclesiastical institutions became deeply indebted to the principal lineages involved in banking (such as the Cavalcanti).[14]

Debt was widespread in the middle of the century, but it was not universal. We must be very careful not to overstate the degree of indebtedness. As Giovanni Cherubini explained regarding this problem in the diocese of Arezzo, it is not true that all the great ecclesiastical lords were ruined. But several were, including the abbey of Santa Fiora. Other lords, including the Aretine bishop, were not indigent, even though they were under great financial pressure. We can say the same about the condition of the Florentine estate. Whereas the bishop of Arezzo, however, was able to escape major debts by selling his public rights and asking for land in return, the bishop of Florence was unable to do so.[15] Not until we have more studies of specific churches in the diocese of Florence will we have a more accurate picture of the overall situation.

The Extension of Florentine Control of the Countryside, 1250–1320

The last quarter of the thirteenth century marked another crucial turning point in the history of the relations between Florence and its *contado*. Prior to 1270 the city was content to rule some areas of the countryside directly, but it left other areas to its surrogates (such as the bishops or rural lords with whom it had made treaties). After that date—given the security threat posed by the Ghibellines, the constant curse of famine, and the weakness of the bishops—the Guelf regime had no choice if it was to survive but to enlarge its sphere of direct control and to weaken pockets of independent jurisdiction. The maintenance of Guelf power in Florence after 1266 required very skillful and firm policies toward its Tuscan neighbors and toward its own *contado*. As many Florentine churches with possessions in the countryside fell into debt, it became clear to the urban elite that it could meet the challenges to its security only by shifting its emphasis from indirect to direct rule of the *contado*. Between 1284 and 1292 the the Guelf elite (organized into an association called the Parte Guelfa) conducted a complex military and diplomatic effort to impose its own hegemony over other Tuscan city-states.[16] To feed its growing population, it needed to have access to a reliable source of grain. In the second half of the thirteenth century the Florentines depended on wheat (*frumentum*) for their bread.[17] In 1258 the city officially forbade the export of grain from the *contado*. Concerns over the food supply were shared by other Tuscan communes. Siena had forbidden the exportation of grain as early as 1223, and Volterra had done the same thing in 1225. By 1262 the Sienese were requiring their citizens to carry their grain into the city (they repeated this requirement in 1274).[18] Most of the grain grown in the *contado*—the Valdarno Fiorentino, the Mugello, the Val di Pesa, and the Valdelsa—was meant for consumption in the city, although most of the grain for the city came from the south. Especially important were the Settimo plain and the Mugello.[19] To assure that the city had a dependable supply of grain, the Captain of the People, a chief urban magistrate, oversaw grain provisioning in the city, set price controls, and maintained security on the roads. By 1274 the Guelf commune had created the office of the *Sei della Biada* to distribute grain in the city, located at Or San Michele.[20] Apparently, there were serious famines in 1276, 1282, 1286, 1291, 1299, 1302–03, and 1305.[21] Consequently, the need to maintain access to an adequate supply of grain inexorably led the Guelf commune to expand its direct jurisdiction over the *contado,* especially in areas of economic and political importance.

As the economic and political pressure increased, the commune acted to limit the access to their landholdings of certain urban lords (including ecclesiastical lords and the houses associated with them) to assure for itself adequate grain reserves and to preserve the security of its major arteries. In 1277 the commune attempted to limit the traditional rights of the Visdomini, Tosinghi, and Aliotti lineages to administer the properties of the episcopate during a vacancy (1275–1286). The year 1276 had been a year of famine, and the commune wanted to assert more direct control over its regional sources of grain. The Visdomini directly administered the areas of the *contado* which traditionally had been under episcopal control. Among those areas were the Val di Pesa, the Valdarno Fiorentino, and the Mugello—three of the four major grain-growing areas of the *contado.* The attempt, however, did not dislodge the Visdomini, the Tosinghi, and the Aliotti from the episcopal *podesteria.* Florence did not have to do that. Through the institution of the office of the *Sei della Biada* in 1274, it gradually succeeded in bringing the grain trade within the *contado* under direct communal control.[22] Nevertheless, this measure was the first communal challenge to the traditional rights of the houses to ecclesiastical property.

The decisive defeat of the Florentine Ghibellines in 1266 solidified Guelf hegemony in the city but created a serious security problem in the countryside. Many Ghibellines took up residence in the *contado* and disrupted the flow of grain into the city when it was in their interests to do so. In periods of famine the exiled Ghibellines posed a particularly serious problem. Allied with the enemies of the Florentine Guelfs, the Ghibellines were a constant threat to order and internal security. Consequently, as the commune systematized its provisioning of the city, it attempted to expand its control of areas deemed militarily and economically sensitive. During the famine of 1276, the Guelf government attempted to prevent *fideles* of convents and rural lords from alienating the land they cultivated to prevent the engrossing of property by powerful lords not supportive of the Parte Guelfa.[23] Shortly thereafter, eager to weaken independent control of areas of the *contado* of strategic and economic importance to the commune, the *podestà* and the General Council of Florence appointed a commission to determine which castles and rural communes were under episcopal jurisdiction and which were under Florentine jurisdiction. This was especially important, because at the time (during the episcopal vacancy of 1275–1286) the Visdomini administrators had jurisdiction over episcopal areas.[24] Furthermore, to prevent any disruption of the grain supply and to assure stability in the countryside, the city relied on lay rectors (*capellani*) in each rural and urban parish to report to the *podestà* about any controversy in their district.[25] After 1276 the commune sent a *podestà* to every *plebatus* of the *contado* to serve the interests of the city. By the end of the thirteenth century the commune had direct jurisdiction over Borgo San Lorenzo. In 1293 Poggibonsi came under the complete subjection of the Arno city. Finally, even San Casciano—the location of the densest concentration of episcopal interests—had passed under the control of the commune by the end of the thirteenth century.[26]

The gradual extension of the direct sphere of urban influence, therefore, was not the result of a predetermined policy. Rather, the Florentines relied on every method available to them to assure their hegemony; they reacted for the most part to circumstances as they arose. After the Guelf return in 1266, however, military and economic realities required a conscious pursuit of direct rule, which the Guelf elite accepted reluctantly. As the costs of supporting the growing military and bureaucratic apparatus escalated, the commune had to devise creative fiscal methods and accept a more centralized form of government to meet its needs.

Church Property and Political Crisis, 1250–1320

The economic pressure on the Florentine church and on the lineages associated with it contributed to the social and political transformation of the city at the end of the thirteenth and beginning of the fourteenth centuries. As we have seen, the commune in the early thirteenth century was highly factionalized and torn apart by conflicts among rival houses of the nobility. Such divisions within the ranks of the *nobiles* had existed before the creation of the commune, but the violence intensified with the gradual subjugation of the countryside (the *comitatinanza*) and the outbreak of war between the emperor and the papacy. In the early thirteenth century, therefore, there emerged throughout central and northern Italy a new organization of non-nobles (*pedites*), the *popolo,* which attempted to put an end to the vicious cycle of violence within the communes. The *popolo* was composed of a wealthy segment of merchants, bankers, and landowners as well as a humbler group of artisans and shop-keepers. It was more than simply an anti-noble class-based movement. It desired good government, a *pax et concordia* which would bring stability and order to a divided commune.[27] Exacerbated by the climate of violence affecting urban life, the *popolo* attempted to create a stable and ordered atmosphere conducive to commerce and trade.

In Florence the split within the *nobiles* among the Guelfs and Ghibellines set the stage for the first triumph of the *popolo*. In 1250 the *popolo* tamed the Guelf elite and created a regime (the *Primo Popolo*) which lasted ten years (1250–1260). Although it was defeated by the Ghibelline nobility at Montaperti in 1260, the *popolo* later allied with prominent Guelfs to expel the Ghibellines in 1266. The years between 1266 and 1282 were crucial years in the social and political history of Florence. Before 1266 the Parte Guelfa had been composed primarily of two groups: a traditional landed aristocracy (*famiglie di antica tradizione* or *cavalleresca feodale*) and descendents of the urban consular aristocracy.[28] Some of the older lineages—the Adimari, Tornaquinci, Lamberti, and Caponsacchi, for example—joined guilds such as the Calimala. After 1267 the *popolo* split into two groups. One faction of bankers increasingly aligned itself with the older aristocracy and became knights, including the Cerchi, the Bardi, and the Mozzi (the *cavalleresca mercantile*). This should not surprise us, since the culture and status of the knighted nobility throughout this period was always the standard point of reference for the elite as a whole. Another faction, however, remained true to their popular origins and stayed with the rich *popolani* (the *popolo grassi*). Between 1266 and 1282 there were therefore three groups composing the urban elite (in order of power): the traditional aristocracy, the knighted mercantile families, and the wealthy *popolani*. Until 1280 the traditional and oldest Guelf families (the *famiglie di antica tradizione*) dominated the city, but after that date, the balance of power shifted to the two groups among the mercantile elite, especially the *popolo grasso.* Less powerful than the *popolo grasso* and generally excluded from power until 1293 were the less wealthy artisans, shopkeepers, and skilled laborers: the *popolo minuto.*[29]

It seems reasonable to suggest that the decline of the traditional aristocracy and the triumph of the newer, "popular" lineages were linked to the history of church property in the diocese of Florence. Indeed, three of the most powerful houses within the Guelf elite and the chief leaders of the major factions after 1266—the Visdomini, the Adimari, and the Tosinghi—had enjoyed long-standing connections with the richest ecclesiastical organizations in the city: the bishopric and the chapter. Within the cathedral chapter—and apparently within the chapter of San Lorenzo as well—the Adimari patrilineage was the major power.[30] Relying largely on ecclesiastical resources to maintain their political connections and alliances, these powerful houses faced growing economic pressures stemming from the factors described above: the emergence of rural communes, papal and communal taxation, the ability of many *fideles* to escape paying their rents on church lands, restrictions by the commune on their ability to dispose of their property as they wanted, and increased debt. At the same time, some members of the *popolo grasso,* such as the Mozzi, Bardi, and Strozzi, sought entry into aristocratic ranks by attempting to appropriate ecclesiastical property, patronage rights, and honors to supplement their commercial success.

It is not surprising, therefore, that factional fighting and conflicts within the ranks of those members of the aristocracy with special ties to church property intensified in the 1270's and 1280's. For example, members of the Mozzi attacked some members of the Bardi lineage in 1271.[31] In 1278 the Tosinghi and Adimari began a serious feud which eventually evolved into a vendetta in 1293. It involved their close allies as well and was linked to disputes over property associated with the cathedral chapter and the chapter of San Lorenzo. Furthermore, during the 1275–1286 episcopal vacancy, the Tosinghi managed to enlarge its power base around the Piazza del Battistero.[32] At the same time, the Adimari were attempting to enhance their power in the center of the city. These rival attempts by the two patrilineages to construct neighborhood power bases for themselves near the Baptistery by using ecclesiastical resources continued throughout the second half of the thirteenth century. When the episcopal see fell vacant in 1275, the two sides supported rival candidates to be the successor of Giovanni de' Mangiadori (1251–1275). The Tosinghi backed one of their own, Lottieri della Tosa, and the Adimari supported one of their allies, Schiatta degli Ubaldini. The escalation of these conflicts led to great concern among the *popolo* and united the *popolo grasso* and *minuto* against such factional disputes.[33]

The threat to social peace convinced the pope to send his envoy, Cardinal Latino, to Florence to reconcile the warring factions. When this attempt at peace-making failed, the *popolo* turned to other methods to control the violence. In 1281 the commune passed the first anti-magnate legislation, requiring those lineages identified as magnates to post bond for their good behavior. Who exactly were these "magnates"? According to Salvemini's reconstruction of the definition of this sub-group of the aristocracy, they were members of the elite in whose houses there had resided a knight within the last twenty years, or they were simply those lineages identified by public opinion as magnates. What set them apart from other members of the ruling class was their tendency to engage in blood feuds and private vendettas, thereby threatening public order and stability.[34] Why should such private conflicts disturb the *popolo* so much? Instability not only interfered with a proper business climate, but it also threatened to create enough political instability to lead to serious *social* disorder. After all, we must remember that the harvests in the following years were especially poor: in 1271–72, 1276–77, and 1281–82.[35] Intramural violence among the elite threatened to call into question and delegitimize the authority of the commune; it had to be restrained if social stability among the lower orders was to be maintained.

Major political changes followed the failed mission of Cardinal Latino and the first anti-magnate measure of 1281. In 1282 the Guelf elite created a new and supreme political institution, the priorate. However, the feuds continued. Competition for office might have exacerbated an already tense atmosphere. In the 1280's several of the older houses, among whom were the Adimari, the Visdomini (*consortes* of the Tosinghi), the Cerchi, and the Pazzi, vied for influence and control in the *sesto* of San Pietro.[36] Furthermore, the clash between certain members of the Tosinghi and Adimari houses over the next bishop of Florence continued to fester into the mid–1280's. After the death of Bishop Giovanni in 1275, the cathedral chapter deliberated to elect a successor but very quickly became deadlocked by the serious divisions between the two lineages and their allies which dominated the chapter: the Adimari and the Visdomini. It was in the interests of the latter to prolong a vacancy, as they were free to use the resources of the episcopate to suit their own interests.[37] The Adimari, on the other hand, wanted to limit the ability of the Visdomini to pillage episcopal property, so they pressed to have their candidate, Schiatta degli Ubaldini, appointed bishop. The

Visdomini presented their own choice, Lottieri della Tosa, and continued to construct a very formidable base of power in the neighborhood around the Baptistery.[38] Determined to end the strife between the two lineages for his own political reasons, Pope Honorius IV simply appointed Jacopo Rainucci (prior general of the Dominicans at Perugia) as the new bishop.[39] Before 1286 the papacy had either been unwilling or unable to end the strife.

The account of the 1286 ceremonial entry of the new bishop of Florence into the city is extremely interesting, as it demonstrates that the factional conflict between the Tosinghi and Adimari (and their respective allies) took place on a ritualistic as well as on a political level.[40] The ceremonial procession took the bishop and his entourage from the southern gate of the city to the convent of San Pier Maggiore, where a ceremonial marriage took place between the bishop and the abbess. The following day, the new prelate followed the Borgo degli Albizzi (past the *Geniculum,* the stone associated with a miracle done by St. Zanobi) to the sacramental center of the city: the contemporary Piazza San Giovanni (see Map 4). According to the account, the first mass traditionally took place in the Baptistery, which was associated with St. John and the bishopric. However, the chapter (influenced by the Adimari faction) convinced the new bishop to offer the mass in Santa Reparata, the principal church of the cathedral chapter. The shift from the Baptistery to the cathedral effectively diminished the status of the Tosinghi and Visdomini and enhanced that of the chapter (dominated by members of the Adimari). Implicit in this dispute was a conflict between the two factions over ecclesiastical honors and over access to the *charisma* of the two saints. Competition over church honors and access to offices (like the episcopate) had intensified as the Guelf aristocracy found itself excluded from the centers of power, particularly the priorate.

Between 1282 and 1292 lineages such as the Visdomini, Adimari, and Tornaquinci held only 3.9 percent of positions in the priorate (or 15 of 381 offices). Nevertheless, they still were very active in other offices: urban councils, *podesterie,* ambassadorships, and the priorate of the Parte Guelfa. The percentage of all magnates (and not just those houses) in the priorate was 12 percent before 1292. The *grandi* also sought entry into the greater guilds. By 1293 half of the magnate lineages had matriculated into those organizations.[41] However, the *popolo* attempted to exclude these older houses from the chief offices of the city (the priorate) because of the threat to civil order posed by their factional traditions. In 1286 the commune passed further anti-magnate legislation, requiring magnates again to post a bond for their good behavior. Simultaneously, many of the newer lineages became the creditors of churches and of the older houses, and they used their newfound wealth after 1250 to appropriate church property in the countryside (as Renzo Nelli has demonstrated in the region around Monte di Croce in the Val di Sieve).[42]

The Ordinances of Justice in 1293 and 1295

In 1293 the Tosinghi and their allies launched a vendetta against the Adimari—an escalation of the conflict which generated intense anti-magnate feeling among the *popolo grasso* and the *popolo minuto*.[43] The Adimari effectively were fighting the Tosinghi and their allies (the Pazzi, Visdomini, and Donati) for control of the city. Each lineage struggled for geographical advantages within the commune, which depended on the formation and expansion of its own enclave. This clash between rival aristocratic lineages, which involved ecclesiastical property and offices, was a key factor setting the stage for the series of measures passed by the communal government that limited the freedom of action of the "magnates" and that culminated in the Ordinances of Justice in 1293 and 1295.

For two years (1293–1295) Giano della Bella, a prior for only two months, was the leading political force in a city dominated by the *popolo minuto* and the middle guilds. Eager to end the factional violence and establish good government, Giano sought to recover property taken by certain nobles, eliminate fraud in the government, and appropriate property of the Parte Guelfa for the commune. Most important, under his leadership the Ordinances of Justice in 1293 and 1295 listed 140 lineages declared magnates and imposed severe restrictions on them: they had to post a 2,000 *lire* bond and swear loyalty to the commune, they could not be elected consul of a guild, nor could they hold other major political offices.[44] Because no one who was not eligible to be elected consul of a guild could also be elected prior, the Ordinances in April 1293 effectively barred magnates from the priorate.[45] Those listed as magnates were not all noble, and some noble houses were not even on the lists of 1293 and 1295 (including the Chiermontesi, Albizzi, Altoviti, della Bella, Importuni, and Baldovinetti). Half the lineages were urban, and half were rural. Furthermore, of the urban magnates, half were merchants. About half the magnate houses mentioned by the chronicler Malespini (52 of 114) had been members of the elite for many generations. Others, like the Cerchi, the Bardi, and the Frescobaldi, were new families which had immigrated into the city. All of these observations indicate that the traditional categories of Italian historiography—urban and rural, "feudal" and bourgeois ("capitalist")—are inadequate to describe these lineages. The houses Giano and his allies apparently listed were only those members of the elite who had been involved in factional feuding.[46]

What this brief overview suggests is that the magnates were indeed a juridical category; it confirms earlier conclusions of Nicolai Rubinstein, Marvin Becker, and Enrico Fiumi. The magnates were those members of the ruling aristocracy known and recognized for their reliance on the vendetta or blood feud to further their interests.[47] Although further research is needed, it is reasonable to suggest that the history of church property was an important and hitherto neglected factor which contributed greatly to the violence-ridden culture of the Florentine magnates. Indeed, it might have been an important common denominator uniting most of the lineages mentioned in the magnate lists, including the most important members of the factions involved in the violence between 1280 and 1293. In other words, what may have distinguished the magnates from other members of the ruling class was the *source* of their political power and the *object* of their political ambitions: ecclesiastical property, honors, and offices.

Since the tenth century the Florentine elite had sought a close association with ecclesiastical resources as a mark of their noble status: it gave them prestige, wealth, access to clientelar networks, and connections with both the city and the countryside. It should not surprise us therefore that access to ecclesiastical resources was a double-edged sword: it helped confer aristocratic status, but it also undercut the standing of those houses associated with them when they came under fiscal pressure. For members of those lineages closely associated with the bishopric and the cathedral chapter, the history of church property was of crucial importance. The Guelf aristocracy at the end of the thirteenth century was continuing the tradition of using church resources to advance themselves economically and socially. For example, those members of the newer lineages—the Bardi, Cerchi, and Mozzi—sought access to ecclesiastical resources, engaged in factional conflict, and found themselves on the magnate lists. A Mozzi became bishop in 1286, and in 1321 the Bardi challenged the Buondelmonti for patronage rights to Santa Maria Impruneta. We must, however, be very careful not to assume that lineages acted in concert as economic units.[48] As we will see, the Tosinghi splintered over church property in the Val di Sieve at the end of the century. Although the economic and political pressures affecting ecclesiastical resources were not the only reasons for the violent feuds, they played a crucial (if not decisive) role in creating the conditions which led to them.[49] A part of the background for the passage of anti-magnate legislation is the crisis in church property.

The developments in Florence in the last decade of the thirteenth century were not typical of events elsewhere in Italy. While the *popolo* was most successful in Tuscany (Pistoia, Prato, Lucca, Siena, and Florence), it exercised significant influence elsewhere only in the following communes: Bologna, Parma, Perugia, Padua, Brescia, and Cremona.[50] Perhaps one of the reasons the history of Florence was so different than that of other communes regarding the *popolo* and the magnate issue was the special role church property played in the history of its elite, relative to that of other communes. Even where the movement against the magnates was successful, it was never really democratic, and its heyday fell between two phases of aristocratic rule in the communes where it emerged (between that of the consular aristocracy and the *signoria*). Moreover, the *popolo* never succeeded in destroying the economic and political base of the magnates. Periodically, the commune of Florence renewed restrictions on the magnate houses, as it did in 1309, 1321, 1324, and 1343. Nevertheless, they survived, even though the Ordinances of Justice had forever stigmatized the 152 lineages as threats to public welfare. Many magnates tried to remove themselves from that designation, and when that did not work some opted for status as *popolani*.[51] Not only did they survive, but they remained the wealthiest group within the ruling elite in Orvieto, Perugia, Arezzo, Padua, Siena, and Florence.[52] In the case of Florence, the reasons for their durability were political and economic, and they had a lot to do with the history of the church. We can examine the history of the bishopric and of the magnate lineages associated with it as a test case of how the church and the houses linked to it were able to re-stabilize their fortunes.

The transformation in the social background of the Florentine bishops during these two generations paralleled the social changes within the Florentine elite itself. It indicates that although the social background of the ruling class changed, the interest of that elite in church property, offices, and honors did not. Bishop Andrea de' Mozzi came from a family which had been made wealthy by banking and which had acquired knightly status. Bishop Lottieri Tosinghi (1302–1309) was member of a magnate lineage which enjoyed extensive urban and rural possessions, deriving for the most part from its association with the bishopric. Lottieri's successor, the *popolano* Antonio degli Orsi (1309–1321), had close familial ties with the Velluti, Frescobaldi, and the Capponi and was a member of the mercantile elite.[53] What they all had in common was the assumption that access to ecclesiastical resources was a pathway into the ranks of the Florentine elite.

The Evolution and Stabilization of Church Property, 1250–1320

Cinzio Violante argues that in the twelfth and thirteenth centuries the bishops of Italy lost their jurisdictional and administrative powers in the cities but conserved their influence in the countryside. Duane Osheim's study of the Lucchese episcopate supports that thesis and demonstrates that the bishops gave up their urban properties gradually in order to concentrate on their holdings in the countryside.[54] In the case of Florence, however, the bishops never fully relinquished their urban properties. In fact, as we shall see, in the late thirteenth century they developed their urban holdings and gained an instrumental role in the expansion and development of the city as a whole. As Appendix D demonstrates, urban leases constituted 25 percent of the total number of episcopal leases between 1301 and 1321. Most of those holdings were houses and shops rented for a year or two for a money rent. Episcopal possessions—originally the grants of Italian kings—were pivotally important to the city as it expanded beyond the second circle of walls at the end of the thirteenth century.[55]

The Making of an Urban Landlord

Leaseable houses and shops appeared in Florence in the middle of the thirteenth century. Responding the the fiscal pressures exerted by both the papacy and the commune,[56] Bishop Giovanni de' Mangiadori began selling property in the Cafaggio to pay for the construction of houses in the area around the Piazza del Duomo, especially in the parish of San Michele Visdomini (see Map 4). Whereas the popular regime in Florence attempted to expand its tax base by taxing ecclesiastical property, the papacy needed money to pay for its military campaigns in southern Italy.[57] On May 28, 1255, Bishop Giovanni sold 140 *piedi* of land in the Cafaggio (near the present church of San Marco) to a certain Consiglio di Lotteringho for 44 *lire*. Receiving permission from the municipal authorities (the Captain of the People), the prelate explained that he sold the property "in order to make and construct houses in the episcopal Cafaggio so that property and resources in that Cafaggio might be better managed and for other uses which please the communal authorities more."[58] Three days later, on June 1, Bishop Giovanni sold another plot at the same location to the same Consiglio di Lotteringho and to one Aretino di Bencivenni di Aretino for 100 *lire*. The reasons given for the sale were the same.[59] Nine months later, in February of 1256, the prelate sold more property in the Cafaggio to the religious fraternity at San Marco in order to repay loans contracted with the Albizzi to pay for his expenses while serving the pope in Apulia.[60]

Not all the sales occurred, however, just to repay contracted loans or taxes. One sale in particular took place simply to develop property for commercial use. In 1269, the bishop transferred property to the Servites of Santa Maria (the present Santissima Annunziata) for 220 *lire* (Florentine). In 1233 seven members of the urban elite constructed a hermitage on Monte Senario, calling themselves the "Servites of Maria." In the middle of the century they returned to Florence to construct their church in the episcopal Cafaggio, now known as the Santissima Annunziata. In 1265 the Servites were building their church in the Cafaggio after the bishop had offered indulgences to anyone who contributed to the construction of the sanctuary.[61] The bishop made the sale to finance the construction of shops near the Baptistery. Bishop Giovanni obtained a special papal license from the pope's representative, the abbot of San Salvi, before the 1269 transfer occurred.[62]

Two observations may be made about episcopal property in the city in the third quarter of the thirteenth century. First, by 1269 the bishopric was well under way developing the area around the Baptistery by selling land in the Cafaggio north of the second communal wall and using the proceeds to develop leasable shops and houses in the parishes of Santa Reparata, San Lorenzo, and San Michele Visdomini. Indeed, the sacramental center of the city was becoming by the end of the thirteenth century an area of concentrated episcopal possessions. Second, primarily for political reasons (to promote the interests of the guildsmen and artisans who were their political supporters), the leaders of the commune encouraged and supported the sale of episcopal property in the Cafaggio. Perhaps the Guelf commune preferred to see its citizens buy and develop the Cafaggio to provide more space and meet the needs of the expanding city.

At the end of the thirteenth century the priors possessed a conscious plan for the development of the city based on the construction of public buildings, bridges, and piazzas. Not least in their plans was the construction of the third communal wall, construction of which began around 1284.[63] The new wall would allow the northward expansion of the city. The episcopal Cafaggio, located as it was between the second and third circle of communal walls, was therefore an area of prime real estate. The properties held by the episcopate on the Via dei Frenari, the Via di Balla, and the Via degli Spadai increased in value markedly as the development encroached northward, and the bishops were willing to part with some of that property to pay taxes and build leasable shops and houses. They were unwilling, however, to part with as much property as the commune and its residents wanted to suit the growing commercial needs of the city. It is likely that the prelates concentrated increasingly on developing their urban properties to offset their losses in the countryside, resulting either from the declining returns from marginal lands or from continued challenges to episcopal power from tenants and communes. Until 1320, however, the rents did not appreciate very much.

Usurpation of episcopal property began at the beginning of the last decade of the twelfth century by artisans acting with the support of communal authorities. The desires of craftsmen and artisans to build or lease shops in the city forced them simply to appropriate episcopal land in the Cafaggio. The communal authorities, sensitive to the commercial interests of the artisans, did not actively intervene to stop such behavior as their predecessors had done on episcopal rural properties since 1159. By early 1290, Bishop Andrea de' Mozzi had officially registered his displeasure that the commune had taken his property and sold it to certain artisans. On March 15 the parties reached a compromise. Having appointed three judges to decide the dispute, the bishop and the commune submitted the conflict over the sales to arbitration. The judges (a notary from Prato, the *camerarius* of the bishop, and a surveyor) decided that 40 *piedi* near the Porta di Balla was fully within the possession of the bishop. The artisans were to pay the bishop 75 *lire* and agreed to build walls to delineate clearly their property from that of the bishop.[64]

Disputes like this were common in the 1290's, as the bishops saw much of their land occupied by the commune and sold or encroached on by artisans building walls, shops, and houses. As one can see from Appendix D, the number of documented conflicts involving episcopal property and rights in Florence increased in the last quarter of the thirteenth century (from five instances for the period 1251–1275 to eighteen for 1276–1300). One example reveals the desperation felt by the episcopal officials charged with the responsibility of protecting the episcopal Cafaggio as they faced ever-increasing challenges to their rights. In 1291 the *camerarius* of the bishop went himself to a part of the Cafaggio outside the Via della Porta Nuova to denounce the construction of a wall there by unspecified parties.[65] Although the bishops were not always adverse to selling part of their holdings in the Cafaggio, they did not want to give up their lands as quickly as Florentine artisans and the communal officials apparently wanted. We must remember that in the 1290's the commune was especially sensitive to the interests of the *popolo minuto,* who effectively controlled the city during the time of Giano della Bella.

By the end of the century, the clash between the interests of the bishop (and the families benefitting from access to the *mensa*) and that of the artisans resolved itself when Bishop Francesco Monaldeschi agreed to sell a substantial portion of the Cafaggio to the commune. Although Bishop Giovanni willingly alienated part of the Cafaggio to pay his papal dues and episcopal expenses in Apulia, Bishop Francesco sold a part of the Cafaggio only reluctantly, pressured as he was by political circumstances to satisfy the needs of the communal elite.[66] Since the sale was supposedly contrary to canon law,[67] Bishop Francesco had to obtain papal permission before making the sale. By July of 1297 he had obtained that license through the papal representative, the bishop of Pistoia. In the document, the delegate notes that the bishop wanted to sell part of the Cafaggio in order to purchase other properties and develop other possessions and that the commune needed the property to enlarge the city. Unfortunately, we do not know how much of the Cafaggio he actually sold.[68] On October 28, 1300, the *cappellanus* of Santa Maria Maggiore and the prior of the monastery of Montefanno, the appointed episcopal procurators to receive the money for the lots (*casolare*) sold in the Cafaggio, transferred 284 *lire,* 4 *soldi,* and 11 gold florins to the bishop from the unnamed purchasers.[69]

With the funds resulting from the sale of certain properties in the Cafaggio, the bishops began to build and develop shops and houses on the lands it did not sell. Before 1304 we have no record of the leasing of these shops. After that date the historical record is more complete. As Appendix D indicates, a quarter of the documented leases for the first two decades of the fourteenth century were leases of urban property (161 out of a total of 648 recorded leases).[70] There were two major sets of shops: those around the Piazza del Duomo and those located in three parishes of the Cafaggio. For those renting near the episcopal palace, the majority of those leasing from the bishop were artisans, precisely the same group guilty of appropriating episcopal property at the end of the thirteenth century. They mostly came from the three central parishes of San Salvatore, Santa Reparata, and San Lorenzo, and they counted among their number bakers, silk and cloth craftsmen, and cobblers (who made up the majority). These shops were in the immediate vicinity of the episcopal palace, many of them actually on the ground floor of the

palace itself. Most of the leases lasted one year, indicating that the episcopate was aware of the commercial potential of its real estate.

For the first two decades of the fourteenth century the rent hovered
around 15 *lire* per year (the lessee paid half at mid-year and half at the
end of the year). Many—if not most—of the tenants paid in gold florins,
although their rents were quoted in *lire*. It is possible that the rate of
exchange of *denari* to florins stipulated in the contract required less
denari than the general rate of exchange. For example, in 1305 the bishop
leased a shop to a baker for 24 *lire,* which the tenant was to pay in florins.
The exchange stipulated in the contract was 29 *soldi* for each florin required according to the rate used by the Calimala guild. Apparently, in
1305 the official rate was 59 *soldi*.[71] Similarly, in 1307 a shoemaker paid
13 *lire,* 6 *soldi,* and 8 *denari* for a shop, and he also had to pay the rent
in florins at the same rate.[72] Why was there such a difference in exchange
rates? It appears that the bishop benefitted greatly from this arrangement, as he was able to exchange the florins received from his tenant
for 100 percent more *denari.* In some cases tenants found their rents
expressed exclusively in gold florins. Between the 1280's and 1340's the
debasement of the *denaro* led to a loss of 50 percent of its value relative
to the florin. By requiring the tenant to pay in florins the bishop was
simply protecting his interests.[73]

Occasionally the managers drew up a lease for five or six years to
facilitate the construction of new shops. In that particular lease, the
lessee agreed to build a shop on episcopal property, pay a lower than
average rent (five or six *lire*), and thereby be compensated for his expenses. For instance, on April 21, 1309, the episcopal syndic in the
episcopal palace rented to Saluccio di Brunello from the parish of Santa
Maria di Quarto and to Bettino di Decco da Calenzano a shop (*apotheca*)
under the stone steps of the episcopal palace, which the two had built
earlier themselves. The contract was for five years at six *lire* and eleven
soldi per year. The bishop agreed to reimburse them the thirty *lire* of
their expenses by charging them less rent than market forces could get
for the prelate. He computed the payment into the rent. If the two
individuals did not fulfill the contract, they had to pay a 25 *lire* fine.[74]
This progressive method of estate management indicates that the bishops
were certainly aware of the long-term commercial potential of their
properties and used creative techniques to maximize their long-term
income.

The level of rents for the shops in or near the Piazza San Giovanni
(unlike those of the Cafaggio) remained roughly the same in nominal
terms for the first two decades of the fourteenth century. For instance,

in 1307 Gianuzzo di Corso (a clothmaker from the parish of San Lorenzo) rented the eighth shop listed in the lease book for two years for fourteen *lire* and fifteen *soldi*. Eleven years later that same shop went for thirteen *lire*, ten *soldi*.[75] The rents for the ninth and tenth shops declined slightly as well in nominal terms. Because of the continued debasement of the *denari* from 1280 to 1340, the rents in real terms probably declined, but the income was still quite helpful.[76] In 1307 there were at least fifteen shops being leased by the bishop for cash rents made twice a year. By 1318, as a result of extensive development, there were at least thirty-three episcopal shops. In addition to the shops rented to artisans in the area around the cathedral, the bishops were also leasing property (including houses and land) in the central parishes of Santa Maria Maggiore, San Michele Visdomini, San Lorenzo, and San Pier Maggiore. The rents might not have been initially lucrative, but by developing this property the bishop was in a favorable position to benefit greatly at a later time.

Individuals from the parishes of San Lorenzo, Santa Reparata, and San Michele Visdomini leased property outside the second communal wall in the episcopal Cafaggio (a region between the second and the third circle of communal walls). Leased on longer terms than the purely urban property (leases of 3–23 years instead of 1–2 years), the rents stipulated in the contracts varied from twenty to forty *soldi* per *staio*. A few share-cropping arrangements (*mezzadrie*) appear in the lease books. For example, on January 29, 1308, Bartelmo and Bacchino di Boninsegna (parishes of Santa Reparata and San Michele Visdomini) leased thirty-three *staia* and four *pannora* for six years in return for the payment of half what they produced.[77] The majority of the leases, however, required cash payments.[78] Many of the lessees worked in the clothmaking industry (*tiratoi*), which may account for the rather high rents.[79] In 1319 Ciandro di Dietavito (a *corregiaio* or girdle maker from San Michele Visdomini) rented a house for fourteen *lire* and ten *soldi*.[80] Most of the rents in this area of houses rose at least one *lire* in the first two decades of the fourteenth century, from six to seven *lire* and ten *soldi*.[81] Thirty years before the Black Death, rents on episcopal property were gradually increasing. As a major landlord of property both within and without the second circle of communal walls, the bishop was renting to dyers, bakers, shoemakers, and silk workers. When the commune made plans to build the third circle of communal walls to accommodate a growing city, the rents on the properties situated between the second circle and the future third circle increased accordingly.

The *Libro dei contratti di Ser Benedetto Martini* contains a complete record of the leasing of property at Montughi from 1304. The first lease was for fifty-four *staia* of land, made to Cambio and Lapo di Gianuzzo from the parish of San Lorenzo for four years.[82] There were six leases in all, on terms averaging four years (although one was for twelve years), requiring payments of fifteen to forty-eight *lire* per year. In 1299 Bishop Francesco made a major purchase of property at Montughi from a certain Grazziano (from the parish of San Felice in Piazza), two years after the papacy gave the bishopric permission to sell part of the Cafaggio.[83] Obviously Bishop Francesco consolidated his scattered possessions, making Montughi a center of episcopal jurisdiction at the turn of the fourteenth centuries. His successor, Antonio degli Orsi, constructed an episcopal palace there (now disappeared) in the midst of his landed possessions.[84] This was one of many episcopal residences enjoyed by Bishop Antonio (1309–1321). Aside from Montughi, he had use of the episcopal palace in the Piazza del Duomo, a residence near the Mugnone, the rural residences of the Florentine bishop; he also used the residence of a certain Guadagni near the Porta di Balla. His household included at least thirty people, including the poet and notary Francesco da Barberino.[85] To support such a large retinue, tenants of episcopal properties at Montughi paid rent in the form of provisions. We have record of four leases of property on Montughi, dated from 1308 to 1314 (for four, five, two, and twelve years, respectively).[86]

All in all, the bishops played a very important role in the development of their city, even if they did not always contribute willingly. Like other church lords, they played an especially important role in the area between the second and third communal walls, where they usually divided their properties into narrow units called *casolari,* designed normally for the construction of a house. Their innovative development of urban property helped render church property economically sound well into the next century.[87]

Episcopal Interests in the Mugello

In the late thirteenth and early fourteenth centuries, episcopal jurisdictional power yielded to direct Florentine control. Eager to break the disruptive power of the rural magnates like the Ubaldini, the Florentines continued to protect episcopal interests in the region while at the same time they extended their own jurisdiction. As the economic might of Florence increased markedly in the twelfth and thirteenth centuries, the Florentines continued to struggle with the lineage. As the commune imported more and more foodstuffs from the Romagna through the

Apennine passes and along the roads of the Mugello, it became more and more important to secure those supply routes. In 1251, shortly after the beginning of the Primo Popolo, the Ubaldini adhered to an anti-Florentine league composed of Siena, Pisa, and Pistoia. It is not surprising, therefore, that the Florentines attempted to neutralize the power of the Ubaldini in the western Mugello.

In 1251 the Florentines defeated the Ubaldini at Montaccianico. For the next half-century the commune extended its direct jurisdiction over that part of the Mugello to provide military security for its supply routes and road system. After the exiled Ghibellines made the Mugello their haven, the need to place the area under Florentine control became more pressing. To protect themselves against Ghibelline incursions and assure a constant supply of grain from the western Mugello, the commune forced residents of nineteen localities in the Ubaldini lands to swear obedience and fidelity to the commune in 1274.[88] After the famine of 1276 the government of Florence froze the buying and selling of property in the *contado* by tenants of regional lords. The intent was to maintain stability in the countryside.[89] In 1286 the commune declared the Ubaldini magnates, subject to the same restrictions as their urban counterparts. In 1289 the cathedral chapter attempted to sell its unfree dependents (*fideles*) in the Mugello to the Ubaldini, who might have been closely allied with the Adimari (the lineage which dominated the chapter at that time). Determined to prevent the lineage from consolidating its power at the expense of the commune, Florence welcomed a petition of the *fideles* themselves to prevent their sale to the Ubaldini.[90] On August 6, 1289, the commune passed a law forbidding anyone from selling their *fideles* or any dependent to anyone except to Florence itself. When the cathedral chapter attempted to sell its Mugello properties to the Ubaldini, the commune intervened and forced the chapter to sell to the commune. In 1290 Florence bought the *fideles* of the chapter for 3,000 *lire* to prevent any increase in Ubaldini power at Borgo, Pulicciano, and Ronta. As L. Kotel'nikova has demonstrated, this sale effectively freed the dependents of the adversaries (the Ubaldini) of the city. It was not an altruistic gesture, however; it was essentially a political act (an anti-magnate gesture, if you will), designed to weaken the Ubaldini, add to the labor force of the city, and add citizens to the tax lists.[91] Although the bishops and the episcopal administrators continued to appoint *podestà* after 1321, they did so within the context of a *pax Florentina*.[92]

In spite of these efforts, the western Mugello continued to pose serious security risks for the commune. In the summer of 1302, the White Guelfs and their Ghibelline allies fought the Black Guelfs in the Mugello and attempted to choke off the supply of grain from that area into the city. The Ubaldini also disrupted grain traffic in the Valdigreve and the Val di Pesa in 1302.[93] To put an end to its security problems in the Mugello, the commune embarked on a policy at the beginning of the fourteenth century to destroy the last vestiges of seigneurial power and to construct new settlements under the direct control of the commune.[94] Only military occupation by the Florentines could fully bring outlying areas of the Mugello into the urban sphere of influence.

Because the jurisdictional power of the episcopate in the Mugello was weakened by the emergence of the rural communes in the early and mid-thirteenth century, the Florentines had no choice if they wanted to preserve order and stability in the countryside than to take more direct steps to fill the vacuum of power. Had the Florentines been able to impose their hegemony over the region in other, less costly ways (such as through the bishops), they would have done so. The extension of Florentine power in the Mugello was not part of an inexorable process of conquest; it was a specific reaction to a set of particular circumstances. With the episcopate's political power weakened in the Mugello, the Florentines witnessed the worst nightmares come true at the beginning of the fourteenth century. In league with the Ghibelline exiles after 1267 and with the exiled Whites after 1302, the Ubaldini periodically cut off the supply of grain from the Romagna into the city by closing off the mountain passes which they controlled during the conflict between the Blacks and the Whites.[95] Such actions underscored the importance of securing the roads in and out of the mountains north of the city.

In the early years of the fourteenth century, therefore, the Florentines acted to end Ubaldini and Guidi regional power in the Mugello. They did so by destroying once and for all the military strongholds of the two lineages and by building their own garrisons in the Mugello plains (the terre nuove). First, the Florentines razed Montaccianico in 1306 and built Scarperia between 1305 and 1313 to serve as a garrison in the midst of Ubaldini lands.[96] They freed all remaining fideles of the lineage and made them dependent on the Capitano della Repubblica. They followed a similar policy with the Guidi, humiliating them at Ampinana and constructing a terra nuova in 1324 named Vicchio.

By 1330 the bishops were no longer the powerful lords in the valley, but they continued to draw a significant amount of their income from the Mugello. Although they had to pursue their interests within the framework of parameters imposed by the Florentine elite (with whom they shared common interests), they retained a strong economic presence in the Mugello. As Appendix D indicates, during the last half of the thirteenth century and the beginning of the fourteenth century, the bishops continued to enjoy a great deal of income from their lands in the Mugello. In fact, in terms of the number of documented agrarian contracts (on perpetual terms), the bishops leased more property in the Mugello than anywhere else (198 documented leases, or 31 percent of the total). There were far fewer commercial, fixed-term leases in the Mugello than anywhere else (only 17 percent of the total number of leases).[97] There is no record at all of any donations or purchases of property in the region, and the number of documented conflicts between the bishop and local tenants declined from 21 and 23 instances (1226–1250, 1251–1275, respectively) to 16 and 15 instances (1276–1300 and 1301–1325, respectively). All in all, the seventy years between 1250 and 1320 represented a period of stability and consolidation for the episcopate; there was very little acquisition of new property and no attempt to transform the customary holdings into commercial leases. The stability attained after 1250 assured later generations of bishops and episcopal families that the Mugello would remain a dependable source of income.

The Plebatus *of San Pietro di Vaglia*

Throughout the thirteenth and early fourteenth centuries, all episcopal tenants mentioned in the sources as *fideles* of the bishops continued to pay annual and perpetual rents in grain. As late as 1304 and 1314, several families acknowledged their status as *fideles* and their responsibility to make perpetual payments for certain consolidated properties (*podere*) at Vaglia to the bishop.[98] Episcopal interests in the area around Vaglia went beyond the collection of rents. The office of the arch-priest was within the control of the prelate, which meant that the bishop could elect the priest after the death or renunciation of another. Furthermore, this arch-priest played an extremely important role in the management of the *mensa episcopalis:* at least from the end of the thirteenth century he served as vicar of the bishop, responsible for buying and selling property as well as collecting rents.[99] In the early *trecento* the primary vicar and arch-priest of Vaglia was Parigio.

Episcopal power in Vaglia also included the jurisdictional right to appoint *podestà* for Vaglia, Soli, and Fortuna,[100] and the bishop leased property to the nearby monastery of Buonsollazzo.[101]

The Plebatus *of Pimonte (Monte Buiano) and the*
Plebatus *of San Lorenzo di Borgo*

In 1253 the Monte Buiano requested permission of the bishop to elect its own *podestà*—an appeal perhaps only partially granted by the prelate.

In 1256 Monte Buiano was again swearing *fidelitas* to the episcopal *podestà*, and in 1290 and 1292 Bishop Andrea de' Mozzi compiled a list of all episcopal dependents holding land of the bishop (*nomine fictus et fidelitatis*).[102]

Although the bishops held unrivaled sway in the region around Borgo until the rise of the rural commune, after 1250 they lost a great deal of that power and influence. They continued to appoint *podestà* for Borgo according to the arrangements worked out in the 1240's through the period covered by this book, indicating that the *podestà* functioned largely as a means of assuring the collection of rent and providing income for members of the Visdomini lineages.[103] It is possible that the commune of Florence brought Borgo San Lorenzo within its direct jurisdiction in the last quarter of the thirteenth century. Although his power was circumscribed, the bishop continued to draw a steady income from his holdings at Borgo San Lorenzo. In the early fourteenth century the bishops continued to let out land on customary terms (perpetual dues), but the sources do record several commercial leases for a fixed number of years—an indication that in the second half of the thirteenth century the bishopric was shifting the nature of the contracts to maximize income in grain and permit more flexibility in setting the terms and amount of the *census*.[104] Another clear example of increased sensitivity to the commercial market at Borgo was that the bishop began to lease for a set number of years (ten) in 1311 the right to collect *all* the rents and income for episcopal properties in the curia and district of Borgo San Lorenzo for the annual payment of nineteen *moggi* grain.[105] Such an arrangement was partially a creative response to the heritage of conflict and rent delinquency on episcopal lands in the *plebatus*.

As Appendix D indicates, the number of recorded instances of conflict on episcopal lands sharply rose between 1201 and 1225 and remained at that high level until 1275 (the period of the emergence of the rural communes). Although the intervention of Florence and the compromises arranged between the bishops and the new communities helped stabilize the political situation in the Mugello at the end of the thirteenth century, the bishops still had to contend with the continued withholding of rents by local tenants. The introduction of this new type of lease—of all episcopal income in a given area for a set number of years—placed the burden of collection on the lessee, not on the episcopal officials. The episcopate received in exchange a sum which would remain unchanged regardless of whether all the tenants paid their annual rents or not. Only one type of episcopal income was not included in the lease: the yearly payments or fines (*condemnationes*) that Borgo San Lorenzo made to the bishop every year as a result of the agreements negotiated with the rural communes in the 1230's and 1240's. As was true in the Sienese *contado*, these payments were compensation for lost seigneurial rights.

For the last quarter of the thirteenth century and the early decades of the fourteenth, the bishops continued to exercise power on several levels in the *plebatus* of Borgo (just as they were able to do at Vaglia), but recent political and economic realities weakened and circumscribed that power from what it had been before 1240. The bishop continued to possess the patronage rights to churches throughout the *plebatus:* San Lorenzo di Borgo itself, Santa Maria Olmi, San Miniato Piazzano, and San Martino Vespignano. Furthermore, the episcopate leased property not only to local residents but also to local churchmen. In 1299 the *plebs* of Borgo acknowledged that it was within the *collatio* (estate) of the bishop and was required to pay annually a *census*.[106] Furthermore, the leasing of all episcopal income to a single person created a class of powerful middlemen in the community. Although these arrangements diminished the direct social, economic, and political presence of the bishop in the community, they provided the episcopate with a source of stable and dependable income.

The Plebatus *of San Casciano di Padule*

As elsewhere in the Mugello, commercial, fixed-term leases in Padule first appear after 1250; the episcopate also began to consolidate all its rents into a single lease, rented to an individual in exchange for a single payment of several *staia* of grain. The first fixed-term lease appeared in 1256. Bishop Giovanni de' Mangiadori leased certain lands in the area for twenty-five years for the annual payment of three *staia* of grain. Shortly thereafter, the first *mezzadria* contract emerges in the documents.[107] During the first two decades of the *trecento*, it appears that much if not most of the land was still held by episcopal tenants (*fideles*) in the *plebatus*. Some tenants still held properties according to the customary arrangements. For example, Pacino di Paco da San Bartolo di Molezzano held land on a perpetual lease at Molezzano which his father had had before him, for which he made annual rent payments. On April 16, 1320, Pacino promised the bishop to continue paying that annual rent of twelve *staia* of grain and a pair of capons.[108]

To compel tenants to hold fast to their obligations, each new bishop required every tenant in the *plebatus* of San Casciano di Padule to swear an oath that he was a dependent (*fidelis*) to him and his officials—an oath which was actually a promise to pay the rents. Such *iuramenta* were made at the beginning of the episcopates of Ardingo (1232) at Molezzano and

Loncastro, of Giovanni de' Mangiadori in 1251 and 1273 at Pagliariccio, and of Andrea de' Mozzi in 1287 at Molezzano. These oaths, as we have seen, were especially important, as the tenants used the installation of a new bishop to challenge traditional episcopal rights in the countryside. The tradition of resistance gave rise to the customary requirement of each tenant to pledge obedience in writing to the episcopal *podestà*.

In the three *plebatus* of Botena, Padule, and Corella, conflict between local tenants and the bishops was constant. Collective oaths (*iuramenta*) at Pagliariccio (1251, 1253, 1273, 1312, and 1317); at Molezzano (1253, 1287, 1312, 1317); at Rabbiacanina (1253, 1312, 1317); at Santa Felicità al Fiume (1273 and 1287); and at San Lorenzo di Corniuole (1292) indicate that the episcopate was having trouble collecting its traditional dues. Sometimes the opposition took the form of the withholding of a single rent by an individual, as in the case of Bottrigo di Ricevuto da Pagliariccio in 1253.[109] But more often the opposition took on a collective aspect. In 1287, shortly after the installation of Bishop Andrea de' Mozzi, the episcopate was locked in a dispute with the *iudex* or local official of Rabbiacanina. Apparently, the entire community took the opportunity of the beginning of a new episcopate to refuse to pay the *census*. The problem for the episcopate continued on into the next century, as Bishop Antonio chose to excommunicate all members of the community for their resistance.[110]

Collective opposition also dramatically appeared at Molezzano, Pagliariccio, and Vitigliano. Again the reason was the refusal by local tenants to pay the required rents (*census*). After warning them on June 17, 1299, to swear *fidelitas*, Bishop Francesco Monaldeschi finally resorted to the excommunication of all the men of the three communities. As late as 1320 the dispute was still continuing, this time concerning a conflict over jurisdictional claims. The parishes San Martino di Pagliariccio and Santa Felicità al Fiume elected syndics to meet with the bishop to settle the dispute.[111] Although the sources tell us nothing about the effect of the excommunication, the two parties did reach an agreement over contested jurisdiction at Santa Felicità al Fiume. With surprisingly little intervention by Florence, the bishops managed to make good their claims over much of that tiny valley, perhaps because their presence pervaded every level of the social and economic life of the *plebatus*.

On April 20, 1309, Ser Bindo da Calenzano (episcopal syndic and notary) leased to Rossellino di Arrigho della Tosa all the income in the *plebatus* of Botena, San Casciano di Padule, and San Martino di Corella for five years for a payment of ten *moggi* of grain to be paid into the episcopal granary every August. Notice the identity of the lessee: a principal member of the Tosinghi patrilineage. The "farming out" of episcopal income to a single individual benefitted the bishop because it gave him a stable income, but it also favored the renter (in this case a member of the *consorteria* which traditionally exploited episcopal income). The contract ended a year later (perhaps because of Rossellino's death or the action of the new bishop Antonio), as in the following March (1310) Vanno di Albertino di Malagonella (from the Florentine parish of Sant'Andrea) was leasing the same income but on different terms. He paid ten *moggi* and ten *staia,* and the contract was for four instead of five years.[112] It is possible that Bishop Antonio believed that the terms of the lease to Rossellino were too easy (given the close connections between the bishopric and the Visdomini). Consequently, he could have revoked that lease in favor of one more commercially competitive.

The Plebatus *of San Cresci in Valcava*

Though the bishopric continued to lease out property on a perpetual basis throughout the thirteenth century in the region around Valcava, it gradually began to shift to commercial fixed-term leases in the latter half of the thirteenth century. In 1270 the episcopal syndic leased for fifteen years a piece of land in the *plebatus* for one *staio* grain.[113] Customary leases requiring perpetual rents continued to be made (as in 1272 and 1289), but the commercial fixed-term variety also appeared in the sources (as in 1291). It is possible that the introduction of the new leases was linked to the desire on the part of the bishops to end widespread discontent with the episcopal presence after 1250.

In 1255 the Florentine courts intervened in a major flare-up, resulting in the order issued by the assessor of the Florentine *podestà* to the commune of Valcava to obey the precepts of the episcopally elected *podestà.* Apparently, the commune was refusing to do so.[114] As elsewhere throughout the *contado* on episcopal lands, the appointment of new *podestà* elicited strong opposition from the local community. In the case of the *plebatus* of Valcava, the local residents formed a commune to declare their opposition. After Florentine intervention, the commune had no choice but to acquiesce and pledge obedience to the new episcopal official. It is very interesting to note that the arch-priest of the *plebs* of Valcava, Stuldo, also joined the rebellion. Shortly after the settlement in the courts, Bishop Giovanni de' Mangiadori excommunicated in 1257 all the canons appointed by the arch-priest. The priest might also have refused to alienate or sell land of the *plebs* to the bishop or the Visdomini or to accept the bishop as his lord and patron (*patronus et dominus*).

At Valcava in the 1270's—as elsewhere—there existed a very strong tradition among the tenants of exchanging property among themselves. The episcopal syndic (Chele) was prompted to forbid a resident of San Cresci (Gerio di Sostegno) from selling, buying, or alienating *podere* in the villa of Cignano without episcopal permission. Herein lay one of the root causes of discontent with episcopal lordship: individual peasants were prevented from buying and selling land to consolidate their holdings and from exchanging property with kinsmen or clients.[115]

Shortly after the assumption of office by Bishop Andrea de' Mozzi in 1286, all the discontent and frustration erupted out into the open again. Valcava refused to swear *fidelitas* to the official episcopal representative, the *podestà*. Andrea retaliated by fining the commune 1,000 *lire*. He then arranged compromises with some of the individuals involved in the disturbances. The clashes, however, continued to create problems. Under orders from the prelate, a loyal canon of the *plebs* excommunicated several men who refused to accept the overlordship of the bishop and claimed he had no rights over the lands they cultivated.[116] Ten years later, Bishop Francesco Monaldeschi again excommunicated them for not accepting their dependent status. By the early 1320's several previously excommunicated tenants promised to obey the bishop and accept their responsibilities.[117] In 1321 the Visdomini and Tosinghi administrators sent Fastello della Tosa to San Cresci for one year as *podestà*, to be paid with the normal salary.[118] Episcopal and Visdomini involvement in the area continued, even if it continued to be difficult to maintain order and stability on episcopal lands. Resentment over the meddling of the bishop and the Visdomini in the local affairs of the community also could have aggravated the conflict.

In the early *trecento* customary and fixed-term commercial leases existed side by side, but more and more short-term contracts made their appearance. For example, on January 24, 1310, Dorello di Bellincione da Monte Aceraia rented for five years all the woods and lands at Valcava (including properties at Aceraia and Monterotondo south of Valcava on the summits of the mountains) for nine *moggi* to be paid in August into the episcopal granary.[119] As in the *plebatus* of Padule and Botena, the bishops often transformed a former "fief" after the death of an heirless tenant into a commercial lease (as they had done at Campestri).[120] In 1300 Bishop Francesco charged Pancerio di Benvenuto da Valcava, a syndic, to collect all the income due the bishop from the entire community.[121]

The Plebatus *of Acone, Doccia, and Montefiesole*

By 1300 the bishops of Florence had at least four residences (*palatia*) in this section of the Mugello: Chiasso, Monterotondo, Pievevecchia, and Monte di Croce. In the latter two the bishops had granaries.[122] A survey of the sources relating to episcopal interests in this region reveal extensive episcopal penetration of the economy. Although the bishop of Fiesole had possessions at Montebonello, Rufina, and Petrognano, he posed no threat to the bishop of Florence or to the security interests of the priorate.[123] The two lease books conserved in the Archivio Arcivescovile reveal that the bishops made more leases of property in this area than anywhere else except within Florence itself (and that was because leases of shops lasted only a year or two; hence, the large number of leases in the sources).[124] The rich archival sources allow us to construct virtually a complete picture of episcopal lordship in the region around Monte di Croce. Renzo Nelli's excellent studies of this region of the Val di Sieve demonstrate the type of meticulous research on ecclesiastical property which the Florentine archives make possible.[125]

Nelli's research of the episcopal lordship at Monte di Croce confirms conclusions reached by this author regarding not only Monte di Croce but also other episcopal properties. Indeed, the course of episcopal lordship in that area did not differ greatly from episcopal lordship elsewhere. Although most of the property was given over to the cultivation of grain, many leases also included the cultivation of the vine and the harvest of chestnuts.[126] Most of the rents required—that is to say, according to Nelli's calculations, 66 percent—did not exceed five *staia*. Forty-seven percent of the total did not go beyond two *staia*. As Nelli cogently observes, the bishop of Florence wanted a secure return without imposing a major hardship on the tenants.[127] Most fathers passed the holdings to their sons, and the next generation generally retained the unity of that holding.[128] However, in his survey of 156 perpetual holdings at the end of the thirteenth and beginning of the fourteenth centuries, Nelli discovered that 42 passed into the hands of tenants unrelated to previous tenants. The number of people (not holdings at Monte di Croce) taking new properties was fourteen, and six of those were city dwellers. Two were artisans, and four were from the Florentine elite (members of the Pazzi, the Saltarelli, and the Caponsacchi).[129] The penetration of Monte di Croce by these families (especially by Lapo di Littifredo dei Pazzi and his heirs)—coupled with the fact that all tenants enjoyed a great deal of independence from the bishop—led Nelli to the conclusion that at the end of the thirteenth century and beginning of the fourteenth, the bishopric attempted to regain power over the properties it had previously lost.

Clearly, a revolution in the nature of the management of episcopal property was occurring at the end of the thirteenth century. As Appendix D indicates, there are only two documented donations and one purchase mentioned in the *Bullettone* for the period between 1276 and 1300, whereas after 1300 the number of purchases increased to ten and the number of donations to four. In other words, there was some attempt before 1320 to acquire property. The primary reason appears to have been concern over the growing presence of the Saltarelli, Pazzi, and Caponsacchi. The Caponsacchi were an ancient Ghibelline lineage, and the Pazzi were among the traditional Guelf lineages (along with the Adimari and *vicedomini* lineages). The Saltarelli, however, had a different origin altogether. Like the dell'Antella, the dal Borgo, the Pulci, the Portinari, the del Rosso, and the Strozzi, they rose to prominence in the second half of the thirteenth century as a result of their mercantile connections.[130] Their presence in the Monte di Croce area indicates that they were interested in landed as well as mercantile property. As part of the mercantile elite edging out the older Guelf lineages, the Saltarelli certainly were challenging the power of the episcopate and the Visdomini and Tosinghi in the area. What was going on at Monte di Croce was going on elsewhere in the *contado:* more and more city dwellers were acquiring property in the countryside.[131] Bishop Lottieri della Tosa had real reason to fear them. The change in direction in management took other forms as well. The major difference between the nature of management before 1300 and after 1300 was that the number of short-term commercial leases jumped dramatically from zero for the period 1276–1300 to fifty-six for the period 1301–1325.

Having received Monte Giovi in 1133 as an imperial possession, the episcopate continued to exploit that holding well into the fourteenth century. The *vicedomini* particularly viewed the holding as its own personal possession in the early *trecento,* most likely because of their complete control of episcopal property by the *consorteria* during the vacancy of 1275 to 1286. In a dispute which had enormous repercussions on Florentine internal politics, Bishop Lottieri della Tosa convoked the entire *consorteria* in 1303 to complain about the seizure of Monte Giovi by his own kinsman, Rossellino di Arrigho della Tosa. Though related to the prelate, Rossellino had been a member of the Donati political faction in the early *trecento,* whereas his rival the bishop was a member of the Cerchi faction. Rossellino's occupation of episcopal property certainly played a role in the factional conflicts of this period.[132] Rossellino refused to pay the customary *census* to the bishop, so Lottieri revoked all *locationes* of properties to him, but apparently to no avail.[133] Therefore, he appealed to the patrilineage. This dispute had tremendous ramifications for the political development of Florence after the expulsion of the Whites in 1302. It was this conflict between two members of the Visdomini *consorteria* which led to a further split in the ranks of the Blacks. Whereas Bishop Lottieri della Tosa supported Corso Donati, Rossellino della Tosa formed his own faction. The source of that split was a dispute over the lordship over Monte Giovi. For the bishop, there were limits to the appropriation of episcopal property by the Visdomini *consorteria*. Rossellino had gone too far, although he probably was doing nothing more than holding on to property administered by his branch of the lineage since the vacancy of 1275–1286. For the bishop—even though he was a Tosinghi himself—the *castellum* of Monte Giovi was strategically located between two *plebatus* where the episcopate exercised tremendous power, Valcava and Acone. This dispute underscores a central fact regarding the nature of the complex internal disputes within the Florentine elite: at the center of the conflict was the struggle to retain access to ecclesiastical property.

This controversy should caution the historian from thinking that members of a *consorteria* necessarily saw eye to eye.[134] As the struggle for access to church property and offices among the magnate elite intensified at the beginning of the fourteenth century, even the Tosinghi split into rival camps. One possible reason for the conflict may be that, in the list of episcopal *podestà* appointed to areas of episcopal dominance, there is no record that Rossellino della Tosa ever held such a post.[135] Because it was such a lucrative position, and because the Visdomini normally staffed those positions since the beginning of the thirteenth century, perhaps Rossellino was simply appropriating a portion of the episcopal *mensa* that other members of his *consorteria* had denied him.

As far as renting was concerned, most of the leasing involved land and houses in the parish of Santa Margarita di Aceraia in the *plebatus* of Acone. After 1300, *mezzadrie* were especially common at Aceraia, as they were wherever the bishop possessed a palace (Montughi and Padule, for example). For example, Monte di Biliotto of the parish of Santa Margarita di Aceraia acknowledged he owed half of his produce every year in 1318.[136] The number of residents of Monte di Croce holding customary perpetual leases from the bishop was extremely high.[137] Given the tradition of resistance at Monte di Croce to episcopal lordship, it is not surprising therefore that many tenants refused to honor their annual obligations. In one case before the Florentine courts, Vagliente and

Consilio di Cino da Monte di Croce admitted to the Florentine court that they "wrongfully" exploited the woods and fields of the bishop of Florence. They probably just took wood from the forest or cultivated episcopal land without paying the *census*.[138] In 1254 and 1256 the men of Monte di Croce swore to obey the mandates of the episcopal *podestà*, but in 1256 they were electing their own syndics to settle a dispute with the bishop.[139] In June of the following year the Visdomini *podestà* condemned them, and they were able to subjugate them two months later. Throughout the remainder of the thirteenth century Monte di Croce was pledging to obey the new *podestà*, but in 1298 they stopped doing so. Bishop Francesco Monaldeschi ordered them to desist. By 1302 there was rebellion at Galiga and Fornello, and in 1303 the representative *(vicarius)* of the bishop (himself a Tosinghi) was still fining individuals for recalcitrance.[140] Perhaps the conflict stemmed from opposition to the presence of Tosinghi.

To minimize the problems of collecting rents from unreliable and obstreperous tenants, the episcopate introduced at Monte di Croce and the *plebatus* of Doccia commercial fixed-term leases for grain rents—following the same pattern as emerged elsewhere. For example, in 1310, when Mannello di Amanito da Sant'Andrea di Doccia surrendered his fief to Bishop Antonio because it was apparently not enough to support him and his family *(paupertas)*, the episcopal representative (the *castaldionus et factor*) leased that same fief the next day to Buccio di Benintendo da Doccia for five years. Whereas Mannello was paying a *staio* per year, Buccio agreed to render to the episcopal *castaldus* at the episcopal palace of Monte di Croce half of all the produce.[141] A necessary part of the bishop's lordship at Monte di Croce was his ability to appoint churchmen to the important clerical offices. For example, the bishops controlled the elections of the arch-priest of Sant'Andrea di Doccia, as well as the rectors of Santa Maria di Fornello, San Pietro di Strata, and Santo Stefano di Patrillo.[142]

As at Monte Giovi, several members of the Visdomini patrilineage acquired interests at Monte di Croce, the origins of which extended back to 1270. In that year Uberto di Gherardo dei Visdomini received arable lands (including a vineyard) in the parish of San Lorenzo di Montefiesole from the Florentine courts as compensation for the non-repayment of funds by Fastello and Ciuto di Gualterio and Mantina di Benintendo (from the *curia* of Montefiesole). The court ordered the heirs of the late Gualterio to appear before it, and when they did not, it awarded the property to Uberto dei Visdomini.[143]

During the vacancy of 1275–1286, the Visdomini administrators were extremely active leasing episcopal property, the rents for which they themselves might have pocketed. In 1279, in the first fixed-term leases in the *plebatus*, Bindo di Guido di Aldobrandino dei Visdomini—in his capacity as procurator and manager (*gestor*) of the episcopal estate—leased to Cenno di Giovanni dei Pilandri and his son Bartolino from the parish of Santa Lucia di Pievevecchia for six years four fulling mills (*gualcheriae*) and a grain mill (*molendinum*) at Bisarno, along with sereral houses, lands, and vineyards. Bindo dei Visdomini also leased four fulling mills and a grain mill (with its aquaduct and accompanying property) located at Rivogamberaio to the same individuals for four years for 122 florins.[144] For the next half-century the episcopate continued to lease mills at places like Solalunga, Bisarno, and Rivogamberaio, usually for four to six years.[145]

In the *trecento,* those tenants holding *podere* from the bishop paid all in grain and rented for a fixed number of years (usually for five or six).[146] Among those leasing mills and land along the river in the parish, there was no one renting on perpetual terms. All leased for a certain number of years and paid cash or grain for their leases. The increased commercialization of the local economy is also evident from the fact that those tenants who paid in grain brought their yearly payment (*census*) in August to the episcopal granary in the episcopal palace at Pievevecchia.[147] Nevertheless, at Montefiesole, perpetual leases were common (one lease we have for the fourteenth century is a *mezzadria,* made for two years).[148]

In the parish of San Niccolò di Vico Panzanese—where the bishop also had possession of a *castello*—fixed-term leases begin to appear in the documents in the middle of the thirteenth century (as they do elsewhere). One lease from 1292 is especially interesting, as it was made to a member of the Visdomini lineage, indicating again that it had managed in the course of half a century to insert itself into the economic and social life of the area. We must not forget as well that only Visdomini were serving as episcopal *podestà* in the area.[149] In the *plebatus* of Montefiesole tension between episcopal tenants and the bishops clustered between two dates: the 1230's (see Chapter 3) and the 1290's. After 1230 the episcopate, aware of the tradition of resistance, periodically required formal oaths of dependency (*iuramenta*) from the tenants themselves. These oaths tended to be made at the beginning of the tenure of a new bishop, as we have seen occurred elsewhere: 1231 (Pievevecchia), in 1233 (Vico), 1251 (Montefiesole), and 1287 (Montefiesole).[150] To enforce the collection of these payments, the bishops began sending *podestà* to the region at least as early as 1229, and all of those *podestà* were members of the Visdomini, Tosinghi, or Aliotti lineages. As payment for their services, they probably received one *staio* of wheat per household.[151]

Renzo Nelli estimates that at Montefiesole two lineages held thirteen of the seventy-two perpetual episcopal leases. At Pievevecchia, Vico, and Montefiesole the original episcopal concessions had been divided up among heirs. Nelli therefore concludes that the local lineages supplemented their sparse holdings from the bishop with allodial possessions.[152]

In the last decade of the thirteenth century—for reasons which must remain unknown—rebellion against the episcopal presence spread throughout the region along the Sieve Valley. Bishops Andrea de' Mozzi and Francesco dei Monaldeschi responded by requiring formal lists of payments to be drawn up so as to enforce collection.[153] Apparently, entire communities attempted to forgo the normal *iuramenta,* as Montefiesole did in 1302 at the beginning of the episcopacy of Lottieri.[154] Individual instances of opposition continued to occur, as in 1300 several local men confessed they had been delinquent in paying their *census* for mills (*gualcheriae*) at Solalunga, Rivogamberaio, and Bisarno (which they had leased in 1297).[155]

In the 1290's resistance to the *podestà* had not ended, and local residents recognized that an episcopal presence meant a Visdomini and Tosinghi presence as well. Hence, in the atmosphere of war and conflict during the 1290's, the local inhabitants seized the opportunity to attempt to shake off the last vestiges of dependency on the bishop: their status as *fideles episcopatus.* It was perhaps this new cycle of resistance which spurred the Florentine commune to create a new policy toward the *contado.* Around 1290 Florentine strategy appears to have changed from using episcopal lordship as a way of maintaining hegemony to extending the city's direct jurisdiction over episcopal lands (especially the Mugello and Val di Sieve). In 1290 all episcopal *bona* passed into Florentine *dominium,* although the bishops continued to exercise their power to lease property and receive annual rents. Between 1305 and 1324 the commune finally extinguished the ability of the Guidi and Ubaldini to act independently of the city. After 1290 Florence intervened rarely on behalf of the bishops in their disputes with local communities. For the bishops, however, the challenges were serious.

The Val di Pesa

The Plebatus of Santo Stefano di Campoli

In the Val di Pesa the number of short-term leases increased markedly from one recorded lease for the period 1251–1275 to forty-one for the quarter century between 1301 and 1325 (see Appendix D). This revolution in management is most importantly evident in the leasing together of all episcopal income in the *plebatus* of Campoli to one person for one to three years for the payment of several *moggi*. For example, in 1310 the episcopal representative, Ser Manno, leased (*locavit et concessit ad affictum*) to Ser Salo di Bonavera da Firenze two pieces of land for five years for two *staia* to be paid into the episcopal granary in August.[156] When a tenant (*fidelis*) died without heirs, the bishop was able to change the concession from a perpetual arrangement to a commercial lease to rationalize and enhance his income. In 1313 Cambuizzio di Lottiero da Santo Stefano di Campoli died without heirs. Wishing to make better use of the property (*cupiens condictionem Episcopatus Florentini facere meliorem*), Bishop Antonio rented all his former tenant's property to Losso di Bonaguida for twenty-nine years for the payment of eight *staia* and one pair of capons per year.[157] As we have seen, the bishops followed a similar strategy at Castelfiorentino, in the Mugello, and at Monte di Croce. This arrangement allowed the bishops to collect one payment in grain from a single person who alone was responsible for the collection of all the local income (*affictus, pensiones, feuda, census, et alia que servitia debita in perpetuum*). The sources record at least five of these leases before 1322: one in 1310 (five years for thirteen *moggi*), 1313 (three years for ten *moggi*), 1319 (one year for twenty *moggi*), 1321 (one year for ten *moggi*), and 1322 (two years for ten *moggi* annually). By 1319 Bishop Antonio had extended this method of management to include income from the *plebatus* of Decimo as well.[158]

Bishop Giovanni de' Mangiadori began his tenure in the See of St. Zanobi by requiring collective oaths of fidelity (*iuramenta*) at Montecampolese in 1252 and 1254 before his *podestà*. These oaths were ways by which the bishop perpetuated the flow of grain into the episcopal granary. Early in the episcopacy of Andrea de' Mozzi there was another series of *iuramenta* between February 12 and 21 and on April 7, 1289.[159] During the episcopacies of Francesco Monaldeschi (1295–1301), Lottiero della Tosa, and Antonio degli Orsi (1309–1321), the sources record a series of *recognitiones* of grain payments to the bishop by his tenants. In 1298 there was one commutation of unspecified customary services (*servitia antiqua*) to three *staia* grain as well as a condemnation by the bishop that same year of the exchange (*cambium*) of a house and property at Ripoli Episcopi by an episcopal dependent named Botticini. Deeming the transaction (probably a sale) harmful to his interests (*quia dictum cambium erat dapnosum dicto Episcopatui*), Bishop Francesco Monaldeschi sought to prevent the exchange of episcopal property between local residents without the necessary recognition of annual payments due the prelate or without payment of a tax. Bishop Francesco also required the drawing up of a list of dependents around 1300 from the surrounding area: Fabbrica, San Niccolò di Montecampolese, San Martino di Cofferi, Santa Lucia a Ligliano, Santa Maria di Campoli, San Fabbiano, Santo Stefano di Campoli, San Donato di Luciana, San Bartolo di Ripoli, and Sant'Andrea di Nuovole.[160] Though we cannot assume that the list is complete, the information provided indicates that the prelate was receiving roughly 277 *staia* of grain every August. The collection of those payments and the administration of those properties required a sophisticated bureacracy.

The Parish of Sant'Andrea di Fabbrica

During the episcopate of Giovanni de' Mangiadori, the episcopal administration purchased significant amounts of property from the rector of Sant'Andrea and from local individuals who were tenants (*fideles*) of the bishop. From 1117 to 1298 there were at least twenty-two purchases of property, eight of which occurred during the episcopacy of Giovanni de' Mangiadori (1251–1274). The bishop acquired more property in the parish of Fabbrica than anywhere else in the diocese. The sources record thirteen purchases for the quarter-century of his lordship (see Appendix D). At the beginning of his tenure—as was usual throughout the *contado* at the beginning of a new term—tenants made their pledges of fidelity and obedience (*iuramenta*). In February 1252 four brothers (as well as others) swore *fidelitas* and sold land to him. Cristiano da Fabbrica sold property to the bishop on March 17, and on March 28 he confessed he had always been a *fidelis*. Similarly, on March 17, Braccio di Piero da Fabbrica declared himself a dependent of the bishop and sold him land as well. The *Bullettone* records another sale by Braccio of property (*certae possessiones*) eleven days later.[161] It is possible that these purchases were part of a larger scheme the bishop undertook to regain properties in the region lost in past time, acquire new holdings, and thereby consolidate episcopal holdings. All of those who turned property over to the bishop were local residents.

The likeliest agent for the purchases of land in the parish of Fabbrica was the local episcopally appointed rector. Fabbrica was one area of the diocese where the power of the bishop of Florence was supreme. He possessed extensive properties and the right to appoint the local rector, and he exercised his power by way of the episcopal *podestà*. The policy of acquisition and consolidation between 1252 and 1258 required the active participation of the rector. Apparently, the rector of Fabbrica resented the invasive policies of the prelate and was the focus of local discontent. Appointed by the arch-priest of Campoli, the rector apparently attempted to obstruct episcopal penetration of the area. Conflict between the arch-priest of Campoli and the bishop was inevitable. In 1258 Bishop Giovanni and the arch-priest of Campoli clashed over the election of the rector of Sant'Andrea. On April 12, 1258, Bishop Giovanni nullified the election of Presbyter Amadore (a canon of the *plebs* of Campoli), appointed by the arch-priest of Campoli (Bencivenni).[162] On April 15, the bishop elected Presbyter Marsoppino as his choice, and the new appointee quickly pledged his obedience (*ipse Presbyter iuravit fidelitatem et fecit obedientiam*). Three weeks later the former rector resigned. On May 17 the bishop confirmed the election of Marsoppino, who was a canon from the church of San Felice ad Ema and probably a member of the Tosinghi lineage. That same day Bishop Giovanni excommunicated the arch-priest of Campoli (Bencivenni), and by February 3, 1259, he had removed him from office.[163] A year later the sources indicate that episcopal acquisition of local property resumed. In March and April of 1259, Braccio di Piero da Fabbrica, Palmerio di Ciuto da Fabbrica, Cristiano da Fabbrica, and Chiaro di Bonello da Fabbrica—all *fideles*—sold property to Bishop Giovanni. In mid-March of that same year, the prelate bought property from a certain Riccio, the new episcopally appointed rector of Fabbrica.[164]

According to canonical procedure, the arch-priest possessed the right (*ius*) to approve the election of the parish priests within his *plebatus*. Ultimately the bishop had to approve the election as well. In this case, however, the interests of the bishop conflicted with those of the arch-priest and chapter of Campoli. As a member of the chapter of Campoli and appointed by the arch-priest of that *plebs,* the rector of Fabbrica attempted to maintain the integrity of the parish patrimony and prevent the alienation of local property into the hands of the bishop by resisting the episcopal economic strategy of acquisition and consolidation. As was true in the eleventh through the thirteenth centuries, episcopal lordship relied on several factors: control of local parish appointments (rectors as well as arch-priests) and the possession of *castelli,* jurisdictional rights, and immobile property. In fact, for centuries before 1259 the bishop alone appointed the arch-priest of Campoli. But in 1258 and 1259 something very dramatic occurred: the attempt on the part of Bishop Giovanni to increase and consolidate episcopal holdings in the parish of Fabbrica led to complete fracture between the prelate and his nominally obedient arch-priest of Campoli. Overall episcopal economic strategy clashed with the desire of the chapter of Campoli to retain local control of parish resources. The bishop succeeded because he possessed superior jurisdictional power: as bishop he could excommunicate and depose, and his acquisition of the *castello* in 1098 effectively gave him the right to elect the local priest.

After 1259 purchases of property continued, but they were fewer than prior to that date. In 1275, 1277, 1280, and 1298, episcopal representatives bought more properties (*terrae et possessiones*). All but the last purchase occurred during the eleven-year vacancy between 1275 and 1286 and directly benefitted the *visdomini* lineages. In fact, it is possible that the ever-present shadow of the Visdomini and Tosinghi in these transactions after 1252 might have been the primary reason for the clash in the first place. After all, Marsoppino, the new rector of Fabbrica, was probably Marsoppino della Tosa. The conflict over episcopal penetration of Fabbrica was a cause of the fierce controversy at the end of the century between the bishop and the chapter of Campoli over the right to appoint the arch-priest. Although there is only one single lease mentioned (1298), the *Bullettone* does record a series of *recognitiones* for the years 1289, 1296, 1299, and 1306 and of *promissiones* for 1298 which contain the pledges of local tenants to make annual grain payments. Individual oaths were made at the beginning of the term of office of Giovanni de' Mangiadori (1252), and also in 1259, 1268, and 1272. After 1300 there is much more information about leasing. In the lease books, there were six acknowledgments of yearly payments. In one instance, in March 1305, Bertino di Lando da Fabbrica confessed that he owed retroactively to the episcopal representative, Chele di Curso, eight *staia* for *poderi* and other unspecified properties.[165] The sources indicate that most tenants of the bishop at Fabbrica held their land on a perpetual basis.

Although an episcopal *castaldus* was active buying land for the bishop as early as 1195, only in the late thirteenth century did episcopal surrogates appear with frequency. In 1288 and 1298 episcopal syndics were taking possession of lands at Fabbrica, presumably from delinquent tenants or tenants who died without heirs. Aside from the local men and members of the episcopal household acting on the bishop's behalf, the bishops continued to control the election of the rector. In both April and October 1298, Bishop Lottieri della Tosa appointed a *cappellanus* from the parish of Decimo and a certain Bonavere as rectors, respectively. In 1313 Bishop Antonio deprived Bonavere of his office (no reason given) and put Presbyter Dino da Calenzano in his place. As was apparent from the overview of the controversy of 1258 and 1259, the bishop relied on the rector as his principal representative, responsible for the implementation of episcopal policy.

In 1254, thirty-seven years after the purchase of the *castello* by Bishop

Giovanni da Velletri, Bishop Giovanni de' Mangiadori leased (*locavit et concessit*) for twelve years all the property at Torniano (*omnes domos, iura, possessiones, servitia, redditus, et proventus*).[166] Episcopal possession of Torniano figured very importantly in the Florentine communal measures against the magnates. In 1288 the priorate declared that if any magnate unjustly held ecclesiastical property, the Captain of the People had the right to investigate. In 1289 a Florentine judge (*Iudex Florentie*) proclaimed that the properties of several men (Cavalcanti?) at Torniano were to be given to the episcopal syndic. The enforcement of the 1288 provision regarding Torniano indicates that the communal officials themselves were aware that the conflict between the oldest lineages in the diocese over ecclesiastical resources was at the heart of the civil strife associated with the magnates. Communal intervention in this case protected the integrity of the *mensa episcopalis* during the tenure of Andrea de' Mozzi and effectively removed episcopal property at Torniano from the arena of conflict. This case is a very good example of a situation true of the entire diocese: the crisis facing those members of the Florentine nobility we call magnates led them to tighten their hold on ecclesiastical property, often exacerbating the already serious factional difficulties.[167]

The Plebatus *of Santa Cecilia di Decimo*

In 1256 the *camerarius* of the commune of San Casciano paid 33 *soldi* and four *denari*, a third of the total amount of *condemnationes* it owed the bishop annually, as stipulated in the 1241 agreement. Although the counsellors of the commune (*consiliarii*) continued to obey the episcopal *podestà*, the episcopal official had to request in 1278 that the Florentine authorities force the vicar of San Casciano to cease interfering with his duties. Florence formally placed the commune under its direct jurisdiction in 1272, but it was careful to continue to recognize and protect episcopal rights there.[168] Indeed, a Florentine magistrate (*iudex* and *assessor*) of the Captain of Florence asserted in 1278 that the bishop continued to control (*dominatio*) the commune, even though Florence was sovereign. The episcopal *podestà* continued to serve in the community, but their functions appear to have been limited to the collection of episcopal income.[169] They also enforced the episcopal statutes of 1241, initiated and administered the *iuramenta*, and enforced collection of rents. Most of that income came into episcopal coffers in the form of annual payments by San Casciano to the bishop—an arrangement similar to the situation at Castelfiorentino and in the Sienese *contado*. Our sources do not record all the payments by the *camerarius* of Castelfiorentino of one-third of the taxes of the commune, but we do have records of payments in 1258 (40 *lire*), 1268 (15 *lire*), 1289 (120 *lire*), 1296 (10 *lire*), and 1298 (10 *lire*).[170]

The *podestà* were important episcopal officials in the second half of the thirteenth century, but so were the arch-priests of Decimo and the canons in its chapter. In 1272 the arch-priest of Decimo acknowledged the bishop as his lord and swore obedience.[171] Though there exists no further entry detailing appointments of arch-priests, we can be sure that the bishops kept a tight grip on whom they elected. In 1292 the arch-priest was doing the episcopal business by excommunicating several men guilty of not paying their *census*.[172] Furthermore, the sources indicate that the bishops carefully manipulated clerical appointments to the chapter: in 1287, 1313, and 1315 the bishops elected canons to the chapter of Santa Cecilia di Decimo. As at Fabbrica, Campoli, and Castelfiorentino, episcopal control of all clerical appointments served to protect the bishop's jurisdictional rights and privileges. The first mention of a *podestà* in the parish of San Martino del Vescovo was in 1244, but these officials were still appearing in the documents in 1272 and 1302. Not surprisingly, the two *podestà* for these years were both members of the Visdomini and Tosinghi lineages: Lottieri dei Visdomini (1272) and Goffredo della Tosa (1302). The episcopal *podesteria* was clearly a major source of income and power for the Visdomini and Tosinghi into the early fourteenth century.[173]

As at Castelfiorentino and in the *plebatus* of Campoli, all new leases after 1300 were commercial, short-term, and made for grain rents.[174] For example, in the parish of Santo Stefano di Petriolo, on June 24, 1304, the episcopal syndic, Ser Manno, leased to Ghinuccio di Azzino from San Casciano di Decimo the former fief of the deceased Farenso di Bongianno di Cardolo da Cigliano for five years for five *moggi*.[175] Customary hereditary tenures still persisted, but as Appendix D demonstrates for the entire Val di Pesa, they made up only about 40 percent of the total number of leases. The remaining 60 percent were short-term leases. In the early fourteenth century the first recorded commercial lease at Santa Cecilia di Decimo involved a *podere* in the parish of San Casciano with house, vineyard, and wood, which episcopal officials leased for five years for eight *moggi* (as well as for quantities of meat, eggs, and capons).[176] The increased commercialization of leases at Decimo and San Casciano—whose dues were often difficult to collect because of hereditary division, sale, and outright opposition—led to the leasing of all income in the *plebatus*. The bishop made the first such lease to a local craftsman (Caruccio di Saracino, a baker or *fornaio* from San

Casciano) for eight years for thirteen *moggi*.[177] In 1319 Bishop Antonio degli Orsi combined the income from the *plebatus* of Decimo with that of Campoli into one lease and conferred it on a Florentine, Vanno di Bianco del Canello from the parish of San Simone. The terms specified a lease of one year at a *census* of 20 moggi. The growing presence of Florentines in the *plebatus* mirrored developments at Monte di Croce and Poggialvento near Passignano.[178]

Episcopal Officials in the Plebatus *of Campoli and Decimo*

On the local level the arch-priests, parish rectors, and episcopal *podestà* were the primary episcopal officials. In the *plebatus* of Campoli, the prelate could appoint the rectors of the following parishes in the thirteenth and fourteenth centuries: Fabbrica, San Miniato di Pappiano, San Fabbiano, and San Geminiano di Petroio. The tie with the bishop was especially strong for the rectors of San Gaudenzo, San Geminiano di Petroio, Fabbrica, and San Fabbiano, as at one time or another (the sources do not provide complete information) they leased episcopal property.

Partly as a response to the tradition of resistance by local parishes supporting episcopal tenants (and often supported by other ecclesiastical lords, like the cathedral chapter), bishops in the late thirteenth and early fourteenth century developed a more sophisticated bureaucracy of officials who worked the entire diocese. The mid-twelfth century provides the first evidence that *castaldi* and *procuratores* were acting on behalf of the bishop in the *plebatus*. These earliest representatives appear to be local men, appointed *ad hoc*. By 1300, however, a very elaborate system of administration had emerged, one that relied on the Florence-based episcopal *familia*. Although bishops Lottieri and Antonio continued to oversee directly some of their own business, their syndics (like Chele Cursi or the notary Bindo da Calenzano) worked throughout the diocese, leasing, orchestrating collective oaths, and collecting rent payments. The *podestà*, wherever they continued to be appointed, continued to be paid a *staio* of grain per household. Similarly, the syndics tended to be paid at the expense of local residents. For example, one syndic was able to take possession of property in the parish of Capalle as his own payment.[179] Although the bishops appear never to have systematized the bureaucracy formally, they increasingly relied on managers whose concerns covered the entire *mensa*. One well-documented example serves to explain how the network was organized.

This example brings us back to Fabbrica. Reliance on local officials to orchestrate unpopular measures often elicited strong negative reactions from the people most closely affected. In the case of Sant'Andrea di Fabbrica, local opposition could fuse with the interests of the cathedral chapter to call into question episcopal hegemony in the entire *plebatus*. When the bishop deposed the rector of Fabbrica in 1259, the arch-priest of Campoli (nominally beholden to the bishop) supported the rector and was deposed as well. For the next thirty years there was very little evidence of tension, but the simmering tensions surfaced again in 1286.

Having gained access to the See of St. Zanobi in 1286, Andrea de' Mozzi began immediately to use episcopal property to benefit his kinsmen. In 1291 the arch-priest of Campoli—presumably loyal to the bishop—sold two parts of a *podere* at Campoli to a member of the Mozzi lineage for two hundred *lire*.[180] Apparently, this loss of local property to a Florentine lineage associated with the bishop led to the emergence of a local party of opposition to episcopal lordship in the *plebatus*, centered in the chapter of the *plebs* of Santo Stefano di Campoli. When the arch-priest of Campoli, Teglaio, died in 1295, the chapter acted quickly to appoint an arch-priest who would be sensitive to local concerns and would not act as a surrogate for episcopal policies. Having not forgotten the events of 1259 and the legacy of the 1236 commutations, the chapter attempted to short-circuit the exercise of episcopal control in the area.

Claiming the *ius electionis*, the canons of Campoli designated the abbot of San Casciano di Montescalari in the diocese of Fiesole to elect the new arch-priest.[181] His choice was Stefano da Broy, a canon in the cathedral of Florence who was close to the papacy.[182] As one would expect, Bishop Andrea de' Mozzi opposed the new choice of arch-priest. He appointed his own man, Alessandro da Pugna.[183] From the bishop's point of view, the stakes were extremely high. A loss of the right to control the appointment of the arch-priest of the richest episcopal *plebs* (Campoli) could jeopardize the privileged position of his lineage in the Florentine church. For the canons of Campoli it was a local concern, but for the cathedral chapter the contest was one more incident in a long series of struggles between lineages over church resources. Therefore, the abbot and canons took the dispute to the papal curia and argued for the invalidation of the episcopal election. They received confirmation of their choice from the papal curia and news of the cancellation of the election of Alessandro.[184]

The new bishop, Francesco Monaldeschi, disregarded the papal representative's decision and appointed Talano della Tosa as the new arch-priest on April 30, 1297. Drawing on the language of the legal tradition of church patronage, Bishop Francesco claimed that only he could name the new arch-priest by virtue of his position as lord and patron of Santo Stefano di Campoli.[185] On August 10, 1299 (probably aware that they were able to keep their choice), the chapter of Santo Stefano di Campoli ordered Stefano da Broy to reach an agreement with the bishop. Recognizing the bishop as the rightful lord and patron (*dominus et patronus*) of Santo Stefano di Campoli, the chapter was able to keep Stefano as arch-priest (provided that he swore obedience to and was confirmed by the bishop).[186] To save face, the bishop compelled his previous arch-priest, Talano della Tosa, to resign on August 22 on the grounds that Talano was already an arch-priest in another church and was too busy to serve in both.[187] On August 24, the bishop had Stefano invested with the spiritual possessions of the church, and Stefano pledged obedience to his lord and patron.[188] On August 25 the arch-priest withdrew his suits against the bishop at the papal curia.[189] A day later the episcopal delegate inducted Stefano into the corporeal possessions of the parish. Except for a brief period when the conflict emerged out in the open again, the papal court settled the matter in 1307 by re-affirming the terms of the agreement.[190] Although the bishop had succeeded in being recognized as the sole patron (*dominus et patronus*) in 1299, he was unable to appoint his own man as arch-priest.[191]

The dispute, therefore, was more than just a conflict over the rights of patronage in the *plebs*. It was a struggle for supreme authority, and it took place on four different levels. On one level, the conflict pitted the bishop of Florence against the chapter of Campoli—episcopal lordship exercised from Florence against the desire for local autonomy. The selection of Stefano was an attempt to block further economic penetration by the bishop into the *plebatus* when the bishop was consolidating and concentrating his properties there following several commutations. Second, the clash pitted the bishops against the cathedral chapter of Florence. The reader has seen that after 1275 the bishop and chapter increasingly came into conflict over property and ecclesiastical honors in the city. It is likely that the cathedral chapter—in which Stefano was a prominent member—took the opportunity of the dispute between the bishop and the *plebs* of Campoli to attempt to weaken the bishop's power where he was strongest. Third—although further research is needed—it is possible that the controversy pitted the principal aristocratic lineages and their factions against one another: the Adimari (the cathedral chapter) and the Visdomini (the bishopric). The appointment of Talano della Tosa by Bishop Francesco was part of a pattern of control of episcopal properties by the Visdomini and Tosinghi patrilineages—a pattern resisted by local parish chapters. Fourth, the conflict set the interests of the papacy for direct control of Florentine clerical affairs against those of the Florentine bishop. Although the papal court was able to present itself as an "objective" arbiter, it was anything but neutral. Canon law—in this particular instance, the tradition of church patronage (*ius patronatus*)—was an effective instrument for the creation and reinforcement of a hierarchy of power within the church with the papacy at the apex. The history of this case demonstrates how the papal bureaucracy around 1300 used the legal tradition of patronage (*ius patronatus*) to hasten the subordination of the Florentine episcopate to papal interests. Throughout his pontificate, Boniface VIII sought to neutralize any independent challenge to his authority in Tuscany in order to place it under the exclusive rule of his family, the Caetani.[192] Given the extreme animosity existing between the bishop and the Florentine clergy over embezzlement, the diversion of hospital funds, and the determination of the bishop to tax the clergy to pay for the consecration of his predecessor,[193] Boniface VIII attempted to strengthen his own position with the anti-episcopal clergy by supporting them against the bishop. There was therefore the conjuncture of two separate but interlocking forces interested in weakening episcopal power: the chapter of Campoli wanted to assert independence of the bishop, and Popes Nicholas IV and Boniface VIII wanted to bend the bishops to their will. By 1309 the papacy had succeeded in making the Florentine episcopate an arm of papal policy, and the resolution of this particular case played an important role in that process.[194]

Innovations in Episcopal Administration

Between 1251 and 1321 the Florentine bishops faced great financial difficulties and witnessed a gradual loss of jurisdictional power in the countryside to the commune of Florence. In the face of these fiscal pressures, however, the bishops were able to stabilize income relative to expenses by continuing to adapt the management of the episcopal estate to the demands of an urban commercial economy. Indeed, in the late thirteenth century the bishops and their estate managers continued successfully to integrate the *mensa* into the regional market economy. Most episcopal income continued to come from rents, so the initiatives primarily affected landed property. Overall, these very important innovations effectively shielded the bishopric from the effects of the steady debasement of the Florentine *denaro*, which fell in value by almost 50 percent between 1280 and 1340.[195] Unfortunately, systematic records do not begin until the early fourteenth century, so it is impossible to quantify the data in a precise way before that date.

Several innovations in the nature of the management of the estate are apparent from the records. First, the granting of leases for a limited number of years began in the second half of the thirteenth century, as it had in the diocese of Arezzo as well. This made it easier for the bishops to set the terms of the leases according to market forces. As the population continued to increase until the early decades of the fourteenth century, commercial rents tended to rise (much of the bishops' holdings were located in the fertile bottom lands of the river valleys). This was not an uncommon practice: the monastery of Sant'Ambrogio (Milan) introduced fixed-term leases after 1257. Presumably, the tenants brought most of their grain payments to the city, where the price per *staio* was probably higher than the price at the rural markets. That price fluctuated a great deal, but it did increase more than the *denaro* was debased during the seventy years covered in this chapter (in some cases by 100 percent), giving the bishop a handsome return.[196]

Second, episcopal administrators leased the collection of rents in particular areas of the *contado* to a single individual for a set grain rent to assure themselves that the bishop would receive a determined amount of grain every year (regardless of the number of tenants who either failed or refused to pay their *census*). As on the estates of the cathedral chapter of Cremona, this practice contributed to the creation of a large class of intermediaries between the ecclesiastical lord and those actually working the soil.[197] In Florence most of those intermediaries were urban dwellers. The practice of this type of leasing, therefore, helped spread urban influence into the countryside at the end of the thirteenth century and promoted the integration of the *contado* into the economic and political orbit of the city.

Finally, there developed a very extensive and sophisticated bureaucracy to serve the needs of the episcopate. Modern management techniques initiated in the middle of the thirteeth century minimized the extent of the crisis and stabilized ecclesiastical income into the fourteenth century. As newer lineages (such as the Mozzi, Bardi, and Medici) increasingly displaced the older aristocracy and sought access to ecclesiastical property for themselves, they were were able to take full advantage of these new techniques to enhance their economic and political position within the city. Furthermore, apparently unlike other northern Italian bishops (such as the bishops of Lucca), the Florentine prelates energetically developed urban property, especially around the Baptistery and the episcopal palace. Far from representing a holdover from an earlier age, the Florentine episcopate successfully commercialized its patrimony and created a stable and dependable source of income for generations thereafter. For the rural population, however, the consequences were not as salutary. The successful extension of direct urban jurisdiction into the *contado* occurred simultaneously as more urban residents purchased land in the countryside and as the bishops depended more on urban intermediaries to collect their rents. The stabilization of the fortunes of the urban elite quickened the loss of control by the rural population over their own lives. Between 1250 and 1320 the managers of the *mensa* successfully adapted the estate to the demands of the regional market economy, and assured that the patrimony would continue to function as an economic and political resource for the Florentine elite.

Conclusion

The ancient churches of Sant'Ippolito di Castelfiorentino, Santa Cecilia di Decimo, and San Lorenzo di Borgo stand as mute reminders of a vanished territorial lordship, replaced now by the prosperous towns of Castelfiorentino, San Casciano Val di Pesa, and Borgo San Lorenzo. Where once the episcopal tenants cultivated the grain in the river valleys that went to their lord's granaries, there are now rural factories, vineyards, and second homes for the wealthy. Only San Miniato al Monte, the palace of Andrea de' Mozzi adjacent to that basilica, the sarcophagus of Giovanni da Velletri in the Baptistery, and the abandoned ruins of the *castello* of Monte di Croce remind the contemporary visitor that at one time the bishops played a dominant role in the life of the Florentine city and countryside. Episcopal power from the eleventh to the early fourteenth centuries had both a material and an ideological dimension (*potestas jurisdictionis* and *potestas ordinis*), and the two were inextricably intertwined. The bishop's charismatic authority assisted both him and those members of the elite associated with his office to acquire and maintain power and aristocratic status in the community. Similarly, the economic influence and status enjoyed by both the bishop and the lineages close to him guaranteed them a central place in the principal ceremonial and liturgical rituals in Florence. To those living in the diocese between the eleventh and fourteenth centuries—regardless of class—each side of his identity appeared to "resemble" or reflect the other.[1] The concept of power used in this study, therefore, has been a broad one; it is not limited to material interests. Only in the twelfth century did legal theorists begin to draw distinctions between the bishop's temporal and spiritual powers—powers which were never distinct in practice. In the *Decretum* of 1141, Gratian distinguished the *potestas iurisdictionis* (the supreme legislative, judicial, governmental authority over the clergy and administrative power over properties) from

the *potestas ordinis* (the authority to ordain priests, promote the venera-
tion of saints, issue excommunications, say Mass, or hear confession).[2]
The bishop's fortunes therefore depended not only on his authority as
landlord or banal *seigneur,* but also on his ability to promote the cults of
saints, make clerical appointments, and invent ceremonial processions.
At a time when social theorists and some historians increasingly seem
to emphasize the consensual and ahistorical nature of ritual (almost to
the total exclusion of material concerns), it is very important for us to
remember that at the heart of many (but not all) rituals are real material
interests and conflicts.[3]

The prelates in these three centuries were economic strategists as well
as spiritual leaders, but at least four major factors limited and condi-
tioned the nature of their power. First, rivalry between the bishops and
the rural patrilineages over land, *castelli,* and clients was always present,
even after 1197. Whereas at Lucca the primary conflict for the episcopate
shifted from clashes with the rural lineages to clashes with the rural
communes, in the diocese of Florence there always existed conflict with
the patrilineages in one form or another.[4] Second, throughout this period peasants and merchants residing in the rural communities under the
authority of the bishop constantly resisted the demands he placed on
them for rents, court fines, and taxes. Third, the strategic interests of the
commune of Florence set limits to the functioning of episcopal lordship,
especially after the death of the Countess Matilda. Finally, throughout
this period many Florentines—including Guarino, Giovanni Gualberto,
the Cathars, and even Dante Alighieri—recognized the contradiction
between the spiritual claims of the bishop and the material reality of his
power, and they often acted to oppose his lordship. To the bishop the
dual nature of his power was necessary, but to this long Florentine spiritual tradition it was unacceptable.

Our story of episcopal lordship began in the first half of the eleventh
century, when the bishops began the process of reclamation and preservation of their properties and jurisdictional rights. Their increased
strength led in mid-century to the actual expansion of episcopal possessions into the river valleys of the Florentine countryside. Threatened by
the interests of the Guidi and Cadolingi, who coveted episcopal properties, sensitive to the challenges to his authority issued by Abbot Guarino
of Settimo, and eager to provide a patrimony for his own offspring,
Bishop Ildebrando of Florence set out to preserve and protect the episcopal patrimony by orchestrating a revival of the cult of St. Minias. The
centerpiece of that program was the founding and construction of San
Miniato al Monte, endowed with properties by Ildebrando and his successors in or near areas of Cadolingi and Guidi strength. For the succes-

sors of Bishop Ildebrando, donations to the monastery and basilica continued to serve as a method of reclaiming lost properties as well as of acquiring new domains. When accused of simony by Giovanni Gualberto, Pietro Mezzabarba responded to the challenge by following the paradigm established by his predecessor Ildebrando, but he focused the spiritual and political program on the city, not on the countryside. He consecrated a new urban convent, San Pier Maggiore, and linked himself closely to the *charisma* of two urban saints, St. Zanobi and St. Peter.

It is apparent on the basis of this study that the commonly used phrase *reform movement* actually distorts rather than clarifies our understanding of the radical changes in ecclesiastical life in Tuscany in the first half of the eleventh century. Indeed, many historians have developed their views of this period from the later "reform propaganda" associated with the *Vita Johannis Gualberti* and the work of Peter Damian and Hildebrand (later Pope Gregory VII), which read into early disputes the agenda of the late-eleventh-century reformers. It is very difficult indeed to disentangle the issues of lay investiture, clerical marriage, simony, and the struggle between empire and papacy. However, it is evident that we can get a full understanding of eleventh-century church history only by studying first the local origin of the disputes over clerical marriage or the involvement of churchmen in a monetarized economy. It is important to explain the events in Florence first "on their own terms."

Seen in this light, the term *reform movement* is a misnomer. Rather, there existed at least two "traditions" in Florence to reorder or remake ecclesiastical and social life. They began in the first decade of the eleventh century and consisted of both an episcopal and an anti-episcopal component. Paradoxically, the drive for ecclesiastical renewal in Florence originated on one hand in the policies of Ildebrando and his successors, and on the other hand in the campaigns of the anti-episcopal factions led by Guarino and Giovanni Gualberto. The earliest stages of this movement for renewal took the form of a struggle between two factions within Florence: an anti-episcopal party against clerical marriage led by Guarino, and an episcopal tradition which was determined to reassert the temporal and spiritual influence of the bishop in the light of the emergence of the powerful rural patrilineages. The actual formation of the episcopal *mensa* as it appeared in the twelfth and thirteenth centuries began during the episcopates of Lamberto, Attone, and Gerardo. These bishops also restructured the cathedral chapter to limit the influence of laymen and improve the quality of spiritual life.

By the middle of the century, the anti-episcopal faction—led by Giovanni Gualberto—had embraced the abolition of simony as its primary issue and had successfully expelled the prelate from the city. The common denominator between the parties of Guarino and Giovanni Gualberto was opposition to the temporal authority and material interests of the bishops. Whereas the former was most concerned with clerical marriage and the influence of women in clerical life, and the latter focused on the association of the bishop with money and lordship, they both adhered to a spiritual program that embraced poverty, chastity, and asceticism. Aristocratic rural houses like the Cadolingi continued to support the efforts of this anti-episcopal tradition for their own interests, which were not always spiritual. Indeed, instead of attempting to thwart the efforts of Guarino and Giovanni Gualberto, these aristocratic lineages supported them.[5] Therefore, both of the two traditions or tendencies present in Florence—the episcopal and anti-episcopal—were important formative influences on the later Gregorian reform movement. The papacy of a bishop of Florence, Nicholas II (1059–1061), and the general European interest in the work of Giovanni Gualberto brought the Florentine experience to center stage. Indeed, aspects of both traditions emerged in the program of later eleventh- and twelfth-century reformers: the reclamation and protection of church property from the power of laymen, the abolition of simony, and the promotion of clerical celibacy.[6] What happened in Florence had continental repercussions.

A study of episcopal power not only provides insight into the development of the movement for the "reordering" of ecclesiastical life (to borrow Gerd Tellenbach's phrase), but it also helps us understand the forces behind the appearance of rural communes in the countryside after 1180. From the standpoint of the local rural population, the emergence of episcopal territorial lordships (*signorie territoriali*) represented an intrusive interference in local affairs by an urban bureaucracy and marked the loss of a measure of local autonomy from outsiders. Tenant obligations before 1180 were not onerous. All that changed at the end of the twelfth century. Before 1200 peasant resistance usually involved peasants acting as individuals or as members of a kinship group. After 1200, however, the resistance assumed a collective aspect, pitting the bishops against entire communities. The commutations, the collection of the *datium*, the collection of court fines, the taxation of immovable property (which affected primarily the merchant), the establishment of episcopal *podesterie*, and the dramatic rise in control of the countryside by the bishops through the purchasing and concentration of property led to widespread discontent. Episcopal tenants found that these measures had eroded the amount of marketable surplus available to them. After 1225 donations and purchases of property declined, but the level of conflict increased. Many communities of tenants and merchants took advantage of the disarray in the countryside caused by war (1207–1208, 1227–1235) to seek independence from episcopal control. Later, during the wars with Arezzo and Pisa between 1287 and 1293, the level of conflict increased as well.

The rural communes studied in this book emerged at the end of the twelfth and the beginning of the thirteenth centuries primarily as the result of the the exercise of episcopal lordship. The evidence presented by this study therefore supports recent studies which indicate that the territorial lordship not only set the bounds of the rural commune, but it was actually the stimulus which provoked its formation.[7] As we have seen, the documentation in Florence indicates that the bishops played both a positive and a negative role in the formation of the communes. The large number of purchases of properties by the bishops were the means by which they attempted to harness the already existing social and economic forces in the *contado* for their own benefit. Primarily, the episcopate attempted to dominate the mercantile networks in the Val di Pesa, at Castelfiorentino, in the central Valdarno Fiorentino, and in the central Mugello by making its *curiae* the foci of economic activity. Such policies suited the Florentine elite because they increased the amount of grain available to a growing population. Episcopal policies might not have created all the markets (social and economic forces did that), but they certainly enhanced the market forces already present. Also, the introduction of the oaths of fidelity (*iuramenta*) and the *podesteria* brought the episcopal dependents of rural communities together. They came to realize they had common interests, and the *podestà* gave them a model of self-government. Collective activity in the countryside had an extremely important role in Florentine history, more than has hitherto been emphasized.[8]

The challenge to episcopal lordship posed by the rural communes occurred at the same time that the urban guilds and the commune gradually displaced the bishop as the principal custodian of the urban cults (particularly of St. John) and of the major ecclesiastical establishments. Beginning at the end of the twelfth century, the merchant guilds (especially the Calimala) mananged to insinuate themselves into the management and administration of several of the most important religious entities in the city. Challenges to episcopal spiritual authority took another form as well: the Cathars attempted to undermine the authority of the bishop (the symbol of orthodoxy); their acts contributed to the creation of a vacuum of power in which challenges to episcopal lordship could flourish. Florentine communal authorities (both Guelf and Ghibelline) realized that a challenge to spiritual authority was also a challenge to temporal lordship. By the middle of the thirteenth century, the commune and the urban guilds had shorn the bishop of most of his authority as the protector and custodian of the cults of the principal urban saints. However, the commune was unwilling to preside over the unraveling of the power of a major defender of the interests of the city in the *contado*. The Florentine elite was determined to maintain stability in the countryside and prevent the emergence of autonomous communities over which it would have had no control. Consequently, it protected episcopal interests as long as they did not conflict with its own.

After the middle of the thirteenth century the rural communes continued to challenge episcopal authority. Several other factors contributed to circumscribing episcopal lordship after 1250: periodic taxation by the commune and papacy, the continuation of a tradition of resistance to episcopal policies by tenants, rising expenses relative to income, and the diversion of property to benefit the patrilineages associated with the episcopate (the Visdomini, Tosinghi, and Aliotti houses). As a result, the bishop in particular and the Florentine church in general were unable to increase their income to keep pace with growing expenses. Indeed, the entire Tuscan church seems to have fallen into debt, including the bishoprics of Massa Marittima, Fiesole, Arezzo, and Volterra. As their temporal authority declined vis-à-vis the commune, the bishops and the lineages associated with them attempted to compensate for that political and economic weakness by expanding and embellishing their involvement in ritual, particularly the entry of the new bishops into the city. Episcopal taxation to fund those entries became a major fiscal burden for the entire Florentine clergy.

On the episcopal lands the bishops and their administrators responded to their problems creatively: they introduced the short-term commercial lease, they leased all income in selected *plebes* to a single individual for a single payment in grain (in the Val di Pesa, the Mugello, and Castelfiorentino), and they threw enormous resources into the development of leasable property in Florence itself. The changes in the management and exploitation of the episcopal *mensa* after 1250 diminished but did not arrest the fiscal pressures; they mitigated but did not end the burden of debt. As we have seen, they also contributed to creating a new class of intermediaries between the bishops and their tenants in the countryside—intermediaries who increasingly came from the city and contributed to ending direct management of the episcopal properties by the bishop after 1250. Nevertheless, these innovations placed the episcopal patrimony on a very stable financial footing by the second decade of the fourteenth century. Urban rents appear to have been especially promising for the future. The principal lineages of the city—composed of some of the older *consorterie* who survived as well as some of the newer lineages like the Medici and Bardi—continued to look at the episcopate in particular and the church in general as sources of prestige and power well into the fourteenth and fifteenth centuries.[9]

Episcopal Lords and Aristocratic Lineages in City and Countryside

The rise and fall of many of the Florentine aristocratic patrilineages—both rural and urban—were directly linked to the fortunes of church property, offices, and honors. Indeed, the patrilineage as a novel form of social organization emerged at the end of the tenth and beginning of the eleventh centuries around patrimonies which included ecclesiastical properties.[10] Its eclipse was also linked to the history of ecclesiastical resources.[11] To preserve the coherence of their patrimonies and to encourage kinship solidarity, many of these new patrilineages established proprietary monasteries in the countryside throughout Tuscany. At the same time the bishops of Florence wished to protect and expand the episcopal *mensa*. We can explain much of the subsequent development of the episcopal estate by focusing on the tension between the interests of the agnatic lineages and those of the prelates. When Florentine churches fell into debt in the middle of the thirteenth century, the economic pressures increased greatly for those aristocratic patrilineages most closely associated with ecclesiastical resources. Not only is the history of church property crucial for an understanding of the structural development of the Florentine elite families, it is also a key to understanding the social transformation of the Florentine elite and the relationship of countryside to city.

This study has indicated that the bishops of Florence exercised at least two "ideal" types of lordship (*signoria*) in three separate periods between 1000 and 1320. Labor obligations appear to have been negligible in the period covered by this study. Indeed, they had largely disappeared by 1200. Between 1000 and 1180 the bishops derived their power primarily from the ownership of land and *castelli* (a *signoria fondiaria*), and the dominant unit of exploitation was the *curtis* (estate). They exercised some rights derived from the public powers granted them by the margraves or emperors (possession of certain *castelli* and the ability to collect public taxes), but those powers were not extensive. By the twelfth century the *curtis* and the *castello* together formed the *curia*. In this phase the possession of *castelli* was essential for the maintenance and protection of episcopal interests. By the end of the twelfth century the prelates had established a network of territorial lordships (*signorie territoriali*) in the major river valleys of the diocese. Between 1250 and 1320—challenged by the rural communes and largely stripped of much of their spiritual power—they were forced to revert to a different type of lordship; land-lordship (*signoria fondiaria*). The bishops continued to draw some income from the rural communes with which they had concluded pacts in mid-century. Though they no longer exercised the extensive seigneurial rights over several communities that they had before 1250, they presided over an estate carefully adapted to the exigencies of a regional commercial economy focused around Florence.

In every phase of the development of episcopal lordship, vassalic relations played a minor role in the exercise of episcopal power. In the eleventh and twelfth centuries, certain episcopal vassals (the Buondelmonti, the lords of Petriolo, and the Ubaldini) donated their *castelli* and estates to the bishop and received them back in fief (at Petriolo it is possible they received a disguised loan from the bishop). They apparently held that property in exchange for administrative and military services. These vassals participated in several twelfth-century sieges, including those of Montegufoni and Monte di Croce, and they apparently assisted the bishops to administer *castelli* before the creation of the regional *podesteria* (as the Ubaldini did in the twelfth century). Service to the bishop was synonymous with service to the commune. The next reference comes from a later period. In 1304, the chronicler Simone della Tosa recorded that Bishop Lottieri della Tosa was able to mobilize four thousand men against his kinsman Rossellino della Tosa.[12] Whether all these men were vassals (in the sense that they were fief-holders in exchange for military service) is doubtful. Perhaps many were hired or were episcopal clients. Most *fideles* simply would not have been able to afford miltary service, unless they served as foot soldiers.

After 1180, the bishops drew on the language of feudo-vassalic relations to define and clarify the obligations owed by dependents in the episcopal territories. The introduction of servile oaths (*iuramenta fidelitatis*) did not change the nature of already existing relationships between bishop and dependent. However, it did more than simply clarify a relationship of dependence: it provided written documentation for the Florentine courts that certain individuals were legally bound to fulfill their obligations to the bishop. These courts were sympathetic to episcopal interests. The Florentines supported the continuation of episcopal power in the countryside because until the middle of the thirteenth century the bishops were one of the few urban lords with substantial holdings in the *contado*. As the urban elite pondered how to secure the vital interests of the Arno city, they knew that a key requirement was the perpetuation of episcopal power in the countryside, not its destruction.[13] This concern to preserve episcopal lordship became especially important in the late twelfth and early thirteenth centuries, when the urban elite was determined to preserve its hegemony over the emerging rural communes.

The bishops were urban as well as rural lords. The Visdomini and Tosinghi were urban dwellers and had interests in both city and country. Because Florence never set out to "conquer" or "subjugate" its countryside, it relied on any method available to it to obtain military security, access to a dependable grain supply, troops, and revenue. Uninterested in the emancipation of its rural population, Florence wanted stability, order, and security, not freedom and liberation. This study should caution historians from viewing the relationship of city to countryside as a necessarily conflictual one (as Salvemini believed) that pit a "feudal" elite (the producers) against urban merchants, artisans, and bankers (the consumers). Furthermore, it should prevent us from identifying the commune with the forces of freedom and the rural lineages with the chains of serfdom. The old categories are no longer adequate, and we must create new terms of classification and analysis consistent with the documentary evidence.

Although this study suggests that the relationship between city and *contado* was not as exploitive as Caggese, Davidsohn, and Salvemini thought, neither was it as conflict-free as Fiumi argued. Perhaps it is most accurate to see it as a conflictual relationship before 1250 but as an increasingly symbiotic one after that, for city and countryside were to become unified by an increasingly integrated regional economy, by a growing number of urban landholders in the *contado,* by the immigration of rural residents into the city, and by the political and economic needs of the urban elite.[14] Unlike the local aristocracy in the Casentino and Garfagnana before 1200 (tied politically to Arezzo and Lucca, respectively), the local aristocracy in the Florentine *contado* was not traditionally oriented to the city.[15] Indeed, it continually resisted urban penetration into the countryside throughout the three periods covered by this study. Even the Buondelmonti and Ubaldini, who were episcopal vassals from the eleventh century, often opposed the episcopal and urban presence. After 1250, however, and even more so after 1300, the flourishing urban market drew all areas of the *contado* into its orbit, while at the same time urban lineages increasingly acquired rural property. The ecclesiastical lords were no longer the only major urban lords in the countryside. By the mid-fourteenth century city and countryside formed a symbiotic unit, and the episcopate had played a major role in that process. The lesson from this case-study of episcopal power is clear: in medieval Italy the economic, social, cultural, and political connections between city and countryside were inextricably close. One cannot explain developments in one without making reference to the other.

Unlike Volterra, Pistoia, and Luni, the city of Florence never had to face a formidable political adversary in the bishop during its formative period of development. And unlike the bishops of those communes, the bishop of Florence had never been closely allied with the emperor in the late eleventh and twelfth centuries. Consequently, he never received vast imperial grants of property and jurisdictional power from the emperor. And unlike the bishops of Luni and Arezzo, the bishop had never enjoyed comital powers. The episcopate was too weak to pose a threat to Florence, but it was strong enough to serve as a surrogate of Florentine power in the countryside. When the commune attempted to impose its hegemony over its own territory, it did not have to do so in spite of its bishop. The bishops and the lineages associated with them were tied closely to the interests of the commune. The social and economic history of the estate of the bishops of Florence is consequently in microcosm also the history of the social and economic transformation of the Florentine countryside. The two generations between 1180 and 1250 mark the crucial watershed in Florentine history—a period when the economy of the countryside became oriented and adapted to the urban market. With economic integration came political integration.

The pursuit of communal interests required the maintenance of episcopal power in the countryside—the exercise of which provoked local rural opposition. Resistance to the bishops was often synonymous with resistance to urban influence. There were several sharp upsurges of conflict and disorder on episcopal properties: 1205–1210, 1220–1225, 1235–1240, 1255–1260, 1270–1275, and 1295–1300. Security in the countryside meant that Florence had to contain or control disorder on episcopal lands during these periods of disarray. Furthermore, there were serious periods of war during the following years: 1207–1208, 1228–1235, 1260, 1287–1293, and 1305-1310 (some of which corresponded to the years of disorder). Another factor which contributed to the climate of disorder was the tradition among the peasantry of refusing to accept the lordship of a new bishop after the death of a former prelate and of failing to pay the yearly rents. Hence, whenever a new bishop took office, the documents record an increase in the number of conflicts on episcopal property involving episcopal jurisdiction. Perhaps this is a milder form of the "ritual sackings" of papal and episcopal property in central Italy presently studied by Carlo Ginzburg and his students at Bologna.[16]

From the standpoint of the rural population which had not immigrated into the city, the growing influence of the city in the *contado* carried with it a corresponding loss of autonomy. Florentine defense of episcopal rights at the beginning of the thirteenth century meant that peasants were forced to cultivate a crop, even against their will, to be handed over to an urban authority (the bishop). Many—as in the Mugello—faced military occupation. Others lost their properties to urban creditors or landlords. After 1276 the city had its representatives in every *plebatus*. Finally, with the growing popularity of the *mezzadria*—linked to property-holding by urban landlords—many *contadini* found themselves part of the new class of proletarian laborers.[17] Those who could no longer make a living off the land immigrated into the city to become unskilled laborers.

This study of the Florentine bishops—who played such an important role in the history of the commune—should caution us from assuming that the formation of the territorial state was necessarily benign or inevitable.[18] Furthermore, as the overview of the magnate problem has indicated, we cannot fully explain political changes within the city without taking into consideration what was happening in the countryside.[19] In Florence, the extension of urban hegemony met stiff resistance from rural communities. In fact, as Giorgio Chittolini has argued, the failure of Italian communes like Florence to subjugate fully their *contadi* and provide stable order led later to the formation of new, more centralized, and more bureaucratized regional states.[20]

The Florentine Elite and Feudalism

Defined narrowly in a juridical sense, *feudalism* as a term of analysis is inadequate to describe the nature of Florentine episcopal power and lordship. Indeed, as a recent synthesis has indicated, feudalism defined in this way never really existed.[21] As a description of a mode of production, however, the term does have some relevance. It provides us with a means of charting economic change on the eve of the Black Death. According to this definition, feudalism is the exploitive social and economic relationship between landowners and a subject population in which surplus beyond the needs of subsistence of the latter—whether in direct labor, in rents in money or kind, or in banal exactions—is transferred to the former, often unwillingly. Fief-holding and vassal-age—the hierarchical social organization of the elite—are not necessary components of this mode of production in a given locality. The power of the lord depends on his ownership of land as well as his extra-economic authority.[22] In the case of the bishop of Florence, the charismatic dimension of his power was a crucial component of his lordship. The conflict on episcopal lands that is documented after 1150 resulted from the dialectical interplay of the desire of the bishops and episcopal families to increase the surplus transferred to them on one hand and the determination of peasants and rural merchants to retain that surplus on the other.

The prelates of Florence contributed to the transformation of the economy of Florence into one of the most advanced in Europe. The development of the episcopal estate after 1180 was not only a creative adjustment to economic pressure coming from the new bureaucracies (the commune and the papacy) and from an increasingly commercialized environment; it was also the response on the part of the episcopate to the continued presence of conflict and rebellion on episcopal lands. Using the history of the Florentine episcopal estate as a case-study, we can see that feudalism as a mode of production was extremely adaptable and responsive to the social and economic challenges of the thirteenth and early fourteenth centuries. This study therefore supports the assertion that agrarian change in the thirteenth and fourteenth centuries did not necessarily lead to a feudal crisis and set the stage for a new type of economy.[23] Rather, the economy adjusted to new circumstances, and even after a painful period of re-adjustment (1250–1300) and the mid-fourteenth century crises, it continued to offer a stable and dependable source of income for the Florentine elite. The principal phases in the transition to capitalism in Tuscany were yet to come. In so far as it relates to the episcopal estate, the feudal economy a generation before the Black Death might not have been extremely healthy, but for its beneficiaries it was certainly resilient and adaptable.[24]

A feudal economy is associated with a landed nobility, but the Florentine aristocracy did not derive its power exclusively from its landed possessions. Indeed, those lineages with connections to the episcopate enjoyed access to rural as well as urban property. Who were the members of this aristocracy and where did they come from? More study is needed, but many of the early Florentine *milites* appear to have had a close association with the bishop and his *castelli*. Indeed, the development of the cult of St. Minias might very well have been an attempt to establish patronage relations with and obtain the political support of eleventh-century rural knights. Furthermore, many lineages of the Florentine aristocracy (including many with vast landed possessions) had enjoyed close relationships with the bishops over the three centuries covered by this book: the Visdomini, the Tosinghi, the Buondelmonti, and the Ubaldini. These lineages appear to some extent to have assumed an aristocratic identity through serving as episcopal vassals, *podestà,* and castellans during the period in which Florence drew its countryside into its military and economic orbit. Consequently, this study tends to validate the thesis of Giovanni Tabacco that the Florentine rural aristocracy formed around the rural *castelli* by providing military service during the period of communal expansion.[25] We must add, however, that those lineages associated with the episcopate also achieved aristocratic stature through their administrative services as well, particularly as the *podestà* of the episcopal territorial lordships. It was not only their military service in the *contado* which distinguished them; it was also their close association with church property, offices, and rituals.

The *milites* (knights) and the powerful landowners (*proceres*) came together to form a new hereditary aristocracy or nobility in Florence and elsewhere in northern Italy earlier than they did in northern Europe. Even before the formation of the commune, factional rivalries and vendettas had split this aristocracy into numerous cliques. The conflict between papacy and empire and the subjugation of the *contado* exacerbated already existing conflicts. Such divisions made possible the eventual triumph in the middle of the thirteenth century of the Florentine *popolo.* In northern Europe the knights and landowners were partially successful in creating a common defense against upwardly mobile merchants. In the words of Maurice Keen, the "two poles of the aristocracy drew together" because each one needed the another.[26] This apparently did not happen in Florence.

The study of the episcopal estate indicates several reasons why this was so. First, the "commercial revolution" had created a much more powerful mercantile elite in Florence and in northern Italy than anywhere else in Europe (with the exception of Flanders). The merchant class was able to challenge successfully the older aristocracy. Paradoxically, as occurred elsewhere in Europe from the fifteenth through nineteenth centuries, many of these prosperous *bourgeois* lineages attempted to "ennoble" themselves by seeking aristocratic status. In the case of Florence, a significant segment of the powerful mercantile elite (the Bardi, Cerchi, and Mozzi) attempted to do just that by seeking access to ecclesiastical property, by purchasing rural property, and even by becoming knights. For three centuries association with church property, offices, and honors had been a mark of aristocratic status. Because aristocratic status was so closely linked with ecclesiastical resources, economic pressures on church property in the second half of the thirteenth century helped create a social crisis for many among the Florentine elite. Finding themselves challenged by the *popolani,* many aristocratic houses increasingly fought among themselves for the limited amount of resources—resources often associated with the church. Conflict among members of the aristocracy over ecclesiastical resources is therefore an important and hitherto neglected factor that contributed to the climate of violence associated with the magnates before 1300. Many of the most important factional leaders during the tumultuous decade between 1282 and 1293 had close associations with church property, offices, and honors. Not surprisingly, they appeared on the list of magnates. Third, as Carol Lansing has argued, the overpopulation of males in these elite lineages might also have exacerbated disputes over property and initiated a structual crisis within the lineages. Clashes over access to church resources might have intensified these divisions.[27]

Another reason why at the end of the thirteenth century the aristocracy was so divided may relate to the fact that the Florentine *popolo* never tamed the power of those lineages closely associated with the episcopate (the Visdomini, the Tosinghi, and the Aliotti) nor of others associated with the cathedral chapter (the Adimari). In the last quarter of the thirteenth century these lineages were the leaders of some of the most important factions. Contrasts with the history of other communes is instructive. At the time of the rise of the *popolo,* the communes of Lucca and Siena ended the power of their episcopal *vicedomini* lineages. Conflicts between rival claimants in Lucca in 1241 led the commune to allow only notaries to administer vacant properties. By 1252 the *popolo* had captured the commune and magnates like the Avvocati were proscribed.[28] At Siena, the commune insisted after 1262 that only it had the right to administer the episcopate during a vacancy.[29] Such was not the case at Florence. When the *popolo* took power in 1250, they could not afford to eliminate the Visdomini. There were several reasons why this was so. First, the Visdomini and Tosinghi were fervent Guelfs, unlike their counterparts at Massa. They could rely on papal support.[30] Second, they had integrated themselves thoroughly into the Florentine elite in the twelfth and thirteenth centuries. Third, they were one of the principal urban lineages to have property in the countryside. Their privileged access to episcopal offices and property gave them power in both city and countryside. They served both as episcopal officials and as communal consuls. That continuity of interests helps explain the close association of the bishopric with the commune. The perpetuation of Visdomini and Tosinghi power after 1250 therefore helped set the stage for the political and social crisis in Florence at the end of the century.

Determined to create a climate of stability in which they could pursue their commercial interests, the Florentine guildsmen sought to curb internal conflicts and vendettas among the nobility by passing anti-magnate legislation in 1281, 1286, 1293, and 1295. If further studies of ecclesiastical lordships in the diocese of Florence confirm the conclusions of this analysis, it is reasonable then to conclude that the political dramas associated with the "magnate issue" at the end of the thirteenth and beginning of the fourteenth centuries were directly involved in the social crisis of those lineages whose wealth and power relied to a large extent on access to church property. Once the magnates found themselves forbidden by the Ordinances of Justice access to the major offices of the commune, they were closed out of the most prestigious posts of the city. Disputes over church property intensified as members of the magnate lineages attempted to stabilize their social and economic positions.[31] Comparison with the situation in Genoa is instructive. In that port city, the aristocracy from the twelfth century enjoyed diverse economic interests, including ownership of rights in port areas, markets, tolls, patronage rights, towers, and land. The power of the Genoese patriciate therefore derived from more sources than ecclesiastical resources.[32] If the history of the Florentine episcopate and the lineages associated with it is any indication, the history of church property is an essential and relatively unstudied dimension of Florentine social, economic, and political development. Furthermore, this survey of one church lord emphasizes how exceptional the history of Florence was, relative to other north Italian communes. Historians must therefore beware of extrapolating from the Florentine example to make generalizations about the history of northern Italy as a whole.

The lineages traditionally associated with episcopal and church property were not as powerful after 1300 as they had been before that date, but they did not disappear altogether either. The stabilization of episcopal income after 1250 contributed to a "crossing over" of members of the mercantile elite into the ranks of the magnate nobility sometime at the end of the thirteenth and the beginning of the fourteenth centuries. Increasingly, younger lineages (the Mozzi, the Bardi, and the Medici) associated initially with banking sought aristocratic status and attempted to appropriate for themselves ecclesiastical property. Even after 1295 the Florentine elite continued to approach church property as a major source of wealth, prestige, and power, which were seen to complement its primary interests in banking and trade. In his recent book on the Florentine church in the fifteenth century, Roberto Bizzocchi estimated that of the thirty-eight members of the cathedral chapter in 1500, only three came from lineages that belonged there before 1300. As older lineages lost their rights to church property and offices (like the Ubaldini and Sizi), newer lineages assumed them. Among the latter were the Medici and the Strozzi.[33]

Appalled that the Florentine church was a vehicle for the attainment of worldly ambitions and for the satisfaction of cupidity, Dante Alighieri called for the expropriation of the material wealth of the church.[34] He was echoing a sentiment that harked back to the time of Guarino. That this sentiment remained a relevant one is evident from the career of Antonio degli Orsi. As the papal inquest after his death in 1321 affirmed, the use of ecclesiastical property to benefit the episcopal lineages was continuing in the early decades of the *trecento*. It functioned to provide status, employment, and income for the family of Antonio degli Orsi, just as it had for the sons of Ildebrando three centuries earlier.

Abbreviations

AAF	Archivio Arcivescovile di Firenze
AAF *Aldobrandino*	*Imbreviature notarili di Romeo di Aldobrandino da Calenzano* (Archivio Arcivescovile di Firenze)
AA Fiesole	Archivio Arcivescovile di Fiesole
AAF *Libro*	*Libro dei Visdomini* (Archivio Arcivescovile di Firenze)
AAF *Martino*	*Libro dei contratti dal 1304–1329: estratto fatto di contratti appartenenti all'arcivescovado, segnato a, e rogato per Ser Benedetto di Maestro Martino, cominciando l'anno 1304* (Archivio Arcivescovile di Firenze)
ACF	Archivio del Capitolo Fiorentino
AS	*Acta Sanctorum Bollandistarum.* 3d ed. 62 vol. Brussels, 1863–1925.
ASF	Archivio di Stato di Firenze
ASF *Dipl.*	*Diplomatico* (Archivio di Stato di Firenze)
Archivio Generale	Archivio Generale dei contratti
Cestello	San Frediano in Cestello
Covi-Commenda	Santa Catarina detta dei Covi
Luco	Monastero di San Pietro di Luco di Mugello
Mannelli	Mannelli-Galilei-Riccardi, dono
Manni	Manni, Regio acquisto
Menozzi	Menozzi, acquisto
Mercatanti	Arte dei Mercatanti
Polverosa	San Donato in Polverosa
Ripoli	San Bartolomeo di Ripoli
San Niccolò	San Niccolò di Firenze
Strozziane-Uguccioni	Strozziane-Uguccioni, acquisto
ASF *Not. Ant.*	*Notarile Antecosimiano* (Archivio di Stato di Firenze)
ASI	*Archivio Storico Italiano*
BNF	Biblioteca Nazionale di Firenze
Capitoli	*I Capitoli del comune di Firenze. Inventario e regesto.* C. Guasti and A. Gherardi, eds. 2 vols. Florence, 1866–1893.

MEFRM	*Mélanges de l'Ecole française de Rome. Moyen âge, temps modernes*
MGH SS	*Monumenta Germaniae Historica, Scriptores.* G. H. Pertz et al., eds. Hanover, 1826–1913.
Rat. Dec.	*Rationes Decimarum Italiae nei secoli XIII e XIV: Tuscia II: Le decime degli anni 1295–1304.* M. Giusti and P. Guidi, eds. Vatican City, 1942.
Vita Johannis Gualberti	*Vita Johannis Gualberti adhuc inedita.* In *Forschungen zur älteren Geschichte von Florenz,* vol. 1, pp. 55–60. Robert Davidsohn, ed. Berlin, 1896.

Appendix A
Chronology of Florentine
Bishops to 1321

Ildebrando (Ildebrandus)	1008–1024
Lamberto (Lambertus)	1025–1032
Attone (Atto)	1032–1046
Gerardo (Gerardus) [Pope Nicholas II, 1059–1061]	1046–1061
Pietro Mezzabarba (Petrus Mezzabarba)	1062–1068
Ranieri (Rainerius)	1071–1113
Goffredo (Gottifredus)	1113–1142
Attone (Atto II)	1143–1155
Ambrogio (Ambrosius)	1155–1158
Giulio (Julius)	1158–1182
Bernardo (Bernardus)	1182–1187
Pagano (Paganus)	1187–1190
Pietro (Petrus)	1190–1205
Giovanni da Velletri (Johannis Velletrus)	1205–1230
Ardingo (Ardingus)	1231–1247
Filippo Fontana (Philipus Fontana)	1250–1251
Giovanni de' Mangiadori (Johannis Mangiadori)	1251–1275
Iacopo Rainucci (Jacobus Castelbuono)	1286
Andrea de' Mozzi (Andreas Mozzi)	1286–1295
Francesco Monaldeschi	1295–1301
Lottieri della Tosa (Lotterius della Tosa)	1302–1309
Antonio degli Orsi (Antonius Orso)	1309–1321

Appendix B
Comparison of a *Bullettone*
Entry with Its Model

In order to demonstrate the abbreviated nature of the *Bullettone* entries, I present below one example of the original document in full, followed by the *Bullettone* version. In 1286 or 1287, Bishop Andrea de'Mozzi conducted a series of examinations (*recognitiones*) of episcopal tenants at Castelfiorentino to reaffirm that those individuals owed yearly payments to the episcopate. Michele Cioni published the series of *recognitiones* (see Cioni, 1912, vol. 20, pp. 84–92, 127–151; 1914, vol. 22, pp. 20–50, 189–199; 1915, vol. 23, pp. 16–36; the following is excerpted from Cioni, 1912, vol. 20, pp. 130–131).

In dei nomine. Anno millesimo ducentesimo octuagesimo nono, Indictione secunda, die vigesimo mensis Aprilis. Actum in ecclesia S. Blasii de Castro Florentino praesentibus Arriguccio Venuti, Carduccio Dietisalvi, et Comuccio Iacopi de Castro Florentino testibus ad hec rogatis et vocatis feliciter. Gianni Riccardini Oddi Palmieri populi S. Bartolomei de Sala constitutus in praesentia domini Lottieri quondam domini Rinucci Uberti de Vice dominis sindici et procuratoris venerabilis patris domini Andreae Dei et apostolica gratia episcopi florentini et episcopatus eiusdem. Coram dictus testibus et me Ricovero notaro infra scripto manifeste et ex certa scientia non per errorem, recognovit et confessus fuit quod olim dictus pater suus et eius antecessores tenebantur solvere et soliti erant praestare praefato episcopatui et eiusdem episcopatus rectoribus pro annuo et perpetuo censu et afficutu singulis annis de mense Augusti tres starios grani ad rectum starium florentinum, et quod ipse met usque nunc dedit et solvit similiter, Et promisit et convenit dictus Gianni tamquam haeres quondam dicti patris sui dicto domino Lotterio sindico praefatum censum et afficutum dictorum trium stariorum grani dare solvere et praestare dicto domino episcopo et eius successoribus et episcopatui florentino singulis annis in perpetuum de mense Augusti sub poena eius unde agitur et restitutione dapnorum et expensarum litis et caetera, et post firmum tenere, et obligatione sui et suorum bonorum omnium praesentium et futurorum quae se pro dicto domino episcopo et episcopatu praecarie constituit possidere. Et Renuntiavit in hiis omnibus exceptioni non factae recognitionis confessionis et promissionis praedictarum et non celebrati contractus et condictioni sine causa et ex iniusta causa, doli mali et in fraudem fori, privilegio epistolae divi Adriani omnique alii privilegio et constitutionis et legis auxilio. Cui Gianni praedicto volenti et confitenti praedicta precepi ego Ricoverus notarus infra scriptus nomine sacramenti sicut michi licebat per capitulum constituti communis florentiae Guarentigiae quod praedictum censum et affictum dictorum trium stariorum grani det et solvat et praestet singulis annis in perpetuum de mense Augusti dicto domino episcopo nomine pro dicto episcopatu suisque successoribus et observet hunc contractum et omnia et singula supradicta ut superius promissum et contentum et scriptum est. Et pro praedictis omnibus servandis solepniter corporale praestitit iuramentum; et inde de voluntate partium duo instrumenta unius tenoris fieri rogaverunt, scilicet pro utraque parte unum.

L. S. Ego Ricoverus quondam Aldobrandini de Campoli imperiali acutoritate iudex ordinarius et notarius praedicta omnia coram me acta rogatus scripsi et publicavi feliciter.

The *Bullettone* version (AAF *Bullettone*, 1323, fol. 182v) is tersely summarized:

Qualiter Gianni Riccardini Oddi Palmieri populi sancti Bartolomei de Sala fuit confessus et recognovit olim pater suus et eius antecessores solvebant annuatim Episcopatui florentino nomine fictus perpetui de mense Augusti ad rectum starium florentinum, et ipse tamquam haeres dicti patris sui solvit et solvere promisit annis singulis in futurum. Carta manu dicti notari, dicti die.

Appendix C
Episcopal *Castelli* in the Diocese of Florence, 1000–1250

I have organized the following list of episcopal *castelli* in the diocese of Florence chronologically, according to the years in which they appear in the sources. In the third column I have identified the bishop during whose episcopacy the *castello* (or portions of it) first was mentioned as an episcopal possession. The dates in the second column record when the episcopate acquired, constructed, or leased part or all of the *castello*. *Castelli* whose names appear in *italic* are those with which the bishop also acquired patronage rights to the local parish in the first date mentioned.

Castello	Dates Mentioned in Sources	Bishop
Montalto	1018 (with *curtis*)	Ildebrando (1008–1024)
Montacuto	1018 (half)	Ildebrando
Lancisa	1023 (donation)	Ildebrando
Campiano	1036 (to chapter)	Attone (1032–1046)
Collis Romuli	1037	Attone
Cavagliano	1036 (to chapter)	Attone
Bossolo (Val di Pesa)	1038 (donated to chapter) 1127 (donation) 1214 (construction of *castello*)	Attone
Ampinana (Mugello)	1041 (donation)	Attone
Cercina (Valdarno)	1047 (donation) 1064 (donation) 1072 (1/2 donation) 1074 (part donation)	Gerardo (1046–1061)
Vespignano	1050 1212	Gerardo
Ripoli (Val di Pesa)	1054	Gerardo

Castello	Dates Mentioned in Sources	Bishop
Cerliano (Mugello)	1059 (donation)	Gerardo
Petriolo (Val di Pesa)	1076 (donation)	Ranieri (1071–1113)
	1148 (purchase)	
	1172 (donation)	
	1175 (purchase)	
	1181 (purchase)	
	1195 (purchase)	
	1208 (purchase)	
Casole (Mugello)	1079 (donation)	Ranieri
Borgo San Lorenzo (Mugello)	1080 (donation)	Ranieri
Carza (Mugello)	1080 (donation)	Ranieri
	1123	
Montebuoni (Valdigreve)	1092 (donation)	Ranieri
Fabbrica (Val di Pesa)	1098 (acquired)	Ranieri
	1116 (acquired)	
	1216 (acquired)	
Pagliariccio (Mugello)	1103 (donation)	Ranieri
	1104 (donation)	
	1104 (construction)	
	1197 (patronage rights acquired to parish)	
Decimo (Val di Pesa)	1105 (donation)	Ranieri
	1183–1195 (donations and purchases)	
Linari (Valdelsa)	1126 (donation)	Goffredo (1113–1142)
	1128 (acquired 3/4)	
Timignano	1126 (donation of part)	Goffredo
Aquilone (Val di Pesa)	1127	Goffredo
Vico (Val di Sieve)	1128 (3 donations)	Goffredo
	1142 (donation)	
	1160 (donation)	
	1213 (purchase)	
	1221 (purchase)	
	1244 (purchase)	
Monte Giovi (Mugello)	1133 (imperial donation)	Goffredo
Monte Buiano (Mugello)	1133 (imperial donation)	Goffredo
	1221 (partial purchase)	
Montacuto (Val di Pesa)	1133 (imperial donation)	Goffredo
	1155 (donations)	

Castello	Dates Mentioned in Sources	Bishop
Montazzi (Mugello)	1133 (imperial donation)	Goffredo
Loncastro	1133 (imperial donation)	Goffredo
	1136 (donation with *podium*)	
Tignano	1149 (purchase of part)	Attone (1143–1155)
Montecampolese (Val di Pesa)	1156 (construction of *castello*)	Ambrogio (1155–1158)
Lomena (Mugello)	1159	Giulio (1158–1182)
Petroio (Val di Pesa)	1165	Giulio
Buonsollazzo (Mugello)	1176 (donation)	Giulio
	1187 (purchase)	Bernardo (1182–1187)
Montemasso (Valdigreve)	1193 (sold by bishop)	Pietro (1190–1205)
	1198 (sold by bishop)	
Montefiesole (Val di Sieve)	1196 (bishop leases part)	Pietro
	1244 (purchase)	
Molezzano (Mugello)	1197 (purchase)	Pietro
	1198 (purchase)	
	1202 (purchase)	
Pila (Mugello)	1202 (donation of part)	Pietro
	1219 (purchase of part)	
San Giovanni (Pagliariccio)	1206	Giovanni (1205–1230)
Rabbiacanina (Mugello)	1212 (bishop leases part)	Giovanni
Torniano (Val di Pesa)	1216 (purchase)	Giovanni
	1217 (purchase)	
Arliano (Mugello)	1222 (bishop leases 1/2)	Giovanni
Monte di Croce	1226 (purchases part)	Giovanni
	1244 (purchases part)	
Monterotondo	1226 (purchased with Monte di Croce)	

Sources: AAF *Bullettone;* Francovitch, 1976.

Appendix D
Entries in the *Bullettone*
According to Date, Region, and Type

Donations

Date	Mugello	Pesa	Elsa	Sieve	Valdarno	Flor	Greve	Total
pre–900		1			1	3		5
900–925	1			1				2
926–950						1		1
951–975	2		1					3
976–1000		1			1	2		4
1001–1025					2	3		5
1026–1050	4				1	1	2	8
1051–1075	1	2			3	2		8
1076–1100	2	2				2	1	7
1101–1125	7	1				1		9
1126–1150	2	23	1	4			1	31
1151–1175	6	9		1	1	2	1	20
1176–1200	6	10	1		2	2		21
1201–1225	10	5	2		1	7		25
1226–1250	3	1	1	1	2	2		10
1251–1275	7		2			1		10
1276–1300	2	1		2				5
1301–1325		1	1	4				6

Purchases

Date	Mugello	Pesa	Elsa	Sieve	Valdarno	Flor	Greve	Total
1101–1125		1						1
1126–1150		15	1				1	17
1151–1175		11					1	12
1176–1200	1	12	1	2	1		1	18
1201–1225		18	2	16	18	5		59
1226–1250		4	1	10	5		1	21
1251–1275		13	1	3	1			18
1276–1300	1	9		1	3	7		21
1301–1325				10	1	4		15

Agrarian Contracts

Date	Mugello	Pesa	Elsa	Sieve	Valdarno	Flor	Greve	Total
926–950	2	1	2		10	8		23
951–975		1	2		2	3		8
976–1000	2	1			9	5		17
1001–1025	1	3	3		3	8	2	20
1026–1050	1					2	1	4
1051–1075					11	6		17
1076–1100	2	1			2	9		14
1101–1125	3	2	1		7	2		15
1126–1150	2	15	1	1	3	4	2	28
1151–1175	6	1	1	1	13	3	2	27
1176–1200	5	7		3	5	1	1	22
1201–1225	30	15	15	12	5	12	1	90
1226–1250	4	11	19	25	4	1	3	67
1251–1275	1	13	6	8	4			32
1276–1300	117	229	3	80	2	3	1	435
1301–1325	175	27	95	54	5	9	1	366

Fixed-Term Leases

Date	Mugello	Pesa	Elsa	Sieve	Valdarno	Flor	Greve	Total
1226–1250	1							1
1251–1275	12	1		1				14
1276–1300	4		5					9
1301–1325	23	41		56	10	152		282

Conflict

Date	Mugello	Pesa	Elsa	Sieve	Valdarno	Flor	Greve	Total
1101–1125					2			2
1126–1150	2	1		1	1	1		6
1151–1175			1	2	1			4
1176–1200	1	1			3	4		9
1201–1225	23	14	8	4	8			57
1226–1250	22	28	3	5	7	1		66
1251–1275	24	8	4	7		5	1	49
1276–1300	19	17	1	6	15	18		76
1301–1325	15	6	2	21	2	7		53

Customary (Perpetual) Leases as Percentage of Total Leases, 1301–1321 (All Sources)

Mugello: 175 perpetual leases/198 total = 88%
Val di Pesa: 27/68 = 40%
Valdelsa: 95/100 = 95%
Lower Sieve: 54/110 = 49%
Valdarno: 5/15 = 33%
Florence: 9/161 = 0.06%

The bishops leased all episcopal income in the areas listed below in the following years:

1301	Decimo
1309	Botena, Padule, Corella (Mugello)
1319	Decimo, Campoli
1321	Campoli (except for Fabbrica)
1322	Campoli (except for Fabbrica)

Notes

Full citations for works referred to by author and date are given in the bibliography. Abbreviations of the names of documents and archives are listed on pages 203–204.

Introduction

1. AA Fiesole, *Atti Civili,* folio 1r.
2. The *cognatio* (such as the German *Sippe*), or bilateral kindred, does not appear in the sources in northern Italy. The *agnatio* (or patrilineage) does, and it traced the line of descent through the male line back to a common male ancestor. Property was transmitted exclusively to male offspring. In the patrilineage, fathers and brothers set apart a portion of the patrimony as a dowry to provide for their daughters and sisters. The aim of the patrilineage was to preserve the wealth of male members of the lineage by reducing the number of heirs. The *consorteria* (an association of related males) was a contractual attempt on an ideological level to achieve a solidarity among lineage members that no longer existed because of family disputes over property (Herlihy, 1986, pp. 82–85; Cammarosano, 1975, p. 432).
3.   Oh quali io vidi quei che son disfatti
           per lor superbia! e le palle de l'oro
           fioran Fiorenza in tutt'i suoi gran fatti.
         Così facieno i padri di coloro che,
           sempre che la vostra chiesa vaca,
           si fanno grassi stando a consistoro.

   Dante, *Paradiso,* 1975, p. 182; English translation on p. 183.
4. For the purposes of this study, I define ecclesiastical resources as church honors (participation in processions or rituals, for example), landed property, offices, and jurisdictional rights.
5. In the middle of the twelfth century, Gratian distinguished between purely ecclesiastical properties and rights such as tithes *(res ecclesiasticae)* and properties and jurisdictional rights granted by a king or emperor *(regalia)*. See Benson, 1968, p. 54; and Osheim, 1977, pp. x–xi.
6. Chomsky, 1982, pp. 3–6.
7. For the purpose of this study, I define charisma in the Weberian sense: "a

certain quality of an individual personality by virtue of which he is considered extraordinary and treated as endowed with supernatural, superhuman, or at least specifically exceptional powers or qualities. These are such as are not accessible to the ordinary person, but are regarded as of divine origin or as exemplary, and on the basis of them the individual concerned is treated as a 'leader' (Weber, 1978, vol. 1, p. 241). Furthermore, charisma is "a sign of involvement with the animating centers of society" (Geertz, 1983, p. 124).

8. Lesne, 1910–1943; Herlihy, 1961.

9. Miller, 1951; Duggan, 1978; Bouchard, 1979, 1987; and Dyer, 1980. Of related interest—but not specifically concerned with bishops—are Johnson, 1981a, b; Rosenwein, 1982, 1989; and Bouchard, 1987.

10. For a historiographical overview, see Osheim, 1977, p. 116. For studies on Tuscan bishops, see Davidsohn, 1960–1978, 1896–1908; Barbi, 1899; Santini, 1895b, 1900, 1903; Volpe, 1923, 1961, 1964; and Caggese 1907–1909.

11. Cipolla, 1947.

12. For a review of Wickham's book, see Herlihy, 1989.

13. For some of the more notable studies, see Romeo, 1971; Vannucci, 1963–1964; Chittolini, 1965; Conti, 1965; Ragni, 1970; Kurze, 1973; Fumagalli, 1976, 1978a, b; Grohmann, 1981; Onori, 1984; Delumeau, 1978; Rippe, 1979, and Epstein, 1986. Though not exclusively concerned with property, the unpublished thesis of Milo, 1979, is also useful.

14. For Pistoia, see Ferrali, 1964; and Herlihy, 1967. For Volterra, see Volpe, 1961; and Fiumi, 1961. Volpe also republished studies of the episcopates of Luni and Massa Marittima (1964). On the Lucchese episcopate, see Osheim, 1977; and Wickham, 1988 (also for Aretine episcopal landholding in the Casentino). For the lordship of the Florentine bishops at San Casciano Val di Pesa, see Dameron, 1986. For Florentine episcopal power at Monte di Croce and in the diocese as a whole, see Nelli, 1985, 1988.

15. Ughelli, 1718; Cerrachini, 1726; Lami, 1758; and Cappelletti, 1861.

16. Davidsohn, 1960–1978, 1896–1908; Santini, 1900, 1903. For detailed studies of specific churches, see Paatz and Paatz, 1955. For an examination of the early development of Florentine churches, see Lopes-Pegna, 1972.

17. Becker, 1959; Stephens, 1972; Benvenuti-Papi, 1980, 1987.

18. Nelli, 1985, 1988; Bizzocchi, 1982, 1984, 1987; Benvenuti-Papi, 1988; Bowsky (unpublished).

19. On the broad concept of power, material and spiritual, in this context, see Benson, 1968, pp 5-9. The literature on the lineage in Tuscany is extensive, but for the most important works, see the following: Jones, 1956a, pp. 183–205; Herlihy, 1969, pp. 173–85; Cammarosano, 1975, 1977; Violante, 1977b, 1981; Raveggi et al., 1978; Lansing, 1984; Herlihy, 1986 (with bibliography); and Carol Lansing is completing a study of the Florentine elite patrilineage, to be published by Princeton University Press. On the linkage between the *contado's* and the diocese's borders, see Waley, 1969, pp. 110-111; Osheim, 1977, p. x.

20. See Salvemini, 1899; Caggese, 1907–1909; and Davidsohn, 1960–1978. This tradition obviously extends to earlier historians. For a terse and helpful description of these views, see Herlihy, 1968, pp. 245–246.

21. In Florentine studies, the key historiographical break occurred with the publication of Nicola Ottokar's *Il Comune di Firenze alla fine del Dugento* in 1926 (republished 1974). For a historiographical overview, see Becker, 1967.

22. See Fiumi, 1956, 1957–1959; Jones, 1956a, 1971, 1980a, p. 5.

23. Romeo, 1971, p. 11.

24. Romeo, 1971, pp. 1–13; Wickham, 1988, pp. 131–134.

25. Rippe, 1979, p. 689.

26. In his study of Poggialvento, Conti argued that the majority of landlords in the eleventh century were from the *contado* and that there were few if any urban lords (1965, p. 170; see also Conti, 1985, p. xi). For relevant discussion, see also Wickham, 1988, pp. 130–131.

27. See Santini, 1900, pp. 27–28; Waley, 1969, p. 111.

28. Jones, 1968, pp. 193–241.

29. I define lordship in the general sense of rule or sovereignty in a particular area (*Oxford English Dictionary,* vol. 1, p. 1664). For more specific discussion within the context of Italian historiography, see below.

30. In his recent survey of the European economy before 1200, Georges Duby described three types of lordship:(1) domestic lordship (*seigneurie domestique*—implying the existence of serfdom and exactions such as *formariage* and the *taille*), (2) landlordship (*seigneurie foncière*—requiring a levy on what the peasant produces), and (3) banal lordship (*seigneurie banale*—a type of legitimized pillage) (Duby, 1974, pp. 176–177). In Tuscany during the period covered by this book, the first type was not as important as it was in the north, and by 1200 it had virtually disappeared (Jones, 1968).

31. For background and an excellent bibliography on *signorie,* see Wickham, 1988, pp. xiii–xiv, 105ff.; and Tabacco, 1969, pp. 203–206.

32. For a full discussion of the term, see Cohen, 1978, pp. 79–87.

33. I am adapting Rodney Hilton's Marxist definition of feudalism to the Florentine countryside: "The essence of the feudal mode of production in the Marxist sense is the exploitative relationship between landowners and subordinated peasants, in which the surplus beyond subsistence of the latter, whether in direct labour or in rent in kind or in money, is transferred under coercive sanction to the former" (Hilton, 1978, p. 30). In my definition, I prefer the phrase "subject population" to the "subject peasantry" in Hilton's definition, because in Tuscany many episcopal tenants were town dwellers. Also, "surplus" can take other forms (like taxation on property or court fines) than labor or rent. Hilton's definition therefore is too narrow in relation to Italy.

34. For recent syntheses on European feudalism, see Fossier, 1982, pp. 952, 958; Poly, 1980, p. 9; and Cheyette, 1968. For the most articulate argument against the continued use of the term *feudalism,* see Brown, 1974. In his recent survey of the literature, Robert Fossier prefers the word *seigneurialism* to *feudalism* (1982, p. 70).

    In its juridical sense, Fossier defines feudalism in the following way: "liens réels établis entre deux hommes avec services, en principe réciproques, à la suite de la concession, normalement provisoire, d'un bien par un seigneur à un vassal au terme d'une serie de rites publics" (p. 952).

35. Fossier, 1982, pp. 952–964; Rippe, 1979, p. 677. Another closely related definition of feudalism as "public power in private hands" is also losing popularity (Peters, 1989, pp. 155, 167).

36. Bloch, 1966, vol. 2, pp. 443–446; Cammarosano, 1981, pp. 837–847; Bisson, 1977.

37. In 1978 the French School at Rome hosted a conference on feudalism in the Mediterranean world, entitled *Structures féodales et féodalisme dans l'occident méditerranéen*. For two evaluations of the proceedings, see Cammarosano, 1981; and Gasparri, 1981.

38. Cammarosano, 1981, p. 868. The situation seems even more diverse in the south. At Capua and Benevento, there were no fiefs or vassalage before the arrival of the Normans. Social relations at Salerno were non-vassalic, archaic, and characterized by reciprocal gift-giving. For Sicily, Sardinia, and the Byzantine lands, feudo-vassalic relations were largely imported (Gaspari, 1981, pp. 634–638).

39. Rippe, 1979, p. 689.

40. Wickham, 1988, pp. xx–xxiii, 160; Cammarosano, 1982, p. 8; Tabacco, 1969, p. 214; Violante, 1974a.

41. Marx, 1977, vol. 1, pp. 877–926; Hilton, 1978; Jones, 1980a, p. 6.

42. Anderson, 1974, p. 156.

43. Kotel'nikova, 1975, pp. 6–12, 401; Vaccari, 1926; Dal Pane, 1959.

44. For recent syntheses and studies of the European nobility, see Flori, 1986, pp. 10–40; Fossier, 1982, pp. 964–970; Génicot, 1978, pp. 26–28; Poly, 1980; and the articles edited by Reuter, 1978.

45. For overviews of the Italian nobility and up-to-date bibliographies, see Fossier, 1982, pp. 977–978; Larner, 1980, pp. 83–105; Jones, 1980a, pp. 61–75; Génicot, 1978, pp. 23–25; Toubert, 1973. For full discussion of the northern Italian *milites*, see Keller, 1982; Moore, 1980; Tabacco, 1976.

46. Génicot, 1978, p. 31 (citing Fiumi, 1957–1959); Tabacco, 1976, pp 47–48.

47. See Marx, 1965; Mauss, 1967; and Polanyi, 1975. Economic anthropologists have argued for decades over the proper methods for the study of non-capitalist or pre-capitalist economies. For the neo-classical approach, see Leclair and Schneider, 1968; and North and Thomas, 1973. Polanyi and his followers, the substantivists, have argued that cultural values and social structure are the predominating influences in pre-capitalist societies but that the market system predominates in capitalism. For the Marxists, social or class relations are the dominant influences in all economic formations—even in capitalism. Few historians have tried to profit from this debate.

48. Cammarosano, 1975, pp. 432–434; Lansing, 1987.

49. Borghini's assertion that the most ancient documents perished in the fire (1809, part 2, p. 579) was later repeated by Lami (1758, vol. 2, p. 1429). Christopher Wickham estimates that there are 20,000 documents in the Florentine archives for the period before 1300 (personal correspondence).

50. The present archivist in the Archivio Arcivescovile di Firenze, Dom Carlo Celso Calzolai, thinks that the name of the manuscript derives from the fact that the register catalogued the *bullette*, annual payments made by tenants to the bishop (1957, p. 164). According to Cassell's Italian dictionary, however, *bullettone*

means "large tack," a reference to the large tacks used to bind together the folios (1977, p. 76).

51. For information on specific contents of the *Bullettone,* a comparison between the 1323 register and its 1384 copy, a history of its manuscripts, see Dameron, 1983, pp. 341–346, 1989.

52. There is some disagreement about the date of his death. Whereas Gams believes July 1322 to be the correct date (Gams, 1873, p. 747), Davidsohn places the date sometine between June 9, 1320, and February 6, 1321 (1960, vol. 4, p. 847n). Ughelli (1718, vol. 4, p. 140), Lami (1758, vol. 3, p. 1686), and the ASF *Bullettone* put the death in July of 1321. My view is that July 1321 is the correct date.

53. Davidsohn, 1960, vol. 4, p. 848; Rotelli, 1978, pp. 210–211. For details on the early history of the lineages associated with the administration of the vacant estate, see Chapter 1.

54. The AAF *Libro* records the series of selections of administrators during the 1321–1323 vacancy. Every two months the Visdomini chose four new administrators from the three families of the *consorteria.* The entries began July 18, 1321, and ended June 30, 1323. See the AAF *Libro,* folio 1r.

55. ASF *Bullettone,* p. 395.

56. AAF *Bullettone,* end folio. Palandri unfortunately mistook the beginning of the ASF *Bullettone* (the model for the *Bullettone* published in Lami's *Monumenta*) for the beginning of the original. Also, Palandri wrongly dated the commissioning of the *Bullettone* at February 10, 1322, whereas the notary clearly dated it February 10, 1323 (sixth indiction). Palandri had failed also to take into account that the Florentine year began on March 25; therefore, February 1322 was really February 1323.

57. Trexler, 1978, p. 24.

58. AAF *Bullettone,* folios 281v–282r.

59. Palandri (1926, p. 186) divided the *Bullettone* into several parts: the *regesti, affitti,* and *obbligazioni;* the entry of Bishop Jacopo in 1286; the list of oaths (*iuramenta*); and the inventory of episcopal possessions ("Inventarium masseritiarum et rerum episcopatus Florentini"). He left out, however, the two introductory and final notarial sections, as well as the collection of documents relating specifically to the Visdomini.

60. In the original 1323 *Bullettone* in the Archivio Arcivescovile di Firenze, this material is placed at the end of the book and not at the beginning (as it should be). A later notary must have rearranged the folios.

61. "Qualiter Martinus et Corsus fratres filii quondam Lombardi tenentur et debent dare et solvere annuatim perpetuo Episcopatui Florentini pro dimidia poderis Bencivennis avi eorum quam ipsi tenent starios tres grani" (AAF *Bullettone,* folio 206r). See Appendix B for comparison.

62. For the history and comparison of these published and manuscript versions, see Dameron, 1989.

63. ASF *Bullettone,* p. 400.

64. Cioni, 1912, pp. 130–131. See Appendix B for the full text, along with the abbreviated *Bullettone* entry.

65. Conti, 1985, p. xiii.

66. Renzo Nelli attempted to fix a date for the surveys of payments made by the episcopal representatives at Monte di Croce, since many of those lists have no date. He hypothesized that the bishops did them between 1295 and 1302. See Nelli, 1985, pp. 12–13. For Conti's observation, see Conti, 1985, p. xviii.

67. For the research for this book, I have consulted all of the relevant source collections in the Archivio di Stato di Firenze for the period before 1320, including the *Notarile Antecosimiano* and the *Conventi Soppressi.* Only those collections cited in this study appear in the bibliography.

1. The Emergence of the Patrilineage and the Challenge to Episcopal Interests

1. Brentano, 1968, pp.62–64.

2. For a basic geographical orientation, see Barbieri, 1972; and Biagioli, 1975.

3. Plesner, 1979, p. 3. I have borrowed David Herlihy's terms of classification for the geographical features around Pistoia for the region around Florence (Herlihy, 1967, chap. 2).

4. Pallottino, 1982, p. 200.

5. Lopes-Pegna, 1974, pp. 219–242, 285; Lanzoni, 1927, p. 505.

6. Wickham, 1981, p. 13; 1980, p. 11.

7. Nanni, 1948, p. 48.

8. Earlier historians believed the church district was coterminous with the Roman *pagus* (Boyd, 1952, pp. 49–50; Mengozzi, 1911, pp. 174–175). The general concensus today is that the *pieve* did not correspond to the *pagus.* For the most recent study of the *plebs,* see Castagnetti, 1976.

9. Boyd, 1952, p. 51; Forchielli, 1917; Nanni, 1948.

10. For a brief overview of the historiography of the *plebs* (Italian *pieve*), see T. Szabó's introduction to Plesner, 1979, p. x. See also Violante, 1977a, pp. 724, 728, and 731 (quoted by Szabó); and Forchielli, 1917.

11. Lopes-Pegna, 1974, pp. 306–307.

12. Quilici, 1938, p. 68; Stahl, 1965, p. 96. For a complete list of the Florentine *plebes* and their dependent oratories, see *Rat. Dec.;* and Dameron, 1983.

13. Boyd, 1952, p. 159; Brentano, 1968, p. 68. The arch-priest was responsible for collecting tithes, performing baptisms and marriages, and burying the dead.

14. Boyd, 1952, pp. 53–55; Violante, 1977a, p. 678.

15. There exists very little evidence of feudo-vassalic ties in the diocese of Florence at this time. Until the end of the eleventh century in Tuscany it is very rare to find evidence of those ties *within* the rural elite. Indeed, it is difficult to find anything but kinship ties. Nowhere in Tuscany do we find the vast territorial lordships that existed in northern Europe (such as Anjou and Burgundy). Fiefs and vassals were most apparent in the diocese of Arezzo. There is also some evidence of those ties in the dioceses of Volterra, Pistoia, Lucca, and Pisa, but little in the regions around Florence and Siena (Cammarosano, 1982, pp. 1–8).

16. Fumagalli, 1976, pp. 95–96.

17. The bishops of Lombardy, the region to the north of Tuscany, had become exceedingly powerful by the early tenth century after having received grants of

royal estates and public jurisdictional powers from the ninth and early tenth century kings. These powers included urban port taxes, navigational rights, the control of streets and markets, and juridical rights (Fumagalli, 1976, pp. 84–96). For Arezzo, see Delumeau, 1978.

18. Leyser, 1979, pp. 1–3.
19. Kurze, 1973, p. 352; Kehr, 1908, vol. 3, pp. 26–28, 61–65.
20. Davidsohn, 1977, vol. 1, p. 169.
21. Kurze, 1973, pp. 352–57; Milo, 1979, pp. 111–115; Schiaparelli, 1913, pp. 10–17; Kehr, 1908, pp. 444, 166, 61, 365. For the foundation of Marturi, see ASF *Dipl.* Bonifazio, 25 July 998.
22. Wickham, 1981, pp. 184–185; Chiapelli, 1932, pp. 117–133; Pescaglini Monti, 1981, p. 193.
23. Violante, 1981, pp. 2, 37; Wickham, 1981, pp. 181, 185; Shevill, 1961, pp. 35–36.
24. Wickham, 1981, p. 218; Davidsohn, 1977, vol. 1, p. 218n.
25. See the maps of Cadolingi and Guidi possessions in Pescaglini Monti, 1981, p. 204; Milo, 1981, following p. 221.
26. Pescaglini Monti, 1981, pp. 193–94. Cadolo's son, Lotario, later transformed the oratory into the abbey of San Salvatore di Fucecchio, located in the midst of Cadolingi possessions (pp. 194–195).
27. Pescaglini Monti, 1981, pp. 194–195. For a map of their possessions, see p. 204.
28. Pescaglini Monti, 1981, p. 193. As the manorial system (*sistema curtense*) disintegrated in the late ninth, tenth, and eleventh centuries, the *castello* emerged as the most important locus of power in Tuscany (Jones, 1964, p. 331; Toubert, 1973, p. xii). I am grateful to Christopher Wickham for having reminded me that the power of the Cadolingi derived from their public authority.
29. Fumagalli, 1976, p. 41.
30. Repetti, 1833–1846, vol. 1, p. 642.
31. Herlihy, 1986, pp. 32, 51–52, 82–92; Herlihy, 1969, pp. 173–185; Violante, 1977b; Cammarosano, 1975; Wickham, 1981, p. 186; and Kurze, 1973, 1981, p. 259. Two types of agnatic lineage emerged at this time in Europe: the *consorteria* and the "dynastic" descent group. Whereas the former contained several lines of agnatic descent (neither of which was "singled out as senior to the others"), the latter type transferred an indivisible patrimony to a single heir (and included both a "preferred" and a "postponed" branch) (Herlihy, 1986, p. 88). For F. W. Kent, a *consorteria* was "a group of kinsmen tracing descent in the male line from a common ancestor" (1977, p. 6).

Cammarosano suggests that the formation of a *consorteria* was primarily an ideological innovation, designed to prevent the fractioning and subdivision of property (1975, p. 432). The first documented appearance of a juridical formation of a *consorteria* comes from Pisa in 1130 (Violante, 1981, p. 31), but the earliest evidence comes from references to collectively owned property at Farfa (1032) in Lazio, Bobbio (975), and Lucca (1010) (Herlihy 1986, p. 88).

32. Volpe, 1964, pp. 14–5.
33. Osheim, 1977, pp. 6, 14–15.
34. Kurze, 1981, pp. 260, 263–264.

35. Kurze, 1981, pp. 259–262; Kurze, 1973, pp. 359–361.
36. Violante, 1977b, p. 101.
37. Violante, 1977b, p. 93.
38. Davidsohn, 1977, vol. 1, p. 218; Kehr, 1908, vol.3, p. 51; Pescaglini Monti, 1981, pp. 195–196; Kurze, 1973, p. 359. According to Kehr, the Cadolingi founded the monastery at Settimo sometime after 998. For the list of donations made by Lotario dei Cadolingi to San Salvatore di Fucecchio, see Coturri, 1964, pp. 107–145.
39. That the monasteries had a dual purpose is the thesis of Kurze's 1973 article (p. 361).
40. For a brief overview of Benedictine monasticism and of the monastic ideal, see Knowles, 1969; and Tellenbach, 1959, pp. 59–85. On a smaller scale, the Tuscan family monasteries resembled contemporary Cluny, which served to intercede for the whole of society, "in a superb setting and fashion" (Knowles, 1969, p. 52).
41. Tellenbach, 1959, pp. 79–80.
42. Kurze, 1973, pp. 359–361.
43. Guarino first appears in the historical record in a 1011 charter. He served as abbot from 1011 to 1034 (Davidsohn, 1977, vol. 1, p. 220).
44. Davidsohn, 1977, vol. 1, pp. 218–220; Schevill, 1961, pp. 42–43.
45. For a more detailed analysis of the circumstances outlined below, see Dameron, 1987.
46. Violante, 1977b, p. 97.
47. The reader can find the following account in Milo, 1979, pp. 16–25; Davidsohn, 1977, vol. 1, pp. 222–224; Davidsohn, 1896–1908, vol. 1, pp. 38–39; Dameron, 1987, p. 130.
48. The Aliotti do not appear in documents before 1200. For more background on the Visdomini, see Davidsohn, 1977, vol. 1, pp. 507–508; Davidsohn, 1896–1908, vol. 1, pp. 77, 137, 1001; vol. 4, pp. 123–132, 187, 350, 359, 490, 507; Lopes-Pegna, 1974, p. 292; and Santini, 1895a, pp. 501, 584n.
49. Before 1179, the election of a new bishop supposedly included all the faithful: cathedral canons, laymen, and the cathedral monastic clergy (Benson, 1968, p. 27).
50. Moore, 1980, p. 68. There is considerable debate about the date of this argument. Indeed, it is impossible to ascertain the exact date of the confrontation. As Davidsohn observed, it must have occurred between 1011 (the first date Guarino appears) and 1024, when Ildebrando died (Davidsohn, 1977, vol. 1, p. 220). Davidsohn believed 1020 was the correct date. I believe, even though we can never be sure, that circumstantial evidence indicates the clash occurred around 1014.
51. "Per idem tempus celebre nomen religionis et sapientie habebat in Tuscia domnus Guarinus Septimensis cenobii abbas primus. Hic libere cepit loqui contro symoniacos et arguere clericos concubinatos" (*Vita Johannis Gualberti*, p. 56; *MGH SS*, vol. 30, pt. 2, p. 1105). The concern with simony was probably added by the author of the later saint's life.
52. "Nam cum quodam tempore pro quodam negotio accessisset ad Florentinum aepiscopum nomine Ildebrandum cumque perorasset rem pro quo venerat et

expectaret aepiscopi responsionem, conjunx aepiscopi nomine Alberga juxta eum sedens respondit: Domne abbas de hac re, pro qua tu postulas, domnus meus non est adhuc consiliatus; ipse loquetur cum suis fidelibus et respondebit tibi quod sibi placuerit" (*Vita Johannis Gualberti*, p. 56; *MGH SS*, vol. 30, pt. 2, p. 1105). I am grateful to Patrick Geary for having first suggested to me that the presence of Alberga in the episcopal audience was a primary source for Guarino's anger.

53. "Ad hanc vocem abbas zelo dei accensus cepit vehementer contra eam maledictionis verba promere dicens: Tu maledicta Zezabel, tanti conscia reatus, audes loqui ante conventum bonorum hominum vel clericorum que deberes igne comburi, quia tale dei plasma deique sacerdotem deturpare presumpsisti?" (*Vita Johannis Gualberti*, p. 56).

    See Schevill, 1961, pp. 42–43; Davidsohn, 1977, vol. 1, pp. 220–221; Dameron, 1987. The first recorded account of the use of the stake dates from 1022 at Orleans (Russell, 1972, p. 151), a fact which underscores that the account in the *Vita Johannis Gualberti* is anachronistic.

54. This papal privilege unfortunately does not survive (Kehr, 1908, p. 53; Davidsohn, 1977, vol. 1, p. 148), but the *Vita Johannis Gualberti* mentioned it. Both Davidsohn and Kehr dated it between 1012 and 1024. I agree with Milo (1979, pp. 27–28) that it probably appeared the same year that Henry II issued an imperial charter of protection for Settimo in 1014.

55. Milo, 1979, p. 28.

56. Dameron, 1987; Duby, 1980, pp. 195–198; Kurze, 1973, p. 361.

57. Romuald (d. 1027), a "holy man" who fled urban life, later established a community at Camaldoli to escape the "impurity" and corruption of contemporary ecclesiastical life. For background on Romuald and his life, see Davidsohn, 1977, vol. 1, pp. 169–172.

58. The Cadolingi obviously benefitted from the acquisition of property by their proprietary monastery. For a discussion of how this worked on the local level in the Casentino for other monasteries, see Wickham (1988), pp. 214, 259, and *passim*.

59. Chiappelli, 1932, pp. 121–122; Milo, 1979, p. 42; Davidsohn, 1977, vol. 1, p. 219.

60. The bishop had at least one *curtis* at Empoli (Lami, 1758, vol. 1, p. 44; Milo, 1979, p. 264).

61. Stuard, 1976, p. 8.

62. Moore, 1980, pp. 67–68.

63. Moore, 1980, pp. 55–68.

64. "Quapropter meum *seniorem,* scilicet Imperatorem adire studui, quatenus illius consilio, juvamineque animatus perficere valerem, quae desideravi. Qui meo desiderio, divina inspirante clementia, non modice congaudens, monasterium in praenominata Ecclesia, sicut antiquitus fuerat, me constituere admonuit, seque mihi favere promisit" (Berti, 1850, p. 176; also Lami, 1758, vol. 1, pp. 42–43; Ughelli, 1718, cols. 47–48). For background on the meeting see Davidsohn, 1977, vol. 1, p. 197; and Davidsohn, 1896–1908, vol. 1, p. 34.

65. Milo, 1979, pp. 27–28; Davidsohn, 1977, vol. 1, pp. 220–222. Christopher Wickham kindly pointed out to me the importance of 1014 to the reign of Henry II:

he needed as many allies as he could get to fight Arduin (for details, see Nobili, 1981, pp. 101–102).

66. The sources tell us little about the role of *milites* in the few episcopal castles (*castelli*), but elsewhere (Lazio and the Po plain) we know the *milites* were very important (Fossier, 1982, pp. 976–978; Keller, 1982, pp. 81–84).

67. Keller, 1982, pp. 67–96. The transformation of the *milites* into an order of knighthood occurred after 1050 and intensified after the promulgation of the First Crusade. By 1100 they were identified with martial service to the commune. By 1200 they were an *ordo militum*, distinct from the peasantry and acknowledged in communal constitutions.

68. As we shall see, Bishop Attone followed Ildebrando's example and donated two *castelli* (also claimed perhaps by the Guidi) to the cathedral chapter (Cavagliano and Campiano) in 1036.

69. For recent work on how this worked elsewhere in Europe, see Geary, 1978, pp. 18–19; Johnson, 1981a. For recent literature on the role of saints in western life, see Brown, 1982; and Vauchez, 1981.

70. *Enciclopedia cattolica*, 1949–1953, p. 1026; Dameron, 1987; Davidsohn, 1977, vol. 1, p. 200. In Sigebert's life of Deodericus ("Sigeberti Vita Deoderici I," *MGH SS*, vol. 4), we read: "Et horum quippe corpora ab Italia ad nos ab eo translata, fide vera credimus. Miniatem vero cum Proto et Iacinto et Vincentio episcopo ad nos delatum, 6. Nonas Iulii legimus"(p. 476).

71. *Passio Sancti Miniatis Martyris*, 1864, pp. 428–430; "De S. Miniate Martyre Florentine in Tuscia: Commentarius Praevius," 1864, *AS*, Octobris XI, p. 415; Lami, 1758, vol. 1, pp. 41–43; *Biblioteca Hagiografica Latina*, 1911, vol. 2, pp. 5965–5966; Davidsohn, 1977, vol. 1, p. 200; Berti, 1850, p. 181.

72. Berti, 1850, pp. 167–171; Drogo, 1898, pp. 197–198; Davidsohn, 1896–1908, vol. 1, p. 36. To borrow Peter Brown's expression, the prelate was the *impresario* of the revived cult of St. Minias (Brown, 1981, p. 101).

73. "Nec solum tunc temporis Florentiae passum, nec solum in praedicto credimus monte depositum, sed cum multis aliis martyrio coronatum terraeque, sociis adiunctis, commendatum. Licet enim is, quem ego secutus martyris passionem utcumque scribendo complevi, nil de sociis dixerit, tuae tamen, reverendissime pater, sanctitati divina visibiliter hos clementia intuendos concessit, quos ille letterarum compositione, nescio cur, tacuit" (Drogo, 1898, p. 198). See also Davidsohn, 1896–1908, vol. 1, p. 36, for a list of the manuscripts of the *Passio Drogonis*.

74. The following works contain copies of those documents: Lami, 1758, vol. 1, pp. 43–45; Ughelli, 1718, cols. 47–50; Berti, 1850, pp. 175–183.

75. Maps detailing Cadolingi and Guidi possessions are in Pescaglini Monti, 1981, p. 204; Milo, 1981, pp. 222–223; and Milo, 1979, pp. 264–265.

76. *Biblioteca Sanctorum*, 1967, vol. 9, cols. 493–499.

77. Milo, 1981, pp. 222; Ughelli, 1718, col. 49.

78. Wickham, 1988, p. 198.

79. Berti, 1850, pp. 178–181; Ughelli, 1718, p. 49; Wickham, 1981, pp. 181–185; Repetti, 1833–1846, vol. 5, pp. 619–622; vol. 3, p. 276.

80. The 1018 donation contains the first mention of an episcopal castle (*castrum* or *castellum*). For the diocese of Lucca, the historian can trace episcopal possession

of castles back to the first two or three decades of the tenth century (Bishop Peter leased half the *castello* of Anchiano to the lords of the same place in 925) (Osheim, 1977, p. 53).

81. For information on the market established by the bishop, see Davidsohn 1977, vol. 1, p. 204; and Ughelli, 1718, cols. 47–50. Information on San Pietro in Mercato appears in de la Roncière, 1976, vol. 3, p. 344. Apparently the bishop of Pistoia made the Guidi and Cadolingi dependent on the episcopal market (Milo, 1979, p. 142.)

82. Berti, 1850, pp. 178–181; Milo, 1979, p. 29; Davidsohn, vol. 1, 1977, p. 224.

83. Milo, 1979, p. 36.

84. Davidsohn, Schevill, Quilici, and most recently Milo have offered extremely negative assessments of the man.

85. Osheim, 1977, p. 15.

86. In the eleventh century, Passignano received an increasing number of donations: 986–1010 (4), 1011–1040 (7), 1041–1070 (17), and 1071–1100 (36) (Conti, 1965, pp. 160–162).

87. Herlihy, 1957; Violante, 1964; Violante, 1980.

88. Wickham, 1988, p. 213.

89. Wickham's conclusions emerged from his study of the zone around Partina in the Casentino (1988, pp. 214–215, 259). Usually the donations continued until the balance of power among the factions within the communities fueling the donations ended or changed. For an example of how this worked in the diocese of Volterra, see Fiumi, 1961, p. 22.

90. Conti, 1965, pp. 45–49. A medium-sized *curtis* had ten to twenty satellites (or dependent properties). The immediate area around the castle was the *circuitus castri*.

91. Quilici, 1940, p. 79; Davidsohn, 1977, vol. 1, p. 224.

92. For Bishop Lamberto, see Quilici, 1940, p. 79; Davidsohn, 1977, vol. 1, pp. 199, 224; Ughelli, 1718, cols. 50–53. For Bishop Attone, see Quilici, 1940, p. 53; Quilici, 1943, pp. 43–67; Davidsohn, 1977, vol. 1, pp. 246–248; Ughelli, 1718, cols. 53–62. For Bishop Gerardo (Pope Nicholas II), see Quilici, 1943, pp. 67–82; Davidsohn, 1977, vol. 1, pp. 271–274; Ughelli, 1718, cols. 62–72.

93. Milo, 1979, p. 29. The document, published in Piattoli (1938, pp. 87–90), is dated August 2, 1025. The sons of Ildebrando appear as the "filii Alberghe" (Piattoli, 1938, p. 88). The use of the matronymic was a common practice in the tenth and eleventh centuries as a way of hiding the clerical parentage of offspring (Herlihy, 1986, p. 47; Milo, 1979, pp. 29–30).

94. Piattoli, 1938, p. 88. The 1036 document stated, ". . . illam partem eis reddimus quam primicerius contra canonica instituta usurpare visus est" (Piattoli, 1938, p. 105).

95. The convent appeared in the record for the first time in January of 1056 (Milo, 1979, p. 36n).

96. Davidsohn, 1977, vol. 1, p. 204.

97. The July 1028 donation is in Lami, 1758, vol. 1, pp. 45–46; and Ughelli, 1718, cols. 50–53. In the map included in Milo's thesis (1979, p. 264) Cellole appears as a Cadolingi landed holding.

98. For Attone's 1037 donation, see Lami, 1758, vol. 1, pp. 47–48; Ughelli, 1718,

cols. 58–60; Milo, 1979, p. 122. For reference maps, see the maps in Milo, 1979; and Pescaglini Monti, 1981.

99. Ughelli, 1718, cols. 53–62. There was a Guidi castle at Monte di Croce (see the map of Guidi possessions in Milo, 1979, p. 265).

100. The churches included San Pietro Apostoli, San Basilico, and another San Pietro (apparently given originally to Bishop Podo, 989–1002).

101. Milo, 1979, p. 123. For the judgment on San Gavino Adimari, see ASF *Dipl.* Olivetani, 8 March 1038. For the margrave's confirmation, see Lami, 1758, vol. 1, pp. 222–223.

102. Milo, 1979, p. 124.

103. For the original documents of donations before 1113, see ASF *Dipl.* Olivetani, years 1048, 1073, 1091, 1095, 1096.

104. Schevill, 1961, p. 46; Davidsohn, 1977, vol. 1, pp. 246–248. Uberto was abbot from 1038 to 1071, following Abbot Leo (who himself succeeded Drogo).

105. Milo, 1979, pp. 173–175.

106. Moore, 1980, pp. 53–66.

107. Tedicio Rodolfi donated the *castello* of Lancisa to the bishop in early 1023 (ASF *Bullettone,* p. 312).

108. The bishop leased the castle to Fulchardo del fu Ildiberto (Osheim, 1977, p. 56). For reference to the Florentine episcopal *castello* of Pagliariccio, see AAF *Bullettone,* ff. 104r–123v.

109. In this respect, Florentine episcopal acquisition paralleled Lucchese episcopal activity (Osheim, 1977, pp. 55–57).

110. Toubert, 1973, vol. 1, p. xii; Tabacco, 1979, pp. 239–241; Fumagalli, 1978a, pp. 9–10; Toubert, 1973, vol. 2, p. 128; Osheim, 1977, p. 27; Violante, 1964; Herlihy, 1959.

111. Vannucci, 1963–1964. In 1156 the bishop donated San Niccolò to San Salvi. In that same year there is a record that San Salvi was leasing property from the bishop (at 6 *denari*) (ASF *Dipl.* Ripoli 31 October 1156). A papal privilege made the monastery free of any episcopal exaction. See Dameron, 1983, p. 99.

112. Davidsohn, 1977, vol. 1, pp. 277–279, 250–252; Milo, 1979, pp. 172–176. For specific information on the monasteries, see Kehr, 1908. For San Salvi, see Vannucci, 1963–1964.

113. Milo, 1979, pp. 264–265; Pescaglini Monti, 1981, pp. 204–205.

114. Chini, 1875, pp. 219–222; Magna, 1982, p. 27. According to a papal privilege from 1062, the cathedral chapter also had possessions at Ronta (Calzolai, 1973a, p. 20).

THE 1024 list of possessions in the endowment of San Miniato al Monte included a *curtis* at Cavagliano, where the Ubaldini did have some property. It is conceivable that Ildebrando was attempting to reclaim property lost to the Ubaldini.

115. The bishop received *iura* at Ripoli and Monte Aquilone from Gherardo di Adonaldo and Berto, Benedetto, and Guglielmo (perhaps his brothers) (ASF *Bullettone,* p. 244). For the Aldobrandeschi donation, see ASF *Bullettone,* p. 157.

116. See Map 2 for thelocations of and Appendix D for complete information on

these *castelli*. Vespignano is especially interesting because the bishop prohibited the locals from selling any of the castle, indicating that the bishop was having trouble preventing the alienation of his property (Lami, 1758, vol. 2, p. 797). For Ampinana, see ASF *Bullettone*, p. 193.

117. AAF *Bullettone*, fols. 93r–103r; Repetti, 1833–1846, vol. 1, pp. 343–347; Dameron, 1983, p. 118. The earliest lease in that area is a *libellus* dating from the episcopate of Rambaldo (929–964) (Lami, 1758, vol. 2, pp. 781–786).

118. SF *Bullettone*, pp. 311, 313–317.

119. Lami, 1758, vol. 2, p. 798.

120. ASF *Bullettone*, pp. 9–11.

121. Kehr, 1908, p. 58.

122. Repetti, 1833–1846, vol. 1, p. 535; Marconcini, 1972, p. 35; Dameron, 1983, p. 230.

123. AAF *Bullettone*, fols. 32v–33r.

124. ASF *Dipl.* Strozziane-Uguccioni, 11 December 1059; Kehr, 1908, p. 58; Marconcini, 1972, p. 14.

125. Wickham, 1988, p. 295; Settia, 1984, p. 490. In the Lucchesia the bishops and local inhabitants were responsible for the creation of most of the *castelli*. In the central and southern regions of Italy, the initiative came from abbots of the great monasteries (and rarely from the locals and bishops). In the Po Valley, by contrast, the royal fisc and the bishops initiated their construction (Settia, 1984, pp. 488–490; Wickham, 1985).

126. Osheim, 1977, p. 56. Apparently, the bishops leased Anchiano in 925, 1005, and 1062. It eventually fell out of episcopal control by the end of the century.

127. Wickham, 1988, pp. 82, 291–305. See also his study of *incastellamento* in the Volturno valley (Wickham, 1985).

128. AAF *Bullettone*, fols. 104r–123v. The second instance of this type of *libellus* dates from 1156 (Montecampolese in the Val di Pesa).

129. The most recent synthesis (Settia, 1984) argues that the construction of castles proceeded from the north to the south, beginning in the Po plain in the ninth century. The timing of the appearance of *castelli* in the countryside depended on several factors, including the degree of initiative by the local elite, military insecurity, the economic/demographic resurgence, and the local political situation (p. 488). Settia's book contains a full bibliography.

130. Toubert, 1973, pp. xii, 1356.

131. The historiography on Florentine *castelli* is complicated. Davidsohn (1977, vols. 1 and 2) and Caggese (1907–1909) believed *castelli* were territorial fortifications and "feudal" residences. Schneider (1975) believed they had imperial connections and were modelled after Roman and Byzantine camps. Marking a historiographical break, Plesner (1934) believed they were first fortified villages and only later became private possessions. Conti (1965) disagreed with Plesner, concluding that some were private from the beginning and all were originally defensive in nature. Francovitch (1976) concluded that Florentine *castelli* were both fortified villages *and* "feudal" residences.

132. For an example of how this worked in the diocese of Arezzo, see Cherubini, 1963, p. 34.

133. The document is published in Piattoli, 1938, no. 38, pp. 102–109; and Ughelli, 1718, cols. 53–62. For details on Attone's measures, see Milo, 1979, pp. 82–85.

134. Piattoli, 1938, no. 41, pp. 114–116; Ughelli, 1718, cols. 53–62; Quilici, 1943, pp. 52–54; Biadi, 1848, pp. 22–23; Repetti, 1833–1846, vol. 1, p. 16; Biadi, 1848, pp. 40–43; Dameron, 1983, pp. 222–223.

135. ASF *Dipl.* Strozziane-Uguccioni, 13 July 1050. A copy of the 1050 document is in Piattoli, 1938, no. 53, pp. 141–146; and Ughelli, 1718, cols. 62–72. For an overview of Gerardo's reform measures, see Milo, 1979, pp. 59–72; Davidsohn, 1977, vol. 1, pp. 313–319; Quilici, 1943, pp. 67–82. The Visdomini also granted property to the chapter in 1050, enhancing the political and economic connections of the lineage with the chapter.

136. Kehr, 1908, p. 58. In 1059 Nicholas II exempted Castelfiorentino from all jurisdiction except episcopal, and in 1136 Pope Innocent II consecrated it (ASF *Dipl.* Strozziane-Uguccioni, 11 December 1059; Marconcini, 1972, p. 14).

   Although I have not completed a systematic analysis of the information, I can list capitular holdings by 1076. For details, see Piattoli, 1938, no. 91, pp. 231–233.

137. Davidsohn, 1977, vol. 1, pp. 329–331; Milo, 1979, pp. 182–200, 204–208; Quilici, 1943, pp. 97–102.

138. Moore, 1980, pp. 51, 55, 66.

139. In 1048 the church of San Salvi became a Vallombrosan monastery under the direction of Giovanni Gualberto himself (Davidsohn, 1977, vol. 1, p. 277).

140. For the raid on San Salvi, see Milo, 1979, p. 184; Davidsohn, 1977, vol. 1, pp. 339–341.

141. Milo, 1979, p. 192.

142. AAF *Bullettone,* fols. 86r–88v; ASF *Bullettone,* pp. 141–146. See also Davidsohn, 1896, vol. 1, p. 47; Milo, 1979, p. 189.

143. For details, see Davidsohn, 1977, vol. 1, pp. 338–339.

144. Victor Turner has demonstrated that human beings often follow certain behavioral "root paradigms" to pursue their interests. They choose in certain situations to act according to a model of behavior established in the distant past, such as accepting martyrdom for altruistic reasons or going on pilgrimages (Turner, 1974, p. 17).

145. St. Zanobi supposedly resuscitated a dead child near the church when he made his entry into the city. Subsequent bishops—when they made their ceremonial entry into Florence—always paused at that site (the Geniculum) to commemorate the miracle. It was another example of the attempt of the prelates to associate themselves with the *charisma* of the dead saint. For details on the processions and St. Zanobi, see Dameron, 1988.

146. A brief overview of the foundation is in Davidsohn, 1977, vol. 1, pp. 338–339; Quilici, 1943, pp. 97–102. The actual act of foundation is preserved in ASF *Dipl.* San Pier Maggiore, 1066. We know very little about Ghisla and her family.

147. The first document regarding the entry and marriage dates from 1286, but that document noted that the ritual entry and marriage had been an ancient custom by that time.

148. Quilici, 1943, p. 97; Sanesi, 1932, p. 15; Davidsohn, 1977, vol. 1, p. 339. The first documented record of the entry dates from 1286, and it is in the *Bullettone*. I am currently investigating this entry, and therefore my dating the beginning of the entry is at this time only a hypothesis.

149. For information on the entry in Troyes, see Gies, 1978, p. 89. I developed my ideas relevant to San Pier Maggiore in a paper delivered at the 1987 meeting of the American Historical Association. A similar symbolic marriage occurred in Pistoia (Dameron, 1988).

150. Milo, 1979, pp. 184–186.

151. For an account of the complex political considerations, see above. See also Milo, 1979, pp. 194–202. Papal reluctance to side with Vallombrosa stemmed from Giovanni Gualberto's unwillingness to accept papal authority, specifically in relation to the question of whether a simoniac can administer the sacraments.

152. Davidsohn, 1977, vol. 1, p. 367. Gams (1873, p. 747) lists an Elinardo as bishop, but there is no evidence in the sources of a bishop by that name.

153. Davidsohn, 1977, vol. 1, pp. 367–368; Ughelli, 1718, cols. 77–89; Quilici, 1942, pp. 5–11.

154. The re-foundation appears in ASF *Dipl.* San Pier Maggiore, 27 November 1073.

155. ASF *Dipl.* San Pier Maggiore, 27 November 1073.

156. Capiteto at Santo Stefano Pane, San Remigio, San Lorenzo a Castello, Santa Reparata, San Benigne. For general information, see Dameron, 1983, p. 180. For information on the interests enjoyed by San Miniato al Monte in the Valdigreve (San Piero ad Ema), see ASF *Dipl.* Olivetani, years 1044–1045. The bishop acquired the castle at Carza in 1080, located where the convent also had possessions.

157. For Carza, see ASF *Bullettone,* p. 151.

158. Dameron, 1983, p. 183; Kehr, 1908, p. 51; Davidsohn, 1977, vol. 1, p. 425.

159. "Dominus et valde venerabilis Rainerius consecravit eam, scilicet in honore eiusdem Sancte Virginis supradicte et S. Agathe in altari superiori" (ASF *Dipl.* Santa Maria Novella, 30 October 1096). The church became a Dominican stronghold after 1221 and the headquarters of the Inquisition in the 1240's (Dameron, 1983, p. 94).

160. "Porro laborum vestrorum decimas vobis ob pauperum usus retinendas absque episcopi cuiuslibet contradictione concedimus" (ASF *Dipl.* Cestello, 6 March 1102).

161. Quilici, 1942, p. 13.

162. For published copies of each of these documents, see Piattoli, 1938, nos. 76, 112, 139, and 159. For a useful overview, see Quilici, 1942, pp. 17–32.

163. Dated 1085, the document summarized in the *Bullettone* mentions that Rodolfo di Signore made the offering. This is the first documented record of a donation at Montughi (AAF *Bullettone,* fols. 30r–31v).

164. "Qualiter Rainerius quondam Rainerii de Monte Buono remisit se in manibus Episcopi Florentini et iuravit quod Castrum Montis Buono com toto Podio est Episcopatus Florentie, et quod non tollet neque contendet neque consulet aliud, quod preiudicet Episcopatui in dicto Castro (AAF *Bullettone,* fol. 72r). See also Davidsohn, 1977, vol. 1, pp. 422–423.

165. Dameron, 1983, pp. 170–171. Even after the 1092 commendation, the Buondelmonti retained the patronage rights to San Pietro di Montebuoni (see ASF *Not. Ant.* B 1340, fol. 38v).

166. Davidsohn, 1977, vol. 1, p. 617.

167. Properties of the margrave in the area later went to the Badias of Marturi and Florence (Dameron, 1983, p. 258; Schneider, 1975, pp. 262–266). For Campoli, see Repetti, 1833–1846, vol. 1, pp. 430–431.

168. The dates represent the first dates at which the bishopric appears to possess interests in the *castelli.*

169. AAF *Bullettone,* fols. 69r–71r. See also Francovitch, 1976, p. 120.

170. Francovitch, 1976, p. 90; Repetti, 1833–1846, vol. 2, p. 79; Schneider, 1975, p. 266.

171. This information is taken from the AAF *Bullettone,* fols. 93r–103r and 104r–123v.

172. ASF *Bullettone,* p. 151.

173. ASF *Bullettone,* pp. 192, 198.

174. For details, see Magna, 1982. I thank Christopher Wickham for having brought this fact to my attention.

175. Davidsohn, 1896–1908, vol. 4, p. 506.

176. Most of the documentation for the estate of the bishops of Fiesole unfortunately begins only in 1228 (Raspini, 1962, p. 8). Most of the parchments dating before that period are in Ughelli, 1718, vol. 3, cols. 214–217.

177. Ughelli, 1718, vol. 3, cols. 214–217.

178. For details, see Ughelli, 1718, vol. 3, cols. 219–220.

179. Ughelli, 1718, vol. 3, cols. 223–231.

180. Lami, 1758, vol. 1., p. 246.

181. ASF *Bullettone,* pp. 14, 18, 19.

182. For details, see Piattoli, 1938; pp. 87–90, 102–109, 114–116, 141–146, 278–282; and AAF *Bullettone,* fols. 5r–23r.

183. For San Pietro in Mercato, see Lami, 1758, vol. 1, p. 246.

184. The date of the acknowledgment of the payment by San Pietro in Mercato was 1008 (ASF *Bullettone,* p. 14).

185. De la Roncière, 1976, vol. 3, p. 344.

186. Lami, 1758, vol. 1, p. 245 (cited in Davidsohn, 1977, vol. 1, p. 498); Davidsohn, 1977, vol. 1, p. 498.

187. AAF *Bullettone,* fol. 165. During the tenure of Ildebrando, there was only one recorded donation: a *castello* at Lancisa in the Valdarno (AAF *Bullettone,* fols. 86r–88v).

188. Between the ninth and tenth centuries the bishop of Volterra had created a market at San Gimignano (Fiumi, 1961, p. 19).

189. Jones, 1974, p. 1479.

190. Jones, 1964, pp. 330–331; Wickham, 1988, pp. 79–80.

191. For the eleventh and early twelfth century, there are only three leases that might have involved labor obligations: Decimo in 1015 (plus 15 *denari*), Carraia/Careggio in 1068 (plus wine), and Florence (a *libellus* in 1119).

192. Money rents also predominated in the dioceses of Arezzo, Pisa, Pistoia, and

Volterra (Kotel'nikova, 1975, p. 67). In the Casentino money rents continued to dominate until 1250 (Wickham, 1988, p. 229).

193. ASF *Bullettone*, p. 19.

194. Jones, 1954a, p. 18.

195. In 451 the Council of Chalcedon had recommended that each bishop appoint a steward to administer his possessions. Theoretically, the *vicedominus* administered the temporal possessions of the bishop and was supposed to be a cleric. Officially, he was probably originally a member of the cathedral chapter, but after the descendants of Davizio took over the office, the *vicedominus* no longer was a cleric.

196. Osheim, 1977, p. 35. The Avvocati enjoyed a resurgence of their power between 1220 and 1240, but after 1241 they disappeared.

197. Volpe, 1964, pp. 22–29, 15. No Visdomini lineage appeared in the diocese of Volterra (p. 280).

198. For information on the legal aspects of the stewards, see Gilchrist, 1969, p. 30.

199. ASF *Bullettone*, p. 68.

200. For general information, see Osheim, 1977, pp. 33–36. For the Avvocati in Florence, see Quilici, 1940, p. 63.

201. Davidsohn, 1977, vol. 1, pp. 373–380. For a biography of the countess, see Overmann, 1895.

202. Davidsohn, 1977, vol. 1, p. 398. The bishop of Pistoia, Leo, remained faithful to the imperial party until the end of his life (p. 398). Although Bishops Anselmo I (1057–1073) and Anselmo II (1073–1086) were both pro-reform partisans (Anselmo II was Matilda's confessor), the "populus" of Lucca was more concerned with achieving independence from Matilda than reforming the cathedral chapter. In 1080 they forced Anselmo II out of the city (Osheim, 1977, pp. 17, 129).

203. Schevill, 1961, pp. 58–59.

204. Wickham, 1988, p. 132; Cherubini, 1963, p. 9.

205. "Per quel che riguarda Volterra l'impedimento maggiore a questi bisogni urbani viene dal Vescovo; dal Vescovo come Conte del comitato e come nobile pannocchiesco" (Volpe, 1964, p. 167).

206. Davidsohn, 1977, vol. 1, pp. 398–401; Davidsohn, 1896–1908, vol. 1, pp. 62–63; Schevill, 1961, pp. 59–60.

207. Milo, 1979, pp. 151–152.

208. Barbadoro, 1929, p. 4; Santini, 1895b, pp. 22–23.

209. Benvenuti-Papi, 1987, p. 83.

2. The Bishop, the City, and the Contado in the Twelfth Century

1. See Volpe, 1964, passim; Herlihy, 1967, p. 26; Cherubini, 1963, p. 9.

2. Conti, 1965, p. 180; Jones, 1980a, p. 148.

3. Fiumi, 1959, p. 486.

4. Santini, 1895a, pp. xxxiv–xlvii.

5. Santini, 1895a, pp. ix–xxvii. The Scolari of Montebuoni apparently were episcopal *fideles,* and a member of that lineage served as consul in 1186 (p. xxxiv).

6. Waley, 1969, p. 111.

7. Jones, 1978, p. 213.

8. Herlihy, 1967, pp. 29–30.

9. Wickham, 1988, p. 131; Romeo, 1971, pp. 12–13.

10. Waley, 1969, p. 111; Jones, 1978, p. 295.

11. Santini, 1900, vol. 25, pp. 33–35, 43–44; Davidsohn, 1977, vol. 1, p. 535.

12. For complete overviews of this period of Florentine history, see Santini, 1900, vol. 25, pp. 42–45; Davidsohn, 1977, vol. 1, pp. 529–672; Schevill, 1961, pp. 60–62.

13. Santini, 1900, vol. 25, pp. 46–48. Galiga shows up in 1113 as part of the endowment entrusted to San Miniato al Monte (ASF *Dipl.* Olivetani, 1113). Doccia was also part of the endowment. The bishop leased the tithes in its parish in 1141.

14. Stahl, 1965, p. 13; Quilici, 1950, pp. 20–22; Davidsohn, 1977, vol. 1, pp. 568–570.

15. Santini, 1900, vol. 25, pp. 43–48.

16. Santini, 1900, vol. 25, pp. 47–48, 56; Davidsohn, 1977, vol. 1, pp. 582–592; Quilici, 1950, pp. 26–29.

17. Santini, 1900, vol. 25, pp. 59–61; ASF *Bullettone*, p. 7.

18. Santini, 1900, vol. 25, pp. 61–64; Davidsohn, 1977, vol. 1, pp. 616–618; Repetti, 1833–1846, vol. 3, p. 327.

19. Santini, 1900, vol. 25, pp. 64–65; Quilici, 1950, p. 37.

20. Santini, 1895b, pp. 23–29.

21. Quilici, 1950, p. 37–46; Santini, 1900, vol. 25, pp.64–65; Schevill, 1961, p. 80; Davidsohn, 1977, vol. 1, pp. 632–635.

22. Count Arduino dei conti di Pancio was the father of the widow of the last Cadolingi, the wife of the brother of the bishop (Nontigiova). The bishop supported his family and the commune decided to back the bishop. Guido Guerra refused mediation (Quilici, 1950, p. 48).

23. Davidsohn, 1977, vol. 1, pp. 641–668; Santini, 1900, vol. 25, pp. 65–77.

24. Santini, 1900, vol. 25, p. 79.

25. Barbadoro, 1929, p. 5. The *foderum* originally was forage for houses required in certain areas of the diocese (usually in kind). Called *foderum* in Lombardy, it came to be called the *collecta, colta,* or *datium* in Emilia and Tuscany. Normally it was 26 *denari* per hearth (*focolare*). For details, see Brühl, 1968, vol. 1, pp. 722–723; Haverkamp, 1966.

26. Repetti, 1833–1846, vol. 4, pp. 480–481.

27. Davidsohn, 1977, vol. 1, pp. 420–421, 676–682; Dameron, 1983, pp. 216–217. For the papal privilege, see Kehr, 1908, vol. 3, p. 60. Davidsohn mentions that prior to 1155 the local population complained of being oppressively taxed by the bishop.

28. On May 6, 1155, Pope Adrian IV wrote the arch-priest Teodoro, taking the parish under papal protection and forbidding episcopal exactions ("suscipit ecclesiam ad Marturam sub apostolica protectione . . . sancit ut Florentinus episcopus ecclesiam illicitis vel indebitis exactionibus nullo tempore gravare praesumat") (Kehr, 1908, vol. 3, p. 60).

29. Davidsohn, 1977, vol. 1, p. 680.
30. "Qualiter Adrianus Papa quartus revocavit concessionem, quam fecerat Episcopatui Senensi in Monte Bonitii in preiudicem Episcopatus Florentini, sub millesimo centesimo quinquagesimo sexto tertio nonas Decembris" (AAF *Bullettone*, fol. 5r). On December 29, 1182, Pope Lucius III reconfirmed the decision regarding the *plebs* (Kehr, 1908, vol. 3, p. 66).
31. Santini, 1895a, pp. 11–12.
32. "Alexander III . . . confirmat ecclesiam in Monte Bonizzi a bona memoria Raynerio episcopo in fundo, quem bona memoria comes Guido bono Petro concessit, auctoritate Hadriani constructam, dans ei liberam facultatem sicut Hadrianus dedit, eamdem ecclesiam consecrandi et in ea clericos ponendi et ordinandi, non obstante retractione, quam Hadrianus super hoc, levi et vano errore ductus, fecit (quia in locus in episcopatu Florentino consistit)" (Kehr, 1908, vol. 3, pp. 66, 205). *Iura spiritualia* included the right to collect a quarter of the tithes and to elect the rector.
33. "Statuit, ut quicumque de Senensi diocesi ad locum illum transierit, in omnibus spiritualibus ei tantum debeat respondere, censum in bizantio apostolica sedi annualiter persolvendo" (Kehr, 1908, vol. 3, pp. 66, 205–206).
34. Barbadoro, 1929, pp. 14–17.
35. Barbadoro, 1929, pp. 17–21; Stahl, 1965, p. 30.
36. Schevill, 1961, pp. 80–86; Davidsohn, 1977, vol. 1, pp. 673–976. For information on the close relations between Frederick I and the Guidi and Alberti, see Quilici, 1950, p. 74.
37. Stahl, 1965, p. 17.
38. A document associated with the monastery of San Piero a Luco in the Mugello and dated sometime between 1090 and 1093 indicates that thirty-two men paid the tax. See Davidsohn, 1977, vol. 1, pp. 400–401; Brühl, 1968, vol. 1, p. 555.
39. Davidsohn, 1977, vol. 1, pp. 1010–1012; Brühl, 1968, p. 693; Barbadoro, 1929, pp. 21–30; Conti, 1985, pp. xii–xiii.
40. Plesner, 1979, p. 461.
41. Soli, Fortuna, and Vaglia are included in folios 89r to 92r in the AAF *Bullettone*. The *affictus* are on folios 210r–211r; the *iuramenta* on folio 265v.
42. AAF *Bullettone*, fols. 89r–89v, 92r.
43. Violante, 1977a, p. 684.
44. ASF *Bullettone*, p. 17.
45. ASF *Bullettone*, pp. 12–13; Francovitch, 1976, p. 105.
46. The area around Molezzano was within the purview of several kin groups (Repetti, 1833–1846, vol. 3, p. 247).
47. ASF *Bullettone*, pp. 239–240.
48. AAF *Bullettone*, fols. 145r–151r; ASF *Bullettone*, p. 265.
49. A similar process was occurring in the countryside around San Gimignano, where minor landholders were selling jurisdictional rights and lands to the bishop of Volterra to escape the pressures coming from the more powerful lineages (Fiumi, 1961, p. 22).
50. Bishop Giulio purchased Petroio and received the patronage rights to the nearby chapel as well (Francovitch, 1976, p. 121).

51. The bishop purchased properties from several people. These were needed for the construction of a *castello* ("quod ad eos pertinebat de dicto podio Montis Acuti, quantum necessarium erat ad Castellum edificandum super ipso podio de fossa usque ad fossam (AAF *Bullettone,* fol. 54v). See Francovitch, 1976, p. 130.

52. Lami, 1758, vol. 2, p. 808; Davidsohn, 1977, vol. 1, p. 601. The lodging rights added to properties the bishops already possessed in those areas (see AAF *Bullettone,* fol. 41r).

53. ASF *Bullettone,* p. 7.

54. The dates of the major acquisitions were 1076, 1148 (purchase), 1159 (purchase), 1175 (purchase), 1181 (purchase), 1181 (donation), and 1195 (purchase of houses and lands) (AAF *Bullettone,* fols. 69r–71r).

55. There is the record of one *libellus* at Fabbrica, made in 1140. For all the entries in the AAF *Bullettone* regarding Fabbrica, see folios 43r–45v.

56. Biadi, 1848, pp. 23, 83, 16; Repetti, 1833–1846, vol. 1, p. 356.

57. The one example we have dates from 1121, when the arch-priest acknowledged he owed annually to the bishop at Christmas three *soldi* (ASF *Bullettone,* p. 11).

58. "Qualiter Johannis filius Petri vocatus Calzaiuolus et Carina eius filia, donaverunt pro remedio eorum animarum . . . Christ (sic) Ospedalee (sic) del Calzaiuolo cum omnibus edificiis, possessionbus et terris" (AAF *Bullettone,* fol. 61r).

59. All entries are in the AAF *Bullettone,* fols. 61r–64r.

60. "Loco dicto al Peruscello ad molendinum cum aqueductu super ipsa terra hedificandum" (AAF *Bullettone,* fol. 61r).

61. Dameron, 1983, pp. 271–272.

62. Entries regarding the parishes of Percussina, San Cresci, Sant'Andrea di Nuovole, Santa Maria ad Argiano, and Sant'Agnolo ad Argiano are scattered throughout the first 71 folios of the AAF *Bullettone.*

63. AAF *Bullettone,* fols. 57r–60v.

64. AAF *Bullettone,* fol. 51v.

65. Brunetto di Gherardo sold numerous possessions ("omnes casas, possessiones, terras suas et ancillas quas habet et tenet pro se vel per alium in feudum vel ad livellarium") (AAF *Bullettone,* fol. 72r).

66. For the donation itself, see AAF *Bullettone,* fols. 40r–41r.

67. Christopher Wickham suggested to me that Zabollina might have made the donation simply because she was childless. See Fiumi, 1961, p. 22, for a description of how the minor nobility donated to ecclesiastical lords to escape pressure from the greater nobility.

68. See Francovitch, 1976, p. 84, for a brief discussion of the castle of Castelfiorentino. Francovitch does not mention Timignano.

69. AAF *Bullettone,* fol. 35r. See also Cioni, 1912–1915, vol. 20, p. 84.

70. Pietro and Gherardo took out a *libellus* with the bishop for three *denari* a year for property at Capezzano and Terra Rubea (AAF *Bullettone,* fol. 33v).

71. Repetti, 1833–1846, vol. 1, p. 535. According to Marconcini, the area was called Castelfiorentino by 1150 (1972, p. 37).

72. Repetti, 1833–1846, vol. 1, p. 535. Frederick I confirmed those possessions in 1164.

73. The bishop of Lucca had lands at Gricciano a Sala, Nebbiano, and Camiano. The Badia had interests in part of the *castrum* of Timignano. In 1190 the imperial vicar mortgaged the toll on the road to the bishop of Volterra. For details, see Marconcini, 1972, pp. 36–37.

74. This was a *libellus*. See AAF *Bullettone*, fols. 5r–23r.

75. AAF *Bullettone*, fols. 74r–77r. In the Archivio di Stato di Firenze there is an 1190 *libellus* for land, pasture, *curtes*, woods, and houses at Padule in the *plebatus* of Sesto (ASF *Dipl.* Strozziane-Uguccioni March 1190). The *census* was 24 *denari*, to be paid at the feast of St. John.

76. AAF *Bullettone*, fols. 5r–23r.

77. Davidsohn, 1977, vol. 1, pp. 1012–1013.

78. Osheim, 1977, p. 87; Fiumi, 1956, p. 39. Volterra forbade the export of grain outside its *contado* in 1225 (Volpe, 1964, p. 219), and Siena did the same in 1223 (Fiumi, 1956, p. 46). Only in 1258 did the Florentines forbid such exportations (Fiumi, 1956, p. 39), probably because the city was not powerful enough to do so earlier.

79. For descriptions of the many types of contracts, see Kotel'nikova, 1975, pp. 231–275.

80. The Fourth Council of Constantinople (869–70) stipulated that a lessee could be evicted only after two or three years of non-payment (Gilchrist, 1969, p. 30), but it was unlikely that this canon was ever enforceable. See also Kotel'nikova, 1975, p. 273.

81. Herlihy, 1959, p. 5.

82. ASF *Bullettone*, pp. 17, 84, 108; Lami, 1758, vol. 1, p. 618.

83. Kotel'nikova, 1975, p. 40.

84. ASF *Bullettone*, p. 182.

85. ASF *Bullettone*, p. 84.

86. Herlihy, 1961, p. 99; Jones, 1964, pp. 335–342; Kotel'nikova, 1975, pp. 330–331.

87. For discussion of market dues received by the bishop of Lucca, see Osheim, 1977, pp. 89–90. In that diocese the bishop probably drew some income from the markets at Moriano, Santa Maria a Monte, and Montopoli.

88. Fiumi, 1959, p. 440; Conti, 1985, pp. xii–xiii.

89. For details, see Conti, 1985, pp. xi–xiv.

90. ASF *Bullettone*, p. 123.

91. ASF *Bullettone*, p. 111.

92. For references, see Lami, 1758, vol. 2, pp. 761, 773. It was a Tosinghi who bought the property at Vallecchio.

93. Santini, 1895a, p. 501; ASF *Bullettone*, pp. 265, 47. There is the record of a donation of property to the episcopate near Sesto in the AAF *Bullettone*, folio 165.

94. Kotel'nikova, 1975, p. 250.

95. Davidsohn 1977, vol. 1, p. 504.

96. Canon 20, Fourth Council of Constantinople (869–70) (Gilchrist, 1969, p. 159).

97. Lopes-Pegna, 1974, p. 203. Already at the beginning of the eleventh century, Florence had imposed a Florentine administrator to manage the property of the bishop of Fiesole (Davidsohn, 1977, vol. 1, pp. 196–197).

98. It is possible that the bishops were going to communal courts as early as 1130 (Santini, 1895b, p. 32). For the episode, see Santini, 1895a, p. 501. However, there is no evidence that communal courts in Florence existed before 1150. Christopher Wickham tells me that they did exist in Lucca and Pisa before that date, indicating that perhaps they also existed in Florence.

99. The communal ordinance stated that the bishop had the authority to nullify any alienation of church property and that the commune could not inhibit his actions ("si quis de possessione Ecclesie Florentine alienasset, sive modo aliquo contraxisset, ex nunc sint contracti inde facti cassi et nullius valoris et Episcopus Florentinus sua propria auctoritate et arbitrio possit retractare et contravenire, et in predictis nullus Iudex et nullusque offitialis contra hoc debeat aliquod auxilium exhibere") (ASF *Bullettone,* p. 315; Santini, 1952, p. 501). The courts affirmed this assurance in 1233 and 1236.

100. Gilchrist, 1969, p. 159; Santini, 1952, p. 501.

101. In 1179 Pope Alexander III protested the placement of restrictions on the church aimed at removing episcopal jurisdiction over its own *fideles* on its own lands (Davidsohn, 1977, vol. 1, pp. 1001, 1014–1015). For more information, see Davidsohn, 1977, vol. 5, p. 483; Barbi, 1899, p. 83.

102. Santini, 1952, p. 501.

3. Rural Communes and the Challenge to Episcopal Hegemony in the Countryside, 1182–1250

1. Conti, 1985, p. xi. See also Benvenuti-Papi, 1988, pp. 21–24.

2. For the properties of the chapter, see the parchments (*Carte Strozziane*) in the Archivio del Capitolo Fiorentino. For the bishop of Fiesole, see AA Fiesole, *Libri Causarum* XIV.III.A.1 and AA Fiesole *Ordinazioni* VIII.A.1 (5a–85r) in the Archivio Arcivescovile di Fiesole.

3. For example, in 1181 the arch-priest of San Pietro in Pisside sold land to settle some debts as well (ASF *Dipl.* Passignano, 31 July 1181), and in 1205 the abbey of Passignano paid grain to its creditors (ASF *Dipl.* Passignano, 30 December 1205). In 1211 the monastery of Settimo pawned its possessions in the parish of San Martino alla Palma in order to take out a loan of 300 *lire*. Regarding the issue of indebtedness, however, the sources are incomplete and spotty. We can only suggest that whereas some church lords were in debt, others contracted loans to finance property consolidation by way of purchases. I am grateful to Duane Osheim for having cautioned me from making a sweeping generalization.

4. ASF *Dipl.* San Vigilio di Siena, 4 August 1193. For the taxes, see Davidsohn, 1977, vol. 1, pp. 1012–1013.

5. For an example of how the bishop sold property in one area to be able to purchase property in another, see ASF *Dipl.* Strozziane-Uguccioni, 2 September 1217.

6. Personal communication from Christopher Wickham.

7. The cases, published by Santini (1895a), involved the following ecclesiastical institutions: Settimo (1172), Vallombrosa (1181), San Miniato (1183), the cathe-

dral chapter (1183), San Martino Vescovo (1183), Santa Maria Maggiore (1193), Vallombrosa (1202), the cathedral chapter (1204), and the Badia (1206, 1209, 1224, 1226). The last instance involved property at Signa. For the actual documents regarding these cases, see *Capitoli,* pp. 223–314.

8. In 1225 the bishop of Fiesole excommunicated the inhabitants of Figline for having sold episcopal property (ASF *Dipl.* Passignano, 22 June 1225). For information on Arezzo, see Cherubini, 1963.

9. ASF *Dipl.* Cestello, 14 September 1211. The monastery pawned all its tithes, the *accattum* and *datium, servitia,* and *pensiones.*

10. For an excellent discussion of what the status *fidelis* actually meant to episcopal dependents, see Nelli, 1989.

11. ASF *Dipl.* Strozziane-Uguccioni, 13 February 1234. See also Piattoli, 1938, pp. 40–45.

12. Davidsohn, 1977, vol. 1, p. 861.

13. "Qualiter Visconte Sindicus Episcopatus Florentini conquestus fuit coram Consulibus Civitatis Florentie de quibusdam hominibus de Querceto, qui se negabant esse fideles dicti Episcopatus, contra quod sententia lata fuit per dictos Consules in favorem dicti Episcopatus" (AAF *Bullettone,* fol. 76r).

14. The men of Sesto had damaged unspecified episcopal interests: "iniurebant et molestabant ipsum Episcopum et Episcopatum de Iuribus pertinentibus eidem . . ." (AAF *Bullettone,* fol. 75v).

15. AAF *Bullettone,* fol. 75v.

16. "Qualiter Comune de Capalle constituit Sindicum ad causandum cum Episcopatu Florentino" (AAF *Bullettone,* fol. 80v).

17. "Qualiter Comune Florentini de mandato domini Episcopi ordinavit quod facerent [se] mandati dicti Episcopi" (AAF *Bullettone,* fol. 80v).

18. The bishop excommunicated certain men for being perjurors: "excommunicavit quosdam homines de Capalle ut periuros" (AAF *Bullettone,* fol. 79r). For payments required of episcopal dependents in the diocese of Siena, see Redon, 1979, pp. 638–640.

19. Studio Telemugellouno, 1982, p. 124; Chini, 1875, pp. 223–225. For the episcopal castles, see Map 2.

20. Magna, 1982, pp. 15–18, 27. Other lords in the Mugello included several abbeys and monasteries. Barberino had many lords (Magna, 1982, p. 20).

21. The first documented evidence of collective opposition occurred in the *plebatus* of Vaglia. In 1217 and 1218 Bishop Giovanni required a large number of acknowledgments from dependents that they were indeed *homines et fideles* and owed the *servitia consueta.* One of those rebels might have been the arch-priest of Petroio himself, who also acknowledged in 1217 that he was leasing episcopal property in the *plebatus* for a certain money rent (AAF *Bullettone,* folio 90v).

22. ASF *Bullettone,* p. 155.

23. ASF *Bullettone,* p. 156.

24. For the following, see also R. Caggese, 1907–1909, pp. 319–330.

25. All the references to Borgo San Lorenzo are from folios 93r through 103r in the AAF *Bullettone* (ASF *Bullettone,* pp. 152–171).

26. ASF *Bullettone,* p. 166.

27. ASF *Bullettone,* p. 165.

28. Conti, 1985, p. xiii. The *iudex* and rectors of Borgo swore to collect the *datium:* "recolligere et adiuvare recolligi datium et impositionem" (ASF *Bullettone,* p. 153). The wording implies the bishop was collecting it previously. The appropriation of the old imperial *datium* by the bishop after the failure of the imperial cause in 1197 was not at all unusual, and cities often helped the bishop to collect it (Stahl, 1965, p. 49).

29. AAF *Bullettone,* fols. 93r–103r. The entries on which I have relied to reconstruct the conflict are scattered throughout that section of the register.

30. In the *Bullettone,* there is a list of about eighty men swearing *iuramenta et fidelitas* to the bishop on that date (AAF *Bullettone,* fol. 262v).

31. For a list of *podestà,* see Santini, 1895a, pp. lxiii ff.

32. Santini, 1895a, p. lxiii.

33. Magna, 1982, p. 38.

34. The relevant sections in the AAF *Bullettone* are folios 217v–227v, 104r–123r, and 269r–270v.

35. Repetti, 1833–1846, vol. 3, p. 247.

36. In 1224, Belincione di Uberto di Bernardo dei Adimari sold all his lands, *fideles,* and possessions in the *curia et castellum* to Bishop Giovanni, though he kept the *ius patronatus* in the local church. The bishop of Fiesole and one Ugo di Ranieri also had land there (see Repetti, 1833–1846, vol. 3, p. 276).

37. It is impossible to know when the episcopate began making those appointments. For information on the relationship of rural churches to the episcopate, see AAF *Bullettone,* fols. 5r–23r.

38. "Qualiter Episcopus Florentinus absolvit Guidonem Iannis della Via et suos descendentes a prestatione multorum et diversorum servitiorum Episcopatui hactenus debitorum et per eosdem reduxit ea servitia in praestationem unius scefigli grani ad starium burgensem" (ASF *Bullettone,* p. 192).

39. See the ASF *Bullettone,* p. 383, for a list of forty men who swore *iuramenta* in 1231.

40. Duane Osheim has also suggested to me the possibility that the tenants enjoyed a close relationship with the bishop, since they might have felt the Guidi were not much of a threat.

41. Unless otherwise cited, all references are from the AAF *Bullettone,* fols. 131r–140r (ASF *Bullettone,* pp. 233–258).

42. ASF *Bullettone,* p. 239.

43. This sale included all properties and possessions (*possessiones, terras, fideles, colonos, servitia, pensiones, fictus, et iura*) in the *curia et districtus* of Uliveta (ASF *Bullettone,* p. 236); Lami, 1758, vol. 1, p. 613.

44. Lami, 1758, vol. 1, pp. 618, 611.

45. ASF *Bullettone,* p. 239.

46. This *podestà* had jurisdiction over Valcava, Pagliariccio, Monte Acutolo, Botena, Monte Rinaldi, Pievevecchia, Vico, and Montefiesole. See the section on the *plebatus* of Montefiesole, below.

47. The payment for each male came to ten *soldi* or one *lire* (Conti, 1985, p. xiii). The residents of Valcava acted as other episcopal tenants did in the *contado*

following the death of Bishop Ardingo: they took the opportunity to deny any
episcopal control over their lives.

48. "Quod illa observarentur, que dictus Dominus Episcopus approbaret" (ASF
    Bullettone, p. 234).

49. The relevant sections in the AAF *Bullettone* are the following: folios 141r–144r,
    145r–147v, 148r–151r, 152r–154r, 156r–161v, 155r–155v, 167r, 236r–242v,
    243r, 244r–246r, 246v–248r, 249r–254r, 266r, 266v, 267r–268r, 271r.

50. Repetti, 1833–1846, vol. 3, pp. 397–398.

51. Repetti, 1833–1846, vol. 3, pp. 397–398; ASF *Bullettone*, p. 282 (or AAF *Bullettone*, fol. 152r).

52. Barbadoro, 1929, p. 16.

53. ASF *Bullettone*, p. 289.

54. Like other *podestà* appointed in other areas of episcopal power in the *contado*,
    Marsoppino was a member of the Visdomini or Tosinghi houses. I have reconstructed the chronology of the sale from the entries in the AAF *Bullettone*, fols.
    236r–242v.

55. AAF *Bullettone*, fols. 148r–151r. The entry is also on page 271 of the ASF
    Bullettone.

56. Dameron, 1983, p. 155.

57. ASF *Bullettone*, p. 267.

58. The earliest mention of episcopal *fideles* at Vico dates from 1212 (see ASF
    Bullettone, p. 267).

59. The introduction of the urban *datium* of 26 *denari* per household was therefore
    late at Monte di Croce (Barbadoro, 1929, p. 30).

60. ASF *Bullettone*, p. 287.

61. There were three *reductiones* and one *permutatio*.

62. ASF *Bullettone*, p. 260. The *podestà* was Guido di Aldobrandino dei Visdomini.

63. ASF *Bullettone*, p. 270.

64. Plesner, 1934, p. 30.

65. Salvini, 1969, pp. 5–101.

66. AAF *Bullettone*, fol. 33r.

67. Calzolai, 1973b, p. 19.

68. "Qualiter Dominus Johannis Episcopus supradictus excommunicavit commune,
    et homines de Castro Florentino, quia nitebantur auferre dictum Castrum Episcopatui Florentino" (AAF *Bullettone*, fol. 33v).

69. AAF *Bullettone*, fol. 32v.

70. The conflict between San Gimignano and Volterra concerned control of several
    episcopal castles (Montevultraio and Montignoso). A mediator in the dispute
    was the bishop of Florence (Volpe, 1923, pp. 115–116; 1964, p. 234; Fiumi,
    1961, pp. 24–27).

71. Marconcini, 1972, p. 9. For a roughly analogous situation in the *contado* of Siena
    (rural commune of Tintinnano), see Redon, 1979, p. 638.

72. ASF *Dipl.* Poggibonsi, 5 November 1231. The parchment is severely damaged.
    There are only two entries in the *Bullettone* which deal with the agreement (fols.
    33v and 35r).

73. See also Marconcini, 1972, for a complete survey of the conflict. The episcopate
    was still receiving these taxes as late as 1315 (AAF Aldobrandino, fol. 58r).

74. "Tertiam partem omnium pecuniarum bannorum et dirictuarum causarum" (ASF *Dipl.* Poggibonsi, 5 November 1231).

75. ASF *Dipl.* Poggibonsi, 5 November 1231. See also Marconcini, 1972, p. 9.

76. AAF *Bullettone,* fols. 261r, 262r.

77. All information on the Val di Pesa and San Casciano comes from the AAF *Bullettone,* fols. 40r–66v. For the most detailed account of the events described, see Dameron, 1986.

78. The arch-priest was also renting episcopal property, just as the arch-priest of Valcava was doing. In 1224 he was paying the bishop four *staia* of grain, one *salma* of wine, two loaves of bread, and six *denari* for possessions including a house. In 1232 the arch-priest of Campoli resigned and the bishop appointed another (AAF *Bullettone,* fol. 47r).

79. Dameron, 1986, p. 144.

80. Dameron, 1983, p. 268.

81. De la Roncière, 1976, vol. 3, p. 343.

82. Dameron, 1983, p. 274; 1986, p. 143.

83. "Qualiter Guarnelloctus, Chiantes, et Mattafellone, fratres olim Mazzalombardi, et Mazzalombardus et Rinerius fratres, filii olim Baracterii, vendiderunt Episcopatui Florentino turrim et palatium et omnes casas et plateas, et res alias pertinentes ad eos, et in cassero et in castro de Torniano, sive eius burgis et omnes colonos ascriptos et inquilinos, et homines cuiusque sint generis cum eorum patribus, filiis, descentibus, et familiis, et peculiis, que habent in dicto castro et eius curia et districtu" (AAF *Bullettone,* fol. 46r).

84. Dameron, 1986, p. 144. A transaction like this resembled a loan.

85. The eleventh section of the *Bullettone* (following Campoli) is "Montis Campolesi et Ripoli Episcopi" (fols. 50r–56r, 198r). For general information, see Repetti, 1833–1846, vol. 1, p. 430.

86. Dameron, 1983, p. 277. The 1214 purchase was for fifteen *lire* and ten *soldi.*

87. Dameron, 1983, p. 277.

88. Dameron, 1986, p. 140.

89. There were at least eight acquisitions of property (land, *fideles,* houses, and vineyards) at Petriolo (Dameron, 1986, p. 141).

90. Francovitch, 1976, p. 77; Dameron, 1983, p. 301.

91. Though the residents of Bossolo pledged to rebuild the *castello,* they never did. For more information, see Biadi, 1848, pp. 21–23. Bossolo was not the only episcopal castle destroyed by the Florentines. The others were Colle Ramola and Cercina (1202).

92. AAF *Bullettone,* fol. 69v; Dameron, 1983, p. 299.

93. "Qualiter Commune Florentie condepnavit homines de Petriuolo quia non obedierunt Potestati electo per Episcopum Florentinum in dicto loco de Petriuolo" (AAF *Bullettone,* fol. 69r).

94. AAF *Bullettone,* fol. 67r; Dameron, 1983, p. 303.

95. Dameron, 1983, pp. 288–289.

96. Dameron, 1986, p. 148; 1983, p. 289.

97. Elsewhere in the Val di Pesa, the bishops had been requiring rents in grain since the twelfth century: Montecampolese (1142) and the Ospedale del Calzaiuolo (1149).

98. ASF *Bullettone*, p. 81. At Montecampolese in 1213 Gherardo di Baroncetti received all the lands of his father from the bishop for a yearly payment of half of what he produced. This is the earliest *mezzadria* I have found in the *Bullettone* (ASF *Bullettone*, p. 83).

99. The *Bullettone* indicates that this *podestà* served only at San Martino Argiano, but the AAF *Libro* (fol. 10r) from 1323 indicates that the *podestà* served all those communities. The appearance of an episcopal *podestà* in 1212 pre-dates the first appearance of *podestà* in the diocese of Volterra by thirteen years.

100. AAF *Bullettone*, fol. 66r.

101. AAF *Bullettone*, fol. 69v; Dameron, 1983, p. 298.

102. "Qualiter Prebyter Bene plebanus plebis de Campoli renuntiavit ipsum plebem in manibus domini Ardinghi Episcopi Florentini. Et qualiter idem Episcopus eandem plebem contulit et recommendavit domino Bernardo plebano de Ponzano" (AAF *Bullettone*, fol. 47r).

103. A typical entry reads: "Qualiter dominus Ardhingus Episcopus Florentinus permutavit cum Cambio Mercati et suis consortibus unum denarium et certa alia servitia olim per ipsos debita Episcopatui Florentino, et ipsum denarium et servitia redegit in uno staio grani solvendo annis singulis in futurum Episcopatui predicto per dictum Cambium et consortes" (AAF *Bullettone*, fol. 51r).

104. AAF *Bullettone*, fol. 65r; Dameron, 1983, p. 301.

105. Dameron, 1983, p. 278.

106. "Item qualiter dominus Rolandus potestas Florentinus commisit domino Iacopaccio Iudici suo ut conoscat causam vertentem inter Episcopum Florentinum ex una parte and homines de Sancto Cassiano ex altera" (AAF *Bullettone*, fol. 57v). The previous Florentine *podestà* had refused to assist the bishop with the case. Rolando, however, swore to uphold ecclesiastical rights. The chapter, meanwhile, was sharply disputing the right of the bishop to issue excommunications and absolutions (probably concerning San Casciano) without conferring with them. Rolando, in effect, was siding with the bishop (Davidsohn, 1977, vol. 2, pp. 307–308). I have reconstructed the conflict from the AAF *Bullettone*, fols. 57r–60v.

107. "Bonactus sindicus Domini Ardinghi Episcopi Florentini erat legiptimus, non obstante quod Capitulum Florentinum non consenserit" (AAF *Bullettone*, fol. 57v).

108. "Qualiter homines de Sancto Cassiano et eius curia debeant stare et subesse domino Episcopo et Episcopatui Florentino et recognoscant eum in dominum temporalem et eidem prestare debeant iuramenta fidelitatis" (AAF *Bullettone*, fol. 57v).

109. Davidsohn, 1977, vol. 2, p. 308.

110. This is the first indication that the dispute concerned withheld payments or rents as well as opposition to the power of the *podestà*.

111. "Qualiter dominus Marsoppus vicedominus Episcopatus Florentinus pro domino Ardingo Episcopo Florentino potestas et rector Montis Campolesis et Ripolis Episcopi eorumque curiarum et districtus cum consensu hominum dictarum contractarum ordinavit forum publicum et solempne in curte Monte Campolesis loco dicto Beccamorto" (AAF *Bullettone*, fol. 51v).

112. AAF *Bullettone*, fol. 70v. See also Dameron, 1983, p. 307; 1986, p. 147.

113. Dameron, 1986, p. 148; 1983, p. 291. The entry stated that no one could enter into any agreement that was harmful to episcopal interests: "quod nullus de Sancto Cassiano faciat, nec fieri faciat aliquem contractum in preiudicum Episcopatus Florentini" (AAF *Bullettone,* fol. 58r).

114. "Ad conservationem iurisdictionis Episcopatus in castro, curia, et districtu Decimi" (AAF *Bullettone,* fol. 59v).

115. Dameron, 1986, p. 153n.

116. Martines, 1972, p. 335; Waley, 1969, p. 53; Martines, 1979, pp. 331–335; Davidsohn, 1977, vol. 2; Larner, 1980, pp. 107–108, 113, 119–120.

117. In the twelfth century there were only three "popular" families in the consulate; the rest were aristocratic (Jones, 1980a, pp. 126–128; Stahl, 1965, pp. 56, 72).

118. Martines, 1972, pp. 341–342.

119. For a recent study of St. Zanobi, see Benvenuti-Papi, 1988, pp. 127–178.

120. Davidsohn, 1977, vol. 6, pp. 73, 251, 271, and 273.

121. For background, see Davidsohn, 1977, vol. 2, p. 50. A copy of the agreement is in the ASF (*Dipl.* Mercatanti, November 1217). See also Dameron, 1983, p. 95.

122. "Opera sancti Miniatis cum bonis sibi pertinentibus perpetuo conservetur separata ab aliis bonis dicti monasterii et semper sit in ea operarius qui dictam Operam et bona ipsius administret, et nullo tempore abbas vel monaci ipsam Operam et eius possessionem retrahant in alium usum vel utilitatem dicti monasterii aut alenet *{sic}* vel subponant aut obligent, sed semper dictam Operam et eius possessionem ac iura per operarium qui pro tempore in ea sicut infra dicitur fuerit institutus administrari et gubernari libere et quiete permictant pro constructione refectione atque reparatione ecclesie gloriossimi martiris sancti Miniatis, pro quo dicta Opera ab ipso primordio potissime dingnoscitur instituta" (ASF *Dipl.* Olivetani di Firenze, 16 May 1228, published in Santini, 1895a, p. 393).

123. Davidsohn speculates that indeed Giulio, responding to serious political pressures, did render homage to the anti-pope (Davidsohn, 1977, vol. 1, pp. 703–704, 716).

124. Davidsohn, 1977, vol. 1, p. 23; 1977, vol. 2, pp. 84, 254; Benvenuti-Papi, 1988, p. 22.

125. Davidsohn, 1977, vol. 2, pp. 253–255; Benvenuti-Papi, 1988, p. 26. For the date of Ardingo's death, see Benvenuti-Papi, 1988, p. 103.

126. Davidsohn, 1977, vol. 2, pp. 203–205.

127. For background on Umiliana, see Benvenuti-Papi, 1980; Davidsohn, 1977, vol. 2, p. 182.

128. Davidsohn, 1977, vol. 2, pp. 153–203.

129. "Absolvimus, eximimus et liberamus ab omni onere prestationem reddituum et servitiorum et qua nobis et Florentino episcopatui prestat prestare aut facere deberetis" (ASF *Dipl.* San Domenico nel Maglio, 1229). See Davidsohn, 1977, vol. 2, p. 198.

130. Davidsohn, 1977, vol. 2, p. 200.

131. Davidsohn, 1977, vol. 1, pp. 907–911.

132. Davidsohn, 1977, vol. 2, pp. 50, 79. Between 1215 and 1225 the *podestà* of Florence also settled the dispute between the bishop of Florence and Lucca (Santini, 1903, p. 36).

133. Benvenuti-Papi, 1987, pp. 82–85.

134. Ronzani, 1983.

135. Davidsohn, 1977, vol. 2, pp. 133–136; Benvenuti-Papi, 1988, p. 99. Bishop Ranieri of Fiesole had died in 1220, leaving behind him large unpaid loans and dissipated church endowments. Much of the property of the bishops, therefore, had fallen into the hands of Florentine creditors as security for the loan. The commune fined the successor of Ranieri, Ildebrando, 10,000 *lire*, forcing him into exile to Pistoia. By 1225 the commune resisted papal pressures and came to an agreement with the bishop. The compromise had strong repercussions on the Florentine episcopate as well.

136. Santini, 1903, vol. 32, pp. 40–57.

137. Barbadoro, 1929, p. 36; Santini, 1903, vol. 32, pp. 30–32; Conti, 1985, pp. xix–xxi. The city divided the residents of its territory into two categories: the unfree (*coloni* and *masnaderi*) were taxed 26 *denari*, and knights and freeholders paid 12 *soldi* (Conti, 1985, p. xx).

138. Conti, 1985, p. xx. As we have seen, however, commutations began much *earlier* than 1233. The communal tax might have led to opposition to the *datium*, but it was not the only factor behind rural opposition to the bishops.

139. Davidsohn, 1977, vol. 2, p. 271.

140. ACF *Carte Strozziane*, 108 (also published in Lami, 1758, vol. 3, pp. 1653–1654). For details, see Benvenuti-Papi, 1988, pp. 34–37.

141. ACF *Carte Strozziane*, 162. The document is dated 3 kalends January, 1236 (December 29, 1235). The chapter protested the bishop's introduction of innovations in the management of episcopal property without proper consultation with the chapter, his failure to offer meals to the kinsmen of the canons on feastdays, and the excommunication of canons or their kin (specifically the archpriest of Signa). See also Santini, 1903, vol. 32, pp. 58–62.

142. Santini, 1895a, p. lxiii; Davidsohn, 1977, vol. 2, p. 307.

143. Davidsohn, 1977, vol. 2, p. 307; Santini, 1895a, p. 511.

144. Davidsohn, 1977, vol. 2, p. 328.

145. The author follows Malcolm Lambert's definition of heresy as "whatever the papacy explicitly or implicitly condemned during the period" (1977, p. xii).

146. Dondaine, 1950, p. 300.

147. Lambert, 1977, pp. 65, 73.

148. Violante, 1972, pp. 363–365; Lambert, 1977, p. 117.

149. Stephens, 1972, p. 28.

150. Lambert, 1977, pp. 117–139. See also Violante, 1972.

151. Dondaine, 1950, p. 300.

152. For a selected overview of studies on heresy in Florence, see Corsi, 1979; Dondaine, 1950; Davidsohn, 1977, vol. 1; 1977, vol. 7; Becker, 1974; Manselli, 1964; Violante, 1972.

153. For details on these miracles, see Benvenuti-Papi, 1988, pp. 21–24.

154. Corsi, 1979, pp. 70–72; Benvenuti-Papi, 1988, p. 27.

155. Davidsohn, 1977, vol. 2, pp. 368–399.
156. Davidsohn, 1977, vol. 2, pp. 411–437; Housley, 1982, pp. 198–199; Manselli, 1964, pp. 262–263; Benvenuti-Papi, 1988, pp. 81–85.
157. Santini, 1895a, pp. lxiii–lxiv.
158. For San Casciano, see Santini, 1895a, p. 514.
159. Davidsohn, 1977, vol. 2, pp. 457–465.
160. Barbadoro, 1929, pp. 50–60. For the taxation of parishes, see Davidsohn, 1977, vol. 3, p. 163.
161. ASF *Dipl.* Cestello, 29 April 1247; Davidsohn, 1977, vol. 2, p. 448.
162. Benvenuti-Papi, 1988, p. 91.
163. AAF *Bullettone,* fols. 26v–27v.
164. Dameron, 1983, p. 77.
165. AAF *Bullettone,* fols. 26v–27v.
166. ASF *Dipl.* Mercatanti, November 1217.
167. Sznura, 1975, p. 78; Davidsohn, 1977, vol. 1, pp. 79–80, 96–97; Davidsohn, 1977, vol. 2, pp. 404–405; ASF *Dipl.* Covi-Commenda, 26 September 1239.
168. "Non possint commode artem suam videlicet lanificium texere pannos et vendere ac alia operari ex quibus possint percipere" (ASF *Dipl.* Covi-Commenda, 11 September 1251). In return for using the location, the order paid the bishop 15 *soldi* per year.
169. Dameron, 1983, p. 97; Davidsohn, 1977, vol. 2, p. 502.
170. "Considerantes insuper quod ipsarum dominarum conventus minus honeste maneat apud Sanctum Cassianum compensatis circumstantiis loci et aliis incommodis que sunt ibi" (ASF *Dipl.* Polverosa, 23 September 1251). The nuns paid the bishop the required pound of wax in 1292, 1299, 1313, and 1317 (according to our sources).
171. The first documented citations of these arrangements are dated 1244 (Valcava) and 1259 (Monte di Croce) (Lami, 1758, vol. 2, pp. 871, 872).
172. As Appendix D demonstrates, the number of purchases in the Val di Pesa, the Valdarno, and the lower Val di Sieve increased in the first quarter of the thirteenth century.
173. Wickham, 1988, pp. 308–315 (concerning the Casentino).
174. Larner, 1980, p. 85. A full copy of one *iuramentum* (dated 1214) survives (ASF *Dipl.* Strozziane-Uguccioni, 3 October 1214): "Augustinus, filius Pieri del Surdo, in presentia Rustichi Bongianelli ordinarii judicis, fuit confessus se esse hominem et colonum Episcopatus Florentini et annuatim eidem Episcopatui dare debere sextam partem unius albergarie et sex denarios et quartuor ova et unum par caponum et unum par de pollatris et operas quas domino episcopo recipere placet, et datium et [?] omnia servitia et redditus predictus Agustinus solempni stipulatione promisit domino Johanni divina providentia Florentino episcopo recipienti vice capones et nomine predicti episcopatus annuatim dare hoc anno dictas in nativitate domini et pollastras in festivitate Sancti Johannis at alia altra [?] [illegible] servitia et redditus tempore usitato. Item promisit eidem domino Episcopo recipienti vice et nomine dicti episcopatus de cetero habitare et stare et morare pro homine et colono dicti Episcopatus in resedio posito Aramagno et alibi ubicumque dicto Episcopo placuerit." The status of

fidelis implied personal dependence but not necessarily seigneurial rights (Nelli, 1988, pp. 246–247).

175. For a description of this process, see Conti, 1965, p. 217; Cherubini, 1974, pp. 63–74.

176. Conti, 1985, p. xiii.

177. Wickham, 1988, pp. 311–315.

178. Fiumi, 1959, p. 472; Redon, 1982, p. 217.

179. Caggese (1907–1909, p. 287) is wrong to suggest that the commutations were random and arbitrary. They were part of a conscious plan.

180. Kotel'nikova, 1975, pp. 28–108; Romeo, 1971, pp. 52–56; Chittolini, 1965, p. 249; Redon, 1979, p. 638; Wickham, 1988, p. 229.

181. No detailed study of commutations like these in northern Italy have been made, although both Herlihy (1959) and Jones (1954, 1956b, 1968) have recognized their importance. All of the references are in the ASF *Diplomatico*. For Buonsollazzo, see ASF *Dipl.* Cestello, 25 February 1204 and 23 January 1228. For Luco, see ASF *Dipl.* Luco 12 March 1235. For the rest, see ASF *Dipl.* Passignano, 1188; Cestello, 6 October 1200; and Olivetani, 1195.

182. Lami (1758, vol. 2, pp. 857–908) claimed that Bishop Giulio (1158–1182) appointed the first rectors or *podestà* (Caggese, 1907–1909, pp. 319–320, agrees). I have found no evidence that the *podesteria* pre-dated 1200.

183. Dameron, 1983, pp. 327–328.

184. Other Tuscan bishops began doing the same. In 1225 the bishop of Volterra began to appoint the *podestà* for the areas under his jurisdiction, as did the bishop of Luni (Volpe, 1923, pp. 88–92).

185. Between those dates the city began to assess the unfree with a 26 *denari* tax (per household) and the knights and free cultivators with a 12 *soldi* tax (Conti, 1985, p. xx).

186. Conti, 1985, p. xiv.

187. Barbadoro, 1929, pp. 29–30. We have records of the commune's extension of the urban *datium* to Figline, Semifonte, and Capraia.

188. Schneider, 1980; Caggese, 1907–1909; Herlihy, 1959, 1961; Fiumi, 1961; Violante, 1980; Tabacco, 1979; Jones, 1964; Wickham, 1988, p. 141. See also Osheim, 1977, and Bognetti, 1978.

189. De la Roncière, 1976, vol. 3, p. 343.

190. Conti, 1985, p. xiv.

191. Conti, 1985, p. xx; Davidsohn, 1977, vol. 5, pp. 330–331. Conti believed the intent of the census was to initiate a new communal tax of 26 *denari* per household, but the city was levying that tax as early as 1197 (Davidsohn, 1977, vol. 1, 1011; Barbadoro, 1929, p. 29). As Conti observed, the urban tax was much less than the episcopal *datium*. It is unlikely, I believe, that the census alone created unrest on episcopal lands. Rather, the initiation of the census might have been a consequence of that unrest. The commune wanted to have a better record of the personal status of its rural residents.

192. Caggese (1907–1909) erroneously characterized the conflicts at San Casciano, Borgo San Lorenzo, and Castelfiorentino as clashes between feudalism and capitalism (pp. 283, 163 ff.).

193. Evidence from Florence supports the conclusions reached by Jones (1964, p. 342) and Osheim (1977) that the rural communes tried but never achieved full jurisdictional autonomy from their traditional lord.

194. In his study of the bishopric of Lucca, Duane Osheim (1977) wrote that the focus of conflict on the episcopal estate shifted from the rural families to the rural commune. In the diocese of Florence, as we have seen, the conflict with the rural patrilineages never went away.

4. Episcopal Property and the Transformation of Florentine Society, 1250–1320

1. Fiumi, 1958, pp. 492–493. We do not possess complete information on urban income and expenses before 1300. The urban *dazio sul focolatico* (the *datium*, descended from the imperial *foderum*) lasted until 1250. The *dazio sulla libbra* (*estimo*) began sporadically in the twelfth century but took off during the Primo Popolo of 1250–1260 (see text, below). At the end of the thirteenth century, indirect taxes supplanted the *estimo* in the city, but the *estimo* remained in the *contado* (Fiumi 1959, pp. 440–444).

2. ASF *Dipl.* Strozziane-Uguccioni 17 September 1257.

3. For documentation regarding the papal tenth, see ASF *Dipl.* Passignano, 12 June 1255; Passignano, 3 December 1296; ASF *Dipl.* Mannelli, 28 October 1297; ASF *Dipl.* Mercatanti, 6 June 1306. In 1296 and 1297 the *Terra Santa* (papal tithes) went to the Mozzi bank.

4. The cathedral chapter was in the same condition. See ASF *Dipl.* Santissima Annunziata, 1 June 1257 and 22 June 1257; Davidsohn, 1896–1908, vol. 4, p. 125; Davidsohn, 1977, vol. 2, pp. 602–629.

5. *Rat. Dec.*

6. ASF *Dipl.* Mercatanti, 6 June 1306; Barbadoro, 1929, pp. 50, 60, 410.

7. The *Bullettone* also contains the accounts of the entries of 1343 and 1383. The 1286 entry appears in Lami, 1758, vol. 3, pp. 1709 ff.; ASF *Bullettone*, pp. 356–359; AAF *Bullettone*, fols. 255r–257r.

8. Davidsohn, 1977, vol. 3, p. 601. Bishop Andrea had wanted the clergy to pay the costs of the entry of his predecessor Bishop Jacopo da Perugia in 1286.

9. ASF *Dipl.* San Pier Maggiore, 8 January 1304.

10. ASF *Dipl.* Olivetani 4 August 1295: "fecit hedificari de suis bonis patrimonialibus et non de bonis Episcopatus Florentiae nec tamquam Episcopus Florentinus sed tamquam privata persona"

11. Vallombrosa was indebted to Florentine creditors (ASF *Dipl.* Passignano, 11 July 1252). The nuns of San Jacopo di Ripoli were indigent (ASF *Dipl.* San Domenico nel Maglio, 22 March 1255), as were the nuns of San Donato a Torri (ASF *Dipl.* Polverosa, 17 December 1256). Other establishments in debt included the following: San Donato in Poggio (ASF *Dipl.* Menozzi, 16 November 1264), Buonsollazzo (ASF *Dipl.* Cestello, 27 February 1300), the *plebs* of Sant'Appiano (ASF *Not. Ant.*, s733, *passim*), Santa Maria Vergine di Torri (ASF *Dipl.* Monticelli, 24 April 1297), San Salvi (after 1290; see Vannucci, 1964); the

Spedale of Santa Maria Nuova (ASF *Dipl.* Manni, 24 August 1296); Santa Maria in Celiaula in 1301 (AAF *Aldobrandino,* fol. 2v); and San Matteo in Arcetri (S. Matteo in ASF *Dipl.* Arcetri, 20 August 1317).

12. ASF *Dipl.* Fontani, January 1255.

13. ASF *Dipl.* Manni, 24 August 1296; ASF *Dipl.* Polverosa, 17 December 1256.

14. ASF *Dipl.* Rosano, 22 June 1261. The four churches affected were Santo Stefano in Calcinaia, San Pietro in Silvio, Santa Maria di Lamole, and San Vito. The episcopal vicar had to intervene to settle the matter (ASF *Dipl.* Polverosa, 11 May 1318).

15. Cherubini, 1963, pp. 6–9.

16. Raveggi et al., 1978, p. 227; Davidsohn, 1977, vol. 3, pp. 428–467.

17. The *contado* produced roughly 5/12 of the grain needs of the city (Davidsohn, 1977, vol. 5, p. 328). In 1280 the city consumed 800 *moggi* weekly. By 1338 the figure had grown to 980 *moggi* (or 140 per day) for a population of 90,000 (Fiumi, 1958, p. 464; Pinto, 1978). Most of the grain for the city came from the south (Pinto, 1981, p. 276; 1978, p. 108). Average grain consumption per man per month was about one *staio* (Jones, 1980b, p. 372).

18. Fiumi, 1956, pp. 39, 46; Volpe, 1964, p. 219; Redon, 1982, p. 217. In years of famine or war the Sienese regularly forbade the exportation of grain out of the *contado* (1225, 1227, 1230, 1250, 1253, 1254, 1257) (Redon, 1982, p. 217).

19. De la Roncière, 1976, vol. 3, pp. 782–783; Pinto, 1981, pp. 258–261, 276. The most important centers of exchange were Empoli, Pontormo, Figline, San Giovanni, Castelfranco, Castelfiorentino, Poggibonsi, and Terranuova-Bracciolini (de la Roncière, 1976, vol. 3, pp. 994–999).

20. Davidsohn, 1977, vol. 5, pp. 238–241.

21. Pinto, 1978, p. 276.

22. Davidsohn, 1977, vol. 5, pp. 240–243. By 1286 the commune had fully systematized the provisioning of grain for the city (Pinto, 1978, p. 108).

23. Davidsohn, 1977, vol. 3, p. 477.

24. ASF *Bullettone,* p. 388. The Visdomini responded to the commune by drawing up a defense of their rights to administer certain castles and rural communes (ASF *Dipl.* Strozziane-Uguccioni, 1276). For more details, see below.

25. Davidsohn, 1977, vol. 3, p. 249.

26. Davidsohn, 1977, vol. 5, pp. 354–362.

27. Jones, 1968, pp. 48, 74, 75, 131, 134, 137; Larner, 1980, pp. 106–113; Jones, 1980a, p. 145.

28. Among this older elite were the Adimari, the Visdomini, the Tosinghi, the Buondelmonti, Cavalcanti, Rossi, Tornaquinci, the Pazzi, and the Donati (Raveggi, 1978, p. 109).

29. Larner, 1980, pp. 119–120; Raveggi, 1978, pp. 153–157; Jones, 1980a, p. 10. In contemporary documents, the word *burgensis* had a very restricted meaning. It designated residents of the *borghi* or *sobborghi,* or it referred to some groups within the *popolani* (not always the wealthiest) (Jones, 1980a, p. 48).

30. Davidsohn, 1896–1908, vol. 4, p. 475. The Adimari were linked closely to Cerchi banking interests and were heavily involved in commerce and banking (Fiumi, 1957, pp. 406–414; Ottokar, 1974, p. 81; Lansing, 1984, p. 43).

31. ASF *Dipl.* Archivio Generale, 5 June 1271, fol. 4r; Villani, 1823, vol. 3, p. 7 (cited in Lansing, 1984, p. 249).

32. ASF *Dipl.* Strozziane-Uguccioni 30 July 1286; Villani, 1823, vol. 3, p. 7; Davidsohn, 1977 vol. 3, p. 165; Lansing, 1984, p. 248.

33. Stefani, 1903–1955, p. 56; Villani, 1823, vol. 3, p. 7; Lansing, 1984, p. 248; Davidsohn, 1977, vol. 3, pp. 165, 189–191. Documents relating to the episcopal vacancy are in the ACF *Carte Strozziane,* parchments 101, 1017, and 1037.

34. Becker, 1965; Raveggi, 1978, pp. 157–60; Salvemini, 1899, p. 118; Lansing, 1984, pp. 228–229; Pampaloni, 1971, pp. 405–406; Rubinstein, 1935, 1939. For a recent bibliography on the magnates, see the article by Klapisch-Zuber (1988).

35. Larner, 1980, p. 154.

36. For a complete overview of the nature of the political changes in this period, see Najemy (1982). For the conflict in the *sesto* of San Pietro, see Ottokar, 1974, p. 78. Competition for office was a major theme in Compagni's chronicle (1986, p. 22).

37. Indeed, as the documents suggest, Ciampi and Davizio dei Visdomini simply divided the episcopal income among the heads of the three lineages (the Visdomini, Tosinghi, and Aliotti) during the vacancy of 1275–1286. For documents relative to Visdomini behavior during the vacancy, see ASF *Bullettone,* p. 388; ASF *Dipl.* Strozziane-Uguccioni 24 February 1276, 8 March 1277, 29 May 1277, 11 December 1279, 30 July 1286; Lami, 1758, vol. 1, p. 250. See also Davidsohn, 1977, vol. 3, p. 165.

38. They built at least one tower for themselves at the episcopal palace, where two Visdomini administrators were living during the vacancy (Davidsohn, 1896–1908, vol. 1, p. 506).

39. Davidsohn, 1977 vol. 3, pp. 189–191.

40. For a detailed analysis, see Dameron, 1988. General treatment of the Florentine episcopal entry is in Sanesi, 1932. For the sociology of ritual processions, see Trexler, 1980; Muir, 1981, pp. 190–223.

41. Becker, 1965, pp. 250, 257. For background and information, see Raveggi, 1978, pp. 157–158, 200–205.

42. Larner, 1980, p. 120; Raveggi, 1978, pp. ix–xxi, 153–160, 203, 228. For Monte di Croce, see Nelli, 1985, 103–104; 1988, p. 256.

43. See Dameron, 1988; Davidsohn, 1977, vol. 3, pp. 189–191.

44. Larner, 1980, pp. 120–121; Salvemini, 1899, pp. 33–34; Najemy, 1982, pp. 43–63; Pampaloni, 1971, p. 408. Salvemini reconstructed the lists from contemporary chronicles (Salvemini, 1899, Appendix, pp. 375–377; cited in Lansing, 1984, p. 300).

45. Najemy, 1982, pp. 9n, 54 (citing Salvemini, 1899, p. 424).

46. Jones, 1980b, p. 375; Becker, 1965, pp. 258, 264; Larner, 1982, p. 121; Jones, 1980a, pp. 135–145; Villani, 1823, vol. 3, pp. 5–24.

47. Rubinstein, 1935, 1939; Becker, 1965; Fiumi, 1959, pp. 437–440. We must bear in mind as well that although the chroniclers blamed the magnates exclusively for factionalism, they were not the only guilty parties (Becker, 1965, pp. 279–281).

48. Lansing, 1987, p. 8; personal conversation with William Bowsky. For patronage disputes, see ASF *Dipl.* Rinuccini, 25 February 1321, 5 March 1321, 7 January 1323, 26 March 1323, 5 December 1326, 16 May 1327. The Bardi, a recent lineage in the magnate ranks, challenged the older Buondelmonti, the traditional patrons of the *plebs.*

49. In her recent thesis (1984), Carol Lansing suggested that at least three factors distinguished the magnates from their contemporaries: a patrilineal kinship organization, association with a chivalrous and knightly cultural tradition, and a long habit of political involvement. In an unpublished paper (1987), she suggests that demographic pressures within the lineages, the declining economic power and status of traditional lineages relative to other lineages, and factional communal politics all contributed to the social and political crisis affecting traditional patrilineages and to the breakup of joint property at the end of the thirteenth and beginning of the fourteenth centuries (pp. 8–17). My views presented here primarily complement rather than dispute her own conclusions.

50. Larner, 1980, p. 122.

51. Becker, 1965, p. 263; Klapisch-Zuber, 1988, pp. 1211–1216.

52. Jones, 1980a, pp. 135–143.

53. Dino Compagni could not stand him: "Bishop Lottieri della Tosa died, and a new bishop was named through simony: a man of low birth, zealous for the Guelf Party and beloved by the *popolo,* but not of holy life" (Compagni, 1986, p. 85). Rosselino della Tosa, the enemy of Corso Donati and Bishop Lottieri, favored him.

54. Violante, 1972, p. 355; Osheim, 1977, pp. 94–95.

55. Fanelli describes in detail the growth of the city in its many complicated stages (1973, vol. 1, pp. 8–67), but the most recent study is Spilner (1987).

56. In 1256 the *estimo* for the episcopal *mensa* was 30,000 *lire* (that of the cathedral chapter was slightly less). Between 1250 and 1260 the bishop was paying 3.25 percent of the *estimo* in taxes (Barbadoro, 1929, p. 60).

57. We have the record of the payment by the abbey of Passignano to the papal collectors of 70 Pisan *lire* (ASF *Dipl.* Passignano 12 June 1255).

58. "Non vel dampnitatem vel lessionem ipsius Episcopatus, sed pro eius utilitate et melioramento et . . . pro faciendis et construendis domibus in Cafadio Episcopatus ut res et fructus ipsii Cafadii magis et melius custodiantur" (ASF *Dipl.* Santissima Annunziata, 28 May 1255).

59. ASF *Dipl.* Santissima Annunziata, 1 June 1255.

60. The amount of property was one *staio,* 8 *pannora,* and 3 *piedi,* and the price was 40 Pisan *lire* (presumably because the bishop paid the papacy in that currency, as did Passignano). The reasons for the sale were explicit: "pro solvendis et exhoneratis debitis usuariis contractis per eundem dominum Episcopum tempore quo erat in Apulea in servitio Romane ecclesie . . . ex bonis ipsius Episcopatus ad praesens per solvere commodius non valebant" (ASF *Dipl.* Santissima Annunziata, 18 February 1255, Indiction 14).

61. In 1250 four Florentines sold land in the Cafaggio to the pope, who gave them (with *plena jurisdictio*) to the bishop to assist the Servites (*disponere et distribuere*

atque facere pro elemosina). See ASF *Dipl.* Santissima Annunziata, 1 July 1250, 16 November 1269; Davidsohn, 1977, vol. 2, pp. 405–406; Benassi, 1977.

62. The bishop explained that his reason for the sale of more Cafaggio property was to build shops (*apothecae*) near the Baptistery (ASF *Dipl.* Santissima Annunziata, 16 November 1269).

63. Sznura, 1975. The author is also indebted to Paula Spilner for information on Florentine urban planning between 1281 and 1400 (public lecture, Villa Spelman, June 8, 1981).

64. ASF *Capitoli* 43, 15 March 1289, fol. 79v. The bishop protested that the commune appropriated the land ("quod commune Florentiae occupaverat de suo et episcopatus Florentiae terreno in magna quantitate, vendendo illud quibusdam frenariis et cassettariis qui ibidem hedificaverunt").

65. AAF *Bullettone*, fols. 26r–27v.

66. Franek Sznura correctly observes that it is difficult to know when the bishop acquiesced in the sales made from the 1260's through the 1290's and when the commune forced him to do so (1975, p. 57).

67. Canon 12, Nicaea II (787) (Gilchrist, 1969, p. 158).

68. ""Et quod terre et possessiones prefati ipsius Episcopi erant ad ampliandum civitatem praefatam . . . ac supplicantibus legato praedicto ut eidem Episcopo concederetur licentiam vendendi terras et possessiones easdem" (ASF *Dipl.* San Niccolò, 18 July 1297). See also AAF *Bullettone*, fol. 27v.

69. AAF *Aldobrandino*, fol. 15v. The *casolare* was a measured building lot (Sznura, 1975, pp. 23–29; Spilner, 1987, p. 274).

70. For rural property, an average of 29 percent of the leases were customary perpetual contracts. The remaining 71 percent of the leases were fixed-term leases like the urban contracts, but they were made for longer terms.

71. AAF *Martino*, fol. 4; Goldthwaite, 1980, p. 429. For another example, see AAF *Martino*, fol. 14r.

72. AAF *Martino*, fol. 15v.

73. AAF *Martino*, fols. 100r, 99v, 97v, 59v, 14r, and 10r for examples. For the debasement of the *denaro*, see Herlihy, 1968, p. 265.

74. AAF *Martino*, fol. 26v. In her study of the activity of other ecclesiastical lords in the city (the abbey of Settimo, for example), Spilner found that contracts of this sort were common (1987, p. 282). Also, like most of the tenants of the buildings of the abbey of Settimo, the two episcopal leaseholders were from the *contado*.

75. AAF *Martino*, fol. 102r.

76. For example, the rents declined in nominal terms from twenty-eight *lire*, fifteen *soldi* in 1307 to twenty-eight *lire* and ten *soldi* in 1318 (AAF *Martino*, fols. 16v and 102r).

77. Bacchino rented the land again in 1314 for ten years for twenty *soldi* per *staio* (AAF *Martino*, fols. 23r–23v).

78. AAF *Martino*, fol. 64r.

79. AAF *Martino*, fol. 98v.

80. AAF *Martino,* fols. 37r and 115r. It is possible that the second lease included more property, but the lease does not specify.
81. One lease included the provisions for the construction of more houses. In 1319 Dolcio di Cenno (from the parish of Santo Stefano) promised to build four more houses (*domus*) on land he would rent from the bishop for ten years, for which the bishop would reimburse him. After that ten years, the houses would return to episcopal possession. A similar arrangement existed in Castelfiorentino (AAF *Martino,* fol. 113v).
82. AAF *Martino,* fols. 1–2r.
83. AAF *Bullettone,* fols. 30r–31v.
84. Davidsohn, 1960, vol. 4, p. 509.
85. Davidsohn, 1960, vol. 4, p. 717.
86. The *Bullettone* provides no information, so the historian must rely on the lease book of Ser Benedetto Martino. Two of the leases were in the parish of San Martino di Montughi.
87. Spilner, 1987, pp. 318–329. I plan to do a systematic study of leasing by church lords in the early *trecento.*
88. Davidsohn, vol. 3, 1977, pp. 143–146; ASF *Capitoli* 29, fol. 260; Magna, 1982, pp. 39–49.
89. Davidsohn, 1977, vol. 3, p. 477.
90. Magna, 1982, pp. 56–58; ASF *Provvisioni* 2, 30 July 1289 and 3 August 1290.
91. For recent discussion of the 1289 sale, see Conti, 1985, pp. xxvi–xxvii; Kotel'nikova, 1975, pp. 194–206; and Magna, 1982, pp. 55–56.
92. The AAF *Libro* lists the appointments of the episcopal *podestà* in the Mugello made on December 28, 1321, for the following places: Valcava, Montefiesole (including Vico, Pievevecchia), Pagliariccio (including Molezzano, Rabbiacanina, Loncastro, Vitigliano, Montagutolo, Guzzano, and Santa Felicità al Flumine); Monte di Croce, Monte Buiano, Borgo San Lorenzo, and Vaglia (fol. 10r).
93. Davidsohn, 1960, vol. 4, p. 328.
94. Studio Telemugellouno, 1982, p. 127.
95. Davidsohn, 1977, vol. 2, p. 101.
96. Studio Telemugellouno, 1982, p. 127.
97. In the Val di Pesa the percentage of fixed-term commercial leases was 60 percent!
98. AAF *Aldobrandino,* fols. 29v–30v, 45r. The payments also included capons and *denari.* The *fideles* brought the grain to the episcopal granary, of which the location is unfortunately unknown. See the lease for 30 October 1304 (fol. 29v).
99. AAF *Bullettone,* fol. 89r. There is the record of an episcopal election of a new arch-priest in 1287 by Bishop Andrea de' Mozzi, and in 1297 Bishop Francesco Monaldeschi appointed a new canon to the chapter of the *plebs* (AAF *Bullettone,* fols. 5r–23r). For an example of some of the duties of the episcopal vicar Parigio at the beginning of the fourteenth century (such as the execution of a will), see ASF *Dipl.* Mercatanti, 11 September 1320.
100. AAF *Libro,* fol. 10.
101. ASF *Dipl.* Cestello, 23 December 1256.

102. There were twenty-one families or individuals acknowledging their tie to the bishop at Monte Buiano, and they were all paying perpetual dues in grain.

103. AAF *Libro*, fol. 10r. Our record of the elections of the rectors is spotty: Olmi (1259, 1280, 1292); Piazzano (1298 and 1315), and Vespignano (1318). See AAF *Bullettone*, fols. 5r–23r. There were appointments of *podestà* for Borgo—all members of the Visdomini *consorteria*—beyond 1323 (Lami, 1758, vol. 2, pp. 882–883; AAF *Libro*, fol. 10r).

104. AAF *Martino*, fols. 42v, 64r; AAF *Aldobrandino*, fol. 37v. One lease was for five years and required a payment of nineteen *moggi;* another was for twenty years for two *staia* (with the additional requirement to build a house of stone for which the bishop would reimburse the tenant). The perpetual holdings were also to be paid for in grain (AAF *Aldobrandino*, fol. 43r; AAF *Martino*, fol. 14v).

105. AAF *Martino*, fol. 64r. The lease on fol. 42v (see above) also rented out all episcopal income in the region.

106. SF *Bullettone*, p. 12.

107. ASF *Bullettone*, p. 187. The *mezzadria* was for property (*petium*) at Pagliariccio.

108. AAF *Martino*, fols. 124r–124v.

109. In the case regarding Bottrigo, the episcopal syndic went to the court of the Florentine *podestà* to compel him to swear *fidelitas* (agreement to make the requisite yearly payments) (ASF *Bullettone*, pp. 192, 197).

110. AAF *Bullettone*, fols. 104r–123r.

111. ASF *Bullettone*, pp. 214–215. The residents did not contest episcopal jurisdiction over some parts of the area, but they resisted accepting all the episcopal claims.

112. AAF *Martino*, fols. 25v and 45r. For unknown reasons, the bishop revoked the latter lease a year later.

113. These leases included a mill and half the *castellum* of Arliano rented to the archpriest in 1222 for 30 *soldi* (Lami, 1758, vol. 1, p. 621).

114. The new *podestà* was a member of the Visdomini *consorteria*, Guido dei Visdomini, who received his appointment in 1253 (Lami, 1758, vol. 2, pp. 882–883). The first *podestà* of the bishop appeared at Valcava in 1229 and 1232. The first documented evidence of the emergence of the commune dates from 1231.

115. See AAF *Bullettone*, entries on fols. 131r–140r.

116. "Quod occupabant quadam iura Episcopatus et non iuraverunt fidelitatem dicto domino Episcopo" (ASF *Bullettone*, p. 233).

117. AAF *Aldobrandino*, fol. 138r. The excommunications initially were for the "occupation" of episcopal land and the refusal to swear an oath of *fidelitas*.

118. AAF *Libro*, fol. 10r.

119. AAF *Martino*, fol. 129r.

120. AAF *Martino*, fols. 67v–68r.

121. "Ad permutandum et redigendum dicta servitia et omnem datium et accattum quod et que ab eis vel eorum altero per episcopum et episcopatum florentinum exigi posset, et potuisset in annum affictum perpetuum solvenda per eos episcopo et episcopatui supradictis prout utilius et decentius pro dictis Episcopo et episcopatu et hominibus et personis predictis videbitur expedire secundam formam" (AAF *Aldobrandino*, fol. 16v).

122. The only other documented granary was in the episcopal palace in Florence and at Pievevecchia. Nelli acknowledges the existence of only one *palatium* at Chiasso (near the *plebs* of Doccia) (1985, p. 44).

123. For information on Montebonello, see Nelli, 1989.

124. The lease books record about 65 leases for the Val di Sieve, compared with 40 in the Mugello and 153 of shops and land in Florence. In the *Bullettone,* the Val di Sieve accounts for about 15 percent of the total number of leases made in the period between 1301 and 1325. The following local notaries also recorded local leases for the bishop: Bernardo Cassi (1311–1315 (*Not. Ant.,* 255) and Jacopo di Vigoroso (1294–1295) (*Not. Ant., filza III, 12*).

125. Nelli, 1985, 1988, 1989.

126. Nelli, 1985, p. 43.

127. Nelli, 1985, pp. 45–48, 57–58.

128. Nelli, 1985, pp. 58–71.

129. Nelli, 1985, pp. 74–75.

130. Raveggi, 1978, pp. 46, 109, and 29. Of the lineages mentioned with the Saltarelli, only the Pulci appeared on the 1293 list of magnates. They did not appear on the 1295 list (p. 46).

131. Nelli, 1985, pp. 74–75; Ottokar, 1974, p. 113.

132. Compagni, 1986, pp. 24, 64, 70.

133. ASF *Bullettone,* pp. 312–313. In the area the bishopric also had the patronage rights (*ius eligendi*) to the local parish of Sant'Andrea di Monte Giovi (elections recorded in 1293, 1298, 1313, and 1313). This right no doubt stemmed back to the original donation of 1133.

134. See Lansing, 1984, 1987.

135. Lami, 1758, vol. 2, pp. 882–883.

136. AAF *Martino,* fols. 30v, 110v. In 1300 a *fidelis* was paying a *staio* every year for a *podere* and houses *nomine fidelitatis* (AAF *Aldobrandino,* fol. 16r).

137. An example was Brunetto di Giovanni da Galiga, who leased (*locavit perpetuum*) lands at Galiga for four *staia* (ASF *Bullettone,* p. 294).

138. AAF *Martino,* fol. 97r. Nelli proposes the thesis that the award by the Florentine *podestà* of property held by rebels constitutes part of an attempt by the bishop to reacquire property which was falling out of his hands at the end of the thirteenth century (1985, p. 108). As this book demonstrates, communal involvement was not unusual; it occurred throughout the thirteenth century and therefore alone does not necessarily constitute evidence of a program of recuperation (*politica di recupero*).

139. "Ad causandum cum Episcopo Florentino" (ASF *Bullettone,* p. 283).

140. ASF *Bullettone,* pp. 287–288.

141. AAF *Aldobrandino,* fol. 29. See also fols. 97r, 116v.

142. There are records of elections of the arch-priests in 1263, 1270, and 1288. There is one mention of the appointment of the rector of Fornello in 1310. In 1288 the office of the *plebanus* of Doccia went to a member of the *vicedomini* lineages. See AAF *Bullettone,* fols. 5r–23r, for the various appointments. The rights to Patrillo were purchased from the Adimari, who probably received them from the Guidi.

143. ASF *Dipl.* Strozziane-Uguccioni, 5 March 1270. The document implies that Uberto gave them the funds (a "loan" is never mentioned) so that they could purchase grain. The property awarded included land and a vineyard ("una petia terre cum domo et vinea posite in populo Sancti Laurentii de Montefesulis in loco dicto podi Gualterii"). In 1255 the brothers of Gualterio were leasing episcopal property at Montefiesole (ASF *Bullettone*, p. 262).

144. ASF *Dipl.* Strozziane-Uguccioni 11 December 1279.

145. An example is the lease by Rustichino from Florence, who paid 200 *lire* per year (see AAF *Martino*, fols. 31r, 135v, 137r; AAF *Aldobrandino*, fol. 13r). The one tenant who did not pay in cash was Tano di Bartolomeo da Pievevecchia, who rented a mill at Bisarno in 1313 for six *moggi* and six *staia* of grain (AAF *Martino*, fol. 84v).

146. AAF *Martino*, fol. 66r; AAF *Aldobrandino*, fol. 6v.

147. AAF *Martino*, fols. 91r and 95r.

148. AAF *Martino*, fol. 138r.

149. ASF Bullettone, pp. 267–268.

150. AAF *Martino*, fols. 266r and 271r.

151. For a complete list for Monte di Croce, see Nelli, 1985, p. 55. In 1321 the Visdomini administrators of the estate after the death of Bishop Antonio degli Orsi were sending two *podestà:* one for Montefiesole, Vico, and Pievevecchia; and the other for Valcava (AAF *Libro dei Visdomini*, fol. 10). Payment to the *podestà* usually took the form of grain. In 1259 it amounted to a *staio* per hearth (Nelli, 1985, p. 25).

152. Nelli, 1988, pp. 253–254.

153. A section of the *Bullettone* dated 1297 made a list of such dues (fols. 160r–165v).

154. Bishop Lottieri fined Montefiesole 100 *lire* (ASF *Bullettone*, p. 261).

155. AAF *Aldobrandino*, fol. 13r.

156. AAF *Aldobrandino*, fol. 31v.

157. AAF *Martino*, fol. 80v.

158. See AAF *Martino*, fols. 51r, 83r, 114v, 133r, 134r, and 140r. The 1319 lease is double the previous leases because it included all the income from the *plebatus* of Decimo. The 1321 and 1322 leases excluded Fabbrica.

159. AAF *Bullettone*, fols. 171r–193v. These oaths were in the parishes of the *plebatus* of Campoli: Fabbrica, Montecampolese, Nuovole, Ripoli, Pappiano, San Fabbiano, Ligliano, Coffari, and the parish of Campoli itself.

160. AAF *Bullettone*, fols. 197r–210v. We can date the survey at the end of the thirteenth century or the beginning of the fourteenth centuries, as many names on the survey appear in dated entries from that period.

161. AAF *Bullettone*, fols. 43r–45v.

162. ASF *Bullettone*, pp. 22–23.

163. SF *Bullettone*, pp. 22–23.

164. See AAF *Bullettone*, fols. 43r–45v for the entries detailing the controversy.

165. AAF *Martino*, fol. 6v.

166. AAF *Bullettone*, fol. 46r.

167. Jones, 1980a, p. 144. For the 1288 provision, see ASF *Bullettone*, p. 76.

168. Repetti, 1833–1846, vol. 1, p. 26.

169. Davidsohn was wrong to state that the last mention of an episcopal *podestà* was in 1278 (1977, vol. 5, p. 354). The *Libro dei Visdomini* documents appointments beyond 1321.

170. AAF *Bullettone*, fol. 33r (for the 1268 entry). There is also preserved a parchment dated December 11, 1268, which records the payment from Castelfiorentino of 15 *lire* (8 *lire* for 1268 and 7 for 1267) representing one-third of all fines collected in the commune: "penarum et bannorum que universitas de Castro Florentino debet annuatim domino episcopo et episcopatui" (ASF *Dipl.* Archivio Generale, 11 December 1268).

171. ASF *Bullettone*, p. 21.

172. AAF *Aldobrandino*, fol. 34v.

173. The *Libro dei Visdomini* lists ten *podestà* for 1321 (including two for the Val di Pesa).

174. Several leases also specified payments in eggs, capons, and meat. Tenants who leased land near episcopal residences normally made such payments.

175. AAF *Aldobrandino*, fol. 28v. The lease included lands, a house, and other unspecified possessions (*domus, curia, resedio, cultus, terrae, et possessiones*). A twelve-year lease to Lapo di Collo di Farolfo for a pair of hens annually is indicative of the same trend of transforming older leases into commercial contracts.

176. An episcopal *castaldionus* collected the payments (AAF *Aldobrandino*, fol. 8).

177. AAF *Aldobrandino*, fol. 1v. See also Jones, 1968, p. 238.

178. See Nelli, 1985; Conti, 1965, vol. 1.

179. AAF *Bullettone*, fols. 79v, 80v. For other examples of how episcopal officials worked, see *Not. Ant.*, U112, fol. 1v, 42r; G393, fol. 46r; R50, fol. 41v.

180. AAF *Bullettone*, fol. 47r; Lami, 1758, vol. 1, p. 287. The sale included property with houses and land ("cum quibus domibus, possessionibus, et terris").

181. "Capitulum et canonici plebis predicte ad quos pertinebat pertinet electio plebani in prefata plebe" (ASF *Dipl.* Cestello, 23 September 1295). The connections between the monastery, the cathedral chapter of Florence, and the chapter of Campoli require more study.

182. Stefano served as canon in the chapter of Prato before becoming a canon in Florence. He was an accomplished jurist and diplomat, and later (in the fourteenth century) served as the Florentine ambassador to the papal curia. See Davidsohn, 1977, vol. 3, 1977, pp. 602–606; vol. 7, pp. 15–17.

183. "Sed venerabilis pater dominus Andreas Episcopus Florentinus post electionem predictam ut dicitur de facto cum de iure non posset, prefatum dictum Alessandrum elegit" (ASF *Dipl.* Cestello, 23 September 1295).

184. The curia ruled that the election of Stefano was just ("confirmandum esse et ipsam firmaliter confirmamus ac ipsum dominum Stefanum in plebanum instituimus ecclesie seu plebis predicte") (ASF *Dipl.* Cestello, 23 September 1295).

185. "Volentes ipsam plebem nostram de plebano et pastore ydoneo prout ad nos tamquam unicum dominum et patronum in spiritualibus et temporalibus dicte plebis pertinere dignoscitur reformari" (ASF *Dipl.* Certosa, 30 April 1297). This is the first instance that the term *ius patronatus* appears in a document relating to this dispute.

186. "Ius conferendi eamdem ad dictum Episcopatum Florentinum tamquam ad

verum dominum et patronum plenarie pertinere" (ASF *Dipl.* Certosa, 10 August 1299). For Stefano's investiture, see ASF *Dipl.* San Francesco di Firenze, 24 August 1299.

187. "Quod propter occupationem negotiorum dicte plebis sue de Sexto non potest intendere circa administrationem dicte plebis de Campoli" (ASF *Dipl.* Certosa, 22 August 1299). When Talano died, the *plebs* of Sesto fought with the bishop for the right to name the new arch-priest of Sesto (ASF *Not. Ant.*, L76, fols. 29v–30r).

188. ASF *Dipl.* San Francesco di Firenze 24 August 1299; ASF *Dipl.* Certosa 24 August 1299; and AAF *Aldobrandino*, fol. 1r. In all of these documents, the notary recorded that the bishop noted that previously Stefano had been a rebel against his authority: "rediens de omne contumatia et rebellione integre satisfecit."

189. ASF *Dipl.* Certosa, 25 August 1299.

190. ASF *Dipl.* Cestello, 26 August 1307 ("arbitramus laudamus pronunciamus et firmaliter diffinimus quod dictus plebanus dictum dominum episcopum vel eius successorem super predictis vel occassione predictorum vel quibuscumque aliis rebus quas idem plebanus usque ad hodiernum diem petere vel exigere posset ab Episcopo supradicto in iudicio vel extra de cetero non molestet perturbet vel inquietet et super ipsis dicto plebano perpetuum silentium duximus imponendum").

191. An arch-priest at Campoli (like Stefano da Broy after 1295) was in a position to damage episcopal interests (for example, obstruct the buying and selling of property) in the area if he appointed local rectors loyal to him and not to the bishop. See ASF *Dipl.* Archivio Generale, 4 January 1292 and 19 March 1292.

192. See Davidsohn, 1960, vol. 4, pp. 113–141; Schevill, 1961, pp. 167–168.

193. See Davidsohn, vol. 3, 1977, pp. 600–613.

194. Rotelli, 1978, pp. 189–211.

195. Herlihy, 1968, p. 265; Goldthwaite, 1980, pp. 429–430.

196. At Impruneta the price per *staio* increased from 4.6 *soldi* between 1276 and 1300 to 9.4 *soldi* between 1301 and 1325 (Herlihy, 1968, p. 251). In the city in 1300 the price was slightly higher, with a range in the fall months of 9.5 *soldi* to 11 *soldi* (ACF *Entrata e Uscita*, fols. 17r–22v).

197. Cherubini, 1963, p. 34. For background on the history of the ecclesiastical estates at Origgo and Cremona, see Romeo, 1971; Chittolini, 1965.

Conclusion

1. Foucault, 1973, pp. 17–23. For a discussion on the "two bodies" of royal authority, see Kantorowicz, 1957.

2. Belief in the efficacy of excommunication and in the worship of saints was shared by all segments of Florentine society. The Florentine bishops cleverly manipulated these popular notions of spirituality when necessary to attract donations and otherwise maintain episcopal hegemony in the areas of the diocese where they exercised lordship. For the approach to popular religion that stresses

a dialectical approach to "high" and "low" culture, see Ginzburg, 1980, pp. 125–126.

3. I am particularly thinking of certain aspects of the work of some post-structuralist theorists, including Clifford Geertz (1983) and Victor Turner (1974). In many other ways, their work is extremely useful. For an extremely good overview of theories of ritual, see Muir, 1981, p. 58.

4. For the Luccan example, see Osheim, 1977, pp. 49–59.

5. In a recent article John Howe (1988) makes the case that the nobility was a major force behind the "reform movement." This study would validate his claim on the local level at Florence, at least for some of the lineages.

6. Osheim, 1977, p. 121. Whereas the movement for renewal at Florence was associated with the bishops, at Pistoia the momentum for reform came from the cathedral chapter. The bishop of Pistoia was loyal to the emperor in the eleventh century, in contrast to the bishop of Florence. The primary reason (but not the only one) for the active leadership role assumed by the bishops of Florence was the determination to overcome the challenge to their spiritual and temporal power posed by the rural patrilineages.

7. "La signoria 'territoriale' dunque non solo predispose l'ambito, ma fu la stimolo che provocò—per reazione—il formarsi del comune rurale" (Violante, 1980, p. 341).

8. Susan Reynolds's book (1984) makes the same case for Europe as a whole.

9. Bizzocchi, 1987, pp. 13–33.

10. For a more general overview of Italy as a whole, see Cammarosano, 1977.

11. See Chapter 4 and Lansing, 1987, pp. 8–17.

12. Cited in Davidsohn, 1960, vol. 4, p. 363.

13. This was a very different situation from that of Pistoia and Volterra, where the commune had to expand into the *contado* at the expense of the bishops. The Florentine episcopal estate was also an important source of revenue. In 1256 the commune assessed its value at thirty thousand *lire* (Barbadoro, 1929, p. 54).

14. For approaches to the problem, see Jones 1980a, 1980b, 1978, 1956a, and 1964; Ottokar, 1974, p. 112–113. I also want to credit some stimulating discussions on this subject with Christopher Wickham.

15. For a description of the situation in the Garfagnana and Casentino, see Wickham, 1988, p. 353.

16. Ginzburg, 1987. My work on the *Bullettone* would tend to confirm that in the "liminal" period between the death of one and the entry of another bishop ecclesiastical dependents systematically called into question the legitimacy of the lord's power by refusing to swear the servile oaths (*iuramenta*) to the bishop.

17. Cherubini, 1974, p. 307; Herlihy, 1968, pp. 270–275.

18. The work of Jacob Burckhardt contributed to elevating the problem of state formation to a high profile in Italian historiography (1958, vol. 1, p. 22).

19. I wish here to support the formal comments of James Grubb on the limits of American historiography on Italy made at the 1989 Meeting of the Renaissance Society of America in Cambridge, Massachusetts, on March 30. I concur with Grubb's observation that many American historians place too much attention on an urban population which is seemingly divorced from its rural counterpart.

20. Herlihy, 1968, p. 267; Chittolini, 1970, pp. 106–109. I detect particularly a "statist" bias among some historians, both American and Italian, who assume that state formation is perhaps a "benign" development (Rubinstein, 1966; Kent, 1978; Goldthwaite, 1980; for a valuable historiographical overview, see Brucker, 1983).

21. See Introduction and Fossier, 1982, p. 952.

22. Hilton, 1978, p. 30. Though my work falls within the radical historiographical tradition, I do not consider myself a Marxist.

23. Jones, 1980a, pp. 111–113.

24. Jones, 1980a, pp. 111–113. For a terse discussion of the social and economic difficulties in the Florentine *contado* at the beginning of the fourteenth century, see Herlihy, 1968, pp. 266–267.

25. Wickham found that the rural aristocracy in the Casentino also "crystallized" around the *castelli* in the eleventh century (Wickham, 1988, p. 291).

26. Keen, 1984, pp. 27–28.

27. Lansing, 1987, p. 8. For a full study of the magnate lineages see the forthcoming book by Carol Lansing cited in the bibliography.

28. Osheim, 1977, pp. 35–36, 121.

29. Mengozzi, 1911, pp. 25–27; Volpe, 1964, p. 108.

30. Volpe, 1964, p. 108.

31. For examples, see AA Fiesole *Mensa Vescovile,* XVII.2, fol. 1, and AA Fiesole *Ordinazioni,* VIII.A, fol. 5b.

32. Hughes, 1975, pp. 6–11.

33. Bizzocchi, 1987, pp. 24, 45–48.

34. Davis, 1984, pp. 43–45.

Bibliography

Primary Sources

Unpublished Materials

ARCHIVIO ARCIVESCOVILE DI FIRENZE

Il Bullettone; Indice storico economico dei beni feudali, 23 vols., March 1800 (Mensa Vescovile Section); *Imbreviature notarili di Romeo di Aldobrandino da Calenzano; Libro dei Visdomini; Libro di contratti dal 1304–29: estratto fatto di contratti appartenenti all'arcivescovado, segnato a, rogati per Ser Benedetto di Maestro Martino, cominciato l'anno 1304; Memoriale di affitti a beni e dei beni del vescovado fiorentino a tempo del Vescovo Antonio dal 1309 al 1319* (Mensa Vescovile Section).

ARCHIVIO ARCIVESCOVILE DI FIESOLE

Atti civili, XIV, III, A 25, fols. 1–81; *Ordinazioni; Mensa Vescovile.*

ARCHIVIO DEL CAPITOLO FIORENTINO

Carte Strozziane; Quadernuccio di spese (1270); *Libretto degli affitti* (1300); *Copie di cartapecore,* 3 vols.; *Libretto del Tesoriere Machiavelli* (1300); *Inventario e spoglio delle cartapecore originali che sono nell'archivio del Capitolo fiorentino ordinate da me, Luigi Strozzi, decano del medesimo* (1681); *Entrata e Uscita.*

ARCHIVIO DI STATO DI FIRENZE

CAPITOLI. *Capitoli,* 29 and 43.
CONSIGLI DELLA REPUBBLICA. *Provvisioni,* register 2.
DIPLOMATICO. Archivio Generale dei Contratti; Arte dei Mercatanti; Bonifazio; Certosa; Santa Maria dei Covi (Covi-Commenda); Fontani; Mannelli-Galilei-Riccardi, doni; Manni, Regio acquisto; Olivetani; Passignano; Poggibonsi; San Bartolomeo di Ripoli; San Domenico nel Maglio; San Donato in Polverosa; San Matteo in Arcetri; San Niccolò di Firenze; San Pier Maggiore; Monastero di San Piero di Luco di Mugello; Santa Maria Novella; Santissima Annunziata; San Virgilio di Siena; Strozziane-Uguccioni, acquisto; Mennozzi, acquisto; Monticelli; Rosano; Rinuccini; San Frediano in Cestello; San Francesco di Firenze.

NOTARILE ANTECOSIMIANO. Benintendi di Guittone (1292–1348), B1340; Bernardo Cassi (1311–1315), C255; Giovanni di Gino da Calenzano (1313–1319), G393 (*filza* 2); Iacopo di Vigoroso (1294–1295); Lapo Gianni (1298–1327), L76; Ranieri di Toso da San Casiano (1305–1317), R50; Uguccione di Berto da San Casciano (1311–1319), U112 (*filza* 4); and Simone di Dino da Pontassieve (1288–1303), S733.

Published Works

Berti, G. 1850. *Cenni storico-artistici per servire di guida e illustrazione di San Miniato al Monte*. Florence.

Biblioteca Riccardiana di Firenze 223, folios 155–156.

Bibliotheca Hagiographica Latina antiquae et mediae aetatis. 1911. Vol. 2. Brussels.

Bibliotheca Sanctorum. 1967. Vol. 9. Rome: Istituto Giovanni XXIII.

Caggese, Romolo. 1910. *Statuti della repubblica Fiorentina*. Vol. 1, *Statuto del Capitano del Popolo 1322–25*. Florence.

I Capitoli del comune di Firenze. Inventario e regesto. 1866–1893. 2 vols., ed. C. Guasti and A. Gherardi. Florence.

Cioni, Michele. 1912–1915. Una ricognizione di beni feudali a Castelfiorentino. *Miscellanea storica della Valdelsa* 20 (1912): 84–92, 127–151; 22 (1914): 20–50, 189–199; 23 (1915): 16–36.

Compagni, Dino. 1986. *Dino Compagni's Chronicle of Florence*. Trans. Daniel Bornstein. Philadelphia: University of Pennsylvania Press.

Dante Alighieri. 1975. *The Divine Comedy: Paradiso*. Princeton: Princeton University Press.

Drogo. 1898. *De Passione S. Miniatis a Drogone conscripta*. In *Analecta Bollandiani*, vol. 17.

Kehr, Paul. 1908. *Italia Pontifica*. Vol. 3, *Etruria*. Berlin.

Lami, Giovanni. 1758. *Sanctae Ecclesiae Florentinae Monumenta*. 3 vols. Florence.

Liber Extimationum. 1956. Ed. O. Brattö. *Goteborgs Universitets Arsskrift*, vol. 62. Gotenborg.

Mosiici, Luciana, ed. 1969. *Le Carte del monastero di Santa Felicità di Firenze (Fonti di Storia Toscana)*. Florence.

Passio Sancti Miniatis Martyris. 1864. In *AS*, Octobris XI, pp. 415–432. Brussels.

Piattoli, Renato, ed. 1938. Le carte della canonica della cattedrale di Firenze (723–1149). *Regesta chartarum italiae*, vol. 16. Rome.

Potthast, A., ed. 1874–1875. *Regesta pontificum romanorum ad annum 1304*. 2 vols. Berlin.

Santini, Pietro, ed. 1895a. *Documenti dell'antica costituzione del comune di Firenze*. Florence.

—— 1952. *Documenti dell'antica costituzione di Firenze: Appendice*. Florence.

Schiaparelli, Luigi, ed. 1913. *Le carte del monastero di Santa Maria in Firenze (Badia)*. Vol. 1, *Fonti di storia fiorentina*. Rome.

Sigeberti Chronica. In *MGH SS* 6: 351.

Sigeberti Vita Deoderici I. In *MGH SS* 4: 476.

Stefani, Marchionne di Coppo. 1903–1955. *Cronaca Fiorentina*, ed. N. Rodolico. In *Rerum Italicarum Scriptores*, new ed., vol. 30, pt. 1. Città di Castello.

Ughelli, Ferdinando. 1718. *Italia Sacra,* vol. 3. Venice.

Villani, Giovanni. 1728. *Cronache fiorentine.* Ed. L. A. Muratori. In *Rerum Italicarum Scriptores,* vol. 13. Milan.

———— 1823. *Cronica,* vol. 3. Florence.

Vita Johannis Gualberti adhuc inedita. 1896. In *Forschungen zur Geschichte von Florenz,* ed. Robert Davidson, 1: 55–60. Also in *MGH SS* 30 (pt. 2): 1104–1110.

Secondary Sources

Anderson, Perry. 1974. *Lineages of the Absolutist State.* London: New Left Books.

Barbadoro, Bernardino. 1929. *Le Finanze della repubblica fiorentina: imposta diretta e debito pubblico fino all'istituzione del Monte.* Florence.

———— 1965. *Firenze di Dante.* Florence.

Barbi, A. S. 1899. Delle relazioni tra comune e vescovo nei secoli XII e XIII. *Bullettino Storico Pistoiese,* 81–94.

Barbieri, Giuseppe. 1972. *Toscana.* Turin.

Barraclough, Geoffrey. 1968. *The Medieval Papacy.* Norwich, Eng.: Harcourt, Brace and World.

Becker, Marvin. 1959. Some Implications of the Conflict between Church and State in *Trecento* Florence. *Medieval Studies* 21: 1–16.

———— 1965. A Study in Political Failure: The Florentine Magnates, 1280–1343. *Medieval Studies* 27: 246–308.

———— 1967. *Florence in Transition,* 2 vols. Baltimore: Johns Hopkins University Press.

———— 1974. Heresy in Medieval and Renaissance Florence: A Comment. *Past and Present* 62 (February): 153–161.

Benassi, Vincenzo. 1977. *Diamante a sette facce.* Florence: Edizioni Comunità di Monte Senario.

Benson, Robert L. 1968. *The Bishop-Elect: A Study in Medieval Ecclesiastical Office.* Princeton: Princeton University Press.

Benvenuti-Papi, Anna. 1980. Umiliana dei Cerchi. Nascità di un culto nella Firenze del Dugento. *Studi Francescani* 77: 87–117.

———— 1987. San Zanobi: Memoria episcopale, tradizioni civiche e dignità familiari. In *I Ceti dirigenti nella Toscana tardo comunale,* ed. D. Rugiardini, 79–115. Florence: Francesco Papafava.

———— 1988. *Pastori di popolo. Storie e leggende di vescovi e di città nell'Italia medievale.* Florence: Arnaud.

Biadi, Luigi. 1848. *Memorie del Piviere di San Pietro in Bossolo.* Florence.

Biagioli, Giuliana. 1975. *L'Agricoltura e la popolazione in Toscana all'inizio dell'Ottocento.* Pisa.

Bisson, Thomas. 1977. The Organized Peace in Southern France and Catalonia, ca. 1140–1233. *American Historical Review* 82: 290–311.

Bizzocchi, Roberto. 1982. La dissoluzione di un clan familiare: i Buondelmonti di Firenze nei secoli XV e XVI. *Archivio Storico Italiano* 140: 3–45.

———— 1984. Chiesa e aristocrazia nella Firenze del Quattrocento. *Archivio Storico Italiano* 142: 191–282.

———— 1987. *Chiesa e potere nella Toscana del Quattrocento.* Bologna: Mulino.

Bloch, Marc. 1966. *Feudal Society*, 2 vols. Trans. L. Manyon. Chicago: University of Chicago Press.

Bognetti, G. P. 1978. *Studi sulle origini del comune rurale*. Ed. F. Sinatti d'Amico and C. Violante. Milan.

——— 1927. Sulle origini dei comuni rurali nel medio evo. *Studi nelle scienze giuridiche e sociali*, vol. 11. Pavia.

Bois, Guy. 1984. *The Crisis of Feudalism: Economy and Society in Eastern Normandy, 1300–1550*. Trans. of *La crise de féodalisme*. Cambridge: Cambridge University Press.

Borghini, Vincenzo. 1809. *Discorsi*, vol. 4. Florence.

Bouchard, Constance. 1979. *Spirituality and Administration: The Role of the Bishop in Twelfth Century Auxerre*. Cambridge, Mass.: Medieval Academy of America.

——— 1987. *Sword, Miter, and Cloister: Nobility and the Church in Burgundy, 980–1180*. Ithaca: Cornell University Press.

Bowsky, William. 1981. *A Medieval Italian Commune: Siena under the Nine, 1287–1355*. Berkeley and Los Angeles: University of California Press.

Boyd, Catherine. 1952. *Tithes and Parishes in Medieval Italy*. Ithaca: Cornell University Press.

Brentano, Robert. 1968. *Two Churches: England and Italy in the Thirteenth Century*. Princeton: Princeton University Press.

Brocchi, Giuseppe Maria. 1969. *Descrizione della provincia del Mugello*. Bologna.

Brown, Elizabeth. 1974. The Tyranny of a Construct: Feudalism and Historians of Medieval Europe. *American Historical Review* 79: 1063–1088.

Brown, Peter. 1981. *The Cult of the Saints: Its Rise and Function in Latin Christianity*. Chicago: University of Chicago Press.

Brucker, Gene. 1983. Tales of Two Cities: Florence and Venice in the Renaissance. *American Historical Review* 88 (June): 599–616.

Brühl, Carlrichard. 1968. *Fodrum, Gistum, Servitium Regis*, 2 vols. Cologne: Böhlau-Verlag.

Burckhardt, Jacob. 1958. *The Civilization of the Renaissance in Italy*, 2 vols. New York: Harper and Row.

Caggese, Romolo. 1907–1909. *Classi e comuni rurali nel Medio Evo Italiano: saggio di storia economica e giuridica*, 2 vols. Florence.

Calzolai, Carlo Celso. 1957. Notizie degli archivi: l'archivio arcivescovile. *Rassegna Storica Toscana* 2 (April-June): 127–181.

——— 1973a. *Ronta, Pulicciano, Razzuolo nel Mugello*. Florence: Libreria Editrice Fiorentina.

——— 1973b. *Castelfiorentino*. Florence.

——— 1974. *Borgo San Lorenzo*. Florence.

——— 1977. *San Michele Visdomini*. Florence.

Cammarosano, Paolo. 1975. Aspetti delle strutture familiari nelle città dell'Italia comunale (secoli XII-XIV). *Studi Medievali* 16: 418–435.

——— 1977. Les structures familiales dans les villes de l'Italie communale, XIIe-XIVe siècles. In *Famille et parenté dans l'Occident médiéval*, ed. G. Duby and J. LeGoff, 181–194. Rome.

——— 1981. Le strutture feudali nell'evoluzione dell'occidente mediterraneo: note di un colloquio internazionale. *Studi Medievali* 22: 837–870.

———— 1982. *Feudo e proprietà nel medioevo toscano.* In *Nobiltà e ceti dirigenti in Toscana nei secoli XI–XIII: strutture e concetti,* ed. Donatella Rugiadini Speroni. Florence: Francesco Papafava.

Cappelletti, Giusseppe. 1861. *Le Chiese d'Italia,* vol. 16. Venice.

Capponi, Gino. 1875. *Storia della repubblica di Firenze,* 3 vols. Florence.

Caprara, Stefania. 1975. Note diplomatiche sui documenti dell'episcopato ai tempo di Dante. *Dante nel Pensiero e nella Esegesi dei secoli XIV e XVI,* pp. 417–421. Florence.

Cassell's Italian Dictionary. 1977. Comp. Piero Rebora. New York: Macmillan.

Castagnetti, Andrea. 1976. *La pieve rurale nell'Italia padana: territorio, organizzazione patrimoniale e vicende della pieve veronese di San Pietro di Tillida dall'alto medioevo al secolo XIII.* Rome.

Castellini, Alessandro. 1943. L'Affrancazione del feudo del Vescovado. *Bullettino Senese di Storia Patria* 50: 156–159.

Cerrachini, L. 1726. *Cronologia sacra dei vescovi e arcivescovi.* Florence.

Cherubini, Giovanni. 1963. Aspetti della proprietà fondiaria nell'aretino durante il XIII secolo. *ASI* 121 (63): 3–40.

———— 1974. *Signori, Contadini, Borghesi: ricerche sulla società italiana del basso medioevo.* Florence.

Cheyette, Frederick. 1968. *Lordship and Community in Medieval Europe: Selected Readings.* New York: Holt, Rinehart, and Winston.

Chiapelli, Luigi. 1932. I conti Cadolingi, i conti Guidi e il 'Comitatus Pistoriensis'. *Bullettino Storico Pistoiese* 34: 117–133.

Chini, Lino. 1875. *Storia antica e moderna del Mugello,* 2 vols. Rome.

Chittolini, Giorgio. 1965. I beni terrieri del capitolo della cattedrale di Cremona fra il XIII e il XIV secolo. *Nuova Rivista Storica* 49: 213–74.

———— 1970. La crisi delle libertà comunali e le origini dello stato territoriale. *RSI* 82 (March): 99–120.

Chomsky, Noam. 1982. *Towards a New Cold War.* New York: Pantheon.

Cioni, Michele. 1911. *La Valdelsa: guida-storico-artistica.* Florence.

Cipolla, Carlo. 1947. Une crise ignorée: comment s'est perdue la propriété écclésiastique dans l'Italie du nord entre le XIe et le XVIe siècle? *Annales* 2: 317–327.

Cohen, G. A. 1978. *Karl Marx's Theory of History: A Defense.* Princeton: Princeton University Press.

Cohn, Samuel K. 1980. *The Laboring Classes of Renaissance Florence.* New York: Academic Press.

Compact Edition of the Oxford English Dictionary, 2 vols. 1971. Oxford: Oxford University Press.

Conti, Elio. 1965. *La formazione della struttura agraria moderna nel contado fiorentino,* Vol. 1. *Studi Storici* 51–55. Rome.

———— 1985. Le proprietà fondiarie del vescovado di Firenze nel Dugento. In *Signoria ecclesiastica e proprietà cittadina: Monte di Croce tra XIII e XIV secolo,* by Renzo Nelli, xi–xliii. Comune di Pontassieve.

Corsi, Dinora. 1974. Aspetti dell'inquisizione fiorentina nel '200. In *Eretici e ribelli del XIII e XIV secolo,* ed. Domenico Masselli, 65–92.

Coturri, Elio. 1964. Ricerche e note d'archivio intorno ai conti Cadolingi di Fucecchio. *Bullettino della academia degli Euteleti della città di San Miniato* 36: 109–45.

Dal Pane, L. 1959. L'economia bolognese del secolo XIII e l'affrancazione dei servi. In *Giornale degli Economisti e di Economia* 18, no. 9–10.

Dameron, George. 1983. *Social Conflict and "Iurisdictio Episcopalis" in the Florentine Contado: A Study of the Episcopal Estate, 850–1321.* Ann Arbor: University Microfilms International.

———— 1986. Episcopal Lordship in the Diocese of Florence and the Origins of the Commune of San Casciano Val di Pesa, 1230–47. *Journal of Medieval History* 12 (June): 135–54.

———— 1987. The Cult of St. Minias and the Struggle for Power in the Diocese of Florence, 1011–24. *Journal of Medieval History* 13 (June): 125–141.

———— 1988. Family Power and the Defence of Lordship in the Diocese of Florence, 1000–1350. In *Proceedings of the American Historical Association 1987.* Reference n. 10485.

———— 1989. Manuscript and Published Versions of the 1323 Florentine Episcopal Register (the *Bullettone*). *Manuscripta* 33 (March): 40–46.

Davidsohn, Robert. 1896–1908. *Forschungen zur älteren Geschichte von Florenz,* 4 vols. Berlin.

———— 1960–1978. *Storia di Firenze,* 8 vols. Florence: Sansoni.

Davis, Charles. 1984. *Dante's Italy and Other Essays.* Philadelphia: University of Pennsylvania Press.

De la Roncière, Charles. 1976. *Florence: Centre économique régional au XIVe siècle: le marché des denrées de premiers nécessité à Florence et dans sa campagne et les conditons de vie des salaries (1320–80),* 5 vols. Aix-en-Provence.

Delumeau, Jean Pierre. 1978. L'Exercice de la Justice dans le Comté d'Arezzo (IXe–Début XIIIe siècle). *MEFRM* 90 (2): 563–605.

De S. Miniate Martyre Florentiae in Tuscia: Commentarius. 1864. In *AS,* Octobris XI, pp. 415–418. Brussels.

Dinelli, G. 1915. Una signoria ecclesiastica nel contado lucchese dal secolo XI al XIV. Contributo alla storia delle giurisdizioni e dei comuni rurali nel medioevo. *Studi storici* 23: 187–291.

Dondaine, A. 1950. La hiérarchie cathare en Italie. *Archivum Fratrum Praedicatorum* 19: 280–312.

Duby, Georges. 1971. *La société aux XIe et XIIe siècles dans la région mâconnaise.* Paris: Ecole Pratique des Hautes Etudes.

———— 1974. *The Early Growth of the European Economy.* Trans. Howard B. Clarke. Ithaca: Cornell University Press.

———— 1980. *The Three Orders: Feudal Society Imagined.* Trans. Arthur Goldhammer. Chicago: University of Chicago Press.

Duggan, Lawrence. 1978. *Bishop and Chapter: The Governance of the Bishopric of Speyer to 1552.* New Brunswick: Rutgers University Press.

Dyer, Christopher. 1980. *Lords and Peasants in a Changing Society: The Estates of the Bishopric of Worcester 680–1540.* Cambridge: Cambridge University Press.

Enciclopedia cattolica. 1949–1953. Rome.

Endres, Robert. 1916. Das Kirchengut im Bistüm Luccas vom 8. bis 10. Jahrhundert. *Vierteljahrschrift für Sozial und Wirtschaftsgeschichte* 14: 240–92.

Epstein, Stephan. 1986. *Alle origini della fattoria toscana: l'ospedale della Scala e le sue terre (metà 200–mèta 400).* Florence: Salimbeni.

Eubel, Konrad. 1898. *Hierarchia Catholica (1198–1431)*. Regensburg.

Fanelli, Giovanni. 1973. *Firenze architectura e città*, 2 vols. Florence: Vallecchi.

Ferrali, Sabatino. 1964. Le temporalità del Vescovado nei rapporti col comune a Pistoia nei secoli XII e XIII. *Vescovi e diocesi in Italia nel medioevo (secoli IX–XIII)*, 365–408. Italia Sacra, 5. Padua.

Fiumi, Enrico. 1956. Sui rapporti economici tra città e contado nell'età comunale. *ASI* 14: 18–68.

———— 1957–1959. Fioritura e decadenza dell'economia fiorentina. *Archivio Storico Italiano* 115: 385–439, 116: 443–509, 117: 427–502.

———— 1961. *Storia economica e sociale di San Gimignano*. Florence.

Fliche, A. 1978. *La Réforme grégorienne*, 3 vols. Geneva: Slatkine Reprints.

Flori, Jean. 1986. *L'Essor de la chevalerie XIe–XIIe siècles*. Paris.

Forchielli, Giuseppe. 1917. *La Pieve rurale. Biblioteca della rivista di storia del diritto italiano*, vol. 17. Bologna.

Fossier, Robert. 1982. *Enfance de l'Europe Xe–XIIe siècles: aspects économiques et sociaux*, 2 vols. Paris.

Foucault, Michel. 1973. *The Order of Things*. New York: Vintage Books.

Francovitch, Riccardo. 1976. *I Castelli del contado fiorentino nei secoli XII e XIII*. Florence.

Fumagalli, Vito. 1976. *Terra e società nell'Italia padana: i secoli IX e X*. Turin.

———— 1978a. *Coloni e signori nell'Italia settentrionale: secoli VI–XI*. Bologna.

———— 1978b. *Il Regno italico*. Turin.

Gams, Bonifaz. 1873. *Series Episcoporum Ecclesiae Catholicae*. Ratisbon.

Gasparri, S. 1981. Il feudalismo nell'Occidente mediterraneo. *Studi storici* 19: 631–645.

Geary, Patrick. 1978. *Furta Sacra: Thefts of Relics in the Central Middle Ages*. Princeton: Princeton University Press.

Geertz, Clifford. 1983. Kings, Centers, and Charisma. In *Local Knowledge: Further Essays in Interpretive Anthropology*. New York: Basic Books.

Génicot, Léopold. 1978. Recent Research on the Medieval Nobility. In *The Medieval Nobility*, trans. and ed. T. Reuter, 17–35. Amsterdam and New York: North-Holland.

Gies, Frances, and Joseph Gies. 1980. *Women in the Middle Ages*. New York: Harper and Row.

Gilchrist, J. 1969. *The Church and Economic Activity in the Middle Ages*. New York: St. Martin's Press.

Ginzburg, Carlo. 1980. *The Cheese and the Worms: The Cosmos of a Sixteenth Century Miller*. Harmondsworth: Penguin.

———— 1987. Saccheggi rituali. Premesse a una ricerca in corso. *Quaderni Storici* 65 (August): 615–636.

Goldthwaite, Richard. 1980. *The Building of Renaissance Florence*. Baltimore: Johns Hopkins University Press.

Grohmann, Alberto. 1981. *Città e territorio tra medioevo ad età moderna: Perugia secc. XIII–XVI*, 2 vols. Perugia.

Haverkamp, Alfred. 1966. Die Regalien-, Schütz- und Steuerpolitik in Italien unter Friedrich Barbarossa bis zur Entstehung des Lombardbundes. *Zeitschrift für bayerische Landesgeschichte* 29: 3–156.

Herlihy, David. 1957. Treasure Hoards in the Italian Economy, 960–1139. *Economic History Review* 10: 1–14.

—— 1959. The History of the Rural Signory in Italy, 751–1200. *Agricultural History* 33: 58–71.

—— 1961. Church Property on the European Continent, 701–1200. *Speculum* 36: 81–105.

—— 1964. Direct and Indirect Taxation in Tuscan Urban Finance, 1200–1400. *Collectio Historie* 7: 385–402.

—— 1967. *Medieval and Renaissance Pistoia*. New Haven: Yale University Press.

—— 1968. Santa Maria Impruneta: A Rural Commune in the Late Middle Ages. In *Florentine Studies*, ed. N. Rubinstein, 242–276. Evanston: Northwestern University Press.

—— 1969. Family Solidarity in Medieval European History. In *Economy, Society, and Government in Medieval History*, ed. D. Herlihy, Robert S. Lopez, and Vsevold Slessarev, 173–85. Kent Ohio: Kent State University Press.

—— 1986. *Medieval Households*. Cambridge: Harvard University Press.

—— 1989. Review of C. Wickham's *The Mountains and the City. Journal of Interdisciplinary History* 19 (Spring): 662–664.

Hilton, Rodney. 1978. *The Transition from Feudalism to Capitalism*. London: Verso.

Housley, N. 1982. Politics and Heresy in Italy: Anti-Heretical Crusades, Orders and Confraternities, 1200–1500. *Journal of Ecclesiastical History* 33 (April): 193–208.

Howe, John. 1988. The Nobility's Reform of the Medieval Church. *American Historical Review* 93 (April): 317–339.

Hughes, Diane Owen. 1975. Urban Growth and Family Structure in Medieval Genoa. *Past and Present* 66 (February): 3–28.

Hyde, J. K. 1973. *Society and Politics in Medieval Italy: The Evolution of Civil Life, 1000–1350*. New York. St. Martin's Press.

Johnson, Penelope. 1981a. Pious Legends and Historical Realities: The Foundations of La Trinité de Vendôme, Bonport, and Holyrood. *Revue Benedictine* 9: 184–193.

—— 1981b. *Prayer, Patronage, and Power: The Abbey of la Trinité, Vendôme, 1032–1187*. New York: New York University Press.

Jones, Philip J. 1954a. A Tuscan Monastic Lordship in the Later Middle Ages: Camaldoli. *Journal of Ecclesiastical History* 5: 168–183.

—— 1954b. An Italian Estate, 900–1200. *Economic History Review*, 2d ser., 7: 18–32.

—— 1956a. Florentine Families and Florentine Diaries in the Fourteenth Century. *Papers of the British School at Rome* 24: 183–205.

—— 1956b. Le finanze della badia cisterncense di Settimo nel XIV secolo. *Rivista di storia della chiesa in Italia* 10: 90–122.

—— 1964. Per la storia agraria italiana nel Medio Evo: lineamenti e problemi. *Rivista Storica Italiana* 76: 287–348.

—— 1966. Medieval Agrarian Society at Its Prime: Italy. In *Cambridge Economic History*, 2d ed., ed. M. Postan and H. J. Habakuk, 340–431. Cambridge: Cambridge University Press.

—— 1968. From Manor to Mezzadria: A Tuscan Case-Study in the Medieval Origins of Modern Agrarian Society. In *Florentine Studies*, ed. N. Rubinstein, 193–241. Evanston: Northwestern University Press.

———— 1974. La Storia economica dalla caduta dell'Impero romano al secolo XIV. In *Storia d'Italia,* vol. 2, part 2. Turin.

———— 1980a. Economia e società nell'Italia medievale: il mito della borghesia. In *Economia e società nell'Italia medievale,* 3–189. Torino: Einaudi.

———— 1980b. Forme e vicende di patrimoni privati nelle 'Ricordanze' fiorentine del Trecento. In *Economia e società nell'Italia medievale,* 345–376. Torino: Einaudi.

Kantorowicz, Ernst. 1957. *The King's Two Bodies: A Study in Medieval Political Theology.* Princeton: Princeton University Press.

Keen, Maurice. 1984. *Chivalry.* New Haven: Yale University Press.

Keller, Hagen. 1979. *Adelherrschaft und stadtische Gesellschaft in Oberitalien, 9 bis 12. Jahrhundert.* Tübingen.

———— 1982. Militia, Vassallität und frühes Rittertum im Spiegel Oberitalienischer Miles-Belege des 10. und 11. Jahrhunderts. *Quellen und Forschungen* 62: 59–118.

Kent, Dale. 1978. *The Rise of the Medici Faction in Florence, 1426–1434.* Oxford: Oxford University Press.

Kent, F. W. 1977. *Household and Lineage in Renaissance Florence.* Princeton: Princeton Unviversity Press.

Klapisch-Zuber, C. 1981. Mezzadria e insediamenti rurali alla fine del medioevo. In *Civiltà ed economia agricola in Toscana nei secoli XIII–XV: problemi della vita delle campagne nel tardo-medioevo,* 149–164. Pistoia.

———— 1988. Ruptures de parenté et changements d'identité chez les magnats florentins du XIVe siècle. *Annales: Économie, société, et civilisation* 43 (September–October): 1205–1240.

Knowles, David. 1969. *Christian Monasticism.* New York: McGraw-Hill.

Kotel'nikova, L. A. 1975. *Mondo contadino e città in Italia dall'XI al XIV secolo.* Trans. L. S. Catocci. Bologna: Mulino.

Kurze, Wilhelm. 1973. Monasteri e nobiltà nella Tuscia alto medioevale. In *Atti del 5 congresso internazionale di studi sull'alto medioevo,* 339–362. Spoleto.

———— 1981. Nobiltà Toscana e nobiltà aretina. In *I Ceti dirigenti nell'eta precomunale,* 257–265. Pisa: Pacini.

Lambert, Malcolm. 1977. *Medieval Heresy: Popular Movements from Bogomil to Hus.* London: E. Arnold.

Lansing, Carol. 1984. *Nobility in a Medieval Commune: The Florentine Magnates, 1260–1300.* Ann Arbor: University Microfilms International.

———— 1987. Ecclesiastical Rights and Private Power in Medieval Florence. Unpublished paper presented at the 1987 American Historical Association Meeting.

———— Forthcoming. *The Florentine Magnates: Lineage and Faction in a Medieval Commune.* Princeton: Princeton University Press.

Lanzoni, Francesco. 1927. *Le diocesi d'Italia dalle origini al principio del secolo VII.* Faenza.

Larner, John. 1980. *Italy in the Age of Dante and Petrarch, 1216–1380.* Harlow, Eng.: Longman.

Le Clair, Edward, ed. 1968. *Economic Anthropology.* New York.

Lesne, Emile. 1910–1943. *Histoire de la propriété écclésiastique en France,* 6 vols. Paris.

Leyser, Karl. 1980. *Rule and Conflict in an Early Medieval Society: Ottonian Saxony.* Bloomington, Ind.: Indiana University Press.

Limburger, Walter. 1910. *Die Gebaude von Florenz*. Leipzig.

Lombardi, Enrico. 1965. Origini e formazione del feudo ecclesiastico vescovile di Massa Marittima. *Bollettino della Società storica maremanna* 2: 39–51.

Lopes-Pegna, Mario. 1972. *Le più antiche chiese fiorentine*. Florence.

—— 1974. *Firenze dalle origini al Medioevo*. Florence.

Lugano, P. 1902. San Miniato a Firenze. Storia e leggenda. *Studi religiosi* 2 (3): 222–245; 2 (6): 482–505.

Luzzatto, G. 1948. *Storia economica d'Italia*. Rome.

Magna, L. 1982. Gli Ubaldini del Mugello. Una signoria feudale nel contado fiorentino (sec. XII–XIV). In *I Ceti dirigenti dell'età comunale nei secoli XII–XIII: Strutture e concetti*. Ed. Donatella Rugiadini Speroni. Florence: Francesco Papafava.

Manselli, Raoul. 1964. I Vescovi italiani, gli ordini religiosi, e i movimenti popolari religiosi nel secolo XIII. In *Vescovi e Diocesi in Italia nel Medioevo (secc. IX–XIII)*, 315–335. Italia Sacra, 5. Padua.

—— 1963. *L'Eresia del male*. Naples.

Marconcini, Sergio. 1972. *Appunti di storia del Valdelsa*.

Martines, Lauro. 1972. Political Violence in the Thirteenth Century. In *Violence and Civil Disobedience in Italian Cities, 1200–1500*, ed. L. Martines. Berkeley: University of California Press.

—— 1979. *Power and Imagination: City-States in Renaissance Italy*. New York: Alfred A. Knopf.

Marx, Karl. 1965. *Pre-Capitalist Economic Formations*. Trans. and ed. E. Hobsbawm. New York: International Publishers.

—— 1977. *Capital*, vol. 1. Trans. Ben Fowkes. New York: Vintage.

Mauss, Marcel. 1967. *The Gift: Forms and Functions of Exchange in Archaic Societies*. Trans. I. Cunnison. New York: Norton.

Mengozzi, N. 1911. *Feudo del vescovado di Siena*. Siena.

Miller, Edward. 1951. *The Abbey and Bishopric of Ely: The Social History of an Ecclesiastical Estate from the Tenth to Early Fourteenth Centuries*. Cambridge: Cambridge University Press.

Milo, Yoram. 1979. *Tuscany and the Dynamics of Church Reform in the Eleventh Century*. Ann Arbor: University Microfilms International.

—— 1981. Political Opportunism in Guidi Tuscan Policy. In *I Ceti dirigenti in Toscana nell'età precomunale*, 207–222. Pisa: Pacini.

Moore, R. I. 1980. Family, Community, and Cult on the Eve of the Gregorian Reform. *Transactions of the Royal Historical Society*, 5th ser. 30: 49–69.

Muendel, John. 1981. The Distribution of Mills in the Florentine Countryside during the Late Middle Ages. In *Pathways to Medieval Peasants*, ed. J. A. Raftis, 83–115. Toronto: Pontifical Institute of Medieval Studies.

Muir, Edward. 1981. *Civic Ritual in Renaissance Venice*. Princeton: Princeton University Press.

Najemy, John. 1982. *Corporatism and Consensus in Florentine Electoral Politics, 1280–1400*. Chapel Hill: University of North Carolina Press.

Nanni, Luigi. 1948. *Le parrocchie studiate nei documenti lucchesi dei secoli VIII–XIII*. Rome.

Nelli, Renzo. 1985. *Signoria ecclesiastica e proprietà cittadina: Monte di Croce tra XIII e XIV secolo*. Pontassieve.

——— 1988. Feudalità ecclesiastica e territorio: le proprietà del vescovado di Firenze. In *Le antiche leghe di Diacceto, Monteloro, e Rignano. Un territorio dall'antichità al Medioevo*, ed. I. Moretti, 241–260. Florence.

——— 1989. "Vescovo e 'fedeli': qualche note in margine a tre documenti ducenteschi." In *San Miniato a Montebonello*. Comunità parrochiale di San Miniato a Montebonello.

Niemayr, J. F. 1976. *Mediae Latinitatis Lexicon Minus*. Leiden.

Nobili, M. 1981. Le famiglie marchionali della Tuscia. In *I ceti dirigenti in Toscana nell'età precomunale*, 79–105. Pisa: Pacini.

North, Douglas (with R. Thomas). 1973. *The Rise of the Western World: A New Economic History*. New York: Cambridge University Press.

Onori, Alberto Maria. 1984. *L'Abbazia di San Salvatore a Sesto e il lago di Bientina: un signoria ecclesiastica 1250–1300*. Florence: Salimbeni.

Osheim, Duane. 1977. *An Italian Lordship: The Bishopric of Lucca in the Late Middle Ages*. Berkeley: University of California Press.

Ottokar, Nicola. 1974. *Il comune di Firenze alla fine del Dugento*. Florence: Einaudi.

Overmann, Alfred. 1895. *Gräfin Mathilde von Tuscien*. Innsbruck.

Paatz, Walter, and Elisabeth Paatz. 1955. *Die Kirchen von Florenz*, vol. 6. Frankfurt.

Palandri, P. E. 1926. L'Archivio arcivescovile di Firenze. Appunti storici e inventario sommario del materiale più antico. *Rivista delle biblioteche e degli archivi*, nuova serie, 6–12 (July–December): 167–200, 169–191.

——— 1929. Il vescovo Andrea de' Mozzi nella storia e nella leggenda dantesca. *Giornale Dantesco* 32: 93–118.

Pallottino, M. 1982. *Etruscologia*. Milan.

Pampaloni, G. 1971. I Magnati a Firenze alla fine del Dugento. *ASI* 4: 388–423.

Pecci, Giovanni Antonio. 1748. *Storia del vescovado della città di Siena*. Lucca.

Pescaglini Monti, Rosana. 1981. I conti cadolingi. In *I ceti dirigenti nell'età precomunale*, 191–206. Pisa: Pacini.

Peters, Edward. 1989. *Europe and the Middle Ages*. Englewood Cliffs: Prentice-Hall.

Pinto, Giuliano. 1978. *Il Libro del Biadaiuolo: Carestia e annona a Firenze dalla metà del 1200 al 1348*. Florence.

——— 1981. Coltura e produzione dei cereali in Toscana nei secoli XII–XIV. In *Civiltà ed egemonia nei secoli XIII e XIV: problemi della vita delle campagne nel tardo medioevo*, 221–285. Pistoia.

Plesner, Johann. 1934. *L'Émigration de la campagne à la ville libre de Florence au XIIIe siècle*. Copenhagen.

——— 1979. *Una Rivoluzione stradale nel Dugento*. Florence: Francesco Papafava.

Polanyi, Karl. 1975. *The Great Transformation*. New York: Octagon Books.

Poly, Jean Pierre, and Eric Bournazel. 1980. *La mutation féodale Xe–XIIe siècles*. Paris.

Pöschl, Arnold. 1908–1912. *Bischofsgut und Mensa Episcopalis*, 3 vols. Bonn.

Pratelli, F. 1940. *Storia di Poggibonsi*, 2 vols. Florence.

Quilici, Brunetto. 1938. La Chiesa di Firenze nell'alto medioevo. *Annuario del R. Istituto Tecnico Commerciante 'Emanuele Filiberto di Savoia'. Studi in memoria di A. V. Crocini*, 7–87. Florence.

———— 1940. Le Chiese di Firenze nei primi decenni del secolo undecimo. *Annuario del R. Istituto Tecnico Commerciante 'Emanuele Filiberto di Savoia'*, 52–80. Florence.

———— 1942. Il Vescovo Ranieri e la chiesa di Firenze durante la lotta delle investiture. *Annuario del R. Istituto Tecnico Comerciante 'Emanuele Filiberto di Savoia'*, 6–33. Florence.

———— 1943. *Giovanni Gualberto e la sua riforma monastica.* Florence.

———— 1950. La chiesa di Firenze nel secolo dodicesimo. In *Studi in memoria di E. Bocci (Instituto commerciale a indirizzo mercantile "Emanuele Filiberto Duca d'Aosta")*. Florence.

———— 1965a. *Il Vescovo Ardingo e la chiesa di Firenze nel quarto e quinto del secolo XIII.* Florence.

———— 1965b. *La Chiesa di Firenze nei primi decenni del secolo XIII.* Florence.

———— 1969. La chiesa di Firenze dal governo del 'Primo Popolo' alla restaurazione guelfa. *Archivio Storico Italiano* 463 (3): 265–375, (4): 423–60.

Ragni, L. 1970. Le proprietà fondiaria del monastero di San Benedetto in Polirone nei secoli XII e XIII. *Nuova rivista storica* 54: 561–581.

Raspini, Giuseppe. 1962. *L'Archivio vescovile di Fiesole.* Rome.

Raveggi, Sergio, Massimo Tarassi, Daniela Medici, and Patrizia Parenti. 1978. *Ghibellini, Guelfi, e Popolo Grasso.* Florence: La Nuova Italia.

Redon, Odile. 1979. Seigneurs et communautés rurales dans le contado de Sienne au XIIIe siècle. *MEFRM* 91: 149–196, 619–657.

———— 1982. *Uomini e comunità del contado senese nel Duecento*, 177–223. Siena.

Repetti, Emanuele. 1833–1846. *Dizionario geografico fisico della Toscana*, 6 vols. Florence.

Reuter, Timothy, ed. and trans. 1978. *The Medieval Nobility: Studies on the Ruling Classes of France and Germany from the Sixth to the Twelfth Century.* New York and Amsterdam: North-Holland Publishing Company.

Reynolds, Susan. 1984. *Kingdoms and Communities in Western Europe, 900–1300.* Oxford: Oxford University Press.

Richa, Giovanni. 1754. *Notizie storiche delle chiese fiorentine.* Florence.

Rippe, Gérard. 1979. Commune urbaine et féodalité en Italie du Nord: l'exemple de Padoue (Xe-siècle–1237). *MEFRM* 91 (2): 659–697.

Romeo, Rosario. 1971. *La signoria dell'abate di Sant'Ambrogio di Milano sul comune rurale di Origgio nel secolo XIII.* Assisi.

Ronzani, M. 1983. La chiesa del comune nelle città dell'Italia centro-settentrionale (sec. XII–XIV). *Società e Storia* 21 (July–Setember): 499–534.

Rosenwein, Barbara. 1982. *Rhinoceros Bound: Cluny in the Tenth Century.* Philadelphia: University of Pennsylvania Press.

———— 1989. *To Be the Neighbor of St. Peter: The Social Meaning of Cluny's Property, 909–1049.* Ithaca: Cornell University Press.

Rotelli, Elena. 1978. I Vescovi nella società fiorentina del Trecento.In *Eretici e ribelli del XIII e XIV secolo*, ed. D. Maselli, 189–211. Pistoia.

———— 1979. Storia interna del Capitolo fiorentino dalla distribuzione del patrimonio in prebende alla soppressione della carica di tesoriere 1220–1331. *Annali dell'Istituto di storia* 1: 17–27. Florence: Università di Firenze, Faccoltà di magistero.

Rubinstein, Nicolai. 1935. La lotta contro i magnati a Firenze: la prima legge sul "soda-mento" e la pace del Cardinale Latino. *Archivio Storico Italiano* 2 (2): 161–172.

——— 1939. *La lotta contro i magnati a Firenze, II. Le origini della legge sul sodamento.* Florence.

——— 1966. *The Government of Florence under the Medici (1434–1494).* Oxford: Oxford University Press.

———, ed. 1968. *Florentine Studies.* Evanston: Northwestern University Press.

Russell, J. B. 1972. *Witchcraft in the Middle Ages.* Ithaca: Cornell University Press.

Sahlins, Marshall. 1972. *Stone Age Economics.* Chicago.

Salvemini, Gaetano. 1899. *Magnati e popolani in Firenze dal 1280 al 1292.* Florence.

Salvini, Enzo. 1969. *Semifonte.* Florence.

Salvini, S. 1752. *Catalogo cronologico dei canonici della chiesa metropolitana fiorentina.* Florence.

Sanesi, E. 1931. Un ricorso del capitolo fiorentino alla signoria alla fine del secolo XIII. *Rivista storica degli archivi toscani* 9 (July–September): 3–24. Florence.

——— 1932. *L'Antico ingresso dei vescovi fiorentini.* Florence.

Santini, Pietro. 1895b. Studi sull'antica costituzione del comune di Firenze. *ASI* 5 series, 16: 3–59.

——— 1900. Studi sull'antica costituzione del comune di Firenze. *ASI*, 5th ser., 25: 25–88; 26: 3–80; 27: 165–249.

——— 1903. Studi sull'antica costituzione del comune di Firenze. *ASI*, 5th ser., 31 (2): 308–364, 32 (3): 19–72, 32 (4): 310–359.

Sapori, A. 1946. *Studi di storia economica.* Florence.

Schevill, F. 1964. *Siena: The Story of a Medieval Commune.* London. New York: Charles Scribners' Sons.

——— 1961. *History of Florence from the Founding of the City through the Renaissance.* New York: Frederick Ungar.

Schmidt, Karl. 1978. The Structure of the Nobility in the Earlier Middle Ages. In *The Medieval Nobility,* trans. and ed. T. Reuter, 37–59. New York and Amsterdam: North-Holland.

Schneider, Fedor. 1975. *L'Ordinamento pubblico nella Toscana medievale.* Trans. F. Barboloni. Florence.

——— 1980. *Le Origini dei comuni rurali in Italia.* Florence: Francesco Papafava.

Settia, Aldo. 1984. *Castelli e villaggi nell'Italia padana.* Napoli.

Shanin, Teodor. 1971. *Peasants and Peasant Societies: Selected Readings.* Harmondsworth: Penguin.

Spilner, Paula. 1987. *'Ut Civitas Ampletur': Studies in Florentine Urban Development, 1282–1400.* Ann Arbor: University Microfilms International.

Stahl, Berthold. 1965. *Adel und Volk im Florentiner Dugento.* Cologne.

Stephens, C. 1942. *Medieval Feudalism.* Ithaca: Cornell University Press.

Stephens, J. N. 1972. Heresy in Medieval and Renaissance Florence. *Past and Present* 54 (February): 25–60.

Stock, Brian. 1983. *The Implications of Literacy: Written Language and Models of Interpretation in the Eleventh and Twelfth Centuries.* Princeton: Princeton University Press.

Structures féodales et féodalisme dans l'Occident méditerranéen (Xe–XIIIe siècles). Collection de l'École française de Rome, vol. 44 1980. Rome.

Stuard, Susan Mosher. 1976. *Women in Medieval Society*. Philadelphia: University of Pennsylvania Press.

Studio Telemugellouno. 1982. I Castelli del Mugello: origine e dislocazione di questi insediamenti nei secoli XII et XIII. In *I beni colturali dalla conoscenza storica. Una prospettiva per il Mugello*.

Stutz, Ulrich. 1961. The Proprietary Church as an Element of Medieval Germanic Ecclesiastical Law. In *Medieval Germany (911–1250): Essays by German Historians*, trans. and ed. G. Barraclough, vol. 2, 35–70. Oxford: Basil Blackwell.

Sznura, Franek. 1975. *L'Espansione urbana di Firenze nel Dugento*. Florence: La Nuova Italia.

Tabacco, Giovanni. 1969. Fief et seigneurie dans l'Italie comunale. *Le Moyen Age* 75: 5–37, 203–18.

———— 1970. Espansione monastica egemonia vescovile nel territorio aretino fra X e XI secolo. In *Miscellanea Gilles Gérard Meersseman* 1, 57–87. Italia Sacra 15–16. Padua.

———— 1976. Nobili e cavalieri a Bologna e a Firenze fra XII e XIII secolo. *Studi medievali* 17: 41–79.

———— 1979. *Egemonie sociali e strutture del potere nel medioevo italiano*. Turin.

Tellenbach, Gerd. 1959. *Church, State, and Christian Society at the Time of the Investiture Contest*. Trans. R. F. Bennett. Oxford: Basil Blackwell.

Toubert, Pierre. 1973. *Les Structures du Latium médiévale*, 2 vols. Rome.

Trexler, Richard. 1971. *Synodal Law in Florence and Fiesole, 1306–1518*. Vatican City.

———— ed. 1978. *The Liber Cerimoniale of the Florentine Republic. By Francesco Filarete and Angelo Manfidi*. Geneva: Droz.

———— 1980. *Public Life in Renaissance Florence*. New York: Academic.

Turner, Victor. 1974. *Dramas, Fields, Metaphors: Symbolic Action in Human Society*. Ithaca: Cornell University Press.

Vaccari, Pietro. 1926. *L'affrancazione dei servi della gleba nell' Emilia e nella Toscana*. Bologna.

Vannucci, Vanna. 1963–1964. Vita economica di un monastero alle porte di Firenze dal secolo XI al XIII: la Badia di San Salvi. *Miscellanea storica dalla Valdelsa* 69: 7–77, 70: 22–61.

Vauchez, André. 1981. *La sainteté en Occident*. Rome: École française de Rome.

Violante, Cinzio. 1964. I vescovi dell'Italia centro-settentrionale e lo sviluppo dell'economia monetaria. *Vescovi e Diocesi*, 193–217. Padua.

———— 1972. Eresie nelle città e nel contado in Italia dall'undicesimo al dodecesimo secolo. *Studi sulla cristianità medievale*, ed. P. Zerbi, 349–379. Milan.

———— 1974a. *La società milanese nell'età precomunale*. Bari: Laterza.

———— 1974b. Un esempio di un signoria rurale "territoriale" nel secolo XII: la "corte" di Salamona in Valtellina secondo una sentenza del comune di Milano. In *Études di civilization médiévale (IXe–XIIe siècles). Mélanges offerts à E. R. Labande*, 739–749. Poitiers.

———— 1977a. Pievi e parrochie nell'Italia centro-settentrionale durante i secoli XI e XII. In *Le istituzioni ecclesiastiche della 'Societas christiana' dei secoli XI–XII. Atti della VI settimana internazionale di studio {alla Mendola}*, 643–799. Milan.

———— 1977b. Quelques caractéristiques des structures familiales en Lombardie, Émilie, et Toscane aux XIe et XIIe siècles. In *Famille et parenté dans l'occident médiéval*, ed. G. Duby and J. LeGoff, 87–147. Rome.

————— 1980. La signoria 'territoriale' come quadro delle strutture organizzative del contado nella Lombardia del secolo XII. In *Histoire comparée de l'administration (IVe–XVIIIe siècles)*, ed. W. Paravicini and K. F. Werner, 333–344. Beihefte der Francia, 9. Munich.

————— 1981. Le strutture familiari, parentali, e consortili delle aristocrazie in Toscana durante i secoli X–XII. *I Ceti dirigenti nell'età precomunale*, 1–58. Pisa: Pacini.

Volpe, Gioacchino. 1922. *Movimenti religiosi e sette ereticali nella società medievale italiana (XI–XIV)*. Florence.

————— 1923. *Volterra. Storia di vescovi signori di istituti comunali, di rapporti fra Stato e Chiesa nelle città italiane, secoli XI–XV*. Florence.

————— 1961. *Medio Evo Italiano*. Florence.

————— 1964. *Toscana medioevale*. Florence.

Waley, Daniel. 1969. *The Italian City-Republics*. London: McGraw-Hill.

Weber, Max. 1978. *Economy and Society*, 2 vols. Ed. Guenter Roth and Claus Wittich. Berkeley and Los Angeles: University of California Press.

Wickham, Christopher. 1980. Economic and Social Institutions in Northern Tuscany in the Eighth Century. In *Istituzioni Ecclesiastiche della Toscana Medioevale*, ed. Cosimo Fonseca and Cinzio Violante, 7-34. Galatina: Congedo.

————— 1981. *Early Medieval Italy*. London: Macmillan.

————— 1985. *Il problema dell'incastellamento nell'Italia centrale: l'esempio di San Vicenzo al Volturno*. Florence.

————— 1988. *The Mountains and the City: The Tuscan Apennines in the Early Middle Ages*. Oxford: Oxford University Press.

Wolf, Eric. 1966. *Peasants*. Englewood Cliffs: Prentice-Hall.

Index

Abbreviations: bp., bishop; def., definition; mon., monastery; not., notary; p., pope. Standard abbreviations for Italian city-states are also used: AR, Arezzo; FI, Florence; LU, Lucca; MS, Massa Marittima; PI, Pisa; PT, Pistoia; SI, Siena.